TREASURED PAST, GOLDEN FUTURE

*The Centennial History of
The University of Southern Mississippi*

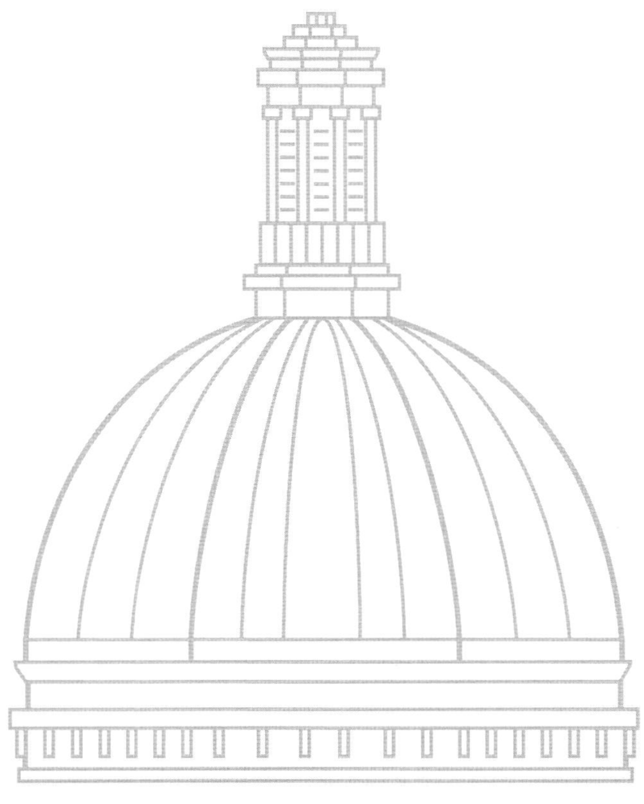

TREASURED PAST, GOLDEN FUTURE

The Centennial History of The University of Southern Mississippi

CHESTER M. MORGAN

The University of Southern Mississippi and University Press of Mississippi www.upress.state.ms.us

The University Press of Mississippi is a member of the Association of American University Presses.

Name of Printing Company: Tien Wah Press (Pte) Limited
Plant Location: Singapore

First printing 2010
∞
Library of Congress Cataloging-in-Publication Data

Morgan, Chester M.
Treasured past, golden future : the centennial history of the University of Southern Mississippi / Chester M. Morgan.
p. cm.
Includes index.
ISBN 978-1-60473-463-8 (cloth : alk. paper) – ISBN 978-1-60473-464-5 (ebook) 1. University of Southern Mississippi–History. I. Title.
LD3425.M673 2010
378.762'18–dc22 2009047985

British Library Cataloging-in-Publication Data available

TABLE OF CONTENTS

FOREWORD

Martha Dunagin Saunders, University of Southern Mississippi President

I once attended a retrospective exhibit of the works of one of America's most prolific artists whose paintings hang in the country's influential galleries and are considered by some as priceless.

Following a few remarks by the artist, a reporter asked him to comment on the magnitude of his accomplishments. His answer was simple: "It hasn't felt like work. It's felt like love."

I think if it were possible today for us to talk with the people who contributed to the building of the University of Southern Mississippi, they would say the same thing. It's hard to read the history of Southern Miss without realizing that this wonderful institution didn't just happen. It is a one-hundred-year-old labor of love.

Within the pages of this book you will read of our early beginnings as Mississippi Normal College, founded in 1910 to provide better training for the teachers in the public schools of this state. (I note that we came into being after one of the most contentious legislative fights in state history, and we've been fighting for quality education ever since.) You will follow our transition from a Normal College, to the State Teachers College, to Mississippi Southern College, to our current designation as the University of Southern Mississippi. You will see us evolve into a place characterized by five distinct forces of innovation bridging us from where we have been to where we will go:

- A spirit of humanity characterized by kindness, compassion, respect, and support for others. At Southern Miss, people look people in the eye. They greet friends and strangers alike. People are real here . . . and gracious.

- A powerful sense of self-efficacy stemming from a belief in our ability to produce results. Our slogan, freeing the power of the individual, emerged from our belief in the potential in all people to do more with their lives.

- A balance between the collective good and the good of the individual as seen in our connections with the community and emphasis on giving back by sharing our gifts.

- A traditional culture with long-established customs and beliefs. We recognize the power of a positive environment and the beauty and power of being at home in the South.

- A diverse culture. We enjoy a rich racial, ethnic, socioeconomic, and disciplinary diversity. As a dual-campus university with six teaching and research sites, we also embrace a unique geographic diversity.

In reading this book, you will learn of our highs and our lows, and the persistent spirit that has brought us to emerge as the premier research university of the Gulf South.

As we move into our next one hundred years of service to the higher mind, we do so with an unrelenting commitment to a climate of academic success, better connections to the bigger world, a culture of healthy minds, bodies, and campuses, and recognition as a top-flight university. As the poet said, "The best is yet to be."

I am most grateful to my friend Dr. Chester "Bo" Morgan for agreeing to write this centennial history. I can think of no one better suited than he to prepare this volume. Bo is a Hattiesburg native, a Southern Miss alumnus, and, most important, a distinguished historian. He has brought to this project an artful blend of scholarly rigor and passion for the subject.

Creative. Bold. Determined.
Southern Miss—To The Top!

Chapter 1

MISSISSIPPI NORMAL COLLEGE

One of the First Observation Classes
Miss. Normal College.
Which Group Is Observing? One Guess.

"The Normal College," said the school's first yearbook, "stands for clean, pure, efficient lives." But for many Mississippians at the dawn of the twentieth century, life was anything but clean, pure, and efficient. More often it was like that of the eighteen-year-old boy whom rural school principal T. P. Scott described as "reared in . . . ignorance, inured to hard . . . labor, and hemmed in by provincialism in its narrowest form." The youngster's long dormant ambition suddenly took life, however, when "he found himself possessed of an opportunity to attend school." Convinced that many other rural children shared this one's "intense earnestness and determination to secure an education," Scott devoted himself to finding some way to allow such earnestness and determination to bear fruit.

Though most Mississippians by 1900 endorsed the principle of public education, the state's public schools still faced enormous practical problems. More than 80 percent of all school-age children lived in rural areas where they depended on country schools, whose terms ran six months at best and often no more than four. Most were one-room schools wherein the frustrations of presiding over all grades drove teachers to a transience rivaling that of the sharecropper families from whence so many of their pupils sprang. More than six teachers in every ten moved annually, while the average tenure at any one school was barely a year and a half. Another 20 percent each year were teaching for the first time anywhere. These harried but devoted educators were the driving force that created Mississippi Normal College.

Mississippi's harried teachers often presided over as many as eight grades simultaneously in one-room schools like Jackson County's old Roberts School, which now stands in the courtyard of Owings-McQuagge Hall on the Southern Miss campus.

Practice School class, 1914 (opposite page).

Before 1912, teacher training was at the mercy of scattered summer normal institutes lasting one to four weeks and offering little more than review courses in preparation for the state examination for teaching licenses. From the day of its founding in 1877, the Mississippi Teachers Association (MTA) worked tirelessly for the establishment of a state normal college. Finally, in 1906, a normal college bill was introduced into the legislature, only to die in the hostile House Education Committee. The following year, MTA president Joseph Anderson Cook devoted his entire 1907 annual address to the issue, sounding a note that would fundamentally alter the tactics of the normal school forces and ultimately lead to success. The lawmakers had rejected pleas for a normal college, Joe Cook suggested, because they did not believe its advocates were "speaking for five thousand teachers and three hundred thousand children. Let us help make the Legislature believe," he urged. "Let us five thousand teachers speak for ourselves and ask the fathers of more than three hundred thousand white children to speak for them!"

Thus began a campaign of organized publicity and personal contact that would eventually overwhelm the opposition in what the *Jackson Daily News* called "one of the great legislative fights of the decade." After a second normal college bill died in committee in 1908, State Superintendent of Education J. N. Powers turned to T. P. Scott, then head of the Brookhaven city schools, to organize a campaign in support of a third bill, which Representative Marshall McCullough intended to introduce in 1910. Scott had served the MTA since 1901 as secretary, vice-president, and

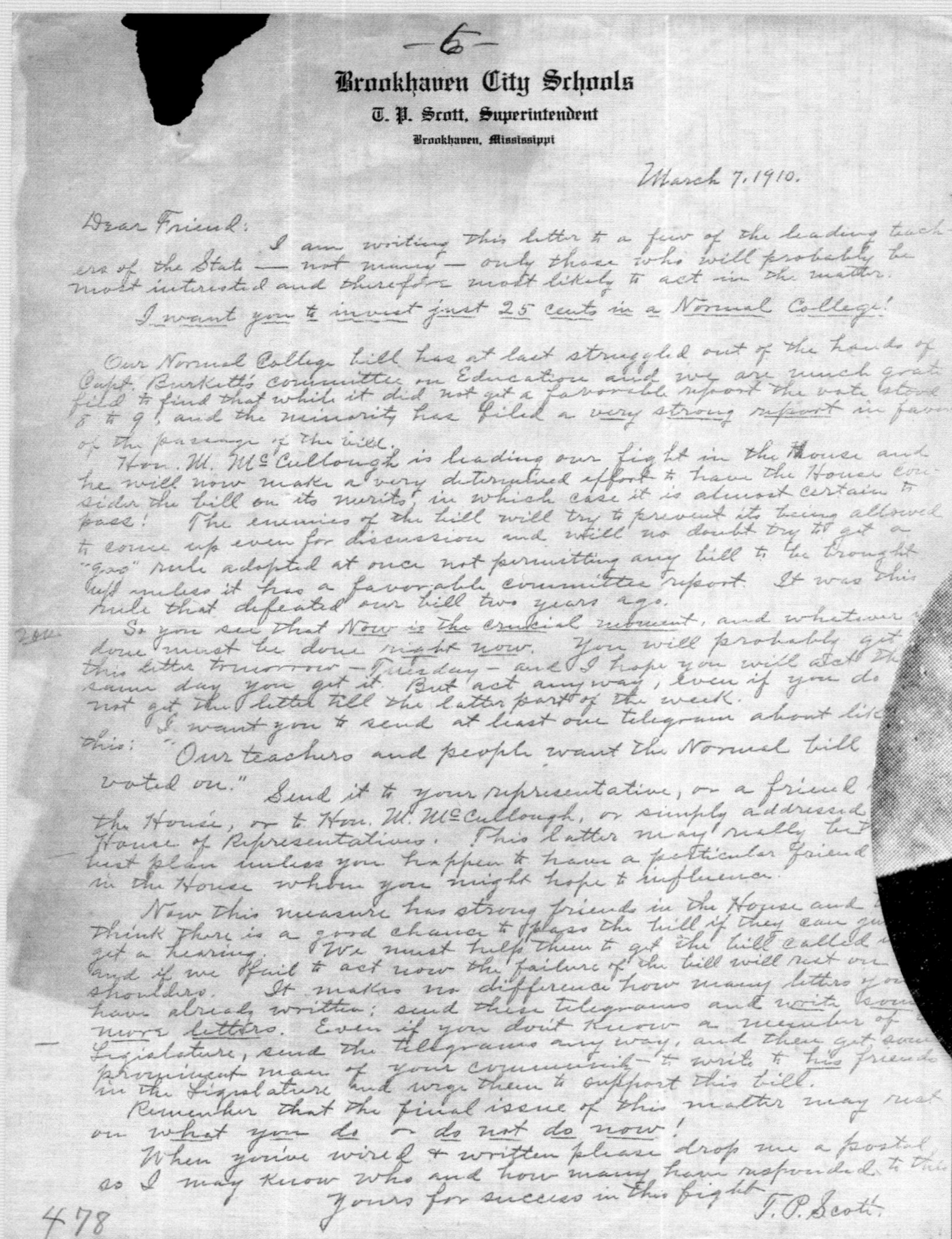

—6—

Brookhaven City Schools
T. P. Scott, Superintendent
Brookhaven, Mississippi

March 7. 1910.

Dear Friend:
I am writing this letter to a few of the leading teachers of the State — not many — only those who will probably be most interested and therefore most likely to act in the matter.

I want you to invest just 25 cents in a Normal College!

Our Normal College bill has at last struggled out of the hands of Capt. Burkitt's committee on Education and we are much gratified to find that while it did not get a favorable report the vote stood 8 to 9, and the minority has filed a very strong report in favor of the passage of the bill.

Hon. M. McCullough is leading our fight in the House and he will now make a very determined effort to have the House consider the bill on its merits, in which case it is almost certain to pass! The enemies of the bill will try to prevent its being allowed to come up even for discussion and will no doubt try to get a "gag" rule adopted at once not permitting any bill to be brought up unless it has a favorable committee report. It was this rule that defeated our bill two years ago.

So you see that Now is the crucial moment, and whatever is done must be done right now. You will probably get this letter tomorrow — Tuesday — and I hope you will act the same day you get it. But act anyway, even if you do not get the letter till the latter part of the week.

I want you to send at least one telegram about like this: "Our teachers and people want the Normal bill voted on." Send it to your representative, or a friend in the House, or to Hon. M. McCullough, or simply addressed House of Representatives. This latter may really be the best plan unless you happen to have a particular friend in the House whom you might hope to influence.

Now this measure has strong friends in the House and I think there is a good chance to pass the bill if they can just get a hearing. We must help them to get the bill called up and if we fail to act now the failure of the bill will rest on our shoulders. It makes no difference how many letters you have already written; send these telegrams and write some more letters. Even if you don't know a member of the Legislature, send the telegrams any way, and then get some prominent man of your community to write to his friends in the Legislature and urge them to support this bill.

Remember that the final issue of this matter may rest on what you do or do not do now!

When you've wired & written please drop me a postal so I may know who and how many have responded to this.

Yours for success in this fight
T. P. Scott.

478

Few but powerful, opponents of the creation of a normal college included Frank Burkitt, Chairman of the House Education Committee, and Speaker of the House H. M. Street of Meridian. A one-time Populist candidate for governor, "Captain" Burkitt now functioned as the self-appointed guardian of the public purse. He labeled Marshall McCullough's Normal College Bill simply a piece of special interest legislation, cooked up by the state's "educational trust" to create well-paying jobs for the leaders of the Mississippi Teachers Association. Though the Education Committee on March 2 voted nine to eight against the bill, McCullough, confident of overwhelming support on the House floor, filed "a *very strong*" minority report. "As long as there is hope or probability of success," he vowed, "I shall fight for the normal college." When rumors surfaced that "Colonel" Street intended to invoke a "gag" rule to prevent consideration of the bill, T. P. Scott decided to fight back and to "hit hard, regardless of where the chips might fly." He "bombarded the county superintendents and the editors (about 200) of all papers in the state with mimeographed letters (left) ... The man I hit hardest," he later declared, "was ... Col. Street." Scott implored the editors not "to let one man ...

T. P. Scott

Representative Marshall McCullough of Lincoln County sponsored legislation that created Mississippi Normal College in 1910.

bring to naught the effort of years on the part of teachers and friends of public education in Mississippi." Stung by public criticism from throughout the state, Street relented. Retiring to the cloakroom for his daily afternoon cigar on March 16, the Speaker relinquished the gavel to a prominent supporter of the normal college, Representative A. C. Anderson of Ripley. Anderson immediately recognized McCullough who called up House Bill 204, which quickly passed by a vote of fifty-nine to thirty-eight.

"You will some day be proud," Scott had assured the state's newspaper editors, "that you did lend a hand toward the establishment of an institution that will be the pride of the state and of untold value to its children." Little did Scott realize how richly the following hundred years would vindicate that promise.

Hattiesburg (above) was in 1910 Mississippi's fastest-growing city. Local businessman W. S. F. Tatum (below) offered several plots of land on which to locate the new college, but the board chose the "Hardy Street site" donated by Dr. T. E. Ross, A. A. Montague, and H. A. Camp (original deed shown right).

State of Mississippi,
Forrest County.

In consideration of One Dollar in hand paid us, the receipt of which we hereby acknowledge, and in consideration of the benefits that will innure to us by the establishment of the State Normal College of the State of Mississippi by the Trustees therefo on the following described land, and for the purpose of locating said College on the hereinafter mentioned land, we bargain, sell, convey and warrant to the Trustees of the State Normal College of the State of Mississippi, and their successors in office forever, the following described land, being and situated in Forrest County, State of Mississippi, towit:

The West Half of the Southwest Quarter of the Northwest Quarter, and the West Half of the Northwest Quarter of the Northwest Quarter, Section Eight, Township Four, North, Range Thirteen, West} and the East Half of the Northeast Quarter of Section Seven, Township Four North, Range Thirteen West, the same containing One Hundred and Twenty Acres.

Witness our signatures this the 26th day of December, 1910.

H A Camp
T. E. Ross
A A Montague

State of Mississippi,
Hinds County.

Personally appeared before me the undersigned authority in and for said county and state, the within named H.A.Camp, T.E.Ross and A.A. ... acknowledged that they signed and delivered the foregoing ... on the day and year above written. ... hand and official signature in the city of Jackson, ...ember, 1910.

Geo. C. Myers
Clerk Supreme Court of Mississippi

president. During those ten years, he had cranked out an endless stream of mimeographed letters to county superintendents of education and newspaper editors throughout the state urging their support for the teachers' association as well as for the general interests of education in Mississippi. The Brookhaven superintendent now trained the sights of his little hand-operated mimeograph machine upon the enemies of McCullough's House Bill 204, who soon found themselves besieged with

Architect R. H. Hunt's original design for the campus.

letters, telephone calls, telegrams, and editorials from all parts of Mississippi urging establishment of the normal college. Gradually Scott's self-proclaimed "propaganda methods" took their toll. With the aid of a strongly worded special message of support from Governor Edmond F. Noel, and after supporters reluctantly allowed opponents to strike the appropriation clause, the bill passed the House on March 16. A week later the Senate approved it, and on March 30, 1910, Governor Noel signed it into law.

It was an act, as T. P. Scott put it, which seemed to its enemies "worth less than the paper on which it was written." Stripped of any appropriation, the bill granted no more than "the bare right" to build a college. Two other bills, however, approved on the last day of the 1910 session, offered supporters at least a possibility of turning "right" into reality. They allowed counties and municipalities to issue bonds to finance land, buildings, or other inducements to aid in "procuring the establishment and location of the Mississippi Normal College." Governor Noel appointed the institution's trustees, who met for the first time on May 7, 1910, in the governor's office. The board decided to solicit bids from cities interested in securing the school but agreed to accept no donation short of $100,000 plus a building site. Three communities made offers: Jackson and Hinds County, $200,000 and a sixty-acre site; Laurel and Jones County, $230,000 and a sixty-acre site; Hattiesburg and Forrest County, $250,000 and a 120-acre site. Several other cities, including Meridian and Artesia, eventually showed some interest, but by September attention focused on the two piney-woods towns, Laurel and Hattiesburg. The board visited Hattiesburg on September 6, Laurel the next day, and then met on the sixteenth to select the location. The vote was Hattiesburg, six; Laurel, two; Jackson, one.

Throughout the fall of 1910, the city and the college board wrestled with the problem of a location for the school. W. S. F. Tatum, a local lumber baron, offered three possibilities, including the campus of old South Mississippi College, which had been founded in Hattiesburg in 1906 and whose main building had burned to the ground earlier in the year. Tatum's most serious challenge came from Dr. T. E. Ross, A. A. Montague, and H. A. Camp, whose so-called Hardy Street site encompassed 120 acres about two and a half miles west of downtown. On December 27, after three months of controversy, the board voted to accept the proposal of the Ross group. The trustees purchased an additional eighty acres—at one hundred dollars an acre—from the same three men who promptly donated the eight thousand dollars back to the school. Tatum later gave his South Mississippi College property to the state's Baptists for a denominational school. Mississippi Woman's College, now William Carey University, began its life a year before Mississippi Normal College opened its doors across town, and the two institutions have prospered together over the last century.

Besides the site, the normal college received several additional considerations from the city and others: extension of both Hardy Street and a parallel streetcar line to the campus; access to the city's gas, sewage, and electrical lines; construction of a railroad spur to the campus by the Mississippi Central Railroad to facilitate movement of building materials; and donation of an additional 640 acres of land to the school by the J. J. Newman Lumber Company. While a special committee of the board toured several campuses around the country to study buildings, grounds, and other physical aspects of comparable institutions, the George Engineering Company of Memphis conducted a topographical survey of the Hardy Street site. To prepare designs for the campus and its first buildings, the board selected R. H. Hunt of Chattanooga, one of the most prominent and productive architects in the South. He had already designed numerous structures in Mississippi, including buildings on almost every college campus in the state and at least four in Hattiesburg itself.

Hunt conceived his plan for the campus around two major axes, one extending northward from the streetcar station on Hardy Street to the opposite end of the site, the other running east and west and intersecting the first at the location of the present Administration Building. Here was the focal point of Hunt's scheme. Though he did not design the existing edifice, its columned porticoes and imposing dome quite faithfully reflect his conception of the structure that should occupy this crucial spot. Well in front of it was a large shady grove, bordered by a semicircular roadway that branched from Hardy Street at the southeast corner of the campus and curved gently toward the rotunda and back out again to rejoin the street at the southwest corner. Along this avenue stood four large academic buildings (of which only two, College Hall and what is now Southern Hall, were ever constructed), overlooking the grove and giving the institution, as architectural historian Ed Polk Douglas put it, "a gracious, ordered 'public front.'" Behind the dome was to be a gazebo in the center of a long, shaded quadrangle extending along the north-south axis to a second semicircle of buildings that anchored the back end of the campus. Three pairs of dormitories faced each other (as Forrest County and Hattiesburg Halls still do) across the quad, women on the east and men on the west.

East of this center campus, Hunt envisioned an almost self-contained secondary complex of buildings for faculty housing. At the south end stood the impressive President's Home (now the Ogletree Alumni House), behind which extended a row of tennis courts and gardens, flanked on either side by seven pairs of buildings. Scattered about the periphery of the campus were smaller auxiliary structures and staff dwellings.

On July 25, 1911, the board approved Hunt's general design and his plans for the first buildings. They included five colonial-style structures of red brick with stone trim: College Hall, the principal academic building, containing classrooms and administrative offices on its first floor, a library and classrooms on the second, and an auditorium and four small rooms on the third; Hattiesburg Hall (in honor of the city's contribution to the college), a three-story dormitory for women; an identical dormitory for men, Forrest County Hall (in honor of the county's gift); a two-story President's Home; and an Industrial Cottage for women students. The board received bids in late August and awarded a contract to I. C. Garber of Jackson for $178,591 to construct all five buildings. Work began in October.

Meanwhile the board encountered some difficulty in securing a president for the college. At the December 27, 1910, meeting at which they had approved the Hardy Street location, the trustees settled on Henry Whitfield, president of Mississippi Industrial Institute and College in Columbus (now Mississippi University for Women). After considering the offer for a month, however, Whitfield decided to remain at II&C. The board then chose W. H. Smith, the state

College Hall

In 1912, the handsome girls' dormitory, Hattiesburg Hall, stood in stark contrast to its desolate surroundings.

A second girls' dormitory, Mississippi Hall, was completed in 1914.

Joseph Anderson Cook was president of MNC, 1911-28.

supervisor of rural schools, who accepted in February 1911 and agreed to supervise preparations for the school's opening on a part-time basis without salary until assuming the full duties of the presidency in February 1912. After eight months of trying to launch a new institution, however, he, too, decided to forego the challenge and remain as rural school supervisor. Finally, the board turned to Joe Cook, superintendent of schools in Columbus, who accepted the job in October 1911, at a salary of $3,500 a year. He would remain almost seventeen years.

Though Whitfield and Smith ultimately rejected the presidency of the college, both had been forceful advocates of its creation and held definite notions about what the school should be and do. Their ideas, along with those of Cook and his handpicked vice-president, T. P. Scott, molded the early character of Mississippi Normal College. That character drew its basic elements from two sources that were common to the background of all four men: educational experience and progressive convictions. All of them had begun their careers as school teachers and had been stalwarts in the fight for education in Mississippi. Whitfield and Smith served as state superintendents of education, Cook and Scott as presidents of the MTA. All but Scott eventually became college presidents: Cook at Mississippi Normal College, 1911–28; Whitfield at II&C, 1907–20; and Smith at Mississippi Agricultural and Mechanical College (now Mississippi State University), 1916–20. A decade after turning down the presidency of Mississippi Normal, Whitfield became governor of Mississippi.

The first decade of the twentieth century witnessed the high tide of American progressivism, and nowhere did progressive currents run deeper than in education. The concept of teacher training that began to take shape at the hands of Whitfield, Smith, Cook, and Scott clearly reflected those currents. Public education, they agreed, should be practical, professional, and democratic, and they designed Mississippi Normal College accordingly.

Whitfield believed that the existing public schools were deficient because they were "not properly related to life." Traditional curricula focused on training the mind alone, "to the exclusion of those subjects which have a direct bearing on the future lives of the children." The common schools, he suggested, should rather take "children with their native endowments and their preschool experiences and . . . grow them into men and women who can perform completely the functions of life in a Christian civilization." The work of the normal school, he concluded, was to equip teachers with "the vision, training, energy, and self-sacrificing spirit" for such work.

Smith concurred, suggesting that such subjects as geography, history, and arithmetic should "be taught as the processes by which the business . . . of life [is] carried on and not as isolated, dead studies." He insisted that only professionally trained teachers could accomplish this task. "Let pedagogy and psychology put on their everyday clothes," he said, "and go to work in earnest on the everyday problems of life among the great common people of Mississippi."

Similarly, Cook was determined "to take pedagogy off of its theoretical perch, bring it to earth, and make it serviceable in the solution of our many rural school problems." No one was more committed to the common people than Joe Cook, and his enthusiasm for the democratic way of life permeated every aspect of his thinking. "Democracy," he said, "not only springs from education but is sustained by education." Throughout his tenure as president, he subordinated all else "to giving more poor boys and girls an opportunity to get an education." He cautioned students against pretension. "Be yourselves," he counseled. "Be what you are. Do not try to be what somebody else is. Do not copy." Following his own advice, he "practiced an informality that at times verged on crudeness," according

President Joe Cook (left) and Vice-president T. P. Scott.

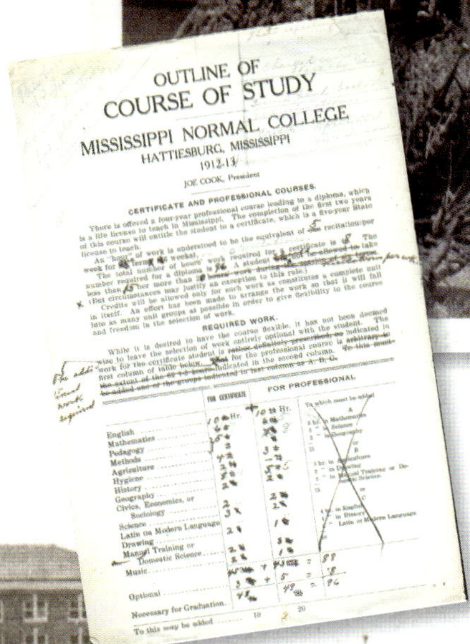

Vice-president Scott's hand-edited copy of the Mississippi Normal College "Course of Study."

to an early faculty member. Social amenities, he thought, smacked of aristocracy and "had no place in democratic living." He even disdained academic credentials, once claiming that the only "D" he ever wanted after his name was "RFD."

As his second-in-command and chief academic confidant, Cook chose one who shared these democratic sensibilities. For T. P. Scott, the principal goal of education was to train not leaders but citizens. He saw the public high school as a kind of "finishing school for the masses," which would "offer a common-sense, practical and efficient preparation for the duties and responsibilities of the life that our boys and girls will of necessity enter upon when they leave." Educators should make students "bold and courageous to grapple with the problems that confront them . . . able not only to pull their own weight, but to 'lend a hand' to the burden of the other fellow." Scott thought this concept required a fundamental change in the traditional course of study, one that would not lower the standard of academic achievement but "raise it . . . breathe life into it, and clothe its dry bones with flesh." Education, he insisted, should "articulate with Life instead of with musty college walls." The early curriculum of Mississippi Normal College was largely the work of Vice-president Scott, and he infused it with these progressive ideals.

The law establishing the institution had defined its purpose clearly: "to qualify teachers for the public schools." The college *Bulletin* set the minimum age at fifteen but recommended that students be several years older than that before entering. The only academic prerequisite was "satisfactory evidence of having completed the common school course," that is, the eighth grade. A stiffer requirement would have excluded one of the college's principal constituencies, the practicing teachers of the state, many of whom could and did pass the state licensing examination with no more than a primary school education. The early curriculum, therefore, included a considerable amount of high school work as well as college-level courses, and experienced teachers and high school graduates often found themselves in classes with young common school graduates. This serious defect could only be corrected as the college itself turned out enough trained teachers to supply the state's needs and allow the institution to raise its entrance requirement. Normal students could receive credit for work beyond the elementary level either by presenting a certificate from "an affiliated high school" (without a formal accreditation system, colleges compiled a list of schools whose work was considered acceptable) or "an approved college," or by passing an examination covering the work done.

The original buildings included College Hall, Forrest County Hall, the dining hall, Hattiesburg Hall, the vice-president's home, the Industrial Cottage, and the President's Home.

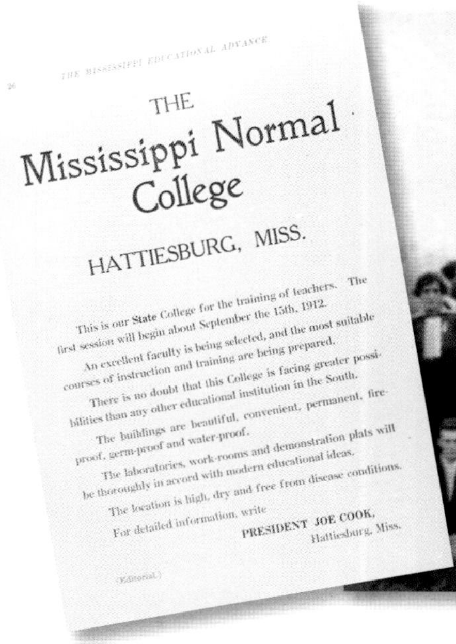

THE MISSISSIPPI EDUCATIONAL ADVANCE

26

THE

Mississippi Normal College

HATTIESBURG, MISS.

This is our **State** College for the training of teachers. The first session will begin about September the 15th, 1912.

An excellent faculty is being selected, and the most suitable courses of instruction and training are being prepared.

There is no doubt that this College is facing greater possibilities than any other educational institution in the South.

The buildings are beautiful, convenient, permanent, fire-proof, germ-proof and water-proof.

The laboratories, work-rooms and demonstration plats will be thoroughly in accord with modern educational ideas.

The location is high, dry and free from disease conditions.

For detailed information, write

PRESIDENT JOE COOK,
Hattiesburg, Miss.

(Editorial.)

The announcement of the opening of the college from the *Mississippi Educational Advance* (left). The faculty and student body, June 1913 (above).

In accordance with its enabling legislation, the college offered two courses of instruction: a two-year certificate program that qualified the graduate for a teaching license good for five years and a four-year diploma program leading to a lifetime professional license. Courses were measured in hours, forty for the certificate and eighty for the diploma. Five forty-five-minute recitations per week for six six-week terms constituted one hour. There was an additional six-week summer term that offered both regular coursework and review courses in common school subjects for teachers wishing to prepare for regular state and county teaching examinations.

Scott chaired the faculty committee that governed the catalog and the curriculum, and his influence was evident in both, right down to descriptions of particular courses. The 1913–14 *Bulletin* announced that all classes should emphasize "the correlation of the work of the school with the community life." The Department of English offered courses in reading, grammar, composition, and literature, as well as, of course, the teaching of English. "The work in composition," said the catalogue, "especially in the lower classes, will be connected as closely as possible with everyday life. Themes connected with country life, with its varied needs, advantages, problems, privileges, and opportunities, will be given a large place in both written and oral composition. . . . It is the aim to make all plans of work genuinely democratic." Upper-level work covered such courses as advanced grammar, Southern authors, Shakespeare, and nineteenth-century poetry.

Mathematics included arithmetic, algebra, geometry, and trigonometry. History courses—ancient, medieval, and modern, English, American, Mississippi, and methods—emphasized, according to the *Bulletin*, "those movements of the past that seem to be most vitally connected with the present. Everything that cannot be vitalized by something from the life of the student is considered out of date pedagogically. Dates, wars, and politics are considered of secondary importance. Social, economic and industrial movements and problems of the past and present are stressed." Professional education courses were both theoretical (principles of teaching, curriculum, psychology) and practical (observation and practice teaching in the training, later Demonstration, school). Science included botany, zoology, general science, physics, and chemistry. Agriculture, civics, hygiene, geography, manual training for boys and domestic science for girls, drawing, and school music rounded out the required curriculum. Optional work included Latin, French, Spanish, German, and piano.

Officials scheduled opening ceremonies for September 18, 1912, and when the faculty, students, and visitors arrived, what they found was hardly R. H. Hunt's vision of a carefully landscaped neo-Jeffersonian "academical village." Those early students remembered their years in Hattiesburg as "the Stump Age," and with good reason. The campus had only recently been carved from a vast cut-over pine forest, untouched by human hands, as a faculty member noted, "except to make it more unattractive." The stump-scarred ugliness stretched as far as the eye could see in every direction except east, where the town lay some two and a half miles distant. Rising from this raw terrain, stark and incongruous, stood the five handsome red-brick buildings, accompanied now by several functional wooden structures in various stage of completion, which were designed, according to Ed Polk Douglas, in what "could only be called "'lumber camp vernacular.'" They included a dining hall, remnants of the contractor's office (later converted into a combination post office and college store), a powerhouse, and several dwellings. Excessive rainfall during the year had delayed construction, and evidence of the contractor's continuing presence lay scattered about: piles of dirt and debris, materials and equipment, a half-unloaded boxcar near the front of Forrest County Hall, and the builder's shack to one side, with several workers digging in an open trench to complete the water and heating systems.

The rains, impervious to the mood of anticipation that surrounded the occasion, continued into opening day, adding a sea of mud to the general unsightliness of the landscape. The steady downpour drenched the crowd but could not dampen the enthusiasm of those who had labored so hard to make this day a reality. By ten o'clock, College Hall's eight-hundred-seat, third-floor auditorium was full, the guests including the board of trustees, Lieutenant Governor Theodore G. Bilbo, State Superintendent of Education J. N. Powers, Rural School Superintendent W. H. Smith, leaders of both houses of the legislature, and assorted local dignitaries. Pastor G. H. Thompson of Court Street Methodist Church invoked the blessing of the Almighty, after which followed the traditional sequence of inaugural oratory: welcoming, thanking, and looking forward to achievement. Joe Cook, presiding, offered special gratitude to the people of Hattiesburg and Forrest County for the land and buildings, adding in an exemplary display of presidential timber, "But, as you see, we need more buildings already." This executive art of yoking thankfulness for past financial favors with urgent pleas for future ones has been refined now through eight subsequent presidencies. Lunch followed the opening exercises, after which came a tour of the campus. The next morning all classes met briefly, but instructors spent the bulk of the day classifying students. On September 20, regular classes began.

"In the final analysis," Alma Hickman said in her memoir, *Southern As I Saw It*, "education involves students, teachers, and books." The 227 students who attended Mississippi Normal College's first term were, according to history professor Willard F. Bond, "the most sober-faced homesick group of people I have ever seen. Some were crying. Many . . . were farther from home than they had ever been." One got off the train and spent the whole day in the depot debating whether or not to go back home. "Hunger finally drove him out to the college." Another's father had opposed his going, certain "he would soon be wearing white shirts, collars, and neckties, which . . . would forever ruin him as a farmer." Most rural parents, however, understood the unique opportunity the normal school afforded: an accessible state school, without the social demands or expenses of a traditional university. Despite these advantages, attending Mississippi Normal College still meant great personal and family sacrifice for many, one of whom Professor Orville Brim later recalled vividly. His clothes were literally worn to the "point of tatters, sometimes held together by common pins," and the entire family of seven lived in a two-room dogtrot cabin. Yet when Brim and his wife accepted an invitation to share Sunday dinner in these modest surroundings, they found not only the expected "atmosphere of family love and devotion," but also "an intense yearning for an education for the children." The example was extreme, but the sentiment was typical. A college education was something precious to Mississippi Normal College's early students, and Brim came to admire them greatly.

There were seventeen on the first faculty: Vice-president Scott (mathematics), J. N. McMillin and Anne H. Augustus (English), W. F. Bond and Kate Brown (history and Latin), W. I. Thames (civics and economics), R. J. Slay (science), Brim and Alma Hickman (pedagogy), T. F. Jackson (agriculture), Annie Faust (primary methods), Willa Bolton (geography), May F. Jones (physiology and resident physician), Maggie De Campbell (domestic science), Delora Hanel (manual training and drawing), Lorena Tomson (school music), and Sadie Chiles (observation school). All but four were Mississippians; Brim and Tomson were from Ohio, Dr. Jones from Virginia, and Hanel from Michigan. All but two had earned bachelor's degrees, while Brim, Augustus, and Jackson, in addition to President Cook, held master's degrees. From September 12 until opening day, they met every afternoon in Hattiesburg High School's auditorium to hammer out educational philosophy, curriculum, and guidelines for student classification. New to each other as well as to the institution, they quickly developed an extraordinary camaraderie. Few, if any, had taught college before; several were recent graduates themselves, teaching for the first time anywhere. But they were amazingly dedicated and fell to their task with an infectious enthusiasm. "From the standpoint of terminal degrees they probably did not rank as high . . . as the college professors of today," one of the early students recalled years later, "but they ranked high in 'educated hearts' and 'understanding attitudes.'" For country boys and girls who were earnest yet unsure of themselves, eager but socially unsophisticated, such teachers were a godsend, and the students loved them for it. Brim, who left after three years to pursue a distinguished career that included several years at Ohio State University, declared, "In my many years of college teaching I have never known a staff more sincere in purpose, more selfless in work, more devoted to the welfare and growth of the student body."

As for the third component of Alma Hickman's educational triad, books, the college was not so well endowed. The first library contained approximately five hundred volumes (the first accessioned being *Webster's Unabridged Dictionary*, purchased for $10.80), a few magazines, and two daily newspapers, housed in two classrooms at the northeast end of the second floor of College Hall. For the first year, students, under the direction of a faculty committee chaired by McMillin, staffed and maintained the facility. In 1913, the college employed a full-time librarian, Pearl Travis, but the library appropriation remained less than that of the college farm for several years. By 1924, the library occupied half of the first floor of the newly opened Science Hall and held six thousand volumes, five daily newspapers, and eighty periodicals.

In 1912, the legislature finally appropriated state money for the college, $76,500 to equip and $50,000 to maintain the existing buildings. It proved less than adequate. For four days during the first session, dormitory residents resorted to hauling water in buckets when sand from the

The original library was on the second floor of College Hall.

campus well clogged the water pump. Had local citizens not come to the rescue, Cook might have been forced to close the school. In an emergency meeting, the Hattiesburg Commercial Club raised $7,000 to link the campus to the city water supply and then supervised the laying of two and half miles of six-inch cast-iron pipe in less than two weeks, a gesture of community support for which the college was profoundly grateful. By the end of the first year of operation, Cook was able to report to the board that initial construction was complete and, thanks largely to student labor, the stumps had been removed and the grounds cleared, leaving "the appearance of the institution, while still crude. . . much more sightly." Prime symbols of the lingering crudeness were the droves of hogs and cows that roamed freely about the campus, bedding down near dormitories where they drew flies, fouled the air, and generally made nuisances of themselves. In the absence of a local stock law, Cook appealed to the board for funds to build a fence, and sometime in 1914 one appeared—supposedly hog-proof with barbed wire and heart yellow pine posts. For sixteen years it remained, enclosing the entire two hundred-acre campus and, according to Alma Hickman, eliminating the problem of cows. Hogs, if the college newspaper offers any indication, were a different matter. The *Normal College News* reported as late as 1920 that several local swine had become such "an accepted institution" that the campus would have seemed "lonesome without their presence and their cheerful grunts." Nor were they without utility, scavenging "bits of lunch dropped by the town students and the fruit peels that are carelessly thrown down near the store." The editors encouraged students to take more notice of these porcine neighbors and to exercise due care in keeping the campus gate closed lest they wander helplessly outside and meet a swift demise under the wheels of the streetcar. A few years later, the *News* again took up the issue, only on a more serious note, urging city officials to help rid the campus completely of animal intruders by imposing a fine on anyone willfully leaving the public gate open.

President Cook labored manfully to beautify the campus. After pushing the grading through to completion in 1916, he planted chinaberry trees along all the roads, oaks in the quadrangle and elsewhere, a few pecan trees here and there, and Bermuda grass all around. Only the chinaberries flourished, but Cook persevered with the oaks for several years and saw some success. The pecans proved hopeless. Grass did well only where the soil had been well prepared, and for several years visitors found the college's main academic building surrounded by pea patches, which not only enriched the soil but supplemented the dining hall fare. Covered boardwalks connecting the dormitories and major buildings on campus provided some relief from the elements and were replaced in 1922 by concrete sidewalks.

In 1914, the campus got its own post office and a streetcar station with brand new cars running a thirty-minute schedule on school days and every fifteen minutes on weekends. The same year, a second girls' dormitory opened to relieve a severe overcrowding problem. The first campus building financed by state funds, it was appropriately named Mississippi Hall. A Laundry (later part of the Industrial Arts and ROTC Building) was constructed in 1918 and equipped with machinery bought from a cleaning establishment in Holly Springs.

Campus life during the early years bore the distinct imprint of two powerful personalities, President Cook and Vice-president Scott. For men with such similar backgrounds and convictions, these two seemed as unlike as any pair could be. Cook was, in Brim's words, "a dynamic, buoyant extrovert," whose pleasant enthusiasm put even "relatively shy students . . . at ease." Almost everyone knew

Female students pose at the campus gate.

SLINGING THE HASH

Mittie Chambers

The original dining hall (opposite page) was a frame wooden structure at the north end of the quadrangle facing south. Resident students paid a board fee, and others could purchase meals daily for fifteen cents each. Students' monthly board statement included an itemized summary of dining hall expenses showing the costs for labor and utilities as well as for food and supplies for that month. Board charges to the students thus varied from month to month. Female residents of the Industrial Cottage, who prepared their own meals and maintained the facility, paid less than those who ate in the dining hall. Student waitresses in the regular dining hall organized a Dining Hall Club, which had its own theme song:

I'm tired of slinging the hash
I want me a man with some cash
A man who is able to wait on his table
I'm tired of slinging the hash

As for the fare, besides hash "they went in heavy for grits and gravy," one dining hall regular later recalled.

While W. I. Thames presided over mealtime activities, Mrs. J. W. Chambers served as stewardess. Throughout the latter months of 1912, future Hattiesburg attorney and two-term state senator Curran Sullivan appeared at the Chambers table with increasing frequency. Friends began to tease him about special treatment, including choice and ample servings of each day's delicacies. It turned out that Sullivan had fallen "desperately in love" with Mrs. Chambers's daughter, Mittie (left), and the two created a mild sensation by eloping before the school year ended.

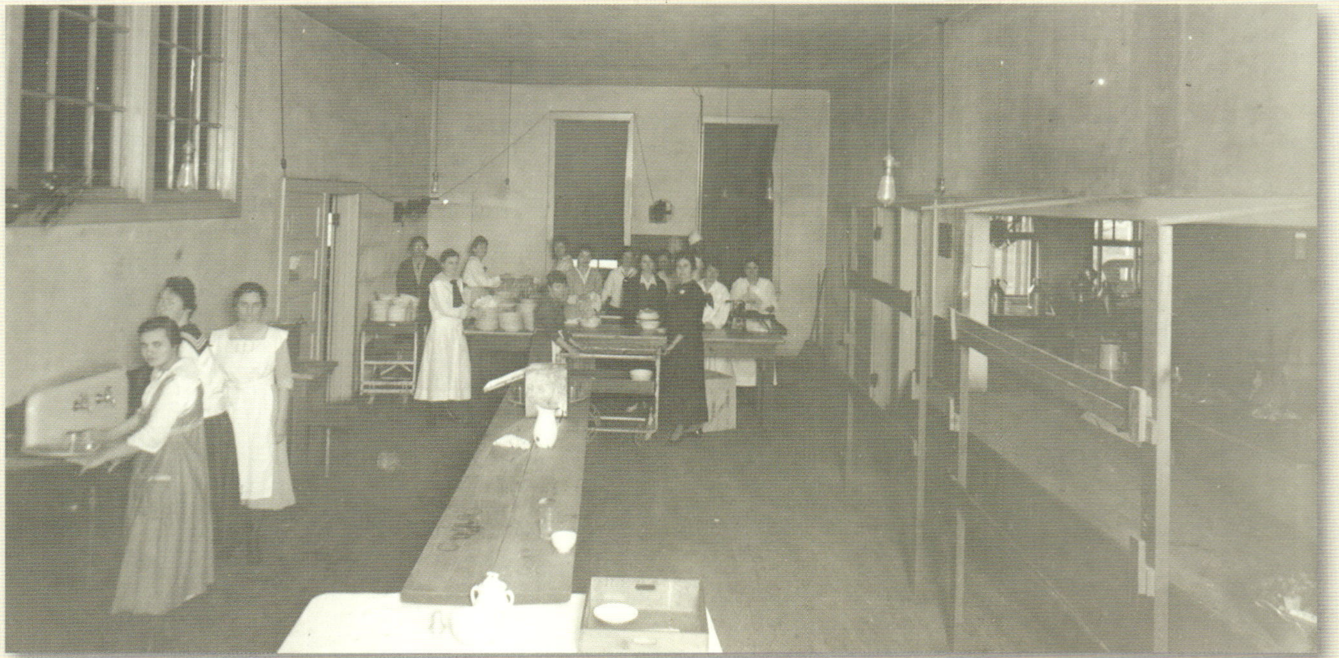

Student workers washing dishes in the dining hall.

The dining hall, as seen from the roof of College Hall.

Vice-president T. P. Scott (front right) and President Joe Cook (third from left, middle row) with students.

him as "Daddy Joe." No student, however, and few adults dared refer to Mr. Scott by his first name, and some surely wondered if even his own children called him Daddy. The two men's mottoes reflected the irony of their relationship. Cook's "get there on time and stay to the end" exuded an optimistic determination that became an almost universal campus slogan. The plaque that hung above Scott's desk also spoke of perseverance, but in a strikingly different tone. "Keep plugging away," it read, "this is not an over-intelligent age."

Colleagues remembered Scott as reserved, cold, austere, and unapproachable. Like Cassius, he "had a lean, hungry look," said Bond. Though many, especially students, feared him, almost everyone respected him. Bond recalled his "rugged honesty" and "devotion to duty," and Brim thought him "a scholar par excellence." Librarian Anna Roberts said that he was "absolutely fearless" as a defender of the college, and Emily Jones, who joined the faculty in 1913, believed that he, more than anyone else, was responsible for the school's academic progress and ultimate recognition by the national education community. Years later, when they had escaped the bite of his wit and the relentless vigilance of his discipline—which extended even to the sage grass that obscured strategic portions of the favorite hillside courting spot—many students even recalled Scott with some degree of affection.

Cook's most striking trait, other than his abiding sense of democracy, was a frugality that bordered on the penurious. As Alma Hickman said, he watched his own and the school's money "like Silas Marner," and his parsimony permeated every aspect of college life. As a young man he had almost lost the family's modest plantation through excessive use of credit, and he was determined to instill the virtue of financial responsibility in those entrusted to his care. Each edition of the school *Bulletin* contained a section on expenses, listing every conceivable penny a student might have to spend, including the fifty cents a week for laundry and the ten-cent streetcar fare for the round trip to town for worship each Sunday.

Cook counseled parents not to allow their children a great deal of spending money and advised students to deposit surplus cash in the business office. "Six bits," he insisted, was "enough for a married man to carry around and two bits enough for a single person." The chapel hour, which remained mandatory—with varying degrees of enforcement—until 1955, offered the president a capital

BOARD STATEMENT.

At the end of each board month (4 weeks) an itemized statement is printed and distributed to the students. The statement for the sixth month of the past session is given below:

TO THE STUDENTS OF MISSISSIPPI NORMAL COLLEGE:—

You will find below a statement of the board account for the sixth scholastic month. The board for the sixth scholastic month is $8.50. This is 20 cents less than last month. I expected an increase instead of a decrease, but the water consumption last month was about what it should have been—40 gallons per day per person. We expect to have only about three weeks more of winter. Continue to co-operate in the management of heat. We are improving in the management of heat. Let us keep on until we learn to manage it scientifically.

The light bill is about as heretofore and the meters do not show any undue amount to any building.

The Cottage girls' board is $5.90—a decrease of 20 cents. They still maintain their good record.

You will note an increase in charge for breakage. This is due to the fact that the charge for breakage heretofore has been found inadequate.

Inspect statement carefully, ask any questions you wish, and send statement home.

Respectfully,

JOE COOK, President.

Statement of Board Account for Sixth Month February 4 to March 3, 1913.

DEBITS

Quantity and articles.	Price	Amount
To amount inventory on hand		$1,387.97
To purchases this month:		

GROCERIES

9 bbls. Flour	$ 5.70	$51.30
1053 lbs. Sugar	4⅞c	51.01
100 lbs. Sugar	5¼c	5.25
172 lbs. B. E. Peas	4¾c	8.17
100 lbs. Lima Beans	7¼c	7.25
100 lbs. Bulk Salt	.70	.70
1 bbl. Pocket Salt	3.00	3.00
1 case Condensed Milk	4.00	4.00
6 cases Oatmeal	1.45	8.70
2 cases Macaroni	1.80	3.60
5 lbs. Tea	.35	1.75
62 lbs. Crackers	.07	4.34
4 bu. Meal	.70	2.80
5 38-lb. sacks Meal	.62	3.10
6 doz. Hominy	.75	4.50
1 bbl. Grits	3.50	3.50
50 lbs. Evap. Apples	$ 9½c	$ 4.75
7½ doz. Canned Goods, asstd.	.85	6.38
2½ doz. Canned Grapes	1.00	2.50
2 1-3 doz. Canned Peaches	1.70	3.97
2-3 doz. Preserves	6.00	4.00
1 case Star Naptha Washing Powder	3.85	3.85
132 lbs. Coffee	23½c	31.02
92 lbs. Coffee	.24	22.08
100 lbs. Rice	5½c	5.50
55 gal. Syrup	.45	24.75
1 bbl. Apples	3.00	3.00
1 case Bon Ami	2.50	2.50
1 case Scouring Soap	3.50	3.50
1 bbl. Washing Powder	9.78	9.78
347 lbs. Lard Comp.	0822	28.52
24 lbs. Cheese	1945	4.67
3150 loaves Bread	3 1-3	105.00

(Total, $428.74)

DEBITS—*Continued.*

MEATS

Bacon	$ .22	$ 44.54
125 lbs. Bacon Rib Bellies	1387	17.34
1457½ lbs. Fresh Pork	.10	145.75
112 lbs. Fore Quarter Beef	.10	11.20
66 lbs. Hind Quarter Beef	.11	7.26
603 lbs. Hind Quarter Beef	1196	72.12
62 lbs. Sirloin Strips	1445	8.96
108 lbs. Hams	17½c	18.90
182 lbs. Beef Liver	0995	18.11
60 lbs. Pork Sausage	.12	7.20

(Total, $351.38)

MILK AND BUTTER

484 lbs. Butterine	.17	82.28
370 gal. Sweet Milk	.30	105.09
.206 gal. Buttermilk	.15	30.90
74 gal. Separated Milk	.15	11.10
Cream		1.80

(To al, $231.08.)

VEGETABLES

100 lbs. Onions	1½c	1.50
2 lots Green Onions		6.00
6 lots Collards		5.03
414 lbs. Turnips	.03	12.42
210 lbs. Cabbage	.02	8.50
10 bu. Irish Potatoes	.85	8.50
31½ bu. Swet Potatoes	.50	15.75

(Total, $53.40.)

EGGS

1 case Eggs	8.00	8.00
71 doz. Eggs	.25	17.75
53 doz. Eggs	.20	10.00

(Total, $36.35.)

COAL AND POWER HOUSE SUPPLIES

2 cars Coal		$ 95.89
Freight on 2 cars coal.		120.51
53 gal. Cylinder Oil	$ .38	20.14
52 gal. Engine Oil	.23	11.96
54 gal. Coal Oil	.10	5.40
Hauling and unloading coal		69.88
2 Brooms		1.30

(Total, $335.08)

MISCELLANEOUS

1 ton Ice	6.00	6.00
6 Floor Brushes	1.50	9.00
5 doz. Brooms	3.25	16.25
2 loads Saw Dust	3.00	6.00
Car Fare of Mail Carrier		5.00
Printing adds for bids		12.00
Printing this statement		8.50
Electric Bill		62.19
Medicines		20.25
Laundry of table linen		4.60
Breakage Fund		30.00
Allowance for E. and O.		12.02

LABOR.

Salary of Steward	50.00
Salary of Cook	40.00
Salary of helpers	84.00
Salaries of 25 dining-room girls	150.00
Salaries Bell, Ringer, Mail Carrier, Physician's assistant and sweepers	56.69

(Total, $380.69.)

Total $3,386.50

The sample board statement from the 1913 *Bulletin* not only illustrates President Cook's meticulous bookkeeping but also reveals much about wages, prices, and dining hall fare.

opportunity to preach economy to a captive audience, and he made the most of it. "Use all of the water you need," he admonished more than one assembly, "but don't let the water run after you use all that is necessary. Keep your bedroom at the required temperature, but don't raise every window as high as you can and try to heat Forrest County." Cook offered opportunity as well as advice. Any student who desired could defray part of his expenses by working a few hours each day—sweeping, digging stumps, waiting tables, or working the college farm—at fifteen cents an hour. And expenses were not very great: five dollars for the matriculation fee (three dollars for summer term only), four dollars a month tuition (which was waived for students who pledged to teach for a specified period in the state's rural public schools), five to eight dollars a year for books, and approximately seventy-five dollars a year for board (excluding laundry). Nonetheless, demand for employment was so great that the school allowed no student more than six dollars a month from student labor.

Discipline at Mississippi Normal College was fairly simple, at least in theory. "Only those of good moral character" would be admitted, and since moral laxity was intolerable in a schoolteacher, any student whose conduct betrayed a lack of self-discipline faced dismissal. "The general rule of the college," the catalogue stated, "is for each student to do the right thing." The vague simplicity of this dictum reflected both the president's ideals and the student body's general makeup. Cook encouraged students "by every possible means," said Alma Hickman, "to think for themselves, speak for themselves, control themselves."

He attributed his success as an educator to the conviction that most young men and women truly desired maturity, intelligence, and the respect of other people. His system of discipline appealed to those desires. "Put boys and girls on their own responsibility," he said, "and they always respond." Most of the early students, having already taught for several years, were older than typical college students and therefore more suited to such an ethic of personal responsibility.

Still, student life was fairly regimented. Each day began with the rising bell at 6:30, followed by breakfast in the five-hundred-seat dining hall. All students dined at the same hour, family style at assigned tables, each of which had a student waitress and a faculty host. A designated faculty member presided at each meal, making announcements and offering thanks for the food. Classes met from 8:30 to 4:00 with chapel at 11:00, where Cook presided over what the *Bulletin* described as "an opportunity to take part in . . . devotional exercises, to hear . . . announcements, and to enjoy many interesting discussions and lectures." The program often included a lecture by some faculty member or prominent visitor or a presentation by a student organization. Usually Cook lectured or led open discussions on topics ranging from practical campus problems to international issues to philosophical inquiries. He encouraged free and full participation by faculty and students. If flagging interest stifled voluntary contributions, he would often call on students by name, a practice which no doubt contributed to persistent attendance problems. In 1925, after what the campus newspaper called the annual "wrangle about chapel and chapel attendance," Cook commissioned the faculty psychologist to prepare and distribute a questionnaire on the issue. A faculty-student committee then evaluated the results and made recommendations to the president. There is no evidence that the administration implemented the suggestions or that chapel attendance improved.

The *Bulletin* noted that "proper social intercourse . . . is encouraged." The rules for decorum suggest, however, that Cook either was a strict constructionist on the meaning of "proper" or that he never intended the "encouragement" to be overly vigorous. The only designated social hours were thirty minutes daily between dinner and the 6:30 social hall bell and Sunday afternoons between 2:00 and 5:30. During the weekday periods, couples were restricted to dormitory lobbies, but on Sundays they were allowed to venture out about the campus. Despite persistent rumors that Mr. Scott kept a spyglass on the roof of College Hall, more than one budding romance blossomed atop the partially wooded hill that sat just barely out of sight of the dormitories. A 6:30 P.M. bell sent students to their rooms for study hours, which lasted until 10:15 and were rigidly enforced. A final bell at 10:30 signaled lights out and the end of the school day.

Students who abused social privileges lost them: kissing could lead to suspension, and anything more daring was likely to be a "shipping offense." The rules explicitly forbade smoking, dancing, and, for girls under twenty-one, riding in automobiles with men. Cook justified the prohibition of cigarettes not on moral or health grounds but because, he said, no school superintendent would hire a man who smoked, an argument the students found less than compelling in light of the president's own inveterate tobacco chewing. By the late twenties, the rule became a dead letter, as did the restriction on automobile riding, once people discovered that a car was, in Alma Hickman's words, "a means of transportation" and not a bordello on wheels. The ban on dancing, interestingly, proved the most durable, lasting until the 1940s.

Students could not leave the campus grounds without special permission, and the administration discouraged them from visiting friends in the city or entertaining guests in the dormitories except during specified times. With special permission, students could go into town to shop on Saturdays but had to return to campus for meals. They were encouraged to attend worship in town on Sunday morning, but as the *Normal College News* advised, "this does not carry with it permission to visit restaurants, refreshment counters, depots, or any other places except the church."

Religion played a central role in life at Mississippi Normal College. The Bulletin urged students to "let no opportunity pass to develop your spiritual nature, since this is even more important than your mental development." And there was no dearth of opportunities: short prayer services each morning in the dormitories, daily chapel devotionals, Wednesday evening prayer services, Sunday morning Bible classes—taught by faculty for credit—Sunday evening campus services, and a series of revival meetings each session. "These privileges constitute an important factor in college life," said the student newspaper. "If you miss them, you are missing the very best part of the college course."

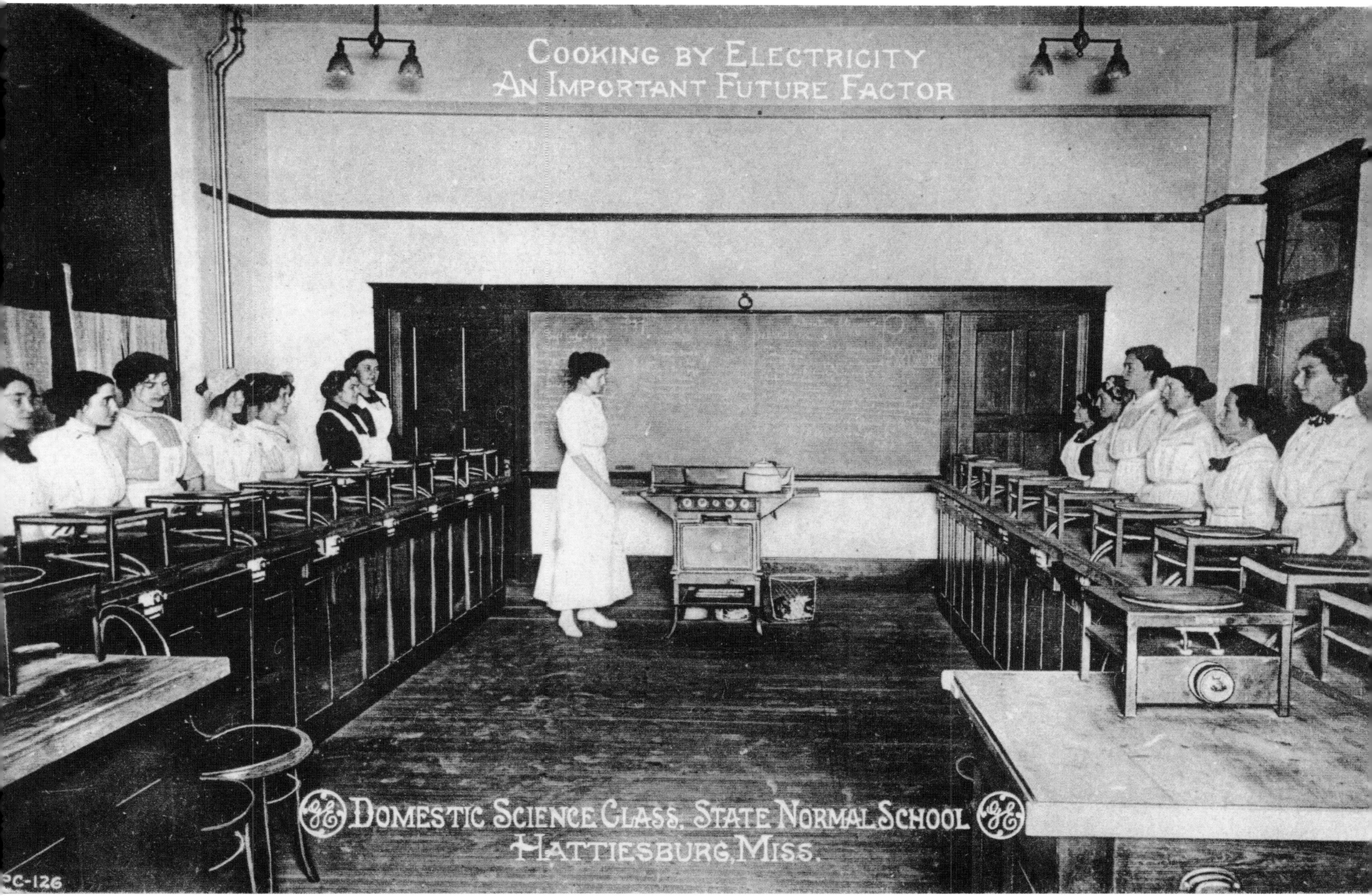
COOKING BY ELECTRICITY
AN IMPORTANT FUTURE FACTOR
DOMESTIC SCIENCE CLASS, STATE NORMAL SCHOOL
HATTIESBURG, MISS.
PC-126

Among the first student organizations formed on campus were Young Men's and Young Women's Christian Associations, founded to unite Mississippi Normal College's students "in loyalty to Jesus Christ, to lead them to accept Him as their personal Savior, to build them up in the knowledge of Christ, especially through Bible study and Christian service that their character and conduct may be in accord with their belief." Even the work of these associations conformed to the general goals of the institution. The YMCA in particular sought to equip men to strengthen and vitalize "the cause of Christ . . . in the rural districts," where graduates, as teachers, would exercise "intellectual leadership." Perhaps more important to the students, however, were the opportunities for fellowship these clubs provided. For simple country boys and girls thrust into an alien social environment, the associations' informal receptions offered a much-needed "means of curing 'the blues.'"

The painted curtain in the chapel auditorium in College Hall depicts progress from one-room school to modern consolidated facility.

Other social outlets included the four literary societies. The Prestonian (named for former state superintendent of education John R. Preston) and the Platonian offered men a chance "to develop themselves along the lines of oratory, debate and a ready ability to act as leaders in public gatherings and to express opinions when opportunity presents or duty demands." The Sherwood Bonner (named for a Holly Springs author of local color fiction) and the Mississippian involved women in programs of "music, readings, discussions, literary criticism, etc." Again, however, the students were perhaps more thankful for the social opportunities that the societies afforded, such as the Leap Year party that the Sherwood Bonners gave for their brothers the Prestonians in January 1924. Held in the lobby of Hattiesburg Hall, it was a girl-invites-boy affair, highlighted by a proposing game, in which, according to the *Normal College News*, "the genus homo was stood around the room" in a ring while the girls circled them, "proposing to each blushing youth in turn. Some of the proposals [were] fraught with earnestness, and genuine pleading was in the tone of the voices and in the eyes of many of the girls who [pleaded] for a husband." Top prize went to Miss Louise Dawson, whose primary inducement was the possession of a job, which allowed her to offer her candidates the prospect of voluntary and leisurely unemployment. "The vote for her," said the *News*, "was almost unanimous."

There were also tomato clubs for girls and corn clubs for boys, which fostered practical skills and prepared the future educators for their roles as leaders in the industrial movement that so influenced rural education during the era. After 1917, when the Smith-Hughes Act provided federal money for vocational education, the college began to train home economics teachers for public schools. Thereafter, the tomato and corn clubs, along with the egg, poultry, and pig clubs, as well as the cooperative dairy association, were consolidated into a Home Economics Club.

In 1922, several faculty members, led by Kate Brown of the history department, organized the World Affairs Club. Affiliated with Andrew Carnegie's Institute of International Education, the club was the first of its kind in Mississippi and was limited to forty members selected by the faculty. Lectures at the monthly programs ranged from Hattiesburg businessman "Pep" Jones's address on international trade to Mabel McMillin's discussion of compulsory employment in Bulgaria. A Lyceum series in the early years also brought to the campus Carl Sandburg, Williams Jennings Bryan, and the Cincinnati Symphony.

Early in the 1912 term, the students, at President Cook's urging, organized a Student Self-Government Association. All students were members of the association, bound by honor to observe its motto: "Every Man a Gentleman and Every Woman a Lady." Officers included a president, vice-president, secretary-treasurer, and an elected council of eight men and seven women whose duty it was to hear cases of student misconduct and recommend punishment to the faculty. The association, which reflected both Cook's democratic ideals and his belief in individual responsibility, lasted until 1926.

In the early years, there were also county clubs, a college quartet, tennis club, debate team, women's glee club, storytellers' league, and Shakespeare club. By 1925, a school orchestra, commercial club, modern language club, dramatic club, American Legion chapter, and Masonic and Eastern Star orders had been added.

The students published the first yearbook, called *Neka Camon* (an Indian term meaning New Spirit), in 1914. The

Organizations for women included the Tomato Club (above).

Normal College News first appeared in December 1918, edited by a faculty-student committee chaired by Scott. Published every Saturday during the forty-two-week session, the newspaper was primarily a means of exchanging information between the college community and teachers in the field, as well as other supporters around the state.

Athletics began modestly at Mississippi Normal College. In September 1912, 150 students organized the Athletic Association and elected science professor R. J. Slay as athletic director. A month later, L. S. Venable, president of the association, "called the student body together . . . for the purpose of selecting suitable college colors." The *Hattiesburg News* reported that the students chose black and gold, "suggested by Miss Stella McLaurin, of Mont Rose." Mrs. Moran M. Pope, however, later recalled being part of a student committee commissioned to make recommendations regarding school colors. She had been involved in a similar task in 1911 as senior class sponsor at the high school in Carson, Mississippi. On that occasion, Mrs. Pope (then Florence Burrow), inspired by the sight of a giant

The postwar frivolity that would characterize America in the 1920s first came to MNC in the form of several unconventional organizations. The Beau Not Club (top right) appeared in response to the administration's wartime restrictions on campus social hours. The club's motto was, "Full many a flower is born to blush unseen and waste its fragrance on the desert air;" its purpose was "consolation and revenge." The Bolshevik Club (below) – only remotely associated with the national "Red Scare" of 1919-20 – aimed "to do as much work as possible to get out of work; to store away knowledge where there is no room; and to furnish information on the values of Campus Course, Volley Ball, Tiddle-de-Wink, and other unnecessary undertakings at the Normal College." The club's color was, of course, red; its song, "Hail! Hail! The Gang's All Here;" its password, "Hunting the Zoo;" and its motto, "Watch Your Step." The Bolsheviks "put on a campaign for 'more beef and less gravy,' [and] voted unanimously that the cooks discontinue washing the mackerel before serving, since water destroys its greatest quality – fragrance." Other exotic organizations included the Jiggs Club (opposite page), named for a popular comic strip character, and the Bobbed Hair Club (below).

Beau Not Club

The "Bolshevik" Club

Bobbed Hair Club

JIGGS CLUB.

Type Writing Class, 1923.

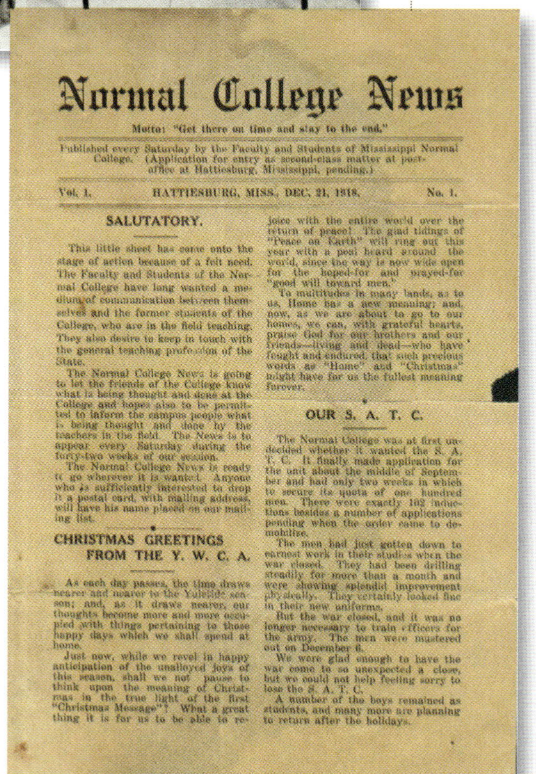

Normal College News

Motto: "Get there on time and stay to the end."

Published every Saturday by the Faculty and Students of Mississippi Normal College. (Application for entry as second-class matter at post-office at Hattiesburg, Mississippi, pending.)

Vol. 1. HATTIESBURG, MISS., DEC. 21, 1918. No. 1.

SALUTATORY.

This little sheet has come onto the stage of action because of a felt need. The Faculty and Students of the Normal College have long wanted a medium of communication between themselves and the former students of the College, who are in the field teaching. They also desire to keep in touch with the general teaching profession of the State.

The Normal College News is going to let the friends of the College know what is being thought and done at the College and hopes also to be permitted to inform the campus people what is being thought and done by the teachers in the field. The News is to appear every Saturday during the forty-two weeks of our session.

The Normal College News is ready to go wherever it is wanted. Anyone who is sufficiently interested to drop it a postal card, with mailing address, will have his name placed on our mailing list.

CHRISTMAS GREETINGS FROM THE Y. W. C. A.

As each day passes, the time draws nearer and nearer to the Yuletide season; and, as it draws nearer, our thoughts become more and more occupied with things pertaining to those happy days which we shall spend at home.

Just now, while we revel in happy anticipation of the unalloyed joys of this season, shall we not pause to think upon the meaning of Christmas in the true light of the first "Christmas Message"? What a great thing it is for us to be able to rejoice with the entire world over the return of peace! The glad tidings of "Peace on Earth" will ring out this year with a peal heard around the world, since the way is now wide open for the hoped-for and prayed-for "good will toward men."

To multitudes in many lands, as to us, Home has a new meaning; and, now, as we are about to go to our homes, we can, with grateful hearts, praise God for our brothers and our friends—living and dead—who have fought and endured, that such precious words as "Home" and "Christmas" might have for us the fullest meaning forever.

OUR S. A. T. C.

The Normal College was at first undecided whether it wanted the S. A. T. C. It finally made application for the unit about the middle of September and had only two weeks in which to secure its quota of one hundred men. There were exactly 102 inductions besides a number of applications pending when the order came to demobilize.

The men had just gotten down to earnest work in their studies when the war closed. They had been drilling steadily for more than a month and were showing splendid improvement physically. They certainly looked fine in their new uniforms.

But the war closed, and it was no longer necessary to train officers for the army. The men were mustered out on December 6.

We were glad enough to have the war come to so unexpected a close, but we could not help feeling sorry to lose the S. A. T. C.

A number of the boys remained as students, and many more are planning to return after the holidays.

First issue of the *Normal College News*.

field of black-eyed Susans, proposed black and gold as the class colors. A teacher bought black and gold hatbands for the two boys in that senior class, one of whom Florence Burrow married in August 1912, a month before the two of them became part of the first class at MNC. Moran Pope proudly wore his straw hat to Hattiesburg, despite some good-natured teasing from classmates about its conspicuous band. When Mrs. Pope sought her husband's counsel about choosing the college's colors, he threw his hat across the room, she said, and exclaimed, "Well, why don't you get black and gold?" After another member of the committee argued for maroon and gray, Mrs. Pope recalled, both sets of colors were submitted to the student body. By whatever process, black and gold became the school colors, and they remain so to this day. Florence Pope later declared, "I don't care who gets credit so long as my children get through school." She got her wish; three subsequent generations of Popes have not only graduated from the institution but served it faithfully in countless capacities.

Football was new to many country boys in 1912, and only after much persuasion did thirteen "stalwart" souls, two of them one-armed, volunteer for the school's first squad. The inaugural game was a 30-0 thrashing of the Hattiesburg Boy Scouts, coached, ironically, by future State Teachers College president Claude Bennett. Another win and a loss filled out the opening season. Students walked the mile or so to Kamper Park where home games were played. In its first decade, the school went through five different coaches—Slay, A. B. Dille, B. B. "Opp" O'Mara, Cephus Anderson, and O. V. "Spout" Austin—all of whom coached on a part-time basis. Scheduling proved difficult, and opponents ranged from nearby agricultural high schools, such as Poplarville and Wesson, to Mississippi College, which pounded the "Normalites" on a somewhat regular basis. "They were from a Baptist school," M. M. Roberts later recalled, "but they were mean."

Highlights of the early years included a 113-0 triumph over Mize and a 13-7 near miss against Ole Miss in 1913. Low points were more frequent, including humiliations at the hands of Mississippi College (75-0 in 1916), Southwestern Louisiana College (66-0 in 1923), and the University of Mississippi (54-0 in 1920). Notable players included "Blink" Anderson, "Puny" Davis, "Mutt" Campbell, "Strut" Venable, and the Busby boys, "Red" and "Black." M. M. Roberts played on the 1916 squad, while Clairborne Meador (1912), Frank Montague (1912), L. E. Gafford (1920–23), Fred "Coon" Leech (1921–24), Nollie Felts (1922–26), and D. C. Leech (1923–24) eventually found their way to the University of Southern Mississippi Sports Hall of Fame. Local support was generally dismal, as indicated by the cancellation of the 1923 game with Ole Miss.

Basketball started at MNC on an outdoor court behind Forrest County Hall. In those early days the black and gold played such powers as the D'Lo YMCA, the Richton All-Stars, Chamberlain-Hunt Academy, and the Bogalusa Gaylords. The school did not field a team in 1917 or 1918

because of the World War, and a flu epidemic wiped out the 1920 season. The 1921 squad traveled to the Gulf Coast for a game against the Gulfport Naval Training Center and found themselves playing on a wooden ballroom floor for which they had no suitable footwear. Undaunted, the "teachers" simply smeared their feet with resin and played barefoot, though their heroic perseverance was no match for the "vacuum bottom sneakers" of the sailors who won 53-17. The lack of an indoor playing facility continued to plague the college until the Demonstration School gymnasium opened in 1934. As with football, however, the real problem was lack of community interest, which led to cancellation of the 1924 season. There was even less interest in other sports, which included tennis, track, and women's volleyball, softball, basketball, and indoor baseball.

In 1920, Audie F. Fugitt, who then occupied the French horn chair in Miss Lorena Tomson's college orchestra, set out to organize a brass band. Help came from college engineer V. C. Cagle and several other students, including J. W. McCleskey and J. B. George. Using instruments donated by the student body, the all-male group rehearsed in classrooms, basements, the powerhouse, and even the college barn, until a frame band building was constructed in 1924. The band made its first road appearance at the Mississippi Teachers Association convention in Meridian in 1923 and by 1925 was playing for chapel programs, athletic events, rallies, fairs, and other public events. Fugitt, as student and later as faculty member, directed the band for most of its first decade and a half. In 1923, fifteen Mississippi Normal College coeds organized the state's first all-female band, which also began to perform at various functions, including the premiere broadcast of Hattiesburg radio station WCBG. In their ankle-length blue pleated skirts, white coat-sweaters, and black and gold hats, they looked, said President Cook, "real tidy."

America's entry into the Great War in 1917 brought the first major changes to the college. Enrollment dropped sharply as 390 students, along with 12 faculty members, marched away to make the world safe for democracy. Six never returned. On October 12, 1918, the school organized a Student Army Training Corps to train officer candidates. The 102 inductees "certainly looked fine in their new uniforms," the *News* reported, but the war ended just as they "were showing splendid improvement" in their drills. They were mustered out on December 6, after less than two months' service. The influx of 40,000 regular troops at

Science professor R. J. Slay (top left) was also the first athletic director and football coach. Above, he demonstrates a farm waterworks to his class. The woman in the foreground is domestic science teacher Maggie De Campbell, whom he married in 1914.

THE FIRST (WOMAN) DOCTOR

Female physicians were rare in 1912. "Dr. Jones . . . was the first woman doctor I had ever met," faculty colleague Willard F. Bond recalled. In addition to her duties as instructor of physiology, May F. Jones served as campus medical officer. She once had Coca-Cola banned from the campus store. The original "hospital" was in Hattiesburg Hall, where it remained despite President Cook's urgent but unsuccessful pleas to the legislature for funds to construct a real hospital. When the world-wide outbreak of influenza struck the campus soon after the war, Cook converted the Industrial Cottage into an infirmary. The epidemic, which killed thirty-eight at Mississippi A & M, claimed not a single life at MNC, thanks largely to the heroic efforts of Dr. Jones.

Dr. May F. Jones

In 1921, the old streetcar station (below) was replaced by a new structure honoring those associated with the college who had served during the World War. The memorial station became home to Rev. and Mrs. W. E. Fail, "Ma and Pa" to the students. Rev. Fail, a Civil War veteran, "guarded the campus at night and chased suspicious automobiles on Sunday."

nearby Camp Shelby led to some precautionary modifications in campus discipline. Cook forbade dating between students and soldiers and hired a night watchman and a day guard to keep unauthorized visitors off the grounds. All student courting rites were restricted to the lobbies, even on Sunday afternoon.

Sometime in 1919, college secretary A. V. Hays suggested that the school erect a campus streetcar station as a memorial to those of the college community who had performed military or civilian service during the war. Cook approved and appointed Kate Brown to direct a campaign to raise funds with Hays serving as treasurer. The president wanted the memorial to command the "most prominent" point on the campus and designated the Hardy Street entrance as the logical spot. Faculty, staff, students, alumni, and friends of the college contributed generously enough to subscribe the necessary ten thousand dollars and lay the cornerstone on July 4, 1921. The ceremony included the performance of a masque, *Memory*, written for the occasion by Alma Hickman.

Significant changes continued after the war. Enrollment again burgeoned, placing a great strain on facilities. By 1919, there were twenty-three instructors but only thirteen classrooms, forcing manual training classes to meet in the basement of Mississippi Hall. Cook renewed a longstanding request for another academic building, and the legislature finally appropriated the money in 1920. A fully-equipped Science Hall (now Southern Hall), identical to and directly across from College Hall, opened two years later.

The college barn

ATHLETICS AT MNC

The 1916 football team included M. M. Roberts (front row, right). Visible in the background are the basketball court and dining hall (left) and the north porch of Forrest County Hall (right).

The girls' band, 1924.

The college orchestra, 1920.

Not all the changes were good. In 1922, Cook had to report to the board the first student deaths, one a swimming accident in the Bouie River, the other a sudden heart attack. A continuing struggle for adequate funds led to a gradual deemphasis of agricultural studies. The campus farm was abolished in 1922 and the entire agriculture department in 1930.

There were also several faculty changes. The three-grade practice school went through three different teachers in its first five years. George G. Hurst succeeded Brim, who took a job at Winthrop College in South Carolina in 1915. When Bond became state superintendent of education the following year, Cook appointed H. L. McCleskey to head the history department. Claude S. Hall replaced Thames, who left in 1916, and O. V. Austin took over science from Slay in 1922. In the 1920s, Cook began to encourage faculty members to take leaves of absence to pursue higher degrees, and by 1928 a majority held master's degrees.

Also by the 1920s, the school's success in its original mission was transforming the institution and expanding its academic horizons. From the very beginning, Cook had sought to improve the college curriculum enough to justify a formal degree program in education, but the academic background of the early students was simply too poor to allow it. For the first decade, the school in reality offered students little more than a review of basic courses in preparation for the state teacher's examination. As the state's education system gradually improved, however, the college was able to stiffen its entrance requirements, accepting only high school graduates after 1917. By 1922, the

Science (now Southern) Hall opened in 1922 equipped with up-to-date laboratory facilities (below).

recitation period was up from 45 minutes to an hour, the certificate requirement from 40 hours to 84, the diploma course from 80 to 150, and the faculty from 18 to 31.

By that time, many normal college graduates found their road to advancement blocked as more and more Mississippi schools required principals to hold degrees. In 1921, the Alumni Association launched an effort to secure legislation allowing the college to offer a baccalaureate program. State representative—and Mississippi Normal College student—Martin L. Riley introduced such a bill, which the lawmakers passed in 1922. In May of the same year, Mississippi Normal College took a major step on the long road to academic distinction, awarding its first bachelor of science degree to Kathryn Swetman of Biloxi. As it matured, however, the institution never lost sight of its original vision, to make life richer for the people of Mississippi.

Mississippi Normal College

Hattiesburg Mississippi

This Certifies that

Kathryn B. Swetman

having completed the Collegiate Course of the Mississippi Normal College is hereby awarded the degree of

Bachelor of Science

which is a professional license, valid for life in accordance with and by authority of Section 13, Chapter 119, Laws of Mississippi, 1910, as amended in Section 1, Chapter 201, Laws of Mississippi, 1922.

Given under our hands and the Seal of the Mississippi Normal College at Hattiesburg, Mississippi, this 26th day of May nineteen hundred twenty-two.

Joe Cook
President Miss. Normal College

Mississippi Normal College awarded its first degree, a bachelor of science (above), to Kathryn Swetman (left) in 1922, a full decade after the school opened.

THE NEW SPIRIT

It is difficult to recapture the mood of passionate optimism that permeated the early years of MNC. Fortunately, Alma Hickman left for posterity a dramatic representation of the institution's early life in the form of a pageant, *Neka Camon*, an Indian phrase meaning "new spirit." The three-act production portrayed allegorically "the magical effects," as the campus newspaper described it, "of the Normal College brand of Education," which subdues four grisly figures who appear on stage chanting:

We are cruel as death and relentless as fate,
We are Ignorance, Poverty, Disease and Hate;
With our chains we shall bind your children free
In the town, on the farm, wherever they be.
We shall banish the light and bring in the dark,
All evil spirits we shall enthrone,
The good cast out, we shall reign, alone.
We are cruel as death and relentless as fate,
We are Ignorance, Poverty, Disease, and Hate.

The play included vignettes of Mississippi history beginning with the author herself as the Spirit of the Pines rising "gracefully," according to a *Hattiesburg American* reviewer, "above the tall

background of green in a magnificent costume, carrying out the symbolism. The stage below teemed with graceful sprites, Pine Needles, Red Birds, Blue Birds, and Rabbits . . . cunningly represented by Miss Hooper's Practice School children." The theme of the pageant was the birth of a "New Spirit" to preside over a new temple which the Spirit of Mississippi builds to honor the Spirit of Education. The "New Spirit" is, of course, MNC:

Oh Spirits fair, please tell to me,
What the name of this new Spirit shall be.
(Spirits sing in distance):
She is Neka Camon, new spirit of knowledge,
Known to mortals as Normal College.

More than 300 college students participated in the production which was filmed to be shown throughout the state as a promotional feature for the institution. A second live performance in Woodlawn Park on campus drew over 3,000 spectators.

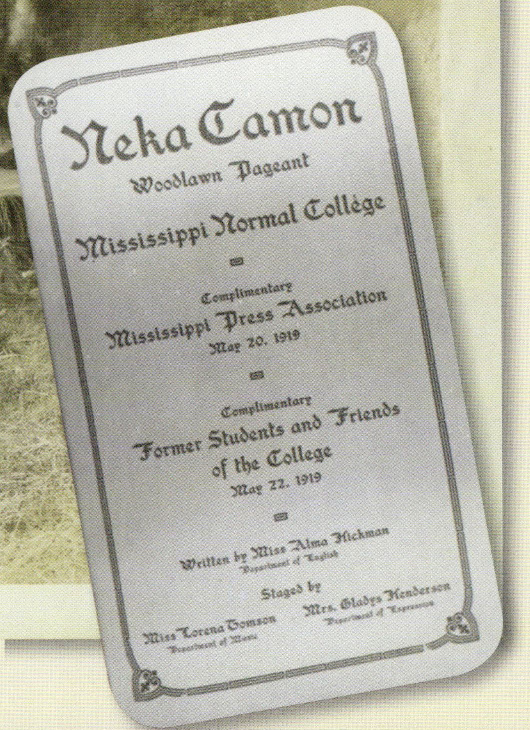

Chapter 2

STATE TEACHERS COLLEGE

College Hall in 1939.

On September 16, 1924, according to the campus newspaper, Joe Cook announced the opening of school much as he had for a dozen years, "with the same lively step . . . the same beam in his eye, and the same smile on his face." Change was in the air, however, for Mississippi Normal College had become, by legislative act of March 7, State Teachers College (STC). The *Teachers College News*, as it was now called, noted another significant change. While the institution retained its original "purpose and spirit," its president seemed to have "allowed that 'standardization bug' to get under his shirt." The comment referred to Cook's determination to conform STC, as soon as possible, to requirements set by the American Association of Teachers Colleges. Spurred by the difficulty students encountered when seeking to transfer work to other colleges, Cook decided that the Hattiesburg institution must pursue accreditation. A first step toward standardization of the curriculum had already occurred earlier in the year when the faculty recommended a shift to the quarter system.

About the same time, Cook engaged Professors Shelton Phelps and Charles A. McMurry of Peabody College in Nashville to conduct an extensive study of the college and recommend changes necessary for accreditation. Their 1924 report focused on three areas: instruction, facilities, and faculty qualifications. A random survey of the records of diploma and degree students revealed several deficiencies. Inadequate classification often placed students with little or no high school training in classes with advanced students, contributing to a high failure rate among the first group, who were ill-prepared for such work, and fruitless repetition of basic college instruction by the second, who should have been doing more rigorous work. The study recommended "complete and accurate classification of all students . . . [with] *no exceptions* whatever" and a restructured curriculum, clearly distinguishing high school, junior college, and senior college courses. "For the present," said McMurry, "the main feature in this institution" should be a two-year program to prepare high school graduates to teach in the common schools. The changes, however, would allow for gradual evolution "into a real not nominal Teachers' College."

The report also called for a second vice-president, with a Ph.D. degree from a standard teachers college, to administer instruction according to policies developed by the faculty through appropriate committees. The consultants endorsed the shift to the quarter system and proposed a significant expansion of faculty and courses. In terms of facilities, said Phelps and McMurry, the institution desperately needed a training school, which should be "a model for consolidated schools" both in structure and in instruction and should become the focus of the entire process of training teachers. The study also called for additional library equipment, including a minimum of "8,000 . . . well distributed, professionally administered volumes" and a fully equipped gymnasium to accommodate "a well organized department of physical education." Every new faculty member, the consultants suggested, should have at least a master's degree in his field of study as well as a graduate minor in education. The administration should allow existing faculty "every opportunity and encouragement" to attain these standards, including a year's leave of absence at half pay to pursue advanced study. Also, the school should establish a salary schedule based on "training, experience and teaching efficiency."

In a letter to Cook accompanying the report, Phelps cautioned that standardization would take time. He insisted, however, that many of the recommendations could be implemented immediately, allowing State Teachers College to "take its rightful place among all colleges of the state, and among the teachers colleges of the nation." Eventually, he concluded, "there is no reason why this cannot be made one of the outstanding teachers colleges of the South." Finally, he offered a tribute to the current faculty, "an earnest determined group," he said, whose "spirit . . . causes them to determine upon standardizing everything about the work of the college, even when some do not actually meet the degree requirements of such a college. Sober judgment must give to those who have worked here for the past twelve years the full credit for the splendid progress already made."

Many of the Phelps-McMurry recommendations proved impractical, primarily for financial reasons. There was no money for a vice-president of instruction, and Alma Hickman insisted that she knew of no faculty member who was ever paid a penny during a leave of absence until well into the 1950s. Nonetheless, several of the suggestions were put into effect fairly quickly. In the 1924–25 academic year, the school adopted a twelve-week quarter system with classes meeting four times each week. Courses of study included a one-year certificate program (48 quarter hours), a two-year certificate program (96 hours), a three-year diploma course (144 hours), and a four-year degree course (192 hours). Renumbered courses reflected clearly defined academic levels: 25–49, freshman; 50–99, sophomore; 100–149, junior; and 150–199, senior. A total of 290 courses were scattered over 19 departments. The degree requirements included 32 hours of education, 20 of English, and 12 each in foreign language, history, and science. Additional hours for a major, two minors, and electives brought the total to 192. Except for minor modifications, this remained the basic curriculum for more than two decades.

Thanks largely to the efforts of the STC Alumni Association, led by president George McLendon and secretary J. B. George, a new $125,000 Demonstration School (now the George Hurst Building) opened in September 1927. The first year's appropriation provided for only eight grades, but the addition of four more the following year made it a full-grade high school. McLendon became the first principal, and George Hurst, as head of the college's Department of Education, the first director. The recommended gymnasium, which for years would serve the college as well as the Demonstration School, was not completed until 1934.

By 1927, Cook was convinced that the college was ready to pursue accreditation, and in November of that year, T. P. Scott attended the annual meeting of the Southern Association of Colleges and Secondary Schools (SACS) in Jacksonville, Florida. SACS would not act on STC's application for membership until the following year, but by that time, Mississippi politics had intervened. Early in 1928, rumors began to circulate that Governor Theodore Bilbo wanted Cook removed. The president at first discounted such talk because, as he later noted, he "had been for 20 years a supporter of the governor." By September, however, realizing that he had misjudged Bilbo's intentions, he addressed a special meeting of faculty and students to clarify his status: "It now seems that the effort to remove me will be pressed. I shall not surrender. I shall not resign." Cook understood power, however, and he sought to prepare his listeners for the worst. "If I am defeated," he warned, "you will have another president. . . . If you love me, I want you, if I go, to rally to the support of the next president with

The new Demonstration School (above) opened in 1927.

The Demonstration School gymnasium (left) was completed in 1934.

GREAT SCOTT

Joe Cook was justifiably "Daddy Joe," but the real "father" of what is now The University of Southern Mississippi was Thomas Percival Scott. One of thirteen children born to a Copiah County family, he eventually earned four degrees from the University of Mississippi. One was in law, but after ten months of legal practice, he turned to education because it seemed more compatible with his Christian ideals. He led the Mississippi Teachers Association in its long and successful crusade for the establishment of Mississippi Normal College, and as an original trustee and secretary of both the MNC board and its building committee, he supervised the minutest detail of construction of the college, from site selection and stump removal to the choice of building materials. When Cook was named president, he persuaded Scott to become his second in command. "I shall want you as my closest advisor," he wrote, "and the man to be in charge when I am away. . . . I have made up my mind on you, and I want you, if necessary, to do as I have done—make sacrifices to come. Now, think over the idea . . . and cut your cards so that you will join me in this work." Scott relented, noting that if the salary proved inadequate, "I shall rent a bob tailed mule and make a 'crop,' I suppose."

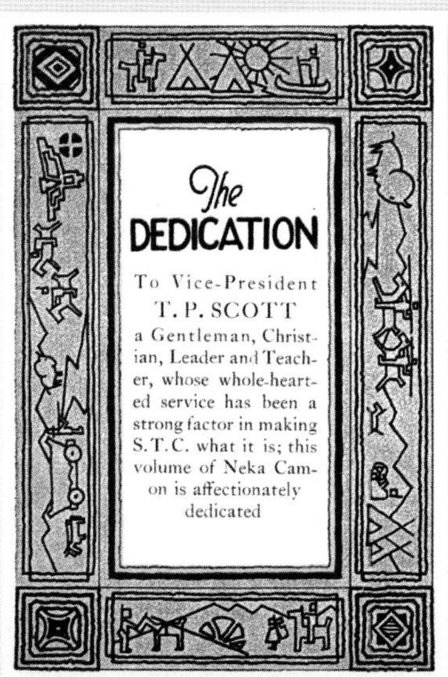

The DEDICATION

To Vice-President T. P. SCOTT a Gentleman, Christian, Leader and Teacher, whose whole-hearted service has been a strong factor in making S.T.C. what it is; this volume of Neka Camon is affectionately dedicated

Dedication page of 1924 *Neka Camon*.

As vice-president, he designed the curriculum, wrote the catalogue, and edited the school newspaper. "He was tireless in his attention to detail," said colleague Willa Bolton, and "some faculty members felt he was too strict and uncompromising in his ideas," not all of which were "progressive." He was advisor to the Honor Council, and one student recalled the case of a married student accused of "slapping" his wife, who was "tall and slender and of a nervous type . . . what was then called 'high strung.'" Scott defended a man's "right to whip his wife" and suggested that she probably "needed more than she received." The council took no action. Another student remembered Scott telling a coed "that everyone knew that we had legs and that he did not want any unusual display of them on the porches of the dormitories. If there was any further display of them by her, she would be on her way home and her trunk would follow her." Students respected Scott, "but they did not like him."

Scott Hall

Antiquated sensibilities notwithstanding, he was, in Claude Bennett's words, "the balance wheel in the operation of the school, [and] he helped shape the destiny of the institution. . . . Many and many a night after the President and other members of the faculty had gone to sleep, the light in Mr. Scott's office could be seen burning. He was working on some problem or doing some work that meant much to the school." In 1959, a men's dorm tory (above) was named in his honor.

even more zeal, if possible, than you have supported me . . . and take the next president into your affection . . . from the start. Your loving him will not detract one whit from your love for me, and your loving help to and co-operation with him will inspire him with a faith from which will be born visions of a greater State Teachers College. . . . Its services and ideals will finally permeate every neighborhood in the State of Mississippi, enter into the life of the people, uplift them, and contribute to the betterment of our civilization." Six hundred students and teachers erupted into a spontaneous and rousing rendition of "Pack Up Your Troubles."

The warning had been prescient, for before the month was out the ax fell, and on October 10, 1928, Claude Bennett became the school's new president. The *Hattiesburg American* praised Cook's selfless dignity. "The greatest moment of his long and useful life," the editorial asserted, "was that in which he rose above the petty prejudices of this finite world and declared that State Teachers College is bigger than any man or set of men, and its future more vital than the fate of its president." Two months later, Bennett accompanied Scott to the annual SACS meeting in Ft. Worth, only to learn that STC's application had been denied because of political interference in the school's administration. Upon returning, they sought assurances from the governor. Scott described a meeting at Jackson's Pantaze Café in December 1928, during which Bennett asked Bilbo to repeat in Scott's hearing the promise he had earlier made to leave personnel decisions at STC to the president. Bennett requested permission to quote the governor to the SACS committee considering the school's application for membership, Scott later insisted, and Bilbo agreed. "I did quote him," Scott said, at the SACS meeting at Lexington, Kentucky, in 1929, "with Claude Bennett seated right in the committee room at the time, and STC did get into the association."

It did not stay long. The following year, Bilbo unleashed a more sweeping purge of higher education that resulted in the expulsion by SACS of every four-year public institution in Mississippi except Delta State Teachers College, whose board defied the governor's efforts to interfere. Among the victims at STC was the vice-president himself, but the board at first agreed only to demote him to registrar. At that point, Scott said, the governor angrily threatened to "clean out this faculty 'from cellar to garret' when he gets complete control of the board next April." Scott insisted

DOWN TO PERKINSTON | STUDENT PRINTZ | DOWN WITH PERKINSTON

Hattiesburg, Miss., October 3, 1928

Joe Cook Is Ousted at S. T. C.

Choctaws Down Yellow-jackets, Score 83 to 0

Mississippians Enjoy Good Program

Simp Jackson Elected Manager

Sherwood Bonners Show Enthusiasm

Claude Bennett New President Teachers College

BEST WISHES OF STUDENTS GO WITH MR. JOE COOK

SOPHOMORE CONVENTION

JUNIORS ELECT OFFICERS

Claude Bennett (left) replaced Joe Cook as president in 1928.

that he would have preferred to force Bilbo's hand, but he informed Bennett in August 1930 that because "you say that you think my remaining here under these circumstances will result in the carrying out of this threat, and that I will be responsible for the wrecking of the college, I have decided to relieve your anxiety and that of others here by tendering you my resignation."

The departure of Cook and Scott ended an era. In its first eighteen years, the school had awarded only 248 degrees, and barely one-fourth of the eleven thousand students who attended earned even a certificate. Those statistics seem to substantiate Alma Hickman's assessment that for much of the Cook era, the institution gave its students little more than "a review of basic elementary subjects" to prepare them for the state teacher's examinations. Nonetheless, she insisted, "Joe Cook could leave the president's office . . . with his head held high," confident, as he stated in his final report to the board, that "this institution from the beginning . . . has been, and is, fulfilling its mission." A 1928 study by alumnus Martin L. Riley found "that a very large majority of graduates go into the teaching service and continue in the profession over a period of time. It is evident that the MSTC is carrying out the purpose for which it was established—namely, to train teachers for the public schools." Cook "never gave a written contract," said Hickman, "but for sixteen years he gave the faculty an almost perfect security. . . . He was honest, fair-dealing, fearless, and a treasured friend to all who worked with him."

While no one could dispute the enormity of Cook's contribution, acclaim for the first president was not quite so universal as Alma Hickman suggests. During the legislative debate over changing the school's name in 1924, Representative J. V. Gibson of Lauderdale County read on the floor of the House a letter, allegedly from a member of the student body, suggesting that Cook was "getting old and . . . losing the respect and confidence of many of the most influential students." The student body and faculty voted officially to repudiate the letter's accusations, but there is little doubt that many students, and some faculty, chafed under the rigor of Cook's discipline.

Sometime in 1926, there appeared on campus a clandestine force of student dissent that scandalized the institution for months. The movement almost certainly included several students, but the conspirators always left a singular and ominous mark of identity: "the Blackbird." Sidewalks, walls, and especially the water tower offered convenient blank space for the paint brush of protest and defiant sloganeering. The age and marital status of several faculty members became favorite topics of comment. Librarian Anna Roberts recalled the shock of exiting the dining hall after breakfast one morning to find "The March of the Dead" scrawled across the sidewalk, and underneath, the names of three prominent elderly professors. More startling was the reference to a not-so-young female instructor

The campus in 1927 included (from left) College Hall, Forrest County Hall, the old dining hall, Mississippi Hall, Hattiesburg Hall and Science Hall. The pavilion behind Science Hall and an identical one behind College Hall became known as "courting sheds" for obvious reasons.

as the "Last Rose of Summer" splashed in mercilessly bright, painted letters across the front of College Hall. Most shocking of all was the cry of "Down with Pimps" emblazoned upon the water tower and visible from virtually any spot on campus. For Roberts, who considered herself "more or less a classicist," the implication of the word pimp was only too clear, and she sternly upbraided one of the boys whom she suspected for insinuating such things in public. Her rebuke seemed lost on the young rebel, who artlessly insisted, "The campus is full of them." Finally, he explained that by pimp he meant simply an informer, a squealer, a collaborator with the administration. At times the rebellion manifested unsettling overtones. "You would be walking along the campus," said Roberts, "and all of a sudden . . . put your hand in the pocket of your sweater and . . . find a note signed, 'The Blackbird.'" Another faculty member linked the protest campaign to Cook's departure, speculating that "the Blackbird did have quite a bit to do with it."

More likely it was the infamous "Dread Scott" decision of November 1926 that really brought the public's attention to student discontent. The Honor Council of the Student Self-government Association convicted several boys, including one of the vice-president's sons, of drinking on campus and recommended their suspension. When Cook rejected the recommendation and exonerated young Edd Scott, the entire Council resigned in protest. Thereafter, all discipline cases were handled exclusively by the administration, ending fourteen years of student self-government, though the student body continued to elect honorary officers. The controversy found its way into the local newspapers and heightened public awareness of growing student discontent with the administration. Obviously, not everyone on campus was sorry to see President Cook go. One professor saw a certain symbolism in Bennett's early removal of the fence that had surrounded the campus for a decade and a half, declaring, "He really unlocked the prison gates" and ushered in "a new day" for the college. "It was like coming out of the middle ages."

Still, Cook remained quite popular with most people, and Bennett wore the albatross of Bilbonic politics throughout his tenure. The association with the governor did, however, carry with it certain advantages, not the least of which was an outpouring of long-needed appropriations that funded a massive construction program. In addition to the Demonstration School, the college added an Auditorium (later named for Bennett), the Administration Building (later named for Aubrey Lucas), a Dining

The new Dining Hall (now The Hub) was completed in 1930.

The college Auditorium (above), later named for President Claude Bennett, and the Home Science Nursery (below), now Fritzsche-Gibbs Hall, were both completed in 1930.

Bertha Fritzsche

Hall (now The Hub), and a Home Science Nursery School (now Fritzsche-Gibbs Hall), all designed by State Architect Vinson Smith Jr. of Gulfport, who also designed Bilbo's "Dream House" in Pearl River County. Smith's buildings, according to Ed Polk Douglas, comport quite well with Hunt's original design, though on a compressed scale, and "are possibly the handsomest on campus." The gravel driveways around the campus loop were paved in 1929, and the following year Bennett hired a horticulturist, Albert Leggett, to improve the campus landscape. Soon azaleas blossomed where pea patches had reigned before, and other flowers and shrubs appeared around the campus.

Despite the unsavory circumstances of his selection, Bennett eventually won acceptance and respect from most students and faculty. He was, after all, well qualified for the post, holding a bachelor's degree from Mississippi College and a master's from Peabody. He had served as vice-president of Mississippi Woman's College, superintendent of the Biloxi school system, and state supervisor of rural schools. Bennett's administration encompassed the worst years of the Depression, and he was kind and humane, almost to a fault. His compassionate indulgence of poor students unable to pay their fees strained a college budget already buffeted by hard times. Through most of the lean years, STC was able to pay salaries on schedule, thanks largely to the resourcefulness of business manager Clarence Woods. In 1932, however, the economy hit bottom. Bilbo's successor, Mike Conner, inherited a mere $1,326.47 of unencumbered funds in the state treasury, and financial institutions refused credit to public agencies. For six months, state employees, including STC faculty, received no paychecks, but the people of Hattiesburg came to the rescue. Banks eased loan policies, and stores extended generous credit. "Old clothes," said Alma Hickman, "were passed around and even became fashionable. Despite the difficulties, we all lived through the winter of our discontent. Spring came, and though our checks did not there was talk . . . of passing a sales tax. . . hope was in

Interior of the new Dining Hall.

Demonstration School director George Hurst (left), who had joined the education faculty in 1915, died unexpectedly in 1929. At his widow's request, his body lay in state in the college library for two days. In 1954, the Demonstration School was renamed in his honor.

the air." Conner did steer through the reluctant legislature a sales tax that by the end of the year restored the state's fiscal integrity.

The economic constraints did not prevent Bennett from achieving a measure of academic progress. Beginning in 1928–29, the degree curriculum distinguished separate courses of study for lower elementary, upper elementary, and high school teacher training. In 1929, the diploma program was abolished and a new Department of Correspondence and Extension created, offering classes in twenty-five Mississippi counties. The same year, W. H. Weathersby took over the education department and Demonstration School following the sudden death of George Hurst, and STC opened the state's first college-operated nursery school. Also in 1929, Bennett established the office of dean of instruction, which the board ratified the following year. J. Lawrence Eason was the first to occupy the new post, but when he left after a very brief tenure, Bennett appointed Colley F. Sparkman. In 1930, the board authorized the college to offer degrees in music and approved the new president's recommendation to place all teachers on nine-month salaries, with every third summer off for advanced study.

To head the music department, Bennett hired Frank E. Marsh Jr., a graduate of the New England Conservatory of Music, who came to STC in 1930 with a master's degree from Syracuse University. He would remain until 1961. In 1932, "two distinguished but elderly native Mississippians," as Alma Hickman described them, joined the faculty, A. A. Kincannon in history and Hubert Shands in English. Their hiring raised some eyebrows, but both made valuable contributions. Kincannon had presided over several institutions, including the University of Mississippi, and Shands held a Ph.D. from the University of Halle in Germany. The former's "wealth of executive experience," said Hickman, proved critical during an anxious faculty assembly amid the national banking crisis of 1933. When someone questioned the prudence of trying to keep the school open under such conditions, Kincannon's ringing affirmation, "Mr. President, we must not close this institution," calmed fears and put the issue to rest. Shands, who was returning to teaching after a career in business, became a scholarly and inspiring campus icon.

Frank E. Marsh Jr. headed the school's music department from 1930 to 1961.

In the early thirties, the history department designed an elaborate landscape map of Mississippi, 186 feet wide and 330 feet long, with a three-inch-wide concrete boundary and scale model replicas of historic buildings. Covering one-eighth of an acre in front of College Hall, it was to have a flowing stream on the west side to represent the Mississippi River and white sand for the gulf on the south. Paved walkways lined with shrubbery were to represent the Spanish Trail, Three-chopped Way, and Natchez Trace. Considerably less sophisticated than originally intended, the project was still quite impressive and took almost three years to complete. The classes of 1929, 1930, and 1932 jointly sponsored construction of a formal, decorative sunken garden, which was dedicated on Class Day in the spring of 1932 and occupied the spot where McLemore Hall now stands.

The same year, the college finally built its own athletic facility thanks largely to Hattiesburg's Central Committee on Unemployment Relief under Chairman L. E. Faulkner. Week by week more than three hundred casualties of the Depression, unemployed workers of all kinds—college graduates, mechanics, railroad men, plumbers, preachers, and multitudes of day laborers—swapped their labor for a modest allotment of groceries. On October 29, at Homecoming, Mississippi's first lady and STC alumna Alma Graham Conner dedicated the new stadium, named Faulkner Field in honor of the relief committee chairman. Relief labor also contributed to the construction of another campus landmark, Lake Byron, named

The Sunken Garden occupied the spot between Science Hall and the President's Home on which McLemore Hall was later constructed.

Built in 1934, Lake Byron has become a campus landmark.

for Byron Green, president of the Forrest County board of supervisors, who helped secure enough federal relief funds to finance the work. The small picturesque pond with an island in the center was a project of the class of 1934. With materials donated by Newman Lumber Company and Hattiesburg Creosote Company, Professor C. E. Thomas's advanced industrial arts class added a scenic arching bridge connecting the island with the mainland.

In 1932, the legislature, in a bill coauthored by Joe Cook, who now represented Lowndes County in the state senate, placed all of the state's colleges under a single new Board of Trustees of Institutions of Higher Learning. Governor Conner served as ex-officio chairman and appointed all nine of the other members to staggered terms. The new board immediately reestablished the office of vice-president at STC and filled it with alumnus J. B. George. The board also made overtures to the Southern Association regarding readmission of the Mississippi schools, and by the end of 1933 the association had restored State Teachers College to full accreditation. The new board was designed to eliminate politics from higher education in Mississippi, but before launching themselves on the road to academic integrity, the trustees disposed of one unfinished bit of blatant political business: they sacked Claude Bennett.

On July 1, 1933, Jennings Burton George became State Teachers College's third chief executive, the first to hold a terminal degree. George was one of the institution's own, having earned a degree in 1923 after eight alternate years of teaching school and attending Mississippi Normal. After securing a master's degree from Peabody College, he returned to STC to teach mathematics for four years. He later spent a year at the University of Chicago before earning the Ph.D. from Peabody in 1932. Since then, he had been vice-president and registrar under Bennett at STC. When he moved up, Mary Pulley took over the registrar's post, which she would retain until her retirement in 1952, and the vice-president's office again disappeared.

The Depression immediately confronted George with a host of pressing problems, but he "proved to be," in Alma Hickman's words, "a frugal businessman and wise administrator." Some of those affected by his austere, but necessary, policies might have described him differently. Among his first economy measures were reductions in employee salaries and increases in student fees.

By 1935, a year at STC cost $246, not including books. The annual budget for the library, which had grown to occupy the entire first floor of Science Hall, stagnated at $1,800 for a dozen years, prompting Anna Roberts to pronounce George "very economically minded" but not very "library minded."

The rise in student expenses and the rapid growth of the state's junior colleges, three of which were within fifty miles of Hattiesburg, forced the college to continue its academic development in order to compete for students. R. G. Lowrey, who replaced Sparkman as dean in 1934, made signal contributions to that end. He immediately organized the various departments into seven divisions:

J. B. George became the school's third president in 1933.

health, language and literature, music, natural sciences and mathematics, practical and fine arts, professional arts, and social studies. With faculty approval, he instituted a quality point system for grading and a system of academic honors. To improve student performance, he implemented an elaborate and effective program of advisement that included a freshman orientation course, student testing, and frequent faculty-student conferences.

Outside the academic sphere, George's major accomplishment, according to Hickman, was "his fight for morality and honesty. He worked harder on these problems than all others." Some thought he worked too hard. In this he resembled Joe Cook, whose devoted disciple he was. George's "approach to education developed into many idiosyncrasies which alienated many people," said Alma Hickman. Another faculty member put it more bluntly: "George was a puritanical Baptist." Students called him Joy Buster or Jitterbug George. A month into his first session as president, he announced to the student body at chapel that there would be "no more leisurely strolling about on remote sections of campus after dark." All "promenading" was thereafter restricted to the area between the main buildings, which was "sufficiently illuminated for propriety" and could be easily patrolled by campus police. Students chafed under George's regimen as they had under Cook's. Several nights after the chapel announcement, according to the campus newspaper, someone painted on the stadium, "in concise slang," a stern criticism of the new administration. Student body leaders called a special meeting to discuss the issue. Acknowledging that most had wanted Bennett to remain, student president Reed Green urged the student leadership, nonetheless, to support the new man, which they did with a censure of the prank and a resounding vote of confidence in George.

The old Laundry (later part of the Industrial Arts and ROTC Building) was converted into a student center in 1933. A sandwich shop named Wimpy's for the Popeye cartoon character was added four years later.

Campus life was not, in fact, altogether barren, despite the reinvigorated social code. In the fall of 1933, the old Laundry was converted into a student social center, with a college store and lounge on the top floor and a barbershop in the basement. The store, operated by student workers, sold all school supplies except books, with the profits going to the athletic program. The black and gold decorated lounge contained tables and chairs, free telephones and newspapers, a radio, games, electric fans, and gas heaters. The student body sponsored a contest to name the facility.

After a faculty committee pared the ninety-five nominations down to five, the students chose "Yellow Jackets' Nest"—Yellowjackets had become the athletic teams' nickname sometime in the mid-twenties—in a special chapel referendum. Sara Weathersby and Kathryn Simmons, who had submitted the winning name, split the grand prize of $2.50 worth of store goods. The center was open until ten o'clock every night except Sunday. In front of the building sat the old band hall, which had also housed the old barbershop. The college Golf Association now acquired this wooden frame structure for a clubhouse and moved it to the recently opened nine-hole course just west of the campus. The band shifted its activities elsewhere.

Religion remained a central aspect of student life. In 1930, President Bennett established a Department of Christian Education, under campus YMCA secretary Henry T. Ware, to supervise all religious and social functions of the student body. Two years later, Ware invited to campus the noted black chemist and fellow of the Royal Academy of Sciences, George Washington Carver. "We feel very fortunate indeed," said Ware, "to be able to present him to our students." Other prominent speakers and performers brought to campus by various organizations included Nelson Eddy, the Vienna Boys Choir, and University of North Carolina sociologist Howard Odum. In 1934, the campus Christian organizations sponsored Religious Emphasis Week, a program of spiritual activities highlighted by morning and evening sermons Sunday through Friday. This modernized version of an interdenominational campus revival became an annual tradition that continued into the 1960s. Also in 1934, the YMCA, with financial help from campus nurse Beedie Smith, built Pinehaven Lodge as a meeting facility for campus religious and social groups. Under President George, a Student Christian Federation replaced the Y associations and in the fall of 1937 took over operation of the campus store. The new proprietors added a pool table, a nickelodeon, and a sandwich shop named Wimpy's after the hamburger-eating Popeye cartoon character. When a new library opened in January

By the late twenties, life at STC included most aspects of the traditional college experience, including freshman hazing.

1940, the entire religious-social center moved into the first floor of Science Hall, and the music department occupied the old Laundry.

As the school grew, student life began to take on the trappings of a typical four-year college, including the hazing of freshmen. By the early thirties, all first-year males faced the annual head-shaving ritual as well as the dreaded dispensation of campus equity by the infamous "Court of Permanent Inter-class Justice." This kangaroo court summoned its accused in a fashion befitting the vermin whose title each freshman bore. "Like the piper of old," said the campus newspaper, "the Judge raps and rats come tumbling, some grumbling, but the worst is yet to come." The highlight of one "rather full docket" was the case of Rats Calender and Therman, who were accused of intelligence, "a serious charge for a rat." The tribunal after very brief deliberation, declared the defendants patently innocent and sentenced them to debate the proposition, "A nut is not what it is cracked up to be." Their performance, of course, proved a thorough vindication of the court, leaving "no doubt . . . as to the correctness of the verdict." Their punishment appears rather mild in light of the correspondent's none-too-subtle report that before adjournment "the upper classmen reduced the seating capacity of some ten freshmen. At the next session, Judge Tumlin promises much weeping and wailing and fanning of seats."

The newspaper, which was now entirely a student enterprise, changed its name in 1927 to the *Student Printz*. The change, according to former editor O. B. Brewer, grew out of a meeting that he and other students interested in improving the publication held in T. P. Scott's classroom in College Hall. After the group had rejected several possibilities, Brewer glanced at the label on his pipe, Student Prince, and suggested that it might make a good title. Alma Hickman, who was also present, liked the sound of the phrase and pointed out that it was also the title of a popular contemporary musical. The group decided to present the idea to the student body, and in a campus referendum the new name won approval, though not without serious opposition. The campus newspaper has been the *Student Printz* ever since. The yearbook, called *Neka Camon* after 1920, did not fare so well. It suspended publication after 1931, a victim of Depression-era finances, and did not appear again until 1938.

1939 State Teachers College Yearbook.

Other activities and organizations, however, flourished throughout most of the STC years. In 1926, the twenty-four-piece college band traveled with the "Know Mississippi Better" train on an extensive tour of the eastern United States and Canada that included a parade down Manhattan's Fifth Avenue and a performance at the Palace Theater. For four years, Audie Fugitt's group was the official band for this annual traveling exhibition of Mississippi boosterism, which took them eventually into almost every state in the union as well as to Canada and Mexico. To raise money for these trips, the young musicians played such events as the Picayune Peach Carnival, the Hattiesburg Water Carnival, and Trades Day fairs in Sumrall, Richton, Wiggins, and New Augusta.

Fugitt left in 1929, and with the onset of the Depression, the school dissolved the band and sold the instruments to raise money. Interest revived the following year with the announcement that John Philip Sousa's sixty-piece band would present two concerts on campus in the fall. Former member and new director Dewey W. Camp returned to reorganize the STC band, which on October 23, 1930, appeared at the Sousa concert to perform one number under the direction of the seventy-six-year-old bandmaster himself. During the thirties the band, under Camp, Fugitt (who returned 1933–36), and William Morgan Keller (1936–43), appeared at Mardi Gras in New Orleans, United Confederate Veterans conventions in Montgomery and Richmond, the Chicago World's Fair, and the 1933 inauguration of President Franklin D. Roosevelt in Washington, in addition, of course, to STC football games and other local events.

Other musical programs flourished, as Frank Marsh began to develop music into one of the college's stronger departments. In 1930, he organized the A Capella Choir, which became the Vesper Choir a year later. Soon afterward Marsh initiated an annual tour that took the young singers into schools and churches throughout the state, generating goodwill for the college and exhibiting the quality of its musical program. In 1932, the choir joined with the Hattiesburg Choral Union to present what would become another annual college tradition, the December performance of Handel's *Messiah.*

Sometime in 1934, another basic element of college life came to the school when seven male students organized the XXX club to "bring about closer fellowship among the fellowmen of State Teachers College." In February of the following year, the club became K.A.T. (Kappa Alpha Tau), the college's first social fraternity. Kappa Phi Sigma appeared in 1937, changing to Zeta Sigma four years later to become the first affiliate of a national fraternity on campus. By that time the college had five sororities, two of them with national affiliation. Sigma Theta Kappa was the first local group, organized in November 1935, followed by Mu Omega two years later. The third local group, Gamma Delta Tau, petitioned to join Sigma Sigma Sigma, and in May 1937, became STC's first national sorority. Alpha Sigma Alpha followed shortly thereafter, accepting another local sorority into its national organization. The fifth women's group was a local sorority, Delta Sigma, founded in 1938.

The advent of a campus Greek community intensified the already mounting pressure on the administration to end the prohibition of dancing. In January 1940, President George finally yielded to the relentless forces of modernity, but it was largely a tactical retreat. The modified rules limited dances to Friday nights, required two faculty or staff chaperones, forbade women students to leave the site of the activity, and excluded nonstudents. "All dances," the new regulation stated, "shall be given for the social welfare of students, faculty, and officers of State Teachers College." Having sanctioned formal dances for fraternities and sororities, the administration could hardly withhold the privilege from others. There was, therefore, a separate code for "informal dancing," which was permitted during designated hours on Monday, Tuesday, Thursday, and Friday afternoons and evenings. Participants again had to provide chaperones, who were to insure that all dancing was "in accord with grace and rhythm and in every respect

The STC band traveled throughout the United States, Canada, and Mexico with the "Know Mississippi Better" train in the late 1920s.

SOUSA EDITION

Student Printz

VOLUME IV | Hattiesburg, Miss., October 17, 1930 | Number 3

WORLD'S GREATEST BANDMASTER HERE THURSDAY

In 1930, the STC band performed with legendary bandmaster John Philip Sousa.

Frank Marsh conducts the Christmas presentation of Handel's *Messiah*. The annual performance became a campus tradition and remains so almost eight decades after its debut in 1932.

Registrar Mary Pulley (far left) helped organize one of STC's early soroities, Alpha Sigma Alpha.

in good taste." In a peculiar stroke of irony, the new guidelines went into effect barely a month before the death of Joe Cook, who would likely never have countenanced any kind of dancing, tasteful or otherwise. When dancing did come to State Teachers College, however, Cook's ghost was there to regulate it. Rule number nine stated: "Each young man attending a dance shall conduct himself as a gentleman, and each young woman . . . shall conduct herself as a lady."

During the STC years, the institution began to emerge as a serious competitor in college football, though not before suffering several more embarrassments, including a 38-6 thrashing at the hands of the Ole Miss freshmen in the midst of a 0-6 campaign in 1925. Herschel Bobo coached the Yellowjackets from 1924 to 1927, compiling a 9-17-4

Legalized dancing finally came to STC in 1939.

record. W. B. Saunders (1928–29) and John Lumpkin (1930–31) followed. The first real success came with former Alabama all-American Pooley Hubert (1932–36), who led the team to a 24-19-5 record during his five seasons. The five victories in 1932, the most in any season in the school's history to that point, were highlighted by a crucial Thanksgiving Day game against Union University of Jackson, Tennessee. A young back from Greene County known as the "Leakesville Express" provided the turning point in that final game of that pivotal season. To the delight of two thousand fans in the newly dedicated Faulkner Field, Reed Green raced eighty-one yards for a fourth-quarter touchdown to seal a 6-0 STC victory. It was a portent of success. Over the next forty years, Reed Green, as player, coach, and athletic director, would lead the school's athletic program to national distinction. After graduating in 1934, Green became an assistant coach and eventually replaced Hubert, who in 1937 accepted a position at Virginia Military Institute. Green hired as his assistant a young Meridian high school coach and former Ole Miss team captain named Thad Vann. These two, Reed Green and "Pie" Vann, would soon construct a football power in Hattiesburg.

The college took a major step toward solving its perennial scheduling problem by joining the Southern Intercollegiate Athletic Association (SIAA) in December 1930. After 1935, only four-year colleges appeared on the schedule. The construction of Faulkner Field in 1932 was another major step, enhanced by the addition of lights two years later and a public address system in 1937. The following year, work began on a stadium dormitory, financed by

As player (above), coach, and athletic director, Reed Green served the institution from 1930 to 1974.

federal public works funds and college revenue bonds and completed in time for the 1939 football season. Despite the increasing respectability of its football program, the college continued to struggle for support. In 1926, the Alumni Association recommended abolishing football, but by the 1930s, both the alumni and the people of Hattiesburg were beginning to recognize that a successful athletic program could be an asset to the college and to the community. The Alumni Association established an athletic advisory council in 1929, and in 1937 several Hattiesburg civic leaders organized the "500" Club to promote STC athletics. These efforts helped the football program to thrive, but other sports continued to lag far behind.

By the end of the 1930s, it was obvious that the college was becoming more than a teacher training institute. President George reminded a state legislator that State Teachers College was the only public "senior college in the southern two-thirds of the state. This being true, we have a great part of the state to serve." George could not have known just how true that statement was about to become. The cataclysm that had erupted only a few months before, halfway around the world in Poland, would soon work a profound transformation in Mississippi. The state's population had already begun to drift southward, but World War II swelled the trickle into a flood. Workers poured into south Mississippi for jobs created by large military

STC football in the 1930s.

Dick Shields, STC's first all-American football player.

Pooley Hubert's 1935 football squad (opposite page) provided not only the first winning season in fifteen years, but the first postseason honors in school history. The Associated Press voted end Dick Shields and halfback J. D. Stonestreet Honorable Mention Little All-American. When Richard Valentine Shields came to State Teachers College from Pelahatchie in the early thirties, he had never seen a football field. He was a quick learner, however, in more ways than one. End and placekicker on the football team, he also lettered in basketball and boxing. A double-major in mathematics and physics, he was also editor and sports editor of the *Student Printz*. His "spare" time was spent working odd jobs to earn money. Twice voted "Most Handsome" at STC, Shields later married his college sweetheart, Erma Paschal of Bessemer, Alabama.

In the days before NCAA scrutiny, athletic stardom carried with it some quaint privileges. During their senior year, Shields and Stonestreet shared accommodations upstairs in the President's Home, eating at the presidential table and sharing the services of the presidential maid. In 1939, Shields became head football coach at Moss Point High School, where Stonestreet joined him as an assistant after World War II. Their Moss Point Tigers were highly successful in the late 1940s, regularly embarrassing larger schools, including Pascagoula and a Mobile, Alabama, team that featured future college coaches Vince and Bill Dooley. As head track coach, Shields also mentored several individual state champions. Shields gave up coaching in 1950 and spent the remainder of his career in management at Ingalls Ship Yard. He and Stonestreet are now in the Southern Miss M-Club Hall of Fame.

State Teachers College subsequently produced other Little All-Americans. A. D. "Sandy" Morgan (1938), A. C. "Mule" Massengale (1938), Reginald Switzer (1939), and Peter "Jabo" Jones (1939) all made Honorable Mention. In 1938, end George Westerfield earned First Team honors.

STC football program.

The 1935 football team was coached by Pooley Hubert (third row, far left) and his assistant Reed Green (second row, far right).

State Teachers College marked its twenty-fifth anniversary in May 1937 with a three-day celebration that included speeches, receptions, garden parties, an alumni reunion, and a parade through downtown Hattiesburg. Helen Wright of Raymond was elected Jubilee Queen, and Ole Miss Chancellor A. B. Butts delivered the commencement address.

Silver Jubilee Edition

Student Printz

S. T. C. Celebrates Full Quarter Century of Worthy Educational Service to State

Past Presidents State Teachers

Lokey Awarded Scholarship

Students, Faculty, Alumni and Citizens of State Join in Colorful Jubilee Events

Helen Wright Elected Queen

FOREWORD

Miss Kate Brown Announces Tour

installations at Camp Shelby and Keesler Field in Biloxi and the huge shipbuilding complex at Pascagoula. Money poured in, too, shifting the state's economic center of gravity southward as well. Even before the war, STC's appeal was reaching beyond aspiring educators, and by 1938 the curriculum included pre-professional training in dentistry, medicine, pharmacy, law, and engineering. Two years later, the school awarded its first bachelor of arts degree to Harry Rollings of Hattiesburg.

Not everyone appreciated the value of the college. In the mid-thirties, some lawmakers sought to abolish STC or to turn it into a branch of the University of Mississippi. Both bills died in committee, but they underscored the precarious nature of STC's existence and convinced the administration and its friends that another name change was essential, both to protect the institution and to reflect its expanding mission. "You know and I know," George wrote to a state senator from Forrest County, "that we are training many people who never expect to teach. . . . If we are to render the service that is demanded of us, we must have the name changed."

Progress did not come at the expense of the institution's original vision, however, and Bell Wiley perhaps best expressed the spirit of that vision as it endured through the State Teachers College era. Wiley first taught at STC in the summers of 1930 and 1931 and, after earning a Ph.D. from Yale, returned in 1935 to head the history department. Three years later, he left again and went on to establish a distinguished career that included professorships at Ole Miss, LSU, and Emory, as well as visiting professorships

1931 graduates filing into the new Auditorium.

at the University of Southern California and Tulane and in 1965–66 the prestigious Harmsworth Professorship at Oxford University.

Despite the international acclaim, his years at State Teachers remained special. As I look back on it," he later said,

> I think maybe that I got more real satisfaction out of teaching during my four years and two summers there than I did at any other place or time in my teaching career. . . . The satisfaction derived mainly from the fact that you could see, in a rather startling

> way, the results of your teaching. You could see these young men and young women come to you unscrubbed from the sandy hills of south Mississippi and take on culture, and you could realize that you were having a part in that. . . . My main concern in history has been the lowly people, the country people, partly because I grew up among them. They are unassuming; they are modest; they are open to suggestion. . . . Many of [these young people] were eager. They wanted to improve themselves. It was fun to be with them.

Perhaps it was the closeness, spatially and otherwise, between faculty and students that nurtured such a spirit. Anna Roberts, like Bell Wiley, lived in a dormitory with students during those years. On first coming to campus, she later recalled, "I . . . took up my residence on the third floor of Hattiesburg Hall, something for which I always—and I stress always—have been very thankful. It was . . . that way that I learned to know so well and appreciate so much the many faculty members and students. . . . I lived there in that dormitory for thirteen years and had the time of my life."

View of the circulation desk inside the Joe Cook Memorial Library.

Librarian Roberts recounted another vivid memory from the 1930s, near the end of the State Teachers College era. During the Christmas holidays of 1939, the 22,250 volumes under her care "were transferred through snow and sleet" from their old niche on the first floor of Science Hall to a new "two story brick building with four identical reading rooms, a large rotunda with eight massive columns supporting [a] lighted dome, a stack area, and several offices." Financed with funds from the New Deal Public Works Administration, the impressive structure represented, in the words of the *Student Printz*, "more than a quarter of a century's efforts and work in one of the most important departments of the college." As the Joe Cook Memorial Library, it stood as a fitting symbol of the institution's continuing union of heritage and progress.

In 1940, the library moved from Science Hall to a new facility named for former president Joe Cook.

Longtime Librarian, Anna Roberts.

Chapter 3

MISSISSIPPI SOUTHERN COLLEGE

MEMORIAL ENTRANCE, MISSISSIPPI SOUTHERN COLLEGE, HATTIESBURG, MISS.—12
MISSISSIPPI S THERN COLLEGE

February 1940 was full of irony for State Teachers College. It was a month of celebration and mourning, of triumph and near tragedy. On February 1, the Mississippi House of Representatives voted 113-0 to change the school's name; a day later, fire almost destroyed Mississippi Hall. The following week the state senate approved the name change, and STC became Mississippi Southern College; the same week, the institution's first president (also a member of that 1940 senate) died. Paradox pursued the school throughout the year, even the decade. In June, the institution awarded its first bachelor of arts degree; before the year ended, the Southern Association placed Mississippi Southern College on probation. In 1941, the football team recorded its first undefeated season; barely a year later, MSC suspended intercollegiate athletics when the United States found itself, for the second time in a generation, embroiled in a profoundly destructive global war. This one almost destroyed the college. Enrollment, which had climbed from its Depression slump to a peak of 1,500 in 1939, plunged by 1944 to a historic low. The male population almost disappeared entirely, as military service took from the campus, in the words of one professor, all but "4-F students and theologues." Colleagues teasingly referred to the dean of students as the "dean of women." The faculty shrank to forty.

World War II and its aftermath dominated college life throughout the forties. The drastic drop in enrollment, especially among men, created unique opportunities for females like star debater Evelyn Gandy who later became Mississippi's first woman lieutenant governor.

What the exigencies of war removed with one hand, however, they gave back with the other, producing by the end of the 1940s immense growth and prosperity for Mississippi Southern College. After the Japanese attack on Pearl Harbor, the war dominated campus life. A hastily organized civilian defense program reflected the mood of anxious uncertainty. Coach Thad Vann became air-raid warden for the college and outlined emergency procedures to the students during a solemn chapel session. "If the raid starts when you are away from home," he said, "lie down under shelter. . . . If an incendiary hits your house, go put it out with a spray (never a stream, jet, or splash) of water." Above all, Vann concluded, "Don't believe wild rumors. Don't crowd. Don't scream. Don't telephone. Don't start disorder or panic. Do what the Air-Raid Warden tells you to do. Be strong, be calm, be orderly. Lick the aggressors—everyone can help. Do your share!"

Fears of immediate danger soon gave way to grim but hopeful determination. In the fall of 1942, the U.S. War Department established an army administration school on campus to train staff for military camps. The 165-member classes rotated through the eight-week school in staggered intervals with two classes on campus all the time, one entering and another leaving every four weeks. One occupied the stadium dormitory and the

Former football standout Andrew Webb was killed in action in the Phillipines on December 8, 1941.

Affectionately called "Granny," Beedie Smith served as campus nurse for over twenty years.

other Forrest County Hall. The army also commandeered the second and third floors of College Hall for classrooms, several offices in the Administration Building, half the dining hall for mess, and the band hall for a quartermaster's building. The twenty-eight student occupants of "The Rock," as East Stadium was called, moved into the campus hospital under the supervision of nurse Beedie Smith, "Granny" to the campus community. "I lost 30 pounds and 11 months sleep the first year," she said, "but I wouldn't have missed it for anything in the world! We fussed, fought, and were friends together." When the army transferred its administration school to Fort Washington in January 1944, the college rented the East Stadium rooms to families of forty-nine men stationed at Camp Shelby, and soldiers continued to overrun the campus and the town until peace returned.

The war years also brought significant administrative changes, culminating in the appointment of a new president. Politics continued to plague higher education in Mississippi, despite the safeguards recently built into the administrative structure. Governors quickly learned to manipulate the new college board almost as effectively as they had the old ones, simply by expanding its membership. The 1936 legislature added three new trustees, giving Governor Hugh White six appointees out of the board's twelve. Holding the tie-breaking ex-officio chairmanship himself, White restored control of the board to the governor's office. His successor, Paul Johnson, persuaded the lawmakers in 1940 that the board needed two additional members, a change that conveniently gave him eight appointments out of fourteen. By then, many MSC faculty members openly referred to themselves as Conner, White, or Johnson appointees. And so it went.

To train staff for military camps, the U.S. War Department established an army administration school at MSC in 1942. Thanks to nearby Camp Shelby and the army administration school, soldiers became a familiar part of college life.

When the college summarily dismissed three professors in the summer of 1940, the Southern Association of Colleges and Secondary Schools (SACS) again intervened to place the school on probation. Likely victims of a Johnson purge, Henry Ware, Truman Lewis, and B. F. Rivers were probably not so much egregious political offenders as simply the most expendable obstacles to the new governor's ability to pay political debts. Johnson needed jobs for his friends, and the positions held by these three must have seemed as good as any. Ware and Lewis had made themselves especially inviting targets by dabbling in interracial activities. Ware even helped organize a Mississippi affiliate of the Southern Commission on Interracial Cooperation, bringing to Hattiesburg an interracial educational institute that featured, among others, Mrs. Jessie Daniel Ames, founder of the Association of Southern Women for the Prevention of Lynching.

During World War II, East Stadium provided temporary housing to families of men stationed at Camp Shelby.

The college's fourth president, Robert Cecil Cook, took office in 1945.

President and Mrs. R. C. Cook greet an unidentified guest as (left to right) Librarian Anna Roberts, geography professor Willa Bolton, and Registrar Mary Pulley look on. The Cooks revitalized campus social life, entertaining as many as five thousand visitors to the President's Home in a single year.

The 1942 legislature again tried to remove the colleges from the political spoils system by making the board a constitutional body. Voters in a November referendum approved an amendment to the state's fundamental law that reconfigured the board into a thirteen-member body whose structure and powers could be changed only by the same cumbersome and difficult amendment process. SACS lifted MSC's probation before the year was out. In January 1945, the new board declined to renew President George's contract, primarily, according to Alma Hickman, because of "his inability to win the support of the students, faculty and alumni." However unpopular his restrictive policies had become, she concluded, the college owed him much, for his steady administrative hand and sound fiscal management preserved the institution through a savage Depression and a wrenching war.

H. M. Craft, who had replaced R. G. Lowrey as dean in 1941, ran the school until June, when the board named Robert Cecil (R. C.) Cook as the college's fourth president. Cook was still on active duty with the army education program in Europe and later claimed that he did not learn of his selection until he arrived in New York in July and a friend showed him the announcement in a Mississippi newspaper clipping. He immediately reported to Camp Shelby, where the army discharged him on July 6, his forty-second birthday. The next day, he paid his first ever visit to the campus, where he found the President's Home occupied by two faculty boarders and its backyard by the remnants of Dr. George's modest poultry farm. After Mrs. Cook evicted the tenants and cleaned out the chicken coops, the college renovated the thirty-three-year-old dwelling, which soon became the centerpiece of the new president's campaign to revitalize campus social life. The Cooks were, it seemed, always hosting various functions to entertain students, faculty, or alumni—as many as five thousand during one particularly busy year.

Cook held a bachelor's degree from Mississippi State College and both master's and doctoral degrees from Columbia University. He had been a teacher and superintendent in Mississippi's public schools and had served the University of Mississippi as principal of its Demonstration School, as well as associate professor and eventually dean of the school of education. His academic credentials were impeccable. Primarily, however, R. C. Cook was a promoter, and he immediately set about promoting Mississippi Southern College. During that first campus visit, Dean Craft assembled an impromptu faculty meeting at which Cook predicted that enrollment would soon top two thousand. His optimism both stunned and amused the fifty-one members of the faculty and staff, who at that moment were serving a student body of barely three hundred. They must have been more stunned, if not more amused, when enrollment quadrupled in two years and did reach two thousand by 1950.

Cook sought especially to attract local students. In those days, as one faculty member acknowledged, most of Hattiesburg's social elite "wouldn't think of sending their children out here . . . they would send them to Ole Miss or to the east." Determined to erase the institution's image as "Hardy Street High," Cook spent much of his time and energy building bridges to the community, too much to suit some on campus. In any case, he hoped to increase MSC's appeal to a broad range of students by promoting excellence in three areas: academics, athletics, and social life. Progress had to begin, he believed, with a "program of superior instruction in a well organized and varied curriculum." The *Printz* reported that "his eagerness for . . . Southern's football future is as intense as the most ardent sportsman of Mississippi Southern College," and in striking contrast to his predecessor, Cook was an enthusiastic advocate of "good wholesome entertainment," including "dances, parties, and other social activities."

To accommodate the flood of returning veterans, the college rented unused apartment facilities at Camp Shelby, which became known as Veterans Village.

The 1946–47 session brought to campus a flood of veterans, who placed a severe strain on college housing. The school imported from Camp Shelby two prefabricated structures, one for married students (later McMillin Hall) and another for married faculty (later McCleskey Hall), and from the National Housing agency, twenty-two trailer units which were placed opposite Faulkner Field. The temporary buildings, said Cook, would provide "adequate light-housekeeping quarters to the GIs who will of necessity have to bring their families with them—but who can't afford to pay high rent." For another 175 couples, the school secured access to a cluster of Camp Shelby apartments that soon became known as Veterans Village. A newly purchased fleet of buses transported the students to campus and back each day. The surge in enrollment strained more than just housing facilities. The fine arts division moved out of the crowded third floor of College Hall into a frame building that Cook also purchased from Camp Shelby and placed on the Demonstration School playground. Several other departments likewise held classes in temporary structures, most of which were "beastly hot," as one faculty member recalled. "It wasn't too uncommon to see a professor under a tree with his students."

The large influx of veterans changed the nature of the college. For the first time, males made up a large percentage of the student population, and Cook felt that the curriculum "had to go in directions other than teaching." The Veterans Administration opened on campus an advisement center that provided education and vocational guidance to former servicemen in a fifteen-county area around Hattiesburg. Business proved especially popular

By 1950, the campus was dotted with temporary white-frame facilities purchased from military surplus.

In 1949, Joseph Greene became chairman of business and commerce. He would later go on to become dean of the College of Business Administration.

with veterans, and in 1946 business education and commerce, which had been a department within social studies, became a separate division. Joseph Greene assumed the chairmanship in 1949 and over the next twenty years developed the program into a highly respected college of business administration. Also in 1946, biology broke away from the physical sciences and mathematics to become an independent division under J. Fred Walker, who had been on the science faculty since 1926. In 1947, the board approved the institution's first graduate program, a master's degree in education with emphases in administration, secondary, elementary, and physical education. To head the new graduate division, Cook appointed former Mississippi College dean W. H. Sumrall. The following year, the legislature defined teacher education as MSC's "principal . . . instead of . . . sole object" and authorized the school's first degree program without a professional teaching component.

The 1949–50 catalogue listed a bachelor of science curriculum with no distinction between teaching and nonteaching degrees. It included composition (ten hours), English literature (eight), speech (four), library science (one), social studies (fourteen), Mississippi history (four), science—biology, chemistry, and physics—(twelve), mathematics (four), science or mathematics elective (four), psychology (four), health and physical education (six). Beginning in 1954, these required courses were administered by a Basic College to which all incoming freshmen were assigned. Major and minor requirements (including professional courses for teachers) and elective courses (which included R.O.T.C. beginning in 1950) filled out the 192 quarter hours required for graduation. Such was the school's general curriculum for the next two decades. Also in the early fifties, the designations "honors" and "highest honors" were added for graduating seniors.

Shortly after the war, Wilbur Stout, chairman of the division of language and literature, established within the speech department a four-year radio course under Mary Tom Colones. She had been a member of Professor Frederick Koch's famous Carolina Playmakers at the University of North Carolina, where she had earned a master's degree in radio and drama. Besides teaching courses in radio, she also assumed direction of major campus theater productions from longtime dramatic club sponsor Alma Hickman. With the cooperation of Hattiesburg station WFOR, the school constructed a fully-equipped studio under the north porch of Mississippi Hall, though it later moved to the third floor of College Hall. By 1951, the radio workshop was producing shows on local stations, and two years later WMS, the college's own ten-watt station, went on the air.

Three new research and service centers emerged during Cook's presidency. In 1946, R. A. Pulliam developed the Reading Clinic, building on the work of Emily Jones, who had organized reading conferences for school teachers as early as the 1920s. As part of the Department of Education and Psychology, the clinic sought to educate teachers, clinicians, and researchers in the whole field of reading. Its diagnostic and treatment services for individual reading problems drew adults and children from throughout Mississippi and surrounding states and in 1953 became available to college students also. In 1947, MSC established a Latin American Institute (now the English Language Institute) to offer intensive language and culture courses designed to smooth the transition of a growing number of foreign students to American university life. When the institute's organizer, Colonel Melvin Nydegger, died suddenly in 1951, Dr. R. C. Reindorp became director. By that time, the institute had become "a two-way street orienting Latin Americans to the American way of life and Americans to the Latin American way of life." In this way it fulfilled Dr. Cook's larger vision of improving "cultural ties and understanding between Latin America and the U.S." The third service unit was the Speech and Hearing Clinic, which opened in 1949, offering clinical therapy for speech disorders, training for student clinicians, and courses for classroom teachers. It also conducted training courses in other Mississippi communities and helped devise a speech curriculum for elementary and secondary schools.

In 1953, after producing shows on local Hattiesburg stations, the college's own ten-watt station, WMS, went on the air.

The rapid expansion of Mississippi Southern College placed a premium on good administrators, and Cook quickly determined that R. A. McLemore "was probably the best academic person on the faculty." When Dean Craft left the school in 1945, Cook appointed McLemore to replace him. "Dr. Mac," as the students knew him, had first come in 1938 to replace Bell Wiley as head of the history department. Except for a brief period as interim president, he continued as dean until 1957. Also during his first year, Cook brought to Southern several people he had known during his days at the University of Mississippi. In December 1945, he named Charles O. (Chuck) Smalling financial secretary, a post he held until his retirement in 1976. In their early days in Oxford, the Cooks had shared a duplex with a young couple from Michigan, Leon and Ivah Wilber. "I knew Mrs. Wilber to be one of the finest women I had ever known," said Cook, and "Dr. Wilber was an excellent teacher," so he brought both to MSC, her as dean of women and him as professor of political science. In 1946, Lena Gough took over as dean of women, but Mrs. Wilber remained as assistant and served the school faithfully in various capacities for many years. Others who came to the school under Cook included Carl McQuagge as principal of the Demonstration School (later dean of education and psychology); Jesse Gore as manager of the bookstore and Wimpy's; Dorothy Lenoir as the first director of placement; Reginald Switzer, who was a little all-American on the 1940 football squad, as dean of student welfare; Ralph Owings as head of educational administration (later dean of the graduate school); Porter Fortune as professor of history (later dean of the college, he went on to become chancellor of the University of Mississippi); Jack Moore as the first director of public relations; Powell Ogletree as executive secretary of the Alumni Association; and O. N. Darby, who replaced Mary Pulley as registrar.

One of Dr. Cook's major accomplishments, according to his successor, was in making Mississippi Southern College "socially acceptable." Having seen Ole Miss attract "a great number of fine girls with national sororities," Cook made the expansion of Greek life at MSC a major objective. The three national women's groups already on campus—Delta Sigma affiliated with Delta Sigma Epsilon in 1940—were all educational sororities. Cook's secretary, Jane McInnis, had been a member of Chi Omega during her college days at the University of Alabama, and with her help, he lured this prestigious national social sorority to Southern in 1949. Kappa Delta came the same year and Phi Mu in 1950. A year later, former Mississippi first lady Corinne Johnson helped organize a Delta Delta Delta chapter, giving the school seven national sororities. Two more local fraternities, Alpha Delta Mu (1947) and Beta Kappa Tau (1948), emerged, but attracting Greek letter organizations for men to Southern proved more difficult, according to Cook, because "the national fraternities took a more standoffish look at schools which had formerly been teachers colleges." Several did come, however: Phi Kappa Tau, Kappa Alpha Order, and Kappa Sigma in 1948; Alpha Tau Omega and Pi Kappa Alpha the following year; Sigma Phi Epsilon in 1953. An interfraternity council was established in 1948.

For $31,000 Cook bought a two-story frame structure from Camp Shelby, moved it on campus near East Stadium, and made it available to the sororities as a Panhellenic building, complete with meeting rooms, a large lounge, and a kitchen. In 1949, Alpha Tau Omega acquired the renovated college barn and turned it into the first fraternity house on campus. Five years later, Phi Kappa Tau broke ground for a building, and a fraternity row began to take shape. The development of fraternities

"MOM, I CAN TALK"

Speech and hearing became not only a field of academic distinction, but a model of institutional service to the community. In 1962, Etoile DuBard (right) came to what was by then the University of Southern Mississippi to establish a School for Preschool Deaf and Aphasic Children. During nine years as an elementary school teacher, her encounter with language disorders among children became for her, she said, "a modern-day burning bush." She returned to school to do master's and doctoral research on the problem, and two years of intensive study at St. Louis' Central Institute for the Deaf exposed her to the "association method," a multisensory teaching-learning strategy that became her passion. Under her direction, the USM School for Children with Language Disorders (SCLD), as it soon came to be called, developed and refined the method while transforming the lives of hundreds of children and their families and providing valuable experience for students studying audiology and speech-language pathology. With an extended waiting list, the school accepted only the most "severely impaired." Most clients came from nearby counties, but families from as far away as Texas and Delaware relocated near Hattiesburg or otherwise rearranged their lives to avail themselves of SCLD's services. Firm but compassionate, DuBard was known to begin a session with, "Sit up straight and quit scratching your nose," but children and parents came to revere her. By the time she retired in 1989, a staff of five served more than thirty fulltime clients while providing others with "outclient therapy" on a part-time basis.

With families waiting as long as three years to get into the school, now named for its founder, new director Maureen K. Martin dreamed of an expanded facility that would accommodate more children. She did more than dream; with the help of a devoted staff and advisory board, she courted potential benefactors relentlessly. USM Foundation director Bill Pace introduced her to what became, in Aubrey Lucas's words, the DuBard School's "fairy godparents," the Kelly Gene Cook Sr., Foundation, which by the mid-nineties had pledged a million dollars toward a new building. With additional support from Blue Cross & Blue Shield of Mississippi, the Asbury Foundation, the Hattiesburg Lions Club and Lions Club International Foundation, and other generous donors, the DuBard School in 2002 moved into a new $3 million facility named for Kelly Gene Cook Sr. Within four years, the School was serving twice as many fulltime clients, though the waiting list remained long.

Etoile DuBard and her colleagues crafted a model of the academic union of teaching, research, and service, but to grateful parents, the last component always shone brightest. "The DuBard School," said one mother, "takes children with no hope and gives them a future. . . . We are able to do things as a family that we never could have done without the DuBard School. My husband and I feel like we literally owe them our lives."

OUR MR. CHIPS

The first new faculty member that R. C. Cook hired was a young history teacher from Louisiana. John Gonzales had earned his master's degree from LSU and had resigned himself to teaching high school when the call came. More than half a century later, he was still teaching history at USM. "He . . . immersed himself totally in the University," said colleague and former student Neil McMillen. "He has . . . devoted himself in a way that seems quite different from professors of today." He rarely missed a home football game and even served as announcer for the Pride's halftime shows 1957-60. For years, he carried the mace at commencement as the senior member of the faculty. He also edited the *Journal of Mississippi History* for three decades and served as drama critic for the local newspaper. In 1973, he became Distinguished University Professor, and he later held the William D. McCain Chair of History.

After teaching more than fifteen thousand students spanning three generations, Gonzalez retired in 1995, though he continued to work part-time. "I never get tired of walking into that classroom and teaching," he said. Piled almost to the ceiling with books and papers, "his office," joked McMillen, "is a national menace." He never married, never owned a car, and lived in a modest apartment across the street from campus. In 1994, friends and colleagues established an endowment in his name, and he later increased it substantially by bequeathing most of his life savings to the university. Ill through much of the spring semester in 1999, he never missed a class until the department secretary took it upon herself to call an ambulance to transport him to a local hospital. Finally, and reluctantly, after more years of service than anyone in the school's history, he gave up the classroom. The following year, the auditorium in the new Liberal Arts Building was named in his honor. "There is only one John Gonzales," said Aubrey Lucas, "and thank God, he's ours. . . . He is our Mr. Chips."

The first home for sorority women was a two-story frame structure relocated from Camp Shelby in the late 1940s.

and sororities during that period, Cook believed, "helped our situation from the standpoint of students better than any other." Other student groups proliferated also. Besides the national leadership organizations, Omicron Delta Kappa and Phi Delta Rho, there were honorary societies in biology, drama, chemistry, commerce, education, mathematics, home economics, literature, music, foreign languages, religion, and speech. New denominational clubs appeared for Catholics, Episcopalians, Methodists, and Lutherans. Service organizations emerged, including the Pan American Student Association, Circle K, and the Yellowjackets, though the latter's primary service seemed to be hazing freshmen. "Mississippi Southern," said Alma Hickman, "was becoming a big college in every way."

Occasionally, being big brought big problems. On a Wednesday evening in May 1952, a crowd of about 150 boys converged on one of the women's dorms in search of ladies' lingerie: a classic panty raid. Conveniently for the intrepid raiders, Cook was on a train somewhere between New York and Birmingham, returning from a meeting of the American Association of Colleges, and the dean of men was in the hospital; no one was quite sure who was in charge of the campus. There had been some drinking, and "several of the students had physical difficulties," as Cook later put it, "with faculty members who tried to intervene." With the girls mostly urging the boys on, there was some minor scuffling, and someone broke down a door. Mostly, however, it was simply the delirium phase of spring fever, harmless, if not altogether innocent, fun. The president, however, according to Leon Wilber, "was very greatly distressed about it . . . afraid it would make a very bad impression around the state." He called a special chapel meeting on Friday morning. Not quite sure how he should begin, Cook suggested that it might be appropriate for the students to pray, so "they had the Lords Prayer," said Wilber. The president then delivered what he later described as "a most impassioned talk about honor and conduct." At the conclusion, honor gushed forth as 141 students voluntarily confessed that they had participated in the prank. More likely, it was fear that was gushing, because the president warned them that "names of participants were in the hands of the administration" already. After lunch, the guilty gathered in the Administration Building to tell their stories to a discipline committee. Several were suspended or put on probation and the rest reprimanded. When asked what the administration would do concerning the "lingerie loss," Cook declared that the culprits would repay the cost "on a pro-rata basis."

Despite a growing reputation as a suitcase college, Mississippi Southern offered students a rich and varied campus life.

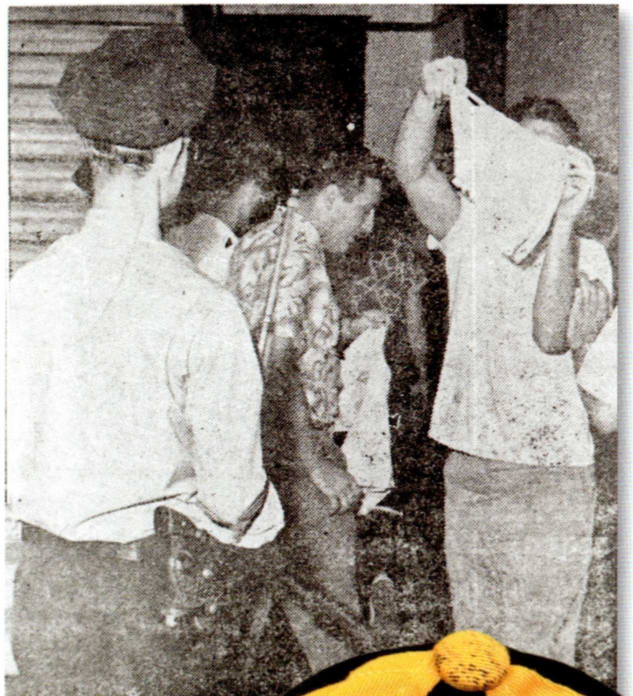
A culprit caught in the daring panty raids of the 1950s.

Cook believed that in addition to a vibrant social life, a strong music program would enhance the college's reputation. "I realized when I came to Southern," he said, "that one of our best contributions (from the standpoint of state-wide recognition) might be in music," so he decided to "put a little extra money into it." Frank Marsh believed that an opera workshop might lure both more and better voice and string students into the music program. He decided to produce a complete opera, *The Bartered Bride*, in the winter quarter of 1948–49 and hired as production director Lloyd Patten, who came officially to head the voice department. "None of us knew anything," recalled one of the cast, "the difference between upstage and downstage or how to use makeup." With Patten's patient encouragement, however, "the Music Department . . . achieved a monumental event," demonstrating that a Mississippi college could produce a fine opera that could be enjoyed by a Mississippi audience. Other campus departments also contributed: a dance director (Laura May Hill) from physical education, sets from art and industrial arts, a lighting technician from English (Wilbur Stout), and publicity from the College News Bureau. Such collegiality was "a happy thing to see," said a local newspaper review, "in this compartmentalized life which we ordinarily feel obliged to lead," and the product was "a thing of elusive and enriching beauty." Except for a brief interruption because of the Korean War and the departure of Patten in 1951, the opera workshop productions became, under the direction of Leonard Stocker after 1952, a fixture of campus life.

The marching band reemerged after World War II but went through five directors in six years. Finally in 1952, Cook imported from Kansas a former University of Michigan assistant band director named Raymond Mannoni. "Before I knew it," the president recalled, "he had recruited over a hundred bandsmen and fifty drum majorettes." In a flash of marketing brilliance, the athletic director suggested that twirling females, if properly attired, might stimulate, among other things, a few extra ticket sales to football games. At Green's urging, therefore, Mannoni organized the Southern Belles to perform with the band, and after their appearance at the football game against Alabama in 1953, a Montgomery reporter referred to them as "those darlings from Dixie." Several months later, "the Pride of Mississippi," as the band was coming to be known, shared the halftime stage at the Senior Bowl with their counterparts from Kilgore Junior College. The entourage from Texas included the Kilgore Rangerettes, a precision dance team that gave Mannoni ideas.

The following summer, he persuaded Joyce Scimeca, a Rangerette from Independence, Louisiana, to transfer to Southern and help transform the Belles. He wanted a spicy name to match the troupe's new persona, and for the first week of practice he called them the Dixie Maids. Still not satisfied, he asked the girls for ideas, and Scimeca suggested Dixie Darlings. Other bands had dancing groups, but Mannoni wanted Southern's girls,

like the Rangerettes, to "dance, strut, and twirl." The Dixie Darlings have since danced and strutted for more than half a century, though they gave up twirling long ago. Introduced with the Pride's stirring new rendition of "Dixie," the Darlings debuted at the 1954 Alabama game in Montgomery. "Few half-time shows ever presented," wrote Montgomery columnist Stuart X. Stephenson, "could match the outstanding performance of the Mississippi Southern group, a marching band of 100 pieces with 16 white-gloved precision beauties, appropriately titled 'The Dixie Darlings.' We'd say [they] are really the South's 'Rockettes of the Gridiron.'" Soon the official band of Mobile's Senior Bowl, the Pride was for two decades arguably the most televised marching band in America.

Mannoni instituted two other events that promoted the college through music. In the summer of 1953, he organized a summer music camp that would become an annual affair, bringing to the campus high school musicians from throughout Mississippi and neighboring states. Many of the campers would later return as MSC students. In the fall of 1953, the school sponsored a band day during which nearby high school and junior high school bands performed with the Pride at a home football game. This, too, became an annual event and a valuable recruiting tool.

As the division of fine arts expanded, it began to outgrow its temporary frame quarters on the Demonstration School grounds. When Cook raised the question of a new fine arts building, Governor Hugh White scoffed at the chances of persuading a legislature highly sensitive to the

Raymond Mannoni (upper left) took over as band director in 1952. Under his leadership, the Pride and Dixie Darlings became a featured part of Mobile's annual Senior Bowl and were for more than two decades arguably the most televised band in America.

Two members of the Gold Notes dance band went on to notable careers: Jimmy Peters as a Grammy Award-winning songwriter and Tommy Senter as a federal district judge.

The annual band camp for high school students began in 1953 and became a valuable recruiting tool for the college's music program.

needs of Delta planters and hill farmers to open the floodgates of the treasury "for a group of fiddlers." Undaunted, Cook invited the lawmakers to a banquet at Jackson's Hotel Heidelberg, where MSC's orchestra, chorus, notable athletes, and others gave them "quite a show." Before the festivities ended, according to Cook, the legislators were solidly committed to a $450,000 appropriation for the needed facility. By the time Cook became president, the Lyceum course had long since disappeared, but the college continued to attract notable speakers and entertainers. The Trapp Family Singers and former Austrian Chancellor Kurt Schushnigg appeared during the forties, and the Anglo-American poet W. H. Auden came in 1952. Two years later the students filled Bennett Auditorium twice, for Harry James in September and Spike Jones in October.

Someone decided that the athletic teams needed a nickname to match the institution's new designation, and people in the community were invited to offer nominations. Among the suggestions were Stumpers, Hubbers, Tough Ombres, Golly Whoppers, Defrosters, Mississippi Scratch Cats, and Southern Beserks. Most latched onto the new word "Southern" in the title with offerings such as Yams, Taters, Cawnpones, and Juleps. Officially, "Confederates" was chosen, but by popular preference and force of habit the teams came to be called Southerners, another of the era's ironies considering a football roster dotted with "Yankees" named Carrozza, Alessandri, Katrishen, Ovca, and Vetrano. Even before the war, Green and Vann had laid a firm foundation for the gridiron squad. In 1940, the Detroit Lions made end Joe Stringfellow the school's first National Football League draftee, but more typical was the story of a young single-wing tailback named C. L. Dews, who came to Southern so small that Green was at first reluctant to play him, afraid he might be injured. Somehow by his junior year, Dews added ten extra pounds, enough to overcome the anxiety of the coaches, who nicknamed him "Dipsey" and unleashed him on opponents whose defenses he riddled with his passing and running. In his final season, Dews led the 1941 squad to nine victories and the school's first undefeated record, marred only by a scoreless tie with Southwestern Louisiana Institute.

The war ended football from 1942 to 1946, as both Green and Vann, along with most of the players, entered military service. Again, however, the war gave with one hand what it had taken with the other. Out of the rental fee that the army paid for using the school facilities, President George set aside $25,000 to rebuild the athletic program after the war. Moreover, returning veterans swelled the pool of available athletes, leaving many prominent football schools with more players than they could use. When Vann and Green returned, they scoured the South for players willing to abandon reserve status on noted teams for almost certain starting opportunities at MSC. To go with such transfers was an abundance of homegrown talent, including a running back known as "Bubber." John Melvin Phillips came to Hattiesburg in 1947 after leading the nation with 235 points the previous year as a senior at Macon High School. In his first college game against the University of Alabama, he scored six more. Trailing 13-0 in the third quarter, Southern halfback Bennie Ray Nobles took a pitch from quarterback Joe Romo and then lofted a pass to end "Spot" Honaker; Honaker in turn lateraled the ball to Phillips, who raced to the end zone to complete a remarkable 71-yard touchdown play. The Crimson Tide went on to crush MSC 34-7, but it would not be long before the ambitious Southerners would learn to hold their own against the likes of

Head coach Reed Green (center), assistant Pie Vann (left), and an unidentified assistant chart plays using pebbles.

Alabama, and in much more conventional fashion. In its very next outing, the team upset Auburn 19-13 in Montgomery's Crampton Bowl and went on to a 7-3 record and the SIAA championship.

The following year, MSC joined Spring Hill College of Mobile and seven Louisiana institutions to form the Gulf States Conference, whose football crown Southern promptly captured. That 1948 season was Green's last as head coach. The next year, he became the school's first full-time athletic director, relinquishing the head coaching duties to Thad Vann. The Reed Green era gave to Southern fifty-four victories (twenty-one losses and four ties) and, in addition to those already mentioned, such memorable names as "Pel" Autry, "Tuffy" Johnson, "Hindu" Reynolds, Jay Smith, brothers Fred and "Bucky" Waters, Maxie Lambright, Mike Katrishen, Pete Taylor, "Ape" Snell, and "Apple" Sanders.

Pie Vann's initiation into the head coaching fraternity was rude in the extreme, administered by a colleague named Paul Bryant, whose Kentucky Wildcats, led by quarterback Babe Perelli, humiliated the Southerners 71-7. Vann and assistants Clyde "Heifer" Stuart and H. A. Smith regrouped their troops, however, who then reeled off six straight wins on their way to a 7-3 season, in which end Cliff Coggin set three national pass catching records. Nineteen-fifty brought a second GSC crown and Coach of the Year honors to Vann, but the team barely broke even for the season. Two of the five losses were embarrassing shutouts at the hands of Southeastern Conference powers Tennessee (56-0) and Alabama (53-0). The school won a third GSC championship in 1951 before withdrawing from the league the following year. Green hoped to turn Southern into a major competitor in college football, and independent status would, he thought, free him to add more prominent names to the schedule.

Playing respectable teams was obviously not enough; the Southerners needed to defeat a national power to make a real mark. They came close in 1951, losing to LSU 13-0, but Alabama remained stubbornly invincible, thrashing MSC the same year 40-7. Vann saw promise in 1952, as his bruising defense forced the Crimson Tide into an SEC record twelve fumbles before finally bowing 20-6 to a team that would go on to crush Syracuse 61-6 in the Sugar Bowl. The squad finished 10-1 that year, scoring fifty or more points four times (including a 55-26 win over a Louisville team led by John Unitas) and making the first bowl appearance in school history, a disappointing 26-7 loss to the College of the Pacific in El Paso's Sun Bowl. Also in 1952, the school joined the National Collegiate Athletic Association.

The big break came the following year, when Southern opened the season against Alabama on September 18 in Montgomery. With Bart Starr at the helm, Red Drew's Tide was a consensus top-ten pick and Grantland Rice's choice to win the national championship. But behind the running of Hugh Laurin Pepper and Bucky McElroy, the passing of Billy Jarrell, and the sensational pass catching of Leonard Williams, Vann's squad stunned Alabama and the football world with a 25-19 upset that gave not only the football team but the institution instant identity from coast to coast. All the publicity was, however, a mixed blessing, as rumors emerged concerning the eligibility of Southern's athletes. In the face of charges that MSC was an "outlaw school," athletic director Green insisted that the program was "clean." President Cook instructed athletic committee chairman Lloyd Milam to collect all information available on the academic standing of every athlete at the school, and the committee kept detailed records thereafter. The team won eight more times in 1953, including a 14-0 shutout of quarterback Zeke Bratkowski and Georgia's Bulldogs before 23,000 fans in Jackson. A 27-13 loss to Memphis State was the only blemish on a record that earned the team its second straight Sun Bowl berth. The trip to El Paso again proved disappointing as Texas Western won handily, 37-14.

Lightning struck again in 1954, as MSC dumped Starr and Alabama, 7-2. "Maybe some day," wrote Vincent

Johnson of the *Mobile Press Register*," the Alabama schedule makers will get it through their thick heads that Southern is no jerkwater school that has to hunt around to find eleven men to fill up a team." The *Atlanta Constitution*'s Furman Bisher heaped praise on Vann, who, he said, "for two years in a row . . . has managed to unzip the Southeastern conference's pride and remove the stuffing." The victories over Alabama were more than football games. As much as anything else, they established MSC as a major institution. Southern would never be considered a "jerkwater school" again.

Under R. C. Cook, the college also established a respectable basketball program. Before 1949, basketball had been little more than something to occupy football players and coaches during the winter, and Vann was the first football coach who did not also run the basketball team.

Players and fans celebrate Southern's victory over powerhouse Alabama in 1953.

Perhaps the most versatile football player in Southern Miss history, John Melvin "Bubba" Phillips (1947–50) still holds several school records in rushing, kickoff returns, and interceptions.

Nick Revon (standing third from left next to Coach Lee Floyd) scored a school record 2,024 career points and led the basketball team to a host of victories, including the 1951 Sun Bowl Tournament championship (above).

When Texas Western graduate Lee Floyd became the first full-time basketball coach in 1949, the school also gave its first full scholarships in the sport. Floyd "revolutionized basketball in Mississippi," according to sportswriter Jimmie McDowell. His "fast-breaking, hell-for-leather type play . . . caught on in rural and city high schools, in every hamlet, community, and town in the southern part of the Magnolia state." Starting four freshmen in his initial season, Floyd coached these "Cinderella Kids" to an 18-6 record and a GSC crown. His teams won twenty or more games in each of the next four seasons, giving him 117 wins (against 46 losses) during his first tour of duty (he would enter private business in 1954 but return to coach the University of Southern Mississippi in 1962). These included championships in the Sun Bowl (1951) and Senior Bowl (1954) tournaments, two district NAIA championships, and another GSC crown—and Coach of the Year honors for Floyd—(1951–52), and victories over Alabama, Texas Western, Memphis State, and New Mexico State. Southern fans, wrote McDowell, "will always remember the beginning—the birth of Mississippi Southern's basketball team, and they'll remember the young Texas poppa. They'll remember the time Jumping Jack Gallagher tossed to Tom (Whiz) Bishop who zipped to Nick (The Cat) Revon in the finest fast-break of all, and they'll remember rebounding Mickey Harrington and battling Billy Allgood and velvet-smooth Jeep Clark. . . . And they'll remember big Mutt Watts and hawk-eyed Stormy Weathers and Jersey John O'Keefe's over-head shot for two points. . . . They'll remember Lee Floyd's boys because they were the pioneers, the products of the early good old days when Mississippi Southern was young and hungry."

Other sports also prospered in the postwar era. In 1947, the college fielded its first intercollegiate baseball team in a dozen years. In 1948, Vann took over the baseball squad

In 1949, President Cook purchased the Camp Shelby field house and had it moved to campus, where it became home to the basketball team until 1965.

from Green and coached them to the school's first win over the University of Mississippi in any sport. The 8-7 victory followed a heartbreaking loss the day before when the Rebels' Barney Poole (who would later serve as a football assistant under Pie Vann) belted a late-inning home run to secure a 2-1 Ole Miss win. Heifer Stuart replaced Vann in 1949 and coached the team until 1958. Several of Vann's and Stuart's players went on to professional careers, including "Mel" Didier, Mickey Harrington, Hugh Laurin Pepper, Bubba Phillips, Fred Waters, and "Peanuts" Davenport, who also later managed the San Francisco Giants. By the 1950s, the school also offered programs in tennis, golf, track, swimming, and boxing.

"So," said Cook, "with a very fine athletic program, a very fine program of music . . . and with fraternities and sororities, we had the basis of what you might call student interest." The interest of the board of trustees was a different matter. There was a definite "pecking order" among the colleges, according to Cook, and Southern remained, with Delta State, far down the line behind Ole Miss, Mississippi State, and MSCW, especially when it came to appropriations. Securing money for salaries was always a struggle; getting funds for construction and equipment was more like a war. "Ole Miss and State would get two or three buildings," said Cook, "and then we would get whatever they had left." For an institution growing as rapidly as Southern, that became a serious problem, forcing the administration to develop novel ways of creating space. Military surplus proved a godsend. In addition to the structures already mentioned, Cook, in 1949, purchased Camp Shelby's field house from the War Assets Commission. Thanks to the influence of Senator James O. Eastland and Congressman William Colmer, the school got the facility at the bargain basement price of $1,927, an 80 percent discount from original construction cost. The state building commission provided $150,000 to dismantle, transport, and rebuild the structure near the southeast corner of Faulkner Field. The stadium itself grew in 1953, when a $350,000 appropriation allowed construction of a five-thousand-seat stadium dormitory on the west side. West Stadium also housed ninety-six male students.

Three new girls' dormitories further eased the campus housing crisis. Weathersby Hall went up in 1946, a dormitory for senior girls (now Hickman Hall) in 1951, and Bolton Hall in 1954. Other construction included an $115,000 expansion of the Home Economics Building (1947), renovation of the Dining Hall, which became a cafeteria (1948), a Women's Physical Education Building (1949), and the ROTC addition to the old Laundry Building (1949). An annex added to the east end of Science Hall in the late 1940s had to be torn down in 1961 because of structural problems.

Two buildings were the fruit of extraordinary labors by Cook. One was a student union, which the president considered essential to his plans for a vibrant social life;

the other was a student religious building. Unable to get the state to fund a student center, Cook decided to raise the money through private contributions. The Alumni Association voted in 1951 to sponsor the project, and Powell Ogletree and President Cook traveled the state soliciting funds from counties, towns, and religious groups, as well as alumni, faculty, students, and friends. Within two years the drive elicited $200,000 in donations, and the state building commission added $50,000 for heat, light, and air conditioning systems. Barely halfway to the $450,000 needed, Cook then appealed to the Forrest County board of supervisors for the balance, noting that the new facility would provide lockers, restrooms, and a gathering place for local students. The supervisors agreed to call a special election, in which the voters overwhelmingly approved a $200,000 bond issue to support construction. Completed in 1956, the building became the R. C. Cook College Union. When the new university union opened in 1976, the name was transferred to that facility and the old Cook Union became McLemore Hall.

The Danforth Chapel resulted from a fortunate visit to campus in 1953 by a representative of the Ralston-Purina company of St. Louis. When Methodist student director Sam Barefield mentioned the school's need for a chapel, the visitor suggested approaching the president of his company, William H. Danforth, whose philanthropic efforts had helped fund college chapels throughout the country. Cook immediately chartered a plane to St. Louis where he persuaded Danforth to contribute $10,000 toward a Danforth Chapel at Southern. The Campus Student Christian Federation raised an additional $20,000 through blood drives, bazaars, and private donations, and the graduating classes of 1955 and 1956 left gifts totaling more than $1,000. The building opened in 1957, complete with furnishings that included a beautiful Thomas organ donated by Roseberry Piano House in honor of J. L. Roseberry.

In the fall of 1954, R. C. Cook stunned the college community by announcing that he was resigning effective December 31, to become vice-president and general manager of a new capital city daily newspaper, the *Jackson State Times*. The offer of a three-year contract at $25,000 a year (he was making $12,000 at MSC) plus 10 percent of the profits, a car, a fifty-dollar-per-week expense account, and membership in two exclusive Jackson clubs proved difficult to resist. Moreover, Cook explained, "I had just enough ink on my hands"—he had edited three nationally known biographical volumes, including *Who's Who in American Education*—"to feel that I was capable . . . it greatly attracted me." So Cook resigned at the end of 1954, the first president to vacate the post voluntarily. "I left Mississippi Southern College," he said, "with a very heavy heart," but his sadness could not have been greater than that of the friends he left behind. "The citizens of Hattiesburg just worshipped the man," one faculty member recalled, as did most of the campus community. "We did hate to see him leave so," said Anna Roberts, "we all cried when he left." Indeed, Cook's contribution to the school had been inestimable. "He found it a small college," said Alma Hickman, "and he left it a much larger one . . . he greatly enlarged and improved the faculty and the academic standards." His decade of leadership left the "institution well on its way toward university status."

Toward that end, the selection of his replacement was, Cook later suggested, "almost providentially inspired." At the time, however, the former president, and others, probably believed that a less benign power had determined the choice, which then seemed more a result of conspiracy than inspiration. Whatever controversy Cook's departure lacked, the board more than made up for in naming his successor. First of all, they delayed a final decision for some time, naming McLemore acting president and Porter Fortune acting dean. Meanwhile, Cook's venture into journalism turned sour as the newspaper struggled financially, and he began to explore the possibility of returning to his old job. By then, campus sentiment had largely swung McLemore's way, and the former president's reentry into the picture left the college community badly divided. It was, said McLemore, "a bad situation for both of us." When the trustees met on May 19, 1955, they, too, were badly split. The board first voted on Cook and rejected his candidacy 6-5 with chairman H. M. Ivy casting the crucial vote. A premature *Hattiesburg American* report that Cook would regain the presidency apparently angered Ivy, who already resented Cook's sudden departure for greener financial pastures. In an effort to unify all factions, the board then decided to go outside the college and chose state archivist William D. McCain.

The college's fifth president was a native of Bellefontaine, Mississippi, and an early graduate of Delta State

College. After earning a master's degree from the University of Mississippi in 1931 and a Ph.D. from Duke four years later, both in history, he taught at East Central and Copiah-Lincoln Junior Colleges, Ole Miss, Millsaps, and Mississippi State. In the 1930s, McCain served as assistant historian at the Morristown, New Jersey, National Historical Park and as assistant at the National Archives. In 1938, he left Washington to become director of the Mississippi Department of Archives and History, where he remained, except for military service, until his selection as president of MSC. McCain began his military career in 1924 as a private in the Mississippi National Guard and ended it forty-three years later as a major general. In between were tours of active duty during World War II and the Korean conflict.

After what McCain described as a week of "bedlam," the president-elect scheduled a visit to the campus. The night before he arrived, students hanged H. M. Ivy in effigy, tossing a dummy of the board chairman from the porch of Hickman Hall into a flaming drum of gasoline, according to the *Printz*, "for his deciding negative vote" on Cook's bid to regain the presidency. Student leaders insisted that their sentiments were not against McCain, only the board's "mistreatment" of Cook. The next day McCain addressed more than six hundred students, faculty, and staff who gathered around the east steps of the Administration Building to get a glimpse of the new president. They seemed favorably impressed. He mentioned few specifics other than his plans immediately to enlarge the library, winning him the undying devotion

THE CHAPEL PLACE

As director of the Student Christian Federation, longtime professor of religion and philosophy John Nau helped raise money for the original construction of Danforth Chapel. Thirty years later, he undertook another campaign to enhance the structure with seven panels of stained glass representing Biblical virtues. At the formal dedication of the addition on October 3, 1987, then president Aubrey Lucas noted that "not only are the virtues depicted, but the flora and fauna native to southern Mississippi are entwined with the spiritual symbolism of the windows' design." By then, another sample of local flora adorned the space just east of the Chapel. A sixty-foot, twenty-three-ton petrified tree, recently unearthed near Ovett, Mississippi, had been moved to the campus for display. Lucas announced that the area surrounding the tree, which had been attractively landscaped, would henceforth be known as "The Chapel Place" in honor of Nau.

USM
Alumni News
Winter, 1988
New windows in Danforth Chapel represent the seven virtues: Faith, Hope, Charity, Justice, Fortitude, Temperance, and Prudence.
The University of Southern Mississippi

In 1955, William D. McCain became the school's fifth president.

of Anna Roberts. Acknowledging the "great responsibility and challenge" of his new position, McCain concluded by predicting that MSC would soon be "a great university."

Back in McLemore's office, the acting president admonished his successor severely for using the word "university" in connection with Mississippi Southern College. McLemore advised McCain that he would get on much better with the board if he would avoid the issue of changing the status of the institution. The new president found out for himself two days later when he met with a committee of the board who informed him "in no uncertain terms," he later recalled, "that I was not to go to Hattiesburg and attempt to transform Mississippi Southern College into a university."

The *Hattiesburg American* had several days earlier charged in an editorial that the board had rejected Cook precisely because of his success at MSC, that supporters of Ole Miss and Mississippi State were "afraid of what further progress Southern might make if he returned." If the trustees hoped that instructing McCain not to pursue university status would dissuade him from such a course, they were mistaken. "My father learned very early," McCain said, "that if he wanted me not to do something, it was wise not to say so, because then I might not think of it on my own."

The new president assumed his duties on August 18 and within a week recommended a reorganization of the curriculum. "There was no hope," he later wrote, "that Mississippi Southern College could ever achieve university status without first being given a university structure. I saw no reason to delay efforts in that direction." The proposal, based on a plan drafted during Cook's tenure, called for the establishment of three undergraduate schools—arts and sciences, education and psychology, and commerce and business administration—to go along with the existing graduate school. When the board rejected it out of hand, McCain decided to focus his energies on broadening and strengthening the graduate program. A year later, he again proposed the reorganization but added a request to offer the Master of Arts degree in English, home economics, applied music, mathematics, and social sciences. "The term 'social science,'" he said, "was used deliberately to confuse, for I intended for it to cover history, political science, sociology, geography, and various and sundry other subjects." He also asked for authority to grant the degree of Doctor of Education. The board referred all three recommendations to committee, effectively delaying any action on them.

McCain continued to push, formulating a third reorganization plan and maneuvering the March 1957 meeting of the board to the Southern campus. The board's education committee met for almost three hours on March 21, during which chairman Reese D. McLendon asked McCain if he was trying to make MSC a university. "I stated truthfully," McCain said, "that the matter had never been discussed during our deliberations on reorganization and expansion." On the recommendation of its education committee, the board authorized Southern "to reorganize administration of instruction so as to provide for a Dean of the College and Graduate School of Education, a Dean of Arts and Sciences, a Dean of Education and Psychology, a Dean of Commerce and Business Administration." Fine arts and home economics continued as divisions. Each of these schools and divisions added various degree requirements to its particular students' Basic College core curriculum—which remained that of 1949–50—after those students declared majors during the sophomore year. The trustees rejected the request for a doctoral program but approved nonteaching master's degrees in social studies, physical sciences, biology, English and literature, home economics, and music.

Without committing itself to the establishment of programs, the board allowed Southern in 1958 to apply, along with Ole Miss and Mississippi State, for federal fellowship money related to doctoral programs in education and marine sciences. Nothing developed from the fellowship application, but the next year, McCain asked the board to approve doctoral programs at MSC in those fields. Marine sciences "was thrown in," said McCain, "for the purpose of giving the board something to disapprove," which it did, but Southern got its doctoral degree

Trio of presidents: (from left) R. C. Cook, W. D. McCain, and R. A. McLemore.

in education with the provision that "requirements for admission and graduation be on a par [with] or better than those of previously authorized institutions." With the aid of the Alumni Association, McCain thereafter continued quietly but effectively "to educate the people of the state to the fact that it was inevitable that Mississippi Southern College would one day be a university."

Several other significant curriculum changes occurred during McCain's early years. In 1957, an Academic Council of elected faculty representatives replaced the old curriculum committee as the primary advisory body for undergraduate studies. Beginning the next year, all students had to pass an English proficiency test, and all males had to pass six hours of military science to graduate. In 1961, the school again renumbered courses according to academic level: 100 courses being freshman, 200 sophomore, 300 junior, 400 senior, and 500 graduate.

Within months of his arrival at MSC, McCain encountered the racial tension that was beginning to envelope Mississippi when Clyde Kennard, a young, black, highly decorated Korean War veteran, sought to enroll for the winter quarter of 1956. When denied admission, Kennard, who had only recently returned to help run his family's chicken farm near Eatonville, declined to press the issue. Three years later, however, he tried again. After consulting with the board, McCain arranged a meeting with Kennard in Governor J. P. Coleman's office on December 19, 1958. Coleman acknowledged past injustices and expressed a desire eventually to see some qualified black students allowed to attend white colleges. With state elections looming in a racially charged atmosphere, however, he insisted that admitting

Clyde Kennard, the first black student to seek admission to MSC. Kennard initially sought to enroll for the winter quarter of 1956.

Student Printz

Negro Warns He Will Seek Admission To MSC

6 Times All American — 8 Times Columbia Medalist

Student Printz

Pacemaker of Southern Journalism

Volume 32 — Mississippi Southern College, Hattiesburg, Mississippi, December 12, 1958 — NO. 10

The Campus Week

★ Get Insurance Forms

★ Alums To Honor Team

★ BW Plans Holidays

By BILL SIMPSON

ust one more week and Bookworm can give a big of relief and head home for two wonderful weeks ristmas vacation on the Gulf Coast. And after a drawn-out 14 week quarter, a little leisure time is inly in order. On BW's agenda for the holidays is irlwind tour of South Mississippi's historical land-s: Spider's, Gus Steven's, Downbeat, Shangrila, etc., etc. If any of you locals happen to be on the drop in and say hello.

— ★ —

ccording to a recent bulletin from campus head-ers, it is the responsibility of the individual student who wishes to make use of the Student Health and Accident Insurance

SGA Starts Book Exchange

By DONALD DANA, JR.

Southern's Student Government Association book exchange program gets underway this week for the first time, according to Billy West Tatum, exchange chairman.

In making the announcement, Tatum said that the program was the result of many months of preparation and planning by the SGA. The purpose of the book exchange

Wants To Transfer From Chicago U.

NAACP May Help

Clyde Kennard, Negro, about 30, of RFD 1 Hattiesburg may make a second attempt to enter Mississippi Southern College.

According to a news release by United Press International, Kennard advised school officials that he would seek to enter Southern when registration begins Monday, January 5, 1959 for the winter quarter.

Kennard first sought admission three years ago, but he was not accepted because his application was not complete. The matter was dropped until about three weeks ago when he telephoned the Admissions Office and related his intentions.

Kennard at that moment would only play into the hands of radical segregationists. Progress, he said, would require patience and cooperation. Courteous but firm, he threatened to close MSC rather than yield to a lawsuit to integrate it. He offered to provide financial assistance for Kennard to return to the University of Chicago, where he had earlier attended, or another school out of state.

Kennard politely declined and the following September made a third attempt to enroll at MSC. McCain, who had at first been favorably impressed with the young man's background and demeanor, if not his intentions, was by now exasperated with his persistence. At a meeting in the president's office on September 15, Kennard was again denied admission. Shortly afterward, while still on campus, he was arrested for possession of whiskey (Mississippi was legally dry until 1966) by a local constable apparently acting on his own with the support of a handful of local segregationist zealots. Coleman, McCain, and most local officials were outraged, not by the injustice but by the potential bad publicity of what had transparently been a setup. Convicted in a justice of the peace court, Kennard unsuccessfully appealed. Several months later, he was again arrested for allegedly receiving five sacks of stolen chicken feed. Found guilty, he was sentenced to seven years in the state penitentiary. Later evidence demonstrated that he had again been framed and this time sent to prison merely for having the audacity to seek an education at his hometown college. While at Parchman, Kennard was diagnosed with terminal cancer, and arch-segregationist governor Ross Barnett mercifully granted

President McCain, pictured above with executive assistant Roger B. Johnson, vowed to keep the campus "dusty or muddy with construction."

The new Cook Library (above) and the first phase of Pinehaven Apartments for married students (below) were completed in 1960.

From this aerial view (opposite page), the multiple campus construction projects of the late 1950s can be seen.

him an early release. He died in 1963, tragically at the age of thirty-six and ironically on July 4.

Upon assuming the presidency in 1955, McCain announced that he intended to keep the campus "dusty or muddy with construction," and he did. One of the most pressing needs was for dormitory space, as the fall quarter's enrollment topped three thousand, forcing the school to refund rent deposits to more than five hundred students for whom no housing was available. "We must do something to take care of the Mississippi boys and girls who are clamoring to attend Southern," McCain declared. The federal government came to the rescue with loans and matching grants that helped the school build five new housing facilities: two dormitories for women, Jones Hall (1959) and Pulley Hall (1962); two for men, Scott Hall (1959) and Bond Hall (1962); and Pinehaven Apartments for married students (1960). Several other buildings opened during McCain's first seven years: a new field house for athletics (1958), a new science building (1959, later named for J. Fred Walker), the new Cook Library (1960), the Commons (1962, later named for J. B. George), and the Beedie Smith Infirmary (1962).

Several important personnel changes occurred also. In 1956, Roger B. Johnson became administrative assistant to the president. For two decades he remained McCain's right arm and was particularly instrumental in the acquisition and management of a flood of federal loans and grants that helped finance the president's building program. Gilbert Hartwig became chairman of the theatre department, Joe Greene dean of commerce and business administration, Claude Fike dean of arts and sciences, Joel Eakins head of the physical plant, and Rader Grantham director of the college union (later dean of men). Porter Fortune replaced McLemore as dean of the college in 1957, and John Allen succeeded him in 1961.

The drum major's backbend became a signature feature of Pride performances.

There were also changes in student life. One of McCain's first acts was the abolition of chapel in 1955. Delta Sigma Epsilon merged with Delta Zeta in 1956, and a new sorority, Pi Beta Phi, appeared in 1961, as did another fraternity, Acacia. The college added honorary societies in economics, accounting, industrial arts, history, business education, band, speech, marketing, psychology, real estate, military science, physics, management, and drama. The reorganized Student Government Association included a student senate as well as men's and women's affairs boards.

Scene from *Hey Daze*, a 1955 original musical production based on life at Southern.

The music program continued to flourish. In 1957, Frances Jellinek became director of the Dixie Darlings, and the band introduced new uniforms, exact replicas of those of the Royal Scots Guards of Buckingham Palace, with red coats and black pants, trimmed in gold, and plaid Scotch tams. In the summer of 1960, the Pride and Dixie Darlings appeared before a national television audience during halftime of the annual College All-Star football game at Chicago's Soldier Field. In 1961, Mannoni became dean of the division of fine arts, and William J. Moody replaced him as director of bands.

Assistant band director Robert Hays and Richard Johnson, cultural relations advisor for the Latin American Institute, had once taught high school together in Alabama, where they had dreamed of putting together a musical theater production. Colleagues again at Southern, in 1955 they persuaded Mannoni to present the idea of an all-campus musical to the president, who appointed an interdepartmental Committee for the Coordination and Integration of School Spirit. The result was *Hey Daze*, a three-act musical based on student life at MSC. Hays composed the show's eighteen tunes, and he, Johnson, Thomas Long, Patricia Hays, and Jacqueline Long collaborated on the story and lyrics. Carl Squitiero, a junior student from Bridgeport, Connecticut, wrote thirty-three pages of dialogue, and a Vicksburg senior, William Don Seay, did the choreography. Charles Ambrose of the art department designed and painted the sets; Wilbur Stout managed the lighting; Mannoni coordinated the general production. Recounting the adventures and misadventures of two student couples and a campus clown during a single academic year, the show featured familiar MSC scenes: Wimpy's, Faulkner Field, classes, and the Dixie Darlings. It was, said the official program, an effort "to symbolize the spirit which has made Southern what it is today." Few people now recall Act III's grand finale, "Hail to the Black and Gold," but the song that concluded Act I has echoed at athletic contests for more than fifty years; it was titled "Southern to the Top."

The *Hattiesburg American* called *Hey Daze* "a smash hit," and the company presented several more performances, including one in Biloxi and another in Jackson. There would be no more original productions after 1955, but Hays and Mannoni, with the help of Robert Treser and Gilbert Hartwig of the theatre department and history professor John Gonzales, revived the all-school musical in 1958. That year's presentation of Lerner and Loewe's 1947 Broadway hit *Brigadoon* began a series of annual productions that included *Guys and Dolls* (1959), *Oklahoma* (1960), and *Damn Yankees* (1961). After 1961, the all-school musical disappeared, as the division of fine arts and the theatre department agreed that each needed to devote more energy to its own programs. Fine arts continued to present musicals, however, including the summer band camp productions that began in 1960 with *H. M. S. Pinafore*.

Basketball coach Fred Lewis (1957-62) and star player Roy Danforth, both of whom later became successful head coaches at Syracuse University.

Under McCain, the athletic program also continued to prosper. In 1955, the football team finished 9-1, winning its last seven games after an early loss at Chattanooga. The 1956 squad extended the streak to 14 before closing its season with a one-point loss at Florida State and a 13-13 tie with Alabama. The 7-1-1 record earned a bid to Orlando's Tangerine Bowl, but West Texas State handed Southern its third postseason loss in as many tries. The 1957 team recorded seven shutouts and finished 8-2 with losses to Houston and Alabama. A second straight trip to Orlando resulted in a 10-9 loss to East Texas State, leaving MSC 0-4 in bowl play.

Nineteen fifty-eight was "a season to remember." United Press International for the first time added a "small college" poll to its weekly rankings, and Southern began the year at number one. After shutouts over Louisiana Tech and Trinity College, MSC entertained Memphis State at Faulkner Field on October 4. Midway through the fourth quarter, the Tigers took a 22-21 lead on a touchdown and a two-point conversion. With five minutes left in the game, the Southerners began a drive at their own twenty-yard line, but two plays later, quarterback George Sekul chipped a bone in his wrist and joined backups Ollie Yates and Willie Coats, who had already been injured, on the sidelines. The team's fortunes rested on the shoulders of fourth-string signal caller, sophomore Billy Larson. "We had a long way to go," he later recalled, "and I felt a little bit nervous because of all the seniors . . . but they just kind of said, 'come on, you call the plays, and we'll do the blocking and running.'" Behind the steady rushing of halfback J. C. Arban, Larson moved the offense into Memphis territory and then completed a critical twenty-seven-yard third-down pass to all-American Bob Yencho, but the drive stalled at the Tiger fifteen. Sophomore Hugh McInnis came on to attempt his first college kick and calmly drilled a twenty-two-yard field goal with forty-three seconds left to seal a two-point victory and preserve Southern's number one ranking.

Upsets over major college opponents North Carolina State and Virginia Tech set up a season-ending showdown against Chattanooga on the road. A special "Chattanooga Choo-Choo" carried three hundred fans to watch their Southerners battle the sixth-ranked Moccasins, who had defeated the University of Tennessee earlier in the year. Despite four turnovers and more than a hundred yards in

"The Golden Giants" in action.

The seniors on the 1958 football team decided to forego a return trip to the Tangerine Bowl, hoping instead that their remarkable season would earn an invitation to a major bowl. There was talk of a Sugar Bowl battle of unbeatens between MSC and LSU, but Tiger coach Paul Dietzel refused to discuss a New Year's Day matchup with "that little team from South Mississippi." In the end, the Southerners went nowhere in the 1958 postseason, remaining, as President McCain put it, "undefeated, untied, and uninvited." It was a disappointing end to an amazing season. At the team's fiftieth reunion, Bob Yencho reflected that "not going to a bowl after the year we had in 1958 just broke our hearts. It still hurts today."

A postseason reward of sorts did come, finally and unexpectedly, some forty-five years later. Among the spectators on that chilly Thanksgiving Day when the visiting Southerners downed Chattanooga to clinch a perfect season, was a shy sixteen-year-old, there no doubt to cheer the hometown

Moccasins. Instead, John Austin Dickey was so taken by MSC's gritty fourth-quarter goal line stand that he became an avid and lifelong fan of Southern Miss football. Unmarried and frugal, he worked for years in the shipping division of Cutter Laboratories in Chattanooga, saving much of his modest income. When he died at age sixty in 2002, his will provided for a gift of $180,000 to the University of Southern Mississippi to endow football scholarships. "He loved that team from the time he saw them," Dickey's sister said, though he never set foot on the campus. Athletic director Richard Giannini lamented "that we never had the opportunity to know him. We'll be indebted to him . . . forever." In 2004, the 1958 players adopted a formal proclamation making John Austin Dickey an honorary member of their national championship team.

Southern fans claim the goal post as a trophy of their victory over Chattanooga in 1958.

The campus as it appeared in 1961.

penalties, MSC clung to a 20-13 lead late in the fourth quarter when disaster struck. A muffed exchange between center Richard Johnston and Sekul gave Chattanooga the ball inside the one-yard line. To preserve its number-one ranking, Southern would have to defend two inches of Chamberlain Field turf for four downs. The amazing goal line stand that followed gave the 1958 football team the only unblemished record (9-0-0) in school history and UPI's first college-division national championship.

The MSC era ended with 6-4 seasons in 1959 and 1960 and an 8-1 mark in 1961. Nineteen fifty-nine included a heartbreaking loss in Mobile's Ladd Stadium, where Southern outgained Texas A&M 368 yards to 195 but could muster only three points to match the Aggies' seven. A 19-14 win over North Carolina State later in the year eased the pain somewhat, but the Wolfpack repaid the debt with interest, winning in 1960 and 1961 behind the strong arm of all-American quarterback Roman Gabriel.

Following Lee Floyd's departure, the basketball program lapsed into mediocrity until Green imported a New Yorker named Fred Lewis to coach the team in 1957. The new man brought with him a "run and gun" style and a new unofficial nickname, the "Golden Giants," which seemed more appropriate than "Southerners" for a lineup strewn with names like Goldberg, Lundberg, Grubar, Delia, and Migliazzo. With these players and others like Roy Danforth, Ken Fortenberry, Don Curry, Sam Hollingsworth, Robert Boothe, Harold Kea, Wayne Pulliam, and Clyde Mills, Lewis built a hardwood program whose success rivaled that of Vann's gridiron squads. In five seasons his teams won eighty-nine games while losing only thirty-eight. The "Magnificent Seven" of 1960–61 finished 23-3 and ranked second in UPI's college division poll. In another twist of irony, however, scandal struck just as MSC seemed poised on the brink of basketball greatness. In the summer of 1961, Hattiesburg police arrested three Golden Giant stars on seven counts of burglary. Lewis cooperated in the investigation, and the players surrendered voluntarily. They were not hardened criminals, the coach insisted, but the incident was a bitter blow to the team, which slumped to 13-13 the following year, Lewis's worst and last at Southern.

As the 1960s dawned, it was obvious that Mississippi Southern College was rapidly evolving into a major educational institution that would soon bid to become the state's largest. Enrollment was approaching five thousand, and there were more than two hundred faculty and staff, many of whom held terminal degrees. Not everyone was ready to acknowledge the school's achievements, however. R. A. McLemore later recalled that "the most difficult job at Southern was to keep financial support adequate to take care of the increasing enrollment. [The legislature] couldn't believe the changes that were taking place. You couldn't convince the powers that there was this much development." The institution's patriarchs had left a rich legacy in dealing with such obstacles. Half a century earlier, a reluctant legislature had finally succumbed to the political potency of T. P. Scott's hand-cranked mimeograph machine. Embracing that heritage, the generation of the sixties would again flex its political muscle and persuade the lawmakers to change the school's name to reflect its growth and progress. "Southern is a school of destiny," Reed Green had said amidst the football eligibility controversy in 1953, "and as we continue to grow rapidly it is only natural that others will label us as outlaws and try to ruin our prestige." Despite temporary setbacks, he concluded, "there is nothing that can stop Mississippi Southern from becoming 'the' school of Mississippi—both athletically and academically."

The Mississippi Southern College era ended as it had begun, in irony. The very year in which the institution became a multipurpose university, 1962, also marked the golden anniversary of its origin as a tiny normal college devoted to the singular task of qualifying teachers for the rural schools of Mississippi. The moment could have been no more poignant for anyone than it was for Alma Hickman, who knew as no one else could have known what the school had been and what it had become. As poet and dramatist of the New Spirit of the Normal College, she had in 1919 prophesied a future in which education would forever banish ignorance, which with its progeny—poverty, disease, and hate—had blighted so much of Mississippi's past. While such an ultimate triumph remained as visionary in 1962 as it had been in 1912, Alma Hickman had seen the institution that she helped establish wage a valiant war against the forces of ignorance, disease, and poverty. She could take comfort in the knowledge that so long as that institution remained faithful to its heritage, the battle would continue. As she reflected on Southern's evolution from a small normal school into a major university, she declared, "It is with great pride that I have watched this development from the beginning. I shall not, of course, live to see all of the future advancements of the school, but I can unequivocally state that I, as part of the small faculty and staff of 1912, take pride in viewing the realization of our dream and toil—superior education for the people of south Mississippi."

Alma Hickman retired in 1954 after more than forty years on the faculty.

Chapter 4

THE UNIVERSITY OF SOUTHERN MISSISSIPPI

THE HUB

Governor Ross Barnett, flanked by President McCain and Lieutenant Governor Paul B. Johnson, signs legislation making Mississippi Southern a university in 1962. Also present were (standing from left) Ralph McDaniels, Stone D. Barefield, Moran M. Pope Jr., Frank Barber, J. K. Tharpe, and Powell Ogletree.

Southern became a university at almost the precise moment that universities were seizing the attention of the nation. "The 1960s became," according to one historian, "the most explosive decade in the entire history of educational expansion, [and] . . . the growth in higher education was most marked." Presiding over this idealistic war on ignorance was a former Texas schoolteacher who had worked his way to a college degree by sweeping the floors of "Old Main" at Southwest Texas State Teachers College, which shortly before young Lyndon Johnson entered it had still been San Marcos Normal. By the mid 1970s, college enrollment had jumped 167 percent in fifteen years, and the United States was spending $45 billion a year on higher education. American colleges exploded in another way during the 1960s, as the confluence of civil rights activism, radical student politics, and an inglorious and protracted war in Southeast Asia helped make "campus unrest" a disturbing and exhilarating part of the American idiom.

In September 1962, only months after the Mississippi legislature gave the Hattiesburg institution its fourth name in fifty years, Southern's sister university at Oxford exploded in violence when James Meredith successfully crossed the color line in Mississippi's system of higher education. State authorities, after long and bitter resistance, finally succumbed to federal power and admitted him to the university, but not before federal marshals and troops quelled a bloody riot that left two dead, scores injured, and Mississippi's public image badly tarnished. Two years later, hundreds of idealistic students from America's most prestigious universities descended upon the state in a "long hot summer" crusade for racial justice. One of them, Maria Savio, returned to the University of California in the fall to lead Berkeley's Free Speech Movement. "Last summer I went to Mississippi to join the struggle there for civil rights," he said. "This fall I am engaged in another phase of the same struggle." In September 1964, Berkeley erupted as had Oxford two years earlier. With the Vietnam War providing an issue fraught with the same kind of moral energy that evoked such passion in the crusade for racial justice, the "student movement" spread across the country etching a host of names and images on the nation's consciousness: draft card burnings, Timothy Leary, Yippies, Bob Dylan, participatory democracy, Che Guevara, Woodstock, SDS, LSD, Hubert Marcuse, and counterculture.

As the 1960s unfolded, Southern's student population increasingly reflected the era's profound social changes.

Against such a backdrop, Southern's entry into the elite fraternity of higher education sometimes seemed a mixed blessing. It was certainly a mixed blessing for William D. McCain, whose fourteen years as a university president were considerably more stormy and unpleasant than his

THE WALKING BLUEPRINT

Richard Gaines holds the distinction of having served the institution under all four of its names. He was a fireman, a plumber, a carpenter, and a general utility man, but he was also a walking blueprint. He first came to Mississippi Normal College in 1916 to visit a nephew who worked in the dining hall, and college secretary A. V. Hays gave him a job firing the boiler. Forty-five years later he was still on the job, though state law required him to retire since he had reached his sixty-fifth birthday. Maintenance superintendent Harry Thomas applied for a year's deferment for him, pleading that "his knowledge of the underground utilities system, of which no record was made at the time of installation, makes it essential that he be retained until this information can be put on a map." It took several thousand dollars and a flock of engineers to design a map to replace the one in Rich's head. Finally on July 1, 1962, he was able to retire, but it took the maintenance crew a long time to break the habit of responding to crises by saying, "Go ask Rich."

Richard Gaines

early tenure at the helm of MSC. Yet USM shared as much, if not more, in the prosperity of the era as in its turmoil. Enrollment continued to grow, by almost a thousand a year from 1964 through 1967. After a brief downturn in the late sixties, it began to inch steadily upward again, topping ten thousand in 1973 (main campus enrollment would not reach that figure until 1979). McCain had to fulfill his "dust and mud" vow just to keep pace. The most pressing problem was housing, and five more dormitories went up before the decade ended: three for women, Wilber Panhellenic Hall (1963), Roberts Hall (1968), and Hillcrest (1964); and two for men, Elam Arms (1964) and Vann Hall (1967). Private interests built and owned Hillcrest and Elam in what the administration hoped would be "a landmark in . . . future development," allowing the university "to concentrate its construction activities in the essential academic fields." Neither dormitory proved profitable, however, and the school eventually acquired both, Elam in 1971 and Hillcrest two years later. A third private company owned Vann athletic dormitory and leased it to the university.

Other construction included the Education and Psychology Building (1964, later named for Ralph Owings and Carl McQuagge), Reed Green Coliseum (1965), Wilbur Stout Lecture Hall (1966), a Business Administration Building (1968, later named for Joseph A. Greene), the Johnson Science Tower (1970), the University Natatorium (1971, later named for M. C. "Tuffy" Johnson), the Performing Arts Center (1972, later named for Raymond Mannoni), and the Nursing School Building (1975, later named for Elizabeth Harkins). After the Commons opened, Wimpy's, the bookstore, and the post office moved into the remodeled Dining Hall, known as The Hub after 1963. A 1968 expansion doubled the size of Cook Library. The old Panhellenic House, renamed East Hall, became home to the departments of geography and religion and philosophy. A similar old Camp Shelby structure known as

Built in 1963, Wilber Panhellenic Hall would be home to USM's sorority women for more than forty years.

West Hall was torn down, though the theater section was moved and renovated and opened in 1966 as the Southern Playhouse (later named for Gilbert Hartwig). Federal loans and grants continued to finance much of the construction boom.

After fire destroyed the Kappa Sigma and Pi Kappa Alpha fraternity houses in 1965, their replacements, along with a Sigma Alpha Epsilon house, inaugurated a new fraternity row just west of the old one in 1968. The Baptist Student Union, the Wesley Foundation (Methodist), the Newman Club (Catholic), and the Southern Christian Student Center (Church of Christ) also built new facilities on or near the campus. In the late sixties as growth cramped existing space, the school began to purchase additional property to the north and west of campus.

When the new Cook Library opened in 1961, the old facility became the Student Services Building.

Named for former athletic director Reed Green, the University Coliseum was built in 1965.

The attainment of university status inaugurated a period of rapid and extensive curriculum changes. The initial undergraduate structure included one college (arts and sciences), two schools (education and psychology and business administration), and two divisions (fine arts and home economics). Fine arts became a school in 1965 as did home economics three years later. In 1966, a special legislative appropriation enabled USM to organize a degree-granting school of nursing with Mary Elizabeth Harkins as its first dean. Education and psychology became a college in 1968. The speech department was divided in 1964, with theatre moving into fine arts while public address joined journalism and radio and television to form a new Department of Communications in the College of Arts and Sciences. Five years later, the offices of public information, duplicating, printing, and photography united with the communications department in a new division of communications. Other new departments emerged during the 1960s: speech and hearing sciences, science education, and educational foundations in 1964; computer science and statistics (the first in the state) in 1965; and polymer science in 1969–70. In 1965, arts and sciences initiated an honors program (later the Honors College), which became university-wide after 1970.

Other developments included publication of *The Southern Quarterly* (1962) and the *Journal of Educational Research* (1968); establishment of a bureau of business research (1964), an office of research and projects (1964), and a computer center; and the inauguration of a free

Dean of Nursing Mary Elizabeth Harkins adjusts nursing student Judie Shanks's cap. Established in 1966, USM's School of Nursing would later boast the sixth largest baccalaureate nursing program in the nation.

textbook service (1964). In the summer of 1962, the university awarded its first doctoral degree, in education. Thereafter, doctoral programs were added in biology, chemistry, political science, science education, music education, English and literature, history, mathematics, speech and hearing sciences, and geography. By 1972, USM offered terminal degrees in twenty-seven fields.

There were also personnel changes. Anna Roberts retired in 1962 after thirty-seven years of service, and Warren Tracy became librarian. In 1969, Charles Moorman became dean of the university when John Allen assumed the presidency of Centenary College in Louisiana, and Peter Durkee replaced the retiring Reginald Switzer as dean of student affairs. In 1971, Robert van Aller succeeded graduate dean Aubrey Lucas, who left to become president of Delta State College. A year later, Sidney Weatherford became director of institutional research, and in 1973 William E. "Bud" Kirkpatrick replaced Forrest Tucker as director of public information.

Moorman's inaugural address invoked a new concept, the career university, which soon brought sweeping and controversial changes to the curriculum. The new dean called for "a new dedication to teaching, a revitalized academic program, a sharpened awareness of public relations and service, and a renewed sense of academic community." Core requirements shrank from ninety-two to fifty-one hours, and the Basic College disappeared as new students enrolled directly in their major areas. A new five-day schedule of seventy-minute classes, adopted in 1972, allowed USM to award semester credit in most courses while retaining the quarter calendar. It also made a significant difference in appropriations after the college board began to allocate funds according to a formula based on credit-hour enrollment. The new schedule "was based on our discovery," McCain advised the board, "that in terms of class contact hours . . . we could quite easily give as much actual instruction per class in a quarter as do semester schools in a semester and . . . graduate our students in ten quarters instead of twelve, thus becoming the first true three-year

In 1969, Dean Charles Moorman introduced a new and controversial "career" curriculum.

university in the United States." Graduation now required 128 semester hours, 35 in the core and 18 in a minor, with the major determined by the appropriate school or college. The streamlined general curriculum included composition (6 hours), humanities and fine arts (9), social sciences (9), mathematics (3), science (6), and physical education (2).

Critics charged that the changes simply reflected an effort to conform to national trends in education and would

Director of Alumni Affairs Powell Ogletree (right) and Hugh Lowery, vice-president of Indurall Paint Company, celebrate the completion of USM's Fourth Street "Welcome" sign over U. S. Highway 49.

After Hurricane Camille devastated the Gulf Coast in 1969 (above), student organizations, such as Phi Mu sorority (right), helped raise money for relief efforts.

lower academic standards. The word "relevant" did seem to appear frequently in defenses of the revised system, and many of the new programs such as American studies, Latin American studies, environmental studies, and black studies were similar to those established at other universities during the era. Other new programs also reflected the career orientation: athletic administration and coaching, hotel and restaurant management, medical technology, linguistics, advertising, medical records, law enforcement, and plastics technology. Additional changes that were more or less related to the new scheme included new programs in dance, jazz, creative writing, aerospace studies, anthropology and comparative religious studies, recreation, microbiology, theatre arts, and art education; an intermediate master of philosophy degree designed to serve junior college faculty; master's programs in criminal justice, nursing, and computer science; a new doctorate in performing musical arts; designation of health, physical education, and recreation as a school (1971); creation of a new graduate school of social work (1974); establishment of an oral history program (1970); and abolition of the English proficiency test and mandatory ROTC. A Career Development Center opened in 1974 to counsel students in choosing career programs. Perhaps the most significant aspect of the career concept was the separation of arts and sciences in 1970. Claude Fike remained dean of the college of liberal arts, and Robert van Aller became dean of the new college of sciences, which three years later became the college of science and technology.

Despite criticisms of the new curriculum, Moorman defended the career university as "a great leap forward in education," one that made the academic program both stronger and more flexible. President McCain called it "another step in our forward march toward becoming the nation's most energetically progressive University. For we are now able to train our young people for active, useful, and profitable roles in society not only better than can more conservative . . . institutions, but faster as well."

The post-World War II enrollment surge finally spent itself by the late 1960s. On-campus registration declined in 1968 and 1969, the first consecutive decreases in a quarter of a century. The most popular explanation was the fading of the postwar baby boom, which left a shrinking pool of high school graduates. Also, higher fees, especially out-of-state tuition, made competing institutions more attractive. The emergence of low-cost universities in New Orleans, Mobile, and Pensacola diminished Southern's yield from those traditionally fertile recruiting fields. Hurricane Camille's economic impact on Mississippi's Gulf Coast after 1969 constricted the student flow from that fruitful source also.

In response to such trends, USM, like other universities, began to reevaluate its services to what became known in the 1970s as "nontraditional" students. Southern had begun, of course, as a service to an atypical college constituency—public school teachers—and had offered home study and correspondence courses since 1912. From 1954 to 1962, MSC sponsored an evening college "to serve adult members of the community" who wanted to "work toward a college degree, improve their occupational skills, study for self improvement, or pursue avocational interests." In 1961, the division of extension and correspondence became the division of continuing education, which by 1969 included four departments: correspondence; conferences, institutes, and workshops; extension and residence centers; and community services. The last named began in 1962 as the Department of Adult Education, "designed to appeal to the professional, cultural, and recreational interests of the adult citizen of the University community."

USM established its first residence center in Meridian in 1952 and a second in Biloxi in 1961. The following year, a third opened in Natchez, primarily in response to that community's appeal for an associate degree nursing program. The university also added permanent extension centers in Jackson (1964) and Jackson County (1972). In 1971, USM acquired the Long Beach facilities of Gulf Park College when that two-year private girls' school closed after a half century of operation. The following year, the residence centers at Natchez (under Dean Bill W. Gore) and Gulf Park (under Dean Joe E. Holloway) became degree-granting branches of the Hattiesburg campus, offering the bachelor of science in business administration, industrial technical education (Gulf Park only) and elementary and secondary education as well as courses in support of other degrees offered only through the main campus. Natchez continued its associate of science degree program in nursing. In 1973, these branches became part of a new division of extension and public service (under Dean Gomer Pound) that also included the departments of independent study, conferences and workshops, and community services and programs.

The same year, a SACS committee commended USM for extending its "resources . . . into the mainstream of the society it serves . . . enhancing the quality of the lives of its constituency." In 1971, McCain predicted that possibly "within a very few years, our off-campus population will be larger than that on campus." That prediction proved far too optimistic, but by the end of the decade, more than two thousand students, 20 percent of total enrollment, were taking courses away from the Hattiesburg campus.

The pulse of campus life during the sixties also reflected the dynamism of a developing university. The Greek community continued to thrive. Acacia disappeared early in the decade, but two new fraternities emerged: Sigma Alpha Epsilon in 1965 and Sigma Nu three years later. In 1971, another sorority, Delta Gamma, appeared. The prestigious scholastic honorary society Phi Kappa Phi came to the university in 1967, and the number of religious, service, and professional organizations mushroomed.

The music program remained one of the university's strongest. Alan Drake became director of bands in 1966 and was followed by Raymond G. Young in 1969 and Joe Barry Mullins in 1973. By 1975 there were, in addition to the marching, concert, and symphonic bands, a symphonic wind ensemble, chamber ensembles, a percussion choir and marimba ensemble, an ROTC band, and a jazz laboratory band. The University Singers appeared with the New Orleans Symphony Orchestra in 1964 and again in 1969. In 1967, the Summer Theatre, which had moved into the renovated Red Barn Theatre the previous year, merged with the Summer Musical Theatre to become the Southern Stage. Frank Monachino's production of *The Mikado* won a Mississippi Arts Council grant that financed a five-city

In 1971, USM acquired the Long Beach facilities of Gulf Park College, which had been a two-year private girls' school.

tour of Mississippi in the fall of 1967. In 1970, Mannoni shifted the opera workshop from music to a new theatre arts department that encompassed all the performing arts including dance. The American Educational Theatre Association chose USM's production of *A Funny Thing Happened on the Way to the Forum*, directed by Blaine Quarnstrom, for a 1975 USO tour of American military bases in Greenland, Newfoundland, Labrador, and Iceland. In 1972, the new Raymond Mannoni Performing Arts Center opened with a production of *A Midsummer Night's Dream* that veteran *Jackson Daily News* critic Frank Hains called "the most striking technical achievement I have seen on a Mississippi stage." Two years later, Robert Mesrobian directed USM's third production of *Die Fledermaus* in fifteen years, which became the first complete opera televised by the Mississippi Educational Television Network.

As a growing university, Southern was able to offer its students better and more varied entertainment. The Lettermen were annual favorites of the early sixties, and in 1965 Pete Fountain presented the premiere concert in the new Reed Green Coliseum. Among the others to appear on campus were Bob Hope, Glen Campbell, Ray Charles,

Football star Ken Avery and 1967 Miss Mississippi Robbie Robertson of USM.

The establishment of new sororities and fraternities during the 1960s helped to sustain a thriving Greek community.

Chicago, Ike and Tina Turner, and the Temptations. Lecturers included ABC newsman Peter Jennings, U.S. Senator and former astronaut John Glenn, former Supreme Court Justice Tom Clarke, and consumer advocate Ralph Nader.

Athletics remained a vital part of student life. Pie Vann's 1962 football squad bade farewell to small college status by winning the school's second national championship in that division with a 9-1 season marred only by a loss to Memphis State. Vann's troops quickly established a reputation for gruesome defensive play that bore the distinct imprint of P. W. Underwood, who joined the staff in 1963. Behind a savage linebacking corps, which included Doug Satcher and Ken Avery, USM's "Vandals" led the nation in total defense in 1963, 1965, and 1966. Despite carving a remarkable 39-13-1 record from 1962 to 1967, Vann found victories over Southeastern Conference foes frustratingly elusive, a problem aggravated by the return to the schedule of Mississippi State and Ole Miss in mid-decade. The renewal of the State series in 1964 was a

Coach Pie Vann with 1960s standouts linebacker Doug Satcher and quarterback Vic Purvis.

48-7 embarrassment. Quarterback Vic Purvis led the nation in rushing through much of the early season, which strangely included, because of scheduling problems, two games against Memphis State, both victories. The next year brought another loss to Mississippi State, though the SEC jinx, which had lasted since the 1954 Alabama win, finally ended against Auburn. The victory over the Tigers was one of three consecutive 3-0 games in 1965, the last of which unfortunately was a loss to William and Mary.

October 1966 was perhaps Pie Vann's most excruciating month as head coach. After a painful 6-0 loss to Memphis State, his team dropped back-to-back heartbreakers against in-state rivals on the road. At Starkville, the defense held Mississippi State to 85 total yards from scrimmage, but in a brutal contest marred by 211 yards in penalties against both teams, a stray extra point handed the Bulldogs a 10-9 victory. The following week, Southern and Ole Miss met for the first time since 1939. After turning a blocked punt into an early touchdown, USM nursed a 7-0 lead deep into the fourth quarter when the nation's leading punt returner, Doug Cunningham, ran one back 57 yards to tie the score. Another late touchdown gave the Rebels a 14-7 lead and handed Vann a crushing loss, the third in fifteen days. His team rebounded to win four of its last five games to finish 6-4, but it would be the dawn of a new decade before another October afternoon in Oxford would finally remove the bitter taste of 1966.

Unfortunately, Pie Vann would not be there to enjoy it, for 1968 would be his last and only losing season. After winning three of its first four games, including a 47-14 thrashing of Mississippi State, Southern lost another heartbreaker in Oxford that seemed to demoralize Vann's squad. They dropped the next four games including a homecoming loss to Maxie Lambright's Louisiana Tech squad—quarterbacked by Terry Bradshaw—and a 68-7 humiliation at the hands of Don Coryell's San Diego State Aztecs led by Dennis Shaw and Fred Dryer. A victory over the University of Tampa in the season finale was not enough to erase the disappointment of a 4-6 record that, along with health problems, led to Vann's retirement. His winning percentage over twenty years as head coach (70.2) ranks him among the nation's best, but his contribution went far beyond the 139 games his teams won. Whatever football success The University of Southern Mississippi would later achieve would be built upon the solid foundation he laid, as a coach and as a gentleman. To replace him, Reed Green chose former Ole Miss team captain and one-time Pie Vann assistant Roland Dale. When Dale, who had apparently accepted the job, changed his mind, Green turned to P. W. Underwood, who had left Vann's staff in 1967 to coach linebackers at the University of Tennessee. Underwood got off to a rocky 5-5 start in his first campaign, which included embarrassments at Alabama (63-14) and Ole Miss (69-7). One of the few bright spots was a one-point victory over Louisiana Tech, the only blemish on the senior season of Terry Bradshaw, who would soon be the first player chosen in the 1970 National Football League draft.

Nineteen-seventy's disappointing 5-6 season ironically would produce three major contributions to Southern's

Throughout the 1960s, Vaught's Rebels remained frustratingly invulnerable to Southern's efforts to claim its initial victory in this bitter cross-state rivalry.

struggle to become a major football power. One was a lanky defensive back and kicking specialist from Thomson, Georgia, who celebrated his debut as a college punter by fumbling his first snap from center. It was one of the few mistakes young William Ray Guy ever made in a USM uniform. That night against Southwestern Louisiana, he went on to kick three field goals and an extra point and intercept a pass to lead USM to a 16-14 win. But it was

Two of football's finest coaches and gentlemen, USM head coach Pie Vann (left) and Ole Miss coach Johnny Vaught.

neither his placekicking nor his defensive play that riveted the attention of the sportswriters, as well as everyone else, in Lafayette that night. During the fourth quarter, he launched a school record 77-yard punt that actually rolled dead 97 yards from where he stood. The greatest punter in the history of college football had declared himself over the sophomore jitters, finishing the night with a 49.8-yard average on 7 punts. The second notable feature of 1970

In 1968, P. W. Underwood (left) replaced his old mentor Pie Vann as head football coach.

was a five-foot four-inch, 145-pound bolt of lightning from Purvis named Willie Heidelburg. Not the greatest running back in USM history, he was among the fastest, but his chief contribution actually had nothing to do with athletic skill at all. He was the school's first black football star, and his courage and affability helped make USM's transition to an integrated athletic program exemplary.

These two, the rangy white boy with the cannon leg and the diminutive but fleet black, had much to do with the third great achievement of 1970, which occurred at Oxford on October 17. That day, John Vaught's nationally ranked Ole Miss Rebels christened Hemingway Stadium's new artificial playing surface against USM. Fresh from back-to-back wins over Alabama (48-23) and Georgia (31-21), Archie Manning was seeking his third consecutive

Ray Guy's famous, and unstoppable, kick. In 1973, the Oakland Raiders made Guy the only pure punter ever chosen in the first round of the NFL draft.

Southeastern back-of-the-week honors on his way, everyone assumed, to the Heisman trophy. The sports pundits predicted not the score but how long the brilliant redhead from Drew would get to shine before yielding to his understudy to prevent a massacre more unseemly than the previous year's 62-point rout. Well into the second half, however, Manning found himself still very much in demand thanks to two 11-yard touchdown scampers by Heidelburg and a 47-yard Guy field goal that helped put Ole Miss on the short end of a 30-14 score. As the third quarter drew to a close, Manning drove his team to a first down at the USM 4-yard line. Three plays later, on fourth down at the one, defensive end Hugh Eggersmen sliced through the Rebel forward wall, pinned Manning high on his shoulder pads, and dumped him, along with hopes for a national championship and the Heisman trophy, onto the plush green Astro Turf floor.

"Don't you call it no upset," growled a proud Underwood to sportswriters after the game. "We took it to their butt and we whipped their butt." But it *was* an upset, perhaps the biggest in either school's history, and it overshadowed a magnificent performance by Manning, who completed 30 of 56 passes for 341 yards and 2 touchdowns in

In 1970, Willie Heidelburg became the first black athlete to play varsity-level football at USM.

Hugh Eggersman's (96) goal line stop of Archie Manning helped seal USM's upset victory over Ole Miss in 1970.

the game. The triumphs of the 1950s, ironically, had vindicated Southern's credentials everywhere but Mississippi, but this win earned for USM within the Magnolia State what the 1953 victory over Alabama had earned elsewhere, instant respectability, and not just as a football team but as a university. By defeating not any Ole Miss team but this particular Ole Miss team, Southern served notice that it was no longer the state's institutional stepchild but was moving forward to stake its claim to the family football inheritance.

Brutal reality, wearing maroon and white, ended the celebration in short order with a 51-15 drubbing from Mississippi State the next week, and the team limped to its second losing season in three years. The misery continued into 1971, but USM rallied to win the last five games and give Underwood that elusive first winning season at 6-5. Prosperity was short-lived, however, as 1972 turned into a 3-7-1 disaster, typified by a late-season game at Utah State. In a blinding snowstorm, Guy kicked a school-record 61-yard field goal, only to have the Aggies block a punt on the game's final play and recover the ball in the end zone to win 27-21. The record improved over the next two years (6-4-1 and 6-5), but the frustrations seemed to grow worse, especially against Ole Miss, who thrashed USM 41-0 in 1973 and the next year converted a fourth-down play with twenty-two yards to go on their way to a last-second 20-14 victory.

At the end of the 1974 campaign, during which stadium renovation forced USM on the road for all eleven games, Underwood resigned. "After a great deal of prayerful thought," he said, such action seemed "in the best interest of my family and the University." His last game, like Vann's, was an upset win over the University of Tampa. Affirming his pride in the progress of the football program under his direction, he declared, "I trust that my contributions will mean something in the future and will not be judged by the scoreboard alone." One must indeed look beyond the scoreboard to see how much progress USM football really made under P. W. Underwood. He gave the school a consensus all-American and its first NFL top-round draft choice

Renovation of the stadium sent the football team on the road for all of its games in 1974 and 1975.

in Ray Guy. Underwood had an infectious and enthusiastic devotion to the institution that helped create "Big Gold Country," a phrase and an idea that he brought with him from Tennessee. During his tenure, the athletic program in 1972 boldly defined a distinct identity by adopting a new nickname, Golden Eagles. He helped dissolve the color barrier in respectable fashion, and he held the program together during the difficult time of transition that always follows a living legend like Pie Vann. And even if some choose to judge him by the scoreboard after all, it will probably be the one that reads USM 30, Ole Miss 14.

The task of finding someone to fill Underwood's position fell to the man who had almost held it in the first place, Roland Dale. In December 1973, McCain had named Dale to replace Reed Green, who announced that he would

General Nat gave way to the Golden Eagle as school mascot in 1972.

In 1975, Bobby Collins became the new Golden Eagle football coach.

retire at the end of 1974 after almost half a century of service to USM athletics. The new athletic director came from Southeastern Louisiana University, where he had been head coach since 1972 after spending time as assistant coach at Ole Miss and Tulane in addition to three years on Pie Vann's staff. After a three-week search, Dale chose University of North Carolina assistant Bobby Collins as Underwood's successor. A Laurel native, Collins had lettered four years at Mississippi State, where he was an outstanding quarterback and punter. Thus, a new phase of Golden Eagle football began under the leadership of an athletic director who had been team captain at one cross-state rival and a coach who had been captain at the other.

The basketball program entered the university era under a familiar face, Lee Floyd, who returned as head coach in 1962. His second stint at Southern proved less successful than the first, and his 1962–63 team's 12-14 record gave him his first losing season. Despite two more losing campaigns (1965–66 and 1970–71), to go with six winning ones, Floyd gave USM another flood of memorable events—wins over Mississippi State (1963), Alabama (1966), and Ole Miss (1966); the opening of Reed Green Coliseum (December 6, 1965, against Southwestern Louisiana); a 23-game home winning streak (1966–69)—and players Jackie Laird, Bruce Miller, Charlie Payne, Gary Kochersperger, Gary Hannan, John Vitrano, Rich Corsetto, and Wilbert Jordan (USM's first black athlete in any sport).

The most memorable player was a six-foot five-inch forward who came to USM in 1966 from Necaise Crossing. Wendell Ladner left Hattiesburg four years later with school records for

As USM's first black athlete in any sport, basketball player Wilbert Jordan paved the way for racial equality in athletics.

Basketball standout Wendell Ladner in action (above) and with Coach Lee Floyd (left).

career average in scoring (20.5 per game) and rebounding (an incredible 16.5 per game). Of the top ten rebounding games in school history, nine belong to him, including the record 32 against Pan American University in 1970. Ladner went on to a successful career in professional basketball before a tragic airplane crash took his life in 1975. Perhaps the most memorable season was 1967–68, when Floyd's team averaged 97.6 points per game and topped the century mark ten times on their way to a 19-6 record. Berlin Ladner entered the season finale against Samford only 39 points short of the 1,000-point club, and teammates spent much of the night helping him reach that milestone. With "little" brother Wendell sweeping the offensive board and shoveling the ball back out to him, Berlin led the team to a 109-90 rout with a school-record 45-point performance.

With his health declining and the team sinking to a 7-19 record, Floyd retired after the 1970–71 season. His 128-100 record after 1962 gave him an overall mark of 246-147. Eugene "Jeep" Clark, who had been Floyd's assistant since 1964, succeeded him as head coach. Clark's first campaign was a 0-24 disaster from which he would never really recover. After an 8-16 record the next year followed by three consecutive 11-15 seasons, he resigned in 1976. Highlights of Clark's tenure included wins over Ole Miss, Georgia Tech, and City College of New York and the play of Glenn Masson, Casey Price, Danny Thornsberry, and John Prince.

Baseball remained largely a nonscholarship sport, yet C. J. "Pete" Taylor, who replaced Clyde Stuart as coach in 1958, produced several outstanding teams. The 1964–65 squad finished 15-4 and defeated Mississippi State, Ole Miss, Alabama, and Arkansas. Memorable players included Frank Baker, Bruce Miller, Gary Hannan, Jimbo Green, Ed Assaf, John Flint, and Wilson Plunkett.

Pete Taylor coached USM baseball for almost three decades, from 1958 to 1985.

While the college experience of most USM students remained much like that of earlier generations, campus life in Hattiesburg was not impervious to the sweeping changes that the sixties loosed upon American society. After the Meredith incident at Ole Miss, McCain apparently realized that integration must come to USM, and he was determined that it come peacefully. A black applicant, John Frazier, was denied admission in the spring of 1964 on the grounds that he had failed to complete the necessary paperwork. On September 6, 1965, the following letter from the president to the students, faculty, and staff appeared in the *Student Printz*:

> Ladies and Gentlemen:
>
> Two Negro students have been admitted to this institution. These students will be participating in the various orientation activities on campus beginning Monday, September 6, 1965.
>
> It is expected that all personnel connected with the University will go about their affairs in a "business as usual" manner. We are certain that the fine conduct and spirit of our people will manifest itself during these times of change and that the University community will continue to show that we are "the biggest and the best."

And so segregation ended at the university without incident.

McCain was not so fortunate with USM's introduction to "student unrest" in 1967. Superficially, it began with all

—The BOOKWORM—

● Moonstruck BW pops question
● Pershing Rifles compete at LSU
● WMSU purchases new equipment

By Bob Wilson

12 Times Columbia Medalist — 7 Times All-American

Student Printz

Pacemaker of Southern Journalism

Volume Thirty-Seven — University Of Southern Mississippi, Hattiesburg Mississippi — Friday, March 20, 1964 — Number Eighteen

SCF plans Sunrise services

Solons may revise USM traffic code

Proposed bill aimed at fines; cabinet appointments approved

Executive Cabinet Members

JOHN FRAZIER . . . to try again

Frazier's attempt to matriculate is unsuccessful

Students hurt in auto mishap

Students, alums to celebrate University Day

Coed's contacts are drain dried

Women's Friday curfew changed

Hayslett to head Yellow Jackets for '64-65 session

The initial March 20, 1964, issue of the *Student Printz* carried a front page story concerning black applicant John Frazier's denial of admission to the university. Within hours of their release, however, copies of the newspaper were confiscated by the administration, and a second edition appeared with the conroversial article replaced by a notice regarding changes in women's curfew hours.

the trappings of a typical pre-final examination fling. Shortly after midnight on May 10, residents of Bond and Scott Halls began to congregate in the parking lot that separated the two men's dormitories. Their enthusiasm and courage grew with their ranks, which quickly reached several hundred. Finally someone uttered the catalytic phrase, "panty raid," and the crowd jubilantly struck out for Mississippi Hall. Before reaching the target, however, they encountered dean of men Rader Grantham and security chief Willie Oubre at the head of a campus force now supported by several Hattiesburg police units complete with riot dogs. The mob splintered into smaller contingents that ventured off to perpetrate individual pranks. One substantial group reformed in front of Panhellenic dormitory, whose window-rattling residents added shrieks, whistles, and a few pairs of underwear to the excitement. Across campus, two city fire engines appeared to extinguish a large wooden cross burning behind the gutted remains of the recently destroyed Kappa Sigma house. Flying rocks and bottles shattered a few car windows, and someone hurled a flaming roll of toilet paper to the roof of Bond Hall. By 1:30 A.M. the rampaging had largely subsided, though shouts and exploding fireworks sporadically punctuated the growing quiet through the rest of the night. Traumatic as the disturbance must have been for school officials, it was puny by national standards and paled even in comparison to an incident the same night ninety miles away where local police sealed off a twenty-block area around Jackson State College as 1,500 students seized control of the campus and surrounding area.

The following night, things turned uglier at Southern. Dean Allen told 1,500 students gathered in front of Bennett Auditorium that the administration would meet with leaders of the protest the next morning to discuss grievances. By 9:30, all seemed calm. Within an hour, however, the mob again began to grow rowdy. Someone tossed a chain across an electrical transformer, darkening the campus for some time, and eggs began to fly. The crowd seemed to swell and then boil out like spilt liquid into scattered pockets that at times appeared to blanket the entire campus, only to re-form again elsewhere. About 11:30, the students began to converge on the home of the president, who had just returned to town from a speaking engagement. McCain met them near the parking lot behind the Student Services Building and summarily advised them to go home and go to bed. They responded with catcalls and shouts of "duck killer." (One of the students' charges against McCain was that he had ordered the slaughter of an overpopulation of ducks around Lake Byron.) Amid the continued jeers and quacking, someone hurled a light bulb that barely missed the head of the president, who shrugged cooly and finished his talk as several more missiles sailed overhead. After a half hour or so, students began to drift away but reassembled in front of The Hub. Soon after midnight, order returned but not before police had made some twenty arrests for inciting to riot, destruction of property, and resisting arrest.

At ten o'clock the next morning, McCain again met with students at a special convocation in the coliseum. Several student spokesmen catalogued complaints that included bad food, crowded dormitories, mandatory meal tickets, stringent social regulations, and the stifling of free expression. The president agreed to work with a new faculty-student committee to find mutually acceptable solutions. The close of the quarter brought calm, and the new committee, meeting well into the summer, hammered out several proposals, most of which McCain approved. They included relaxation of restrictions on student publications, women's dormitory curfew, off-campus student housing and visitation, and dress codes for men and women. The riots ended in 1967, but tensions remained between a new generation of students and a president who must have felt betrayed by their apparent indifference to his contributions to the university. Growing national conflicts over racial justice and the Vietnam War heightened these local tensions.

The USM community had generally looked favorably on American efforts in Southeast Asia, but by 1968 antiwar sentiment began to surface. That fall, USM encountered its first real organized dissent in the form of the Student Action Party and its "central committee," the Committee for Student Action (CSA). Most students, however, still seemed more interested in the football game against Alabama or the new campus coffeehouse, Nat's Nook. The coffeehouse lasted only a year, but among those who performed there was an aspiring young student singer from Mobile, Jimmy Buffett.

The CSA, however, spawned other dissident groups such as the United Party and the Progressive Students Association, and by early 1969, politics—campus, national, and international; radical, moderate, and reactionary—was fast becoming a favorite student pastime. Dennis White of the Action Party launched a *Student Printz* column "directed at those students who are thoroughly dissatisfied with American, and especially Southern, society and who are tempted to call themselves 'radicals.'" White dropped out of school after winter quarter but remained active on campus as a distributor of *The Kudzu*, Mississippi's contribution to the era's underground student press. When he defied a school order to remain off campus after business hours, security officers arrested him for trespassing. The administration, White charged, had suppressed "all my attempts to create a more liberal atmosphere and my attempts to win more rights for the students." Student

Among the aspiring musical groups that entertained on campus during the 1960s was the Upstairs Alliance, which included USM students Bill Kehoe (kneeling) and (from left) Scooter Gill, Rick Bennett, and Jimmy Buffett.

conservatives were also organized and vocal, as reflected by another weekly column "Slightly to the Right," which a leader of George Wallace's American Independent Youth (AIY) party contributed to the school newspaper.

Early in 1969, the president of the Interfraternity Council returned from a regional meeting in Miami full of dire warnings about the "menace of the Students for a Democratic Society" with its doctrine of "Marxist Communism" and its antipathy toward Greek social organizations. Soon afterward, arts and sciences dean Claude Fike echoed the alarm, insisting that the SDS was a "menace and not just a nuisance." Such groups were part of the New Left movement, he warned, and sought "to bring down society in general and the university in particular," thriving on the notion that students possess "a natural right to run the college." A student's only natural right, Fike countered, was "being a student," and he encouraged the campus senators to "raise a student responsibility banner against the student power banner."

Bud Kirkpatrick, director of the student union (later director of public relations), recalled that the Progressive Students Association once filed a peculiar student activity form. "They all wanted to get around the administration building," he said, "and levitate it, shake out all of the evil spirits, and let it back down. I denied it on the basis that it was a very old building, and lifting it like that would pull all the plumbing loose. . . . If they succeeded but lost their concentration, they might drop it . . . which would be of great expense to the University. . . . They brought their lawyers in, we haggled about it, and they went on their way, apparently convinced that this was a legitimate reason."

By focusing on the student revolt's threat to fraternities and sororities, the controversy ironically drove independent students on the political left and right into each other's arms in an anomalous alliance against the Greeks. A fraternity leader observed in the *Student Printz* that "students—especially members of the United Party—see SDS as a big, wonderful, revolutionary brother who is about to swoop down and slaughter an imaginary Greek monster." The new student political party, he continued, "would have us believe that Greeks are the sons and daughters of capitalist millionaires—people who drive Cadillacs and hate common people." The response to these charges came not from the political left but from a student spokesman for Wallace's AIY party, who sardonically warned in a newspaper column: "The SDS is coming! The SDS is coming! The SDS is coming!" Invading from LSUNO, he said, they had been sighted somewhere near Poplarville "headed this way." Fellow travelers lurked everywhere; even the girls in home economics, he noted, were supposedly "cooking up something subversive." While the political passions that spawned the student revolt largely faded with the decade, the SDS scare's prime legacy at USM was a Greek-independent split that remained intense well into the 1970s.

There was also dissension within the faculty. Controversial changes in several departmental chairs and the dismissal of a number of professors provoked cries of repression. A *Hattiesburg American* editorial suggested an investigation of the removal of department heads, and an arts and sciences faculty advisory council accused the administration of "unethical and unprofessional conduct in the intimidation of lawfully and responsibly dissenting faculty members." One disgruntled professor later painted a bleak picture of faculty morale during the late sixties and early seventies. Many of his colleagues, he claimed, had spent those years under a cloud of dread and with a sense of impending doom. "They spoke to each other in whispers. Many were on edge and afraid." Another described Southern as "a twilight zone dominated by the Exit 13 syndrome, a place in which fact and fiction, fantasy and reality all became hopelessly entangled," an institution where "academic freedom or freedom of expression for students and faculty is virtually unheard of." Both of these critics placed their indictments of Southern in a more grandiose context. The former saw "Ft. McCain" as "a microcosmic expression of bureaucratized brutality in American life;" while for the latter, Exit 13 represented "a case study showing how a procapitalist ideology permeates every aspect of college life and curriculum in a way that recreates a microcosm of the authoritarianism, racism, and sexism in society itself." And so the political and ideological winds of the age finally drifted over Hattiesburg.

As the end of the sixties approached, the forces of student activism, faculty dissent, and black rights converged. Several professors and black students marched with members of the Progressive Students Association in two antiwar Moratorium Day marches in the fall of 1969. The cooperation extended into the following spring's upheaval over the American military incursion into Cambodia. In the wake of nationwide campus violence that left two

Anti-war demonstrations came to Southern in the fall of 1969 as several USM students and faculty participated in the Vietnam Moratorium Day marches.

Jackson State students—as well as four at Kent State—dead, black activist Julian Bond canceled an appearance scheduled for May 17 at USM. His telegram message to the sponsoring black students that he assumed the university would "be closed in memory of your slain brothers at Jackson State College" sparked tense demonstrations. The administration issued a statement that "Dr. McCain respects your feelings and is sympathetic with your problems. They are the problems of the entire university and the nation." The president agreed to meet with representatives of the protesters but refused to close the school. Four students were later arrested and suspended from the university for distributing notices that classes would not meet on May 18 and 19.

The Student Printz

ALL AMERICAN — ACP — 1970

VOLUME 53—NUMBER 57 | UNIVERSITY OF SOUTHERN MISSISSIPPI | HATTIESBURG, MISSISSIPPI 39401 | TUESDAY, MAY 12, 1970

Progressives Sponsor Indochina Reaction

Estimated 700 Students Gather, Hear Students, Faculty Members

Speakers at the Indochina Reaction Thursday were heckled by some spectators at the otherwise peaceful rally, sponsored by the Progressive Students Association.

William E. Johnson, president of the PSA, presided at the rally, where an estimated 700 students gathered to hear students and faculty members give their views on the recent announcement by President Nixon on U.S. intervention in Cambodia.

The first speaker at the rally was Dr. Robert Smith, assistant professor of political science. "I'm not sure I belong here today," Dr. Smith told the crowd. "I'm opposed to war in Vietnam and Cambodia," he said and labeled the war as "unjustified" and "futile."

Dr. Smith said the war diverts "attention from current problems at home and abroad" and asserted that "no one to this date has offered any reasonable end to the war."

Dr. Smith labeled the deaths of four students at Kent State University as "very tragic" but said "we cannot assign blame for the deaths. We can all learn from what happened at Kent. We can learn the lesson of restraint."

Dr. Smith received almost no heckling as he spoke and received applause when he finish-

Dr. Ira Schwarz, the coordinator of Allied Arts and associate professor of music, urged the observers of the rally to help "bind up the nation's wounds."

Singer Pat Weathers, who provided entertainment throughout the rally, was heckled several times during his performances. While Weathers sang a protest song entitled "Oh, Mary," a group of spectators at the rear of the crowd began to sing Dixie."

Ernie Gregory, a senator, told the spectators that he believed the crowd was "a more relevant body than the Senate because we are discussing more relevant subjects." Gregory urged more communication between students and the administration on campus. "We should talk to each other," Gregory said, and in reference to the heckling, he said, "we're not here to call each other 'redneck.' We should understand each other, not fight with each other. This is merely a rally to express our opinion that we

Football star Fred Cook became the first black Mr. USM in 1974. He is pictured here with Miss USM Lula Fuller.

The university, which had already instituted a black studies program, intensified its efforts to hire black teachers, and the immediate crisis gradually subsided. Critics continued to complain, however, about the small number of black faculty members and administrators, the absence of black fraternities and sororities, and the continued use of what were considered racist symbols: the mascot "General Nat" (Confederate General Nathan Bedford Forrest) and the song "Dixie." General Nat disappeared when Golden Eagles became the school nickname in 1972. The same year, the homecoming court featured a black senior maid, and in 1974, popular football standout Fred Cook became the first black Mr. USM. Greek social organizations for blacks appeared in 1975: two sororities, Alpha Kappa Alpha and Delta Sigma Theta, and one fraternity, Omega Psi Phi.

Controversy also lingered concerning academic freedom and the role of faculty in university affairs. A SACS committee that visited the campus in 1974 noted a low level of faculty morale, which it blamed on a combination of apathy and insecurity among professors. The committee recommended the establishment of a faculty senate or some other form of faculty governance and adoption of "a tenure system that is clearly defined, guarantees academic freedom, and is in keeping with customary university practice in the nation." Despite its criticisms, the SACS report praised the overall progress of the institution, acknowledging that "the character of the University is changing markedly in the shift from a teacher-training college to a university that is far broader in its mission. The University is deserving of commendation for its efforts to meet the needs of business and industry in the region by developing new programs. Similarly the University has done well in striving to meet local community needs." Such an assessment underscored USM's enduring effort to adapt its educational mission to the sweeping social changes of modern life without sacrificing the spirit of the institution's original commitment to make life richer for the people of Mississippi.

In 1972 alumni, faculty, students, and staff were asked to submit new names for the athletic teams. An ad hoc committee appointed by the Alumni Association voted on the submissions and chose "Golden Eagles" as the new mascot.

Several months before the SACS visit, McCain announced that he would retire on June 30, 1975. His

Walter Washington, pictured here with President William D. McCain and Dean Charles Moorman, became the first black student to earn a doctoral degree from a Mississippi institution. He served as president of Alcorn State University 1969–94.

twenty-year presidency, the longest so far, had been as energetic, forceful, and controversial as the man himself. "Pussycats do not become university presidents," one of his critics later observed, "and Dr. McCain was no pussycat. He was . . . a curious, complex man—a walking enigma." A soldier who rose from the enlisted ranks to major general, he could be as cold and hard as steel. In 1972, he boasted before the student senate, "I have worked a long time in this world, and this month I reach complete financial independence, to the extent that I can tell everybody to go to hell." Yet he could be gentle and eloquent, as in his dedication of a genealogical volume: "To the memory of my Father, Samuel Woodward McCain, who taught me the alphabet, and who instilled in me a love for books and for the making of books, and to my Mother, Sarah Alda Shaw McCain, who never said an unkind word to me, who never did an unkind thing toward me, and who never was a party to an unkind act in my presence."

He was a humanities scholar who created a separate college of science and technology and made it one of USM's strongest. "In my experience with Dr. McCain," said a former and longtime faculty member, "you could count on his word. . . . If you'd go to him and ask for something and he said yes, that yes was firm." Yet an ad hoc committee of professional historians appointed by the American Historical Association in 1971 concluded that an article that McCain wrote for a historical journal "represents a violation of 'approved scholarly usage' with respect to another author's literary property." Some detractors accused him of being too conservative, yet he inaugurated some of the most sweeping changes in the school's history. He steered an institution with a remarkably straitlaced tradition through an era of unparalleled social upheaval with a minimum of disruption. Some of his staunchest supporters thought the tone of his administration was too military. "I was an assistant professor when I came here," said one, "and that would be about the equivalent of corporal. Then I became associate professor, and that was about buck sergeant. Then when I became full professor, I figured that was staff sergeant." Even one of his severest critics acknowledged that "the University of Southern Mississippi, on its way to becoming a major academic institution in the South, would not be what it is today had there been no General William D. McCain." He was indeed a complex man, and he served in a complex age.

During his twenty-year tenure (1955–75), President McCain, pictured here with Governor Paul B. Johnson Jr., remained true to his promise "to take a small college and make a good university out of it."

Changing of the guard – Aubrey Lucas is announced as McCain's succesor.

His final year, as the campus newspaper noted in May 1975, included "some of the most disheartening days of his administrative career." They were haunted by "charges of discrimination—between Greek and Independent, white and black . . . campus petitions, threats of outside law enforcement agencies on campus . . . [law]suits. . . grand jury investigations . . . [and] a local publicity-hungry district attorney." The disappointments, however, the *Printz* reporter asserted, would never overshadow the achievements. "My goal," McCain said, "was to take a small college and make a good university out of it." The spectacular fulfillment of that goal seems beyond dispute. In 1955, McCain inherited a 3,000-student college with an annual appropriation of $2 million. He left a major multipurpose university with more than 11,000 students, 470 full-time faculty—almost 60 percent of them with terminal degrees—and a $24 million budget. One professor, who first came to Southern in 1926 under Joe Cook, observed that considering "what McCain has done . . . the total picture, how he has developed the organization, its physical facilities . . . increase in staff, great increase in faculty members with terminal degrees, tremendous increase in salaries . . . we must admit or conclude that he is without any reasonable doubt the best we have ever had."

R. C. Cook echoed that assessment: "When the annals of the University of Southern Mississippi are written, Dr. W. D. McCain will be listed as the outstanding president of the school." His only fault seemed to be a "superfluous" use of the first person singular. "Years ago he made a talk to the Rotary Club," said Cook, "and the man next to me said after the speech, 'That damn fellow can put more I's into one sentence than any person I have ever known.' Scholar, soldier, and administrator that he is, maybe he is entitled to spread a few personal pronouns around." When the board of trustees in October 1974, named Aubrey K. Lucas to succeed him, McCain seemed pleased. "We need him now. We've gone through two decades of bitter, bitter battles; I fit into the battles, he'll fit into the peaceful world." Asked what influence he hoped to have on the new administration, McCain said he intended to keep any advice to himself. After all, he explained, "No one told me anything when I came here."

Aubrey Keith Lucas was no stranger to Hattiesburg. A native of State Line, he received bachelor's and master's degrees from Mississippi Southern College before earning a Ph.D. from Florida State University in 1966. He served USM as director of admissions, registrar, and dean of the graduate school, as well as professor of education, before leaving in 1971 for Delta State College. In July 1975, Lucas returned to his alma mater as its sixth president. Two months later, he delivered an important address that contained a blueprint for his presidency. Speaking to a faculty eager for some insight into the tone of the incoming administration, he gave thanks for the hospitality he had been shown since his arrival. "Your friendliness and helpfulness," he said, "have been matched only by your advice and counsel, all of which I need, and some of which I even appreciate." Aware that the role of the faculty in university affairs was a sensitive matter, he noted that "goal setting *is* important, for truly if we have no vision, we shall perish with aimless wanderings or debilitating arguing and struggling over priorities." He intended only to "sketch broadly," he said, "not because I think specifics are unimportant, but because I believe all of you ought to have some part in planning this institution's future by filling in details through appropriate committee and council work." Those must have been welcome words to his listeners, who heard him go on to speak of "consensus decision making," meaning not that "we consult with everybody or that we vote on every issue," but that he expected his administrators to "be prepared to defend our decisions, and . . . be big enough to modify them if they turn out to be bad ones."

In that initial address, Lucas articulated what would become the theme of his administration. "We must set for ourselves," he said, "no less goal than to become a *distinguished* university. I believe that we can be, and I believe that we ought to serve notice on our competitors and our constituencies that we intend to be so." Distinction had to begin, he insisted, with the faculty, which is "the very heart and soul of a university. . . . It is my intention to interview every prospect. I have asked the deans to search carefully into the backgrounds of faculty to make sure that they are productive scholars who are willing to work hard to help us achieve our goals." Securing good teachers would not be enough, however. "We need to nurture our faculty," he continued, and "find ways and means to reward them properly. It is my goal that the faculty of this university shall be the highest paid in our state." He went on to outline other goals: "establishing an honors college" to attract "the brightest students in our state and region"; creating "opportunities for our students to study abroad"; strengthening the library, going "beyond books [to] develop a learning center where all kinds of instructional aids are available"; and reassessing "our present credit-calendar system." One of the obvious tasks Lucas faced was reconciling the new vision of distinction with the school's career orientation. "I am well aware," he noted, "that there are those in the faculty who feel that the career university and the distinguished university are incompatible. . . . It seems to me that we can define and structure career opportunities in such a way that our larger goal of eminence will be enhanced." Much of the first decade of the Lucas era would be spent refining that definition and structure. "In 1952," he concluded, "I came here from State Line as green a freshman as was ever admitted, expecting and needing a lot and I was not disappointed. In 1975, I'm back, somewhat awed by the challenge but confident that with the great talent assembled here dedicated to conspicuous excellence and to bringing about a true academic community, we will become a distinguished university."

Student life, however, rather than faculty or curriculum, dominated the new administration's attention at first. Students returned in the fall of 1975 to discover a streamlined rules system that granted self-regulating hours to all female dormitory residents and the right to live off-campus to all students over twenty-one. Though the regulations explicitly forbade possession, consumption, or sale of alcoholic beverages on campus, they eliminated university restrictions regarding the use of alcohol elsewhere, yielding that responsibility strictly to the administration of local law. Almost a decade after USM students "rioted" to protest being told "where to live and how to act," the university placed its "boys and girls" where Joe Cook had put them in principle more than sixty years earlier, "on their own responsibility."

In 1976, Lucas reorganized the school's student affairs division, adding to the existing dean of men new deans of student services and student development, all reporting to a vice-president for student affairs Peter Durkee. In the summer of 1976, the president appointed an ad hoc committee to investigate charges of a "double standard" in the university's application of judicial procedures. Some independents complained that Greek students and organizations were subject to Panhellenic and Interfraternity Council judicial boards rather than the university's student affairs committee. Early in 1977, Lucas approved a restructuring of judicial procedures that explicitly protected students' "right to privacy" in their living quarters and established a single discipline system for all students and campus organizations. Despite the controversy, the president insisted that he found no widespread student dissatisfaction, and indeed the new generation of students did seem to be more sedate and content than those of the previous decade. The arrival of two new black fraternities, Kappa Alpha Psi and Alpha Phi Alpha, attested to both the continued vitality and growing diversity of campus Greek life.

Athletics also remained popular. Bobby Collins's first football squad, again playing all its games on the road, finished 7-4, winning more games than any Southern team in a decade. His second team finished 2-9, losing more games than any in school history. A 48-point shutout by East Carolina on opening day began a 9-game losing skid that included a 63-19 pounding by Brigham Young and an embarrassing 28-0 loss to Ole Miss before a capacity crowd in the inaugural game in the new M. M. Roberts Stadium. The misery finally ended with a 14-12 upset over Memphis State, a game that in some sense marked the real beginning of Eagle Fever. A small but vocal home crowd vented a season's worth of frustration in a loud and raucous display

Tailback Ben "Go-Go" Garry (1974-77) finished his career as the leading rusher in Mississippi collegiate football history.

of hometown support that echoed into the next week, a win over Texas-Arlington, and the next year. Through the dark cloud of 1976 at times glimmered several characteristics that both echoed past glory and forecast future success. One was a punishing ground attack that became a hallmark of Bobby Collins football, typified by tailback Ben Garry, who would amass during his career at Southern more rushing yardage (3,595) than any collegiate player in Mississippi history, including Walter Payton.

The second trait was a ferocious defense anchored by a group of linebackers who brought back memories of P. W. Underwood's Vandals of the early sixties. They became known as the Nasty Bunch, and in 1978, when Collins hired his former North Carolina colleague Jim Carmody as defensive coordinator, the defense adopted him as the original Big Nasty. A final characteristic of the 1976 Eagles was a reinvigorated USM tradition of doggedly determined play by athletes with marginal athletic ability but with a wealth of character and grit. The victory over Memphis State was engineered by a sophomore quarterback from Memphis who ironically drew his first starting assignment against his hometown school. Jeff Hammond's unspectacular but steady play that night not only helped break the frustrating losing streak, it also cost the Tigers a bowl invitation. Hammond was one of a seemingly endless stream of Golden Eagle stalwarts who came to USM because few others seemed to think they could play college football.

The climb to respectability began in 1977 when Collins's crew defeated Auburn, Ole Miss, and Mississippi

M. M. Roberts, flanked here by President Lucas and Governor Cliff Finch, dedicates USM's new football stadium named in his honor in 1976. Roberts received a diploma from Mississippi Normal College in 1917 and returned to earn a Ph.D. in 1964. As president of the state college board during the 1960s, he did much to advance Southern's interests.

State (the first of seven in a row against the Bulldogs) to enter a solid claim to the college championship of Mississippi and a somewhat less serious one to the SEC title. A late-season slump turned what began as a remarkable season into a mediocre 6-6. The next year when Collins's first recruiting class became seniors, his program finally turned the corner. Ironically, the pivotal game was a loss, one of three nonvictories that Collins would later describe as among the most important in his tenure at USM. Late in a 13-13 deadlock against Ole Miss in Jackson, junior quarterback Dane McDaniel made a crucial mistake. At the Rebel 36, needing only a yard for a first down, he threw an interception that would have been returned for a touchdown had Eagle reserve James Hale not bolted from the USM sidelines to take the ball carrier down short of the goal line. Despite the ensuing penalty for Hale's desperate tackle from the bench, Ole Miss had to settle for a field goal, but it was enough for a crushing 16-13 win. The following week, however, McDaniel redeemed himself, leading his teammates to a 22-17 victory over Mississippi State on their way to a 7-4 finish.

The Golden Eagles closed the seventies with a 6-4-1 season that included memorable games against Florida State, Ole Miss, Tulane, and Arkansas State. In the season opener in Tallahassee, USM came within a whisker of upsetting a highly ranked Seminole team that would win all of its regular season games on the way to the Orange Bowl. A blocked punt and a punt return for a touchdown, both in the final quarter, allowed FSU to escape with a 17-14 win. The Ole Miss game was memorable because of a newly-installed I-formation that ground the Rebels into submission 38-8 to avenge the previous year's disappointing loss. The Tulane game was another of those nonvictories that proved so important in USM's quest for football distinction. Aided by two crucial pass interference penalties, quarterback Roch Hontas marched the Green Wave 67 yards to take a 20-19 lead with 44 seconds left in the game. A furious Eagle comeback effort fell short with Winston Walker's 41-yard field goal attempt that left the home crowd sitting in stunned silence. Despite the outcome, the game was perhaps the most thrilling ever played on campus and did much to generate a loyal and enthusiastic constituency for Roberts Stadium football. The game against Arkansas State was notable not so much for the 14-6 victory that ended the season as for the debut of quarterback Reggie Collier, whose lithe limbs at times took on the appearance of a young colt. Over the next three years, Collins molded the youngster from D'Iberville into a supple and steady thoroughbred who carried Eagle football fortunes to their pinnacle. Collier not only broke a host of school offensive records, he solidified what Willie Heidelburg had begun a decade before, manfully demonstrating not only that a black athlete could exercise capable leadership but that white athletes would follow it and white fans would applaud it. No football program in the South has done more for racial harmony than Southern's, and for that Bobby Collins and Reggie Collier deserve much credit.

A new era of Golden Eagle basketball also began under Aubrey Lucas when Memphis State assistant M. K. Turk

Men's basketball coach, M. K. Turk.

replaced Jeep Clark as head coach in 1976. It took Turk but two seasons to produce USM's first winning record (13-12) since 1969–70. After a 13-14 season the next year, his troops posted a 17-10 mark in 1979–80, barely missing the school's first National Invitational Tournament bid by dropping its last two games, both by one point. Despite

Sammy Winder and Jeff Hammond were vintage Bobby Collins Eagles, supreme overachievers. Hammond played quarterback (1975-79), and after suffering through the worst season (2-9) in modern school history in 1976, he engineered victories over Auburn, Ole Miss, and Mississippi State the following year. After graduation, he served in the U.S. Army, rising to the rank of Major General and Chief of Staff for the U.S. Army Forces Command, having commanded the 4th Infantry Division (Mechanized) and the Multinational Division Baghdad during Operation Iraqi Freedom. Collins, he said, "set the standards of character and leadership. I learned more about leadership from him than . . . from anyone else. I used to watch every move he made . . . and, believe it or not, to this day I apply the Collins checklist to organization and leadership. . . . Those early Collins years set the tone for where we are today. We were a blue collar team, and we've been that way since. . . . None of us were really highly recruited, and we all kind of had a chip on our shoulder. We wanted to prove that we belonged. It didn't hurt that we had a great football coach."

The youngest of eleven children in a sharecropper family, Winder faced enormous obstacles in securing a college education. He spent much of his youth hauling hay and chasing cows on the family's rented farm near Pocahontas in southwest Madison County, and he walked a mile each day to catch the local school bus, which could reach his house only with great difficulty. Football changed things for him, though there were still days when, as his high school coach recalled, "Sammy came up to me and said, 'Coach, I don't know if I can be at practice today, because I've got to pull corn.'" Valuable as he was to the Madison-Ridgeland High School team—valuable enough that the school bus finally found a way to get to his house, at least on dry days—college scouts seemed uninterested. Winder was determined, however, not only to play college football but to get a degree. "I want an education," he later told a reporter during his USM days. "I remember the guys I hung out

Sammy Winder's leaping touchdown against Ole Miss in 1980.

General Jeff Hammond in Iraq.

with in Pocahontas. Some of them were faster and better than me but they didn't want to go to college, [though] they had the opportunity. I didn't want to do that. They'd have to run me out to get me out of here." With that kind of determination, Winder walked on at USM, eventually earned a scholarship, and became one of the most productive ball carriers in school history. Many of his teammates were, he said, like him, "too small, too short, and too slow, but Coach Collins got them in and worked them into a system that their talents would fit." Winder went on to a successful career in professional football, helping to lead the Denver Broncos to three Super Bowls. He also played in two Pro Bowls and once graced the cover of *Sports Illustrated*. But the image of Sammy Winder that Eagle fans will always remember was the magnificent leaping touchdown against Ole Miss in 1980, because it so perfectly captures the character of the teams that carried USM football fortunes to their grandest heights.

Jeff Hammond (#18) with assistant coach Daryl Moody and fellow 1975 quarterbacks Ken Alderman (#15), Jeff Bower (#7), and Jim Nyers (#12).

Kay James became Lady Eagle basketball coach in 1976, and by 1980 USM varsity athletics included women's volleyball, softball, and basketball.

the disappointment, M. K. Turk's Eagles entered the 1980s poised on the brink of basketball prominence.

Lucas and Dale also revived women's basketball, though for the first two years (1975–77) it was little more than a club sport. Looking for a coach who could build a first-rate program, Lucas called Margaret Wade, who won three national championships at Delta State and whom he had known when he was president there. Wade recommended a young Gulfport native who had just won a small college national championship at Berry College in Georgia, and in 1977 Kay James became the school's first full-time women's basketball coach. Her first recruit, Shirley Jones, recalled that her sense of direction was sometimes less than reliable. Driving the lead van on the way to her first game at the University of New Orleans, James headed north on Interstate 59 until Jones and her teammates got her turned around. Her sense of direction on the court was impeccable, and within four years she had the Lady Eagles in postseason play with a 22-7 record in 1980–81. Along with Jones, who would later become the first female athlete to join the USM Sports Hall of Fame, those early players built a solid base. Three of them (Jones, Nancy Faulk, and Pam McCoy) scored more than a thousand points in their careers, and Diana Lyons still holds the school record for career rebounding average. Kim Dedeaux and Vianne Giddens led the way with assists. By 1980, Dale had also added men's swimming, indoor and outdoor track, and cross country, as well as women's volleyball and softball to an athletic program that began to reflect USM's emergence as a major state university.

During his first year in office, Lucas reorganized the university's administrative structure by instituting a system of vice-presidents. Dean Charles Moorman became vice-president for academic affairs, Peter Durkee vice-president of student affairs, Thomas G. Estes vice-president for business and finance, and Shelby Thames, vice president

Shirley Jones (#12), who later served as assistant coach under Kay James, was the first female inducted into the USM Sports Hall of Fame.

for administration and regional campuses. Also, fine arts became a college in 1975, and the following year a new school of library science was established, the first such program to be accredited in Mississippi. In his second year, Lucas approved a new thirty-two-member elected Faculty Council "to provide for the faculty," according to its charter, "both a forum and a voice and so allow it to assert for the general welfare of the University its distinctive viewpoint and principles." In September 1978, the university ended a fifty-two-year tradition when it abandoned the quarter calendar and adopted a full semester system. Lucas approved the change, he said, "after long deliberation and . . . countless reports and discussions involving all areas of the university." As expected, the faculty generally applauded the new format, but it proved very unpopular among students at first. Nonetheless, as Lucas reported to the board in 1979, USM "made the transition . . . with very little trouble." In fact, the requisite reworking of class lectures, reexamination of procedures, and adjustments in class schedules produced "an updated curriculum, a trimmed-down schedule, and a computerized registration system," all of which proved quite beneficial.

Curriculum changes included new or expanded emphasis programs in paralegal studies, safety education, and environmental design; a new school of professional accountancy; designation of music as a school; graduate programs in nursing, library science, and counseling and clinical psychology. Accreditation of programs by recognized national professional agencies became a major goal in the pursuit of academic excellence, and programs that earned initial accreditation after 1975 included dietetics, professional accountancy, art, art education, dance, theatre, interior design, corrective therapy, journalism, athletic administration and coaching, social work, physical education, psychology, counseling psychology, business, home economics education, and librarianship.

Lieutenant Governor Evelyn Gandy breaks ground for the new Technology Building. Standing to her left is college board president and USM alumnus Bobby Chain, for whom the building was later named.

The new R. C. Cook University Union (above), which opened in 1976, included a spot for Cecil's newspaper stand (right), which had long been a fixture at the campus grill.

Engineering technology blossomed into one of the university's showpieces with accredited programs in architectural, construction, computer, electronics, industrial, and mechanical engineering technology.

Another significant innovation was the university's program in international education, which began in the summer of 1976 when the Department of Criminal Justice sent twenty-six students to England for a firsthand study of British criminal law and procedures. The program soon expanded to include economics, philosophy, political science, sociology, history, finance, English, and library science and by 1979 was exposing more than sixty students from twenty-nine states to the instruction of an array of prominent British scholars in those fields. Meanwhile, the Honors College Forum series brought distinguished speakers to the Hattiesburg campus, including John Barth, Howard Nemerov, George Gilder, Garry Wills, Phyllis Schlafly, Benjamin Hooks, Jerry Rubin, Charles Kuralt, and former British Prime Minister Sir Harold Wilson.

The dust of McCain's construction boom still swirled as Lucas supervised the completion of several major projects begun under his predecessor. These included a new physical plant facility (later named for Gene Henderson), a Speech and Hearing Building, the McCain Library and Archives, the new Cook University Union, and a $6 million expansion of the football stadium (named for M. M. Roberts) to a capacity of thirty-three thousand, all of which opened in 1976. Other construction included a new president's home (1979), the C. W. Woods Art Gallery (1977), the Technology Building (1981, later named for Bobby L. Chain), and major renovations of the old President's Home (which became the Alumni House in 1976 and was later named for Powell Ogletree) and several other older structures.

The invigorated quest for academic excellence placed special emphasis on faculty research and publication. During the 1978–79 year, fifteen members of the college of science and technology were invited to present scholarly papers at professional meetings abroad, as were representatives of fine arts, liberal arts, and business administration. Faculty scholarship increased steadily after 1975 and in the first year of the school's eighth decade reached an unprecedented 54 books, 516 articles in scholarly journals, more than 300 papers delivered at professional meetings, and 20 exhibitions of creative art. For the year, the faculty also generated more than $3.5 million dollars in research grants from outside agencies.

None of this diminished the institution's fundamental commitment, which remained quality education for the people of Mississippi. As vice-president for academic affairs Charles Moorman later put it, "We thought that if a man or woman gave himself wholeheartedly to his profession in terms of teaching, then he would become automatically involved in research. But first and always was teaching—first and always was the idea of training the students, teaching the students to go out into the world and become profitable and useful members of society, and sensitive citizens." And so the dream remained what it had been for almost seven decades, but those early dreamers would have been astounded to see the great university that their beloved little normal college had become. Like those oak seedlings that Joe Cook nurtured so carefully so many years before, The University of Southern Mississippi had, despite the scars of struggle and pruning, blossomed into luxuriant maturity. "No one could have dreamed," said President Emeritus McCain, "that we could have gone from a small teachers college to a major university in less than seventy-five years. No one could have dreamed that."

Hattiesburg mayor A. L. "Bud" Gerrard (second from left) joined President McCain and representatives of the Hattiesburg Area Rose Society for the April 1, 1974, dedication of USM's All-American Public Rose Garden.

Chapter 5

TOWARD DISTINCTION

R C COOK UNIVERSITY UNION

EAGLES
SOAR
INTO
THE
80's

As the 1980s dawned, USM approached both its seventy-fifth anniversary and a critical process of reaccreditation. The latter included a 1983 self-study that underscored the importance of "student and faculty involvement in the changing definition of the University's self-image and their satisfaction with its priorities." A few years later, amidst a wrenching institutional reorganization, President Lucas sounded a similar note. "During the . . . history of this University," he observed, "transition and adjustment have ever been with us. It is a tribute to this institution that throughout these seventy-five years its internal, organizational changes have been initiated and directed from within though the causes may have been external." As the eighties unfolded, however, external pressures, magnified by seismic shifts in the nature of public higher education, especially regarding funding, made it increasingly difficult to remain, as Lucas put it, "masters of our [own] fate."

In 1981, Mississippi's Board of Trustees of Institutions of Higher Learning (IHL) issued mission statements to the eight public universities under its jurisdiction. The boom in education had peaked in the 1970s, and gone were the days when the state seemed awash in money and university expansion appeared unlimited. In a period of growing austerity, the board was attempting to improve higher education by establishing a "direction of excellence" for each university within "differential roles" clearly defined among them. Designating USM, along with Ole Miss and Mississippi State, as a "comprehensive" institution, the board assigned to it leadership roles in communications, computer science, home economics, library science, marine sciences, music, polymer science, psychology, social work, and technology. Responding to the board's new policy, Lucas in 1982 designated communications, computer science, and marine science as areas in which the university would develop "centers of excellence." The board was then to provide specific financial resources to allow these programs to pursue particular regional and national recognition.

In the 1980s, USM developed "centers of excellence" that earned national distinction for its programs in computer science (above), communications, and marine science (left).

Accreditation in photojournalism, along with news-editorial, advertising, and public relations, made USM's department of journalism one of only fourteen in the country fully accredited in all four emphasis areas.

Those efforts suffered a minor setback when the trustees, amid great controversy, removed USM's leadership roles in journalism and computer science in 1984. The board defended its action as a response to academic program reviews that it had commissioned the universities to conduct in connection with the 1981 mission statements. Lucas, who had been out of town when the board made its decision, found himself squeezed between the USM community, especially an outraged faculty, and the trustees to whom he was constitutionally accountable. It was among the most difficult issues of his presidency, and despite obviously severe personal disappointment, he refused to question the trustees' motives. "It's been a tough one," he acknowledged, "because I like my board. They're good people." Though his public response to the decision, according to a Jackson newspaper, "wasn't warmly received" by the board, many among the faculty were disappointed that he had not confronted the trustees even more aggressively. Lucas suggested using the program reviews to reexamine the assignment of other leadership roles, in which case, he argued, "surely the board will assign to USM leadership in English, history, philosophy, anthropology, geography, medical technology, mathematics, speech and hearing science, and perhaps even biology," all of which had initially gone to other institutions. The reviews "imply and in some cases state," he said, that USM offered Mississippi's best programs in those areas. Moreover, USM was the only institution whose programs received no "approval pending," "marginal," or "phase-out" ratings in the review process. Every one of its seventy-four undergraduate programs received an "approval" rating, and three—English, polymer science, and medical technology—earned "commendations," indicating the board's recognition that in those fields USM ranked among the nation's best.

Southern overcame the losses, as its centers of excellence prospered, and the board made no other leadership changes. In 1985, all four emphases in journalism—news-editorial, advertising, photo-journalism, and public relations—received full accreditation, making USM one of only fourteen programs in the nation to share that distinction. The same year, the school lured nationally recognized marine biologist George A. Knauer to direct the center for marine science, which at the same time moved its facilities to the National Space Technologies Laboratory near Bay St. Louis, strengthening its relationship to the prominent marine science community there. Against the odds, USM appeared poised to fulfill Lucas's inaugural vision, as confirmed by the Southern Association of Colleges and Secondary Schools in 1985. Granting full reaccreditation, SACS noted that "today the University is the largest . . . in Mississippi serving more than 13,000. . . . Quality of faculty and students enrolled is significantly moving the institution toward its goal of becoming a distinguished university." With "strong administrative and academic leadership and a positive campus morale . . . the framework . . . is clearly present."

On a more ominous note, the 1985 SACS report warned that "at a time when the institution seems poised for a giant step forward the financial resources available to the state are on the decline." The warning proved prescient, as the budget ax fell before the year was out. With state tax collections falling dangerously below projections, Governor Bill Allain imposed severe midyear budget cuts, including a $12.2 million reduction for IHL. At a November 13 news conference, Lucas announced that USM would lose $1.2 million but declared resolutely, "We will not let these cuts deter us from our very sure progress [in] bringing distinction to this university." The new year brought worse news. The legislative budget office proposed a 21.5 percent cut in funds for higher education in 1986–87, and IHL's response bordered on panic. The board recommended closing Mississippi Valley State University, Mississippi University for Women, Mississippi State's School of Veterinary Medicine, Ole Miss's dental school, and USM operations on the Gulf Coast. Supporters of the universities protested vigorously. On February 26, friends of higher education from throughout the state converged on the Capitol to "call attention," as USM's president put it, "to the impending disaster" facing the universities.

Assistant vice-president for academic affairs David Bodenhamer spearheaded the university's efforts to adjust to severe budget cuts.

Meanwhile, on March 18, Lucas assembled a university priorities team under assistant vice-president for academic affairs David Bodenhamer. Through private discussions as well as forums open to the university community and the general public, the group was to explore available options and recommend specific reallocation of resources to accommodate the budget losses. A month later, the college board set USM's share of IHL's $133.5 million for 1986–87 at $34.1 million, $3.4 million (9.3 percent) below the university's original budget for 1985–86. On April 21, the priorities team reported to the president, who eventually approved most of its thirty-nine recommendations.

At a special convocation on June 19, Lucas outlined the painful measures, which included raising tuition, freezing or eliminating thirty vacant positions, and suspending subsidies to athletics. Mercifully, Lucas was able to fulfill his pledge not to reduce salaries or terminate employees, though several had their contracts reduced from twelve months to nine. Ever master of the "bully pulpit," the president remained cautiously optimistic: "I don't see a great exodus [of faculty and staff] now, but that situation cannot be maintained. We've got to have some help." The situation was all too familiar. From the beginning, as Alma Hickman had long ago observed, Southern's "hardest battle" had always been the struggle for adequate funding. This most recent manifestation produced significant consequences. In 1987, the USM priorities team gave way to a university planning advisory council (UPAC), also headed by Bodenhamer. UPAC's labors ultimately generated a sweeping reorganization designed to convince the legislature that USM, in the campus newspaper's words, "is 'sincere in its efforts' to use dollars wisely." Since the early years of the Lucas administration, changes in structure and personnel had been generally routine and without controversy. In 1982, a vice-president for research and extended services, Karen Yarbrough, replaced the vice-president for administration and regional campuses, and the following year James Sims succeeded Charles Moorman as vice-president for academic affairs. Both reported to the president through a new executive vice-president, Shelby Thames, though that position was eliminated in 1986 when Thames returned to full-time teaching in polymer science.

The reorganization of 1987–88 was of a different order, and it provoked more than a little controversy. The process began with a September 24, 1987, letter from Bodenhamer to the vice-presidents, outlining procedures and calling for "meaningful faculty, staff, and student participation." College-level "select committees" would make recommendations to an academic affairs organizational review committee that, in turn, reported to UPAC. By February 1988, when the review committee made its recommendations, the *Student Printz* reported that "faculty and administrators are beginning to choose sides in the upcoming battle of . . . reorganization." A political science professor described the review committee's report as "a very blunt, ill-conceived, and ludicrous scheme with few redeeming qualities." The committee's proposal to merge political science with geography and area development and criminal justice with philosophy and religion would, he said, make USM not "a distinguished university but a trivia question. Where else would you find a department of law and philosophy? Or geography and political science?"

In late March, UPAC issued its report, two inches thick with scores of recommendations plus appendices. "Perhaps more than any other event during the Lucas presidency," the document declared, ". . . the funding crisis of spring 1986 forced us to face squarely the gap between our ambitions and our resources. . . . How we

will redefine ourselves has become the most important question facing us as we prepare for the 1990s and beyond. . . . We cannot be all things to all people; nor can we expect to promote the interests of all programs and activities simultaneously, or to grant to each program or activity equal resources. We must set institutional priorities for funding and provide special assistance for those programs or activities that offer the greatest potential for meeting our mission and securing our reputation as a university." UPAC was proposing no program eliminations, the report stressed, and only such consolidation as "would retain, enhance, or give new direction to existing programs." The goal had been "self-definition" rather than "retrenchment." Still, the recommendations were sweeping. Ten existing schools and colleges would be reconfigured into just six colleges, including a new college devoted to health and human services; fifty-two administrative units would shrink by ten, saving an estimated $370,000 to be redistributed among academic "areas of greatest need." However imperfect, the report insisted, "the process we chose to follow . . . has been open. . . . We continue to believe that this process of openness is ultimately more salutary for our well-being and sense of community than is reorganization by administrative fiat."

Lucas described the UPAC report as "immensely impressive . . . comprehensive . . . vast and . . . forward looking. . . . I think it gives us direction that can well take us throughout this century, which really is passing quickly, and get us into the 21st century." Others disagreed, some vociferously. The more controversial proposals, according to some critics, compromised the entire report and reinforced suspicions about the process that had spawned it. "This proposal," said a veteran member of the history department, "is illogical, irrational, unprecedented, and incomprehensible. . . . They sure use the word taxonomy a lot." A philosophy professor suggested that "what needs to be reorganized is the reorganizers." Drawing the most intense fire were the makeup of the new college and proposed changes in the college of liberal arts. The former would include the schools of nursing and social work and three unnamed schools cobbled together from rearranged—cannibalized, critics would say—components of the existing schools of home economics and health, physical education, and recreation. In liberal arts, UPAC recommended combining the departments of political science, criminal justice, geography and area development, and philosophy and religion into a new school of public affairs and making speech communication a free-standing department within the college, leaving the other departments within the existing school of communication as a new school of mass communication.

Bodenhamer became a lighting rod for critics' fears and frustrations. "I think it's time we call names," said history colleague William Scarborough. "Bodenhamer is an excellent teacher and scholar, but when he thinks he's right he rolls on no matter what opposition develops." His "inflexible attitude" would "convert" USM into "IBM." In his inimitable way, the president turned controversy into a virtue. "If a university does not have some controversy," he noted, "it pretty well indicates that no one is doing critical thinking. . . . Of course, you hear the charge that 'the council didn't listen to us.' That's what we generally think when we make a suggestion and someone doesn't implement it. The council certainly listened, but it had to make its own judgments." He deemed outspoken criticism "very healthy," he said. "It demonstrates that not only do we permit debate, but we encourage it."

In mid-April, the president and his executive cabinet scrutinized every recommendation in the UPAC report

Established in 1976, USM's Honors College is one of the nation's oldest. In 1985, it was reorganized under the leadership of new dean Peggy Prenshaw (above).

a weekend retreat at Gulf Park. On April 22, 1988, hundreds of anxious faculty, staff, and students filed into Bennett Auditorium to hear the results. "Let me make it very clear," Lucas emphasized, "that the decisions which I am about to announce are mine." He had been "guided," he acknowledged, "by the UPAC report . . . the counsel of the Cabinet," and "many letters . . . telephone calls, and conferences with faculty, staff, students, alumni, and friends of the University. It is now time for this consultation to cease and for the President to take actions." Regarding the sometimes heated criticism, he lamented that such "an open examination of University organization causes such anxiety" and conceded that "if we had to do it again (God forbid), we would, no doubt, do it differently. But the process," he insisted, had "been very open. Everyone . . . has had an opportunity to give . . . suggestions and opinions. We have experienced fear; friendships have been ruptured; and our sense of community has been lessened, but people of goodwill can and will find ways to repair strained relationships and move on." Lucas lauded UPAC for its "energy and courage" and heaped special praise on Bodenhamer. "There is probably no other person in the University," the president insisted, "whose leadership has been more valuable during the past years when we have suffered cuts in funding. . . . Even though there have been criticisms of some aspects of his leadership of the UPAC, I, for one, deeply appreciate his work with this historic effort." The institution had experienced reorganization before, Lucas said, but "the report at hand is, without doubt, the most comprehensive in my memory." While he and the cabinet had approved "many if not most" of UPAC's recommendations, he added, some had been rejected and others deferred for further consideration.

The new college, later named health and human sciences, would include the school of nursing; the school of social work; a third school to include faculties from the existing departments of home economics education/family life studies, environmental design, and institutional administration; and another school to include faculties from the existing departments of sports administration, physical education, health, and recreation and parks. The last mentioned school would be expected to "develop a strong emphasis in Health Sciences that is programmatically separate from the traditional emphases in teacher training, physical education, and sports administration." In liberal arts, the new school of public policy and international affairs would not include philosophy and religion, which would remain a separate department within the college. Moreover, departments within liberal arts would retain their integrity. USM boasted the oldest continuous geography department in the country, and "I was not about to see us give up that particular distinction," Lucas insisted. The school of communication would remain as constituted. In conclusion, Lucas pledged "that if experience convinces us that these changes are not in the best interest of this University, we will look at other options but not until we have made a sincere effort at implementation. . . . I'm relieved to have made the decision and the announcement. Now the hard work begins."

Despite budget woes and structural changes, USM continued to grow and prosper. The student body had grown to more than 13,000, and in the decade after 1974 the average ACT score of incoming freshmen rose from 19.2 to 19.8. Those with scores above 27 increased from 63 to 102, while those below 15 declined from 95 to 69. The 1985–86 academic year began with a reorganized and revitalized Honors College under Dean Peggy Prenshaw. To sustain these advances in the quality of its students, USM adopted stiffer admission and academic progress requirements, along with a new program of academic advisement. In response to a national reemphasis on general education, the university in 1985 instituted an expanded core curriculum that included composition (6 hours), algebra or higher mathematics (3), fine arts (3), world literature (3), world history (6), social and behavioral sciences (6), natural and applied sciences (11), human wellness (2), and electives (6).

The faculty had grown to almost six hundred, 65 percent of them with terminal degrees and 98 percent with at least a master's degree. Lucas sought vigorously to nurture them and to reward them appropriately, and by 1985 he could take pride in having fulfilled one of his earliest promises, to make USM's professors the highest paid in Mississippi. Still, salaries, research funds, and support services all remained well below national standards. With a vice-president now specifically designated to supervise and support faculty research, the university appointed a director of research and sponsored programs with expertise in funded research and patent applications. During the first half of the eighties, USM faculty generated almost $20 million in research grants, and for 1986 alone the figure reached an unprecedented $6.3 million.

The administration expected reward and achievement to go hand in hand. In 1985, Lucas approved a new university policy on tenure and promotion that set standards of excellence for faculty who sought higher rank and continued employment. In the words of the 1983 institutional self-study, "The University now places a growing emphasis on the professional distinction of its faculty; personnel decisions are now directly linked to scholarly and artistic achievement. Competence in the classroom remains important and faculty are also expected to perform a wide range of other institutional and community service, but scholarly, creative, and professional endeavors are valued as never before." The faculty responded admirably to the challenge. In 1985 alone, they collectively contributed to the world of scholarship 60 books, 439 articles, 925

An increased emphasis on faculty scholarship enhanced USM's reputation as a distinguished research university.

artistic performances, 610 professional papers, 7 sound recordings, and 4 patents. The increased emphasis on research and scholarship did not come at the expense of classroom instruction. SACS commended USM for the quality of its teaching and heaped special praise on several departments.

The graduate school also prospered, with enrollment increasing 30 percent between 1972 and 1983. Nonetheless, the staff of the state college board recommended elimination of several doctoral programs in 1986. The board rejected the staff recommendation, recognizing, as SACS had put it, that USM "has a number of extremely strong graduate programs taught by talented, productive faculty. They deserve defense against unwarranted decisions by the Board to downgrade or terminate them. Rather than duplicate programs offered elsewhere in the state, these [provide] healthy alternatives which need and deserve greater support inside and outside the University."

In 1981, a new Center for International Education (CIE) assumed direction of the English Language Institute (ELI), the Office of International Student Admissions and Advisement, the Institute for Anglo-American Studies, and the Office of International Studies. Criminal justice professor William Taylor, who had led USM's first study abroad venture in 1976, was named director. The ELI served more than seven thousand students from forty nations in the decade after 1975, and foreign student enrollment at the university jumped by more than two hundred percent between 1981 and 1984. By the end of

In 1981, a new Center for International Education (above) assumed direction of the English Language Institute, the Office of International Student Admissions and Advisement, the Institute for Anglo-American Studies, and the Office of International Studies. Over the next three years, foreign student enrollment increased by more than 200 percent.

the decade, USM's British Studies Program was the largest of its kind in the United States, offering courses in criminal justice, computer science, speech and hearing sciences, clothing and textiles, hotel and restaurant management, business, and library science as well as the more conventional classes in art, literature, and theatre. Based in London, the five-week summer program allowed students to supplement the standard classroom experience with visits to the city's historical and cultural landmarks, such as Westminster Abbey, the Tower of London, and the British Museum. Also available were excursions beyond London to Oxford, Cambridge, Bath, Stonehenge, Shakespeare's Stratford-upon-Avon, and other sites of interest. Classes included guest lectures by English artists, scholars, business leaders, and public officials. In addition to the British Studies Program, CIE sponsored study abroad opportunities in Austria, France, Japan, Mexico, and Jamaica. Students from other universities could participate through a USM-led consortium that included institutions from as far away as Texas and Vermont as well as the national community college honor society, Phi Theta Kappa. In 1987, Taylor resigned as director of the Center, and geography professor Tim Hudson was chosen to replace him. "International education used to be a luxury," the new director noted, but "it now is a necessity, and that . . . is good news for USM and . . . for the schools we work with because we are on the cutting edge of what is happening in the field of international education."

USM broadened its services to nontraditional students, as the division of continuing education became the division of lifelong learning in 1985. Its independent study program offered a complete high school curriculum as well as almost one hundred university-level courses. The Department of On-campus Noncredit sponsored a variety of camps and clinics, conferences, workshops, institutes, seminars, and other services to employees of business and industry and other professional people, as well as a full array of noncredit courses for the general public. Beginning in 1987, the department hosted the American Legion Auxiliary's annual Girls' State program, which had outgrown the facilities at its traditional home at Hinds Junior College. Lifelong Learning's adult studies program, through expanded evening class offerings and a competent counseling staff, afforded working adults the opportunity to pursue a degree part-time, prepare for an alternate career, or simply develop themselves culturally and intellectually. By the end of the decade, adult students constituted almost 20 percent of USM's undergraduate population, and the average student age was twenty-five. Among the results of the 1988 reorganization was a decision to drop the word "adult" from all "titles of offices and programs" and to "mainstream" such students "into as many University activities as possible without sacrificing" attention to their special needs.

The university was forced to close its Natchez branch in 1985, but USM-Gulf Park continued to thrive. Southern had offered classes on the Gulf Coast as early as 1947, using facilities at the Methodist Camp Grounds in Biloxi and qualified local instructors supplemented occasionally by professors from the main campus commuting

Beginning in 1987, USM became home to the American Legion Auxiliary's annual Girls' State program.

to teach night classes. A decade later, classes moved to Michel Junior High School, and a single permanent instructor/administrator was hired to oversee operations. In 1964, classes moved again, to Keesler Air Force Base. By that time, course offerings were expanding to meet the educational demands of a growing population serving the needs of Keesler, Ingalls Ship Yards in Pascagoula, the NASA space flight facility at Bay St. Louis, and other civil and military operations along the Gulf Coast. Over the next two years, classes were added at Mississippi Gulf Coast Junior College's (MGC) Jefferson Davis campus in Harrison County and its Jackson County center in

In 1982-83, Jackson County officials constructed a classroom building exclusively for USM's use at Gautier.

Gautier. After acquiring Gulf Park in 1972, USM, with IHL approval, designated it, along with the Keesler facility, "an upper level degree completion regional" branch of the main campus. Courses continued to be offered in Gautier, where in 1982–83 the Jackson County Board of Supervisors built and equipped a classroom facility exclusively for USM's use. In 1976, USM and MGC launched an historic Two Plus Two arrangement that allowed students to earn degrees without ever leaving the coast.

In 1988, IHL placed the Gulf Coast Research Laboratory (GCRL) under USM's administration. Founded by the Mississippi Academy of Sciences in 1947 and taken over by IHL the following year, GCRL operated the J. L. Scott Marine Education Center and Aquarium, the Office of Fishery Assistance, and a Seafood Quality and Technology Laboratory at its Biloxi Center, along with laboratories, research facilities, administrative offices, and a library at Ocean Springs. The same year, USM engaged a Florida consulting firm to analyze the educational needs of the growing coast population. Aimed at students, employers, workers, military personnel, civic leaders, and the general public, the survey focused particularly on the link between educational opportunity and economic development in the six-county Gulf Coast region. One direct result of the needs assessment was the introduction of day classes at Gulf Park in 1989–90, and by the second semester, enrollment was up 10.4 percent over that of the previous spring. USM-Gulf Coast was now Mississippi's largest off-campus degree-granting program, serving almost 1,500 students with sixteen undergraduate and eighteen graduate degree programs and a resident faculty of thirty.

On the Hattiesburg campus, USM installed a new mainframe computer in 1984–85 and hired a staff

Advances in technology modernized many aspects of campus life. In 1988, a telephone-assisted registration system eliminated the venerable ritual of standing in line at the coliseum.

President Aubrey Lucas and Alumni Director Powell Ogletree admire USM's seventy-fifth birthday cake (upper photograph). As part of the anniversary celebration, Lucas welcomed several students (above) from the Mississippi Normal College days, including three from the inaugural class of 1912: Fleet Burkett, flanked by sisters Mollie Graham Pickering (to his right) and former first lady of Mississippi Alma Graham Conner. At the far left is 1921 graduate Emily Cook Bickerstaff, daughter of President Joe Cook.

consultant to facilitate faculty and staff access to its benefits, one of which was a computerized early registration system that eliminated the old Coliseum ritual that someone once said pitted "perseverance against Pandemonium." In the fall of 1988, almost eight thousand students took advantage of a new Southern Telephone-Assisted Registration System (STARS) that allowed them to register for spring classes from home or dormitory. All they needed was a touch-tone telephone. The $75,000 system, the first of its kind in Mississippi, was not without its problems, however. The initial sixteen telephone lines proved inadequate, as some students encountered incessant busy signals. Additional lines eased the problem in the spring, and the average registration time fell to less than five minutes. During the eighties, the administration also initiated a computer-augmented curriculum to increase the use of computer technology in all disciplines of study.

March 30, 1985, marked the seventy-fifth anniversary of the founding of Mississippi Normal College, and Alumni Director Powell Ogletree suggested to Lucas a celebration "to run for 30 months," from that day through the anniversary of "the day we started operations [September 18, 1912]." He also proposed a concurrent $7.5 million fund-raising campaign to conclude on December 31, 1987. In conjunction with the seventy-fifth anniversary, the Alumni Association voted to establish an Alumni Hall of Fame with seventy-five members to be chosen for the inaugural class. A committee of former Alumni Association presidents would select the inductees, and only those who had graduated prior to 1972 would be eligible. On October 9–10, 1987, the anniversary celebration culminated in Homecoming ceremonies that Ogletree predicted would be "the biggest and best ever in the 75-year history of this university's existence."

Powell Ogletree came from Neshoba County to Mississippi Southern College in 1941, following in the footsteps of an older brother who had graduated from State Teachers College a decade earlier. Three months after he arrived, the Japanese attacked Pearl Harbor, and by the end of the school year he was one of the few men still on campus. Working for the physical plant, he mowed lawns and opened and closed all the buildings each day. Drafted in 1942, he served with the Fifteenth Air Force Command in North Africa and Italy, but by the fall of 1946 he was back at MSC. He majored in social studies, edited the *Student Printz*, and met Frances Townsend, whom he married a week after graduating in 1948. The couple moved to Monticello, where both taught school until he was appointed principal of an elementary school in Greenwood in 1950. Two years later, R. C. Cook asked him to return to Southern as director of alumni affairs, but he had just been voted Greenwood's "Outstanding Young Man," and the school year had already begun. He told Cook that if the position was still open the following year he would take it.

On June 22, 1953, Ogletree became MSC's first full-time alumni secretary, with a cramped office in College Hall and a staff of one. He inherited address cards on 3,200 graduates, no organized alumni chapters, 158 paid members, and assets of $55.86. When he retired 34 years later, there were computerized records on almost 60,000 alumni, 61 active chapters, 17,562 members, and $260,000 in annual revenue. Under Ogletree's direction, the Alumni Association became a jack-of-all-trades. He later recalled that "if it seemed something needed to be done that was not being done by someone else, we did it." Ogletree helped rally support for a Forrest County bond referendum that financed construction of the original R. C. Cook Student Union (now McLemore Hall), where the Alumni office moved in 1955 after a short stay in the Administration Building. He played a key role in the school's gaining university status in 1962, in changing the nickname to Golden Eagles a decade later, and in securing funds to build a new president's home in 1979. When William D. McCain's family moved out of the old President's Home in 1975, Ogletree persuaded new president Aubrey Lucas to convert it into an Alumni House.

Powell Ogletree as editor of the *Student Printz*.

When he realized that the school provided no scholarship support except for athletes and band members, Ogletree in 1959 persuaded ten men to contribute $100 each to help launch the Foundation. One, Moran Pope Jr., agreed to serve as president until the Foundation raised $2 million in a single year; he was finally able to hand the office to someone else in 1982. "The first year, we took in $33,000," said Ogletree. "It took us three years to get the first $100,000." From 1959 until his retirement in 1987, Ogletree served as both Alumni director and executive secretary

of the Foundation, which by that time had raised $16 million and awarded more than $5 million in scholarships. Its in-kind assets included a registered quarter horse, a three-fourths blood Arabian filly, a thoroughbred race horse, a 17-foot power boat and trailer, and a 6-room house on Thirty-fifth Avenue. After Ogletree's retirement, the Foundation was separated from the Alumni Association with Donald Elam as the first full-time executive director. The Alumni House, which was named in Ogletree's honor in 1987, stands as a monument to his contributions to his beloved alma mater, but he will always be best remembered for his enthusiastic greeting: "It's great to be a Golden Eagle!"

Festivities ended on a somewhat sour note on Saturday when Florida State overwhelmed the Golden Eagles 61-10 in the football clash. Despite the loss, Ogletree, who had earlier announced that he would retire at the end of October, declared the celebration a success. "My departure is coming at the best time in the world," he said. "We will have ended our celebration of a glorious 75 years and a new era will begin." The icing on the anniversary cake came at the end of the year when he was able to announce that the fund-raising effort had exceeded its goal by more than $4 million.

Early in 1987, the administration had named Donald Elam full-time director of development and had placed all fund-raising activities, except alumni dues and the Eagle Club, under his office. Among his first actions was the establishment of an Honor Club to recognize major donors. Following Ogletree's retirement, the Foundation was detached from the Alumni Association with Elam as executive director under the authority of an elected board of directors. In 1989, William Pace replaced Elam, who returned to private business. Later that year, Lucas was able to announce "the largest cash gift in the history of USM," a $1.5 million endowment from the Ottilie Schillig Trust of Port Gibson, administered by Jackson businessman James T. Baird. Reserved for Honors College students, the first Schillig-Baird scholarships were awarded in the fall of 1991.

During the eighties, USM's athletic program also rose to new heights. The 1980 football team celebrated the dawning of the decade with the school's network

Reggie Collier led USM to a 42-14 victory over Mississippi State in 1980, the fourth of seven consecutive wins over the Bulldogs.

television debut, the first bowl invitation since 1957, and the third mythical state championship in four years. The season opened with a 17-14 win over Tulane in the New Orleans Superdome that ABC televised regionally. Later, after a 28-22 victory over Ole Miss in Jackson, Collins marched his troops to Starkville in quest of a second consecutive sweep of the two Mississippi rivals. "The game should have been rated R," wrote Jackson columnist Orley Hood, "children under 17 not admitted without parent or guardian. Southern Mississippi 42, Mississippi State 14. . . . It was about as one-sided as the St. Valentine's Day Massacre. . . . There was nothing graceful about it. . . . Nothing subtle . . . . The Golden Eagles drove up the road, beat the hell out of the Bulldogs, and went home. It was hit-and-run, but it was no accident. Nothing personal, you

USM won its first bowl game in five tries with a 16-14 victory over McNeese State in the 1980 Independence Bowl. Coach Bobby Collins hoists the championship trophy.

know, just business." Sammy Winder rushed for three touchdowns on his way to the national scoring title, and USM ran its record to 5-0 for the season and 7-1 against in-state competition since 1976. "How good is Southern?" asked Hood. "The best in Mississippi. . . . It's not even close."

It was a different matter when the Eagles ventured outside the Magnolia State. After drubbing Arkansas State 35-0 in Hattiesburg the next week, USM crept into the number twenty slot in the Associated Press poll and headed for Tuscaloosa to challenge the top-ranked Crimson Tide. Alabama ended Southern's visit to the top twenty after only a week, crushing Collins's crew 42-7. Two weeks later Auburn added to the chastening with a 31-0 rout, and the Eagles stumbled to an 8-3 finish. But that was good enough for a trip to Shreveport's Independence Bowl, which the Eagles won 16-14 over McNeese State to give the school its first postseason victory in five tries.

The next season proved even better. After four straight wins early in the year, Collins took his undefeated team to face Alabama in Birmingham. Exactly twenty-five years after the same two teams had battled to a 13-13 tie in Tuscaloosa, Steve Clark kicked a field goal with eight seconds left to make 1981's score identical to that of 1956 and once again draw the nation's attention to Southern football. A month later a capacity crowd filed into Jackson's Memorial Stadium to watch one of the most important games in Mississippi college football history,

In 1981, Reggie Collier (# 10) became the first college quarterback to gain a thousand yards both rushing and passing in a single season and finished ninth in the voting for the Heisman Trophy.

USM's 1982 upset of Alabama was only Coach Bear Bryant's second loss ever in Tuscaloosa and the first in nineteen years.

as USM and Mississippi State met with bowl invitations and national rankings on the line. It was a bruising defensive battle reminiscent of the 10-9 State victory in 1966. A Winder touchdown offset two Dana Moore field goals to give the Eagles a 7-6 lead at the half. The Nasty Bunch made that one point hold up, stopping the Bulldogs twice in the fourth quarter on fourth down and less than a yard.

The slim victory nudged Southern back into the top twenty as they headed for Tallahassee to play Florida State in a regional telecast, which ABC interrupted periodically to cover the return of NASA's space shuttle. As *Columbia* touched down in California, the Eagles were taking flight in Florida, in equally spectacular fashion, scoring on their first seven possessions to humiliate a Seminole team that had earlier beaten Ohio State in Columbus and Notre Dame at South Bend. The 58-14 score was shocking, and it catapulted USM into the top ten (ninth in AP, eighth in UPI) for the first time in history. Louisville brought the Eagles back to earth with a 13-10 upset the following week, and a 19-17 Tangerine Bowl loss to Missouri knocked them out of the national rankings completely. Still, it had been a remarkable year, especially for Collier, who finished ninth in balloting for the Heisman Trophy and became the first college quarterback ever both to rush and pass for 1,000 yards in the same season.

Jim Carmody, godfather of the Nasty Bunch, became USM's fifteenth head football coach in 1982.

Less than a month after the Tangerine Bowl, Bobby Collins accepted the head coaching position at Southern Methodist University, where six of nine USM assistants joined him. In a matter of hours, Dale replaced Collins with Big Nasty himself, former assistant head coach and defensive coordinator Jim Carmody. The new Eagle boss inherited a solid football program, but he also inherited allegations of a recruiting scandal that for two years had hung over the program like a pall. "The first day

Basketball coach M. K. Turk, athletic director Roland Dale, and President Lucas look on as Commissioner Larry Albus welcomes USM into the Metro Conference.

With his mother looking on, heralded running back Marcus Dupree of Philadelphia, Mississippi, announces his transfer from Oklahoma at a press conference in the USM Administration Building in October 1983. When the NCAA ruled that he would have to sit out the 1984 season, Dupree signed a professional contract and never played for the Golden Eagles.

I reported for work," he later recalled, "the NCAA was here." The distractions aggravated the normal difficulties involved in a major coaching change and took a heavy toll early in Carmody's first season. After a 1-3 start, the Eagles reeled off five consecutive wins and appeared to be on their way to a third straight bowl invitation when the NCAA ax fell. On the Monday before the Alabama game, USM announced that recruiting violations, some involving "promises of significant financial benefits to prospective athletes," between 1979 and 1982 had resulted in a two-year probation that included sanctions prohibiting television and bowl appearances "This is an embarrassment to me as president," Lucas told reporters. "I wish we didn't have to drink from this cup." Dale shouldered the blame himself, but as Lucas pointed out, none of the infractions involved the athletic director. Nonetheless, Dale acknowledged that "somebody has to be responsible and I am."

One silver lining of the probation cloud was Lucas's determination to improve the university's compliance with not only the NCAA's recruiting regulations but also its academic standards. In 1984, the athletic department added to its traditional study hall sessions a personalized program using qualified and trained student tutors. Two years later, a more elaborate program of academic support services was established under director of compliance Jimmy Farris. Three full-time counselors assisted athletes with scheduling and advisement and supervised the student tutors. They also attended every home athletic event. "You can't expect athletes to be committed to what you are doing," said counselor Nancy Johnson, "if you aren't committed to what they are doing." She also claimed never to have been required to redeem her offer of "a steak dinner for any athlete who went to all the assigned tutoring sessions and didn't improve by a letter grade at least." USM's academic services for athletes would soon become a model for other institutions, and its graduation rates, among the nation's best, would become an identifying aspect of its athletic program.

Probation was a bitter pill for Carmody and his players, who vented their frustrations against the Crimson Tide, handing Bear Bryant his first defeat in Tuscaloosa in fifty-seven games. It was a vintage USM upset that epitomized the best in a long tradition of Southern football. Mickey Spagnola described it well in his *Jackson Daily News* postmortem of the Alabama home win streak. "If you're going to war," he wrote, "and if you get to pick first, choose Southern Mississippi. Always choose Southern Mississippi. . . . Don't fight Southern Mississippi. No matter how hard you fight, those folks will fight harder. They are that way, as if this Hattiesburg, this school of 11,800, is some sort of transplanted inner-city core in the state of Mississippi. Blue collar types, you know. Hard hats, tattoos. . . . These people know sweat. They know work. They know nothing ever came easy, nor will it ever come easy. They are hard . . . hard, I'm telling you."

It had been, as Carmody noted afterward, "an emotional week, which no doubt contributed to the letdown that produced a 13-6 loss to Louisiana Tech in the season

Jeff Davis, whose unconventional antics as the Eagle mascot delighted fans in the early 1980s, went on to a notable career in Hollywood.

finale. Distractions, including more trouble with the NCAA, would not seem to go away. In February 1985, USM found itself on probation for another two years, the second of which the NCAA suspended along with all sanctions because of "the prompt disciplinary action taken by the university." That action had included two controversial firings of assistant coaches, one of whom later won a substantial judgment against the school in a state court. His suit and another for breach of contract by an applicant for an assistant coaching job kept Carmody, Dale, and Lucas in and out of courtrooms frequently during the 1980s.

As a true freshman, Brett Favre led the Golden Eagles to a 31-24 home victory over Tulane in the second game of 1987.

In 1986, a beleaguered Dale announced his retirement. He had seen the best of times and the worst of times, but under his direction USM had established itself as an institution of prominence in college athletics. Perhaps his finest achievement was the school's entrance into the prestigious Metro athletic conference in June 1982. M. K. Turk called it "the single greatest move that this institution has ever made." Lucas underscored Dale's accomplishments when he noted that "our ascendency in athletics has been very beneficial in terms of attracting students, and it has been particularly helpful in focusing the attention of people all over the country on this university, which was really not known outside the Southeast." Ironically, the man chosen to replace Dale, Terry Don Phillips of Southwestern Louisiana, accepted the post only to change his mind, as Dale himself had done when USM first offered him its head coaching position in 1969. USM then turned to former Clemson athletic director Bill McLellan, who in 1986 became only the third director of athletics in school history.

Despite all the upheaval, Carmody's team struggled on. Impressive wins over Ole Miss (27-7) and Mississippi State (31-6)—the seventh in a row against the Bulldogs—highlighted a 7-4 season in 1983, during which Louis Lipps became the second leading pass receiver in school history. He went on to become the Pittsburgh Steelers' top draft choice and NFL Rookie of the Year in 1984. The Eagles opened 1984 between the hedges in Georgia's storied Sanford Stadium, where Rex Banks kicked a school record four field goals, matched by Bulldog Kevin Butler to

In 1987, a record Roberts Stadium crowd of 33,687 saw USM defeat Jackson State 17-7 in the first contest ever between a Division I-A football team from Mississippi and one of the state's historically black schools.

Following the 1987 season, Texas A&M assistant Curley Hallman replaced Jim Carmody as USM's head football coach.

set an NCAA record for the most combined field goals in a single game. Southern's bid for an upset fell short, 26-19, and launched a disappointing injury-plagued year that ended 4-7, Carmody's only losing season at the Southern helm. A 13-10 victory over Ole Miss in Jackson eased the pain somewhat; it marked USM's fifth win over the Rebels (against two losses) since 1976 and ended the series that had been revived in 1966. The Eagles rebounded in 1985, giving Carmody his third 7-4 record since taking over the program, but after that, things seemed to stagnate.

Nineteen eighty-six began tragically as running back Eric Sorey collapsed during the first fall practice and died several hours later from what turned out to be a congenital heart defect compounded by sickle-cell anemia. Despite the pall cast by Sorey's death and a slow 3-4 start, the team won three of its last four games to salvage a winning season. The highlight came against Mississippi State in Jackson, when quarterback Andrew Anderson marched the Eagle offense 98 yards in the final minutes to seal a thrilling 28-24 victory. Carmody's 31-24 record over five seasons gave him the best start of any Southern coach since Pie Vann, but some fans, now measuring success by the remarkable achievements earlier in the decade, began to complain, especially about lopsided losses to Kentucky (32-0) and Florida State (49-13). Barely 11,000 showed up for the final home game, a 31-16 victory over Louisville. In a less than subtle message to the disgruntled, McLellan extended Carmody's contract through 1990.

The 1987 season proved pivotal for several reasons. It marked the debut of arguably the most celebrated player ever to wear the black and gold, as well as the first-ever gridiron match between one of Mississippi's "big three" and one of the state's historically black institutions. It also ended Jim Carmody's tenure as head coach. Things began ominously with a 38-6 shellacking by Alabama in Birmingham. Following an open week, the Eagles returned home to face Tulane, and trailing 16-10 late in the third quarter, Carmody made a desperate but ultimately momentous decision. He replaced veteran quarterback Ailrick Young with a seventeen-year-old true freshman, who seven months earlier had been offered a scholarship only at the last minute. "I was scared to death," Brett

Favre later confessed, but he quickly settled down and engineered three touchdown drives on the way to a 31-24 victory. The freshman was now the starting quarterback, though a month later his youth and inexperience handed Young a poignantly ironic opportunity to redeem himself. Trailing Mississippi State 14-3 into the fourth quarter, Carmody turned the tables and replaced Favre with the veteran, who completed all six of his passes to lead the Eagles to an 18-14 comeback win. "I'm a team player," said Young after the game. "When I lost my job, that made me a better person. . . . I knew I'd get another chance."

USM was 4-3 when Jackson State rolled into town for a historic contest at Roberts Stadium. A record crowd of 33,687 saw a bruising defensive struggle that was scoreless at the half and too close at the end to suit many of the Eagle faithful. Despite the 17-7 victory, only 10,123 returned the following week for the game against I-AA Northeast Louisiana, a 34-24 loss. It was the lowest attendance in a decade and the second lowest since the renovation of the stadium, and the team stumbled to a 6-5 finish. On December 3, matters came to a head, and at an afternoon press conference, Lucas announced that Carmody had resigned. The two had met earlier that day, the president said, to discuss "the issues, the program, and changes which were perhaps needed. The resignation came from that." McLellan was attending a Metro meeting in Atlanta, Lucas explained, but he and the athletic director had communicated frequently by telephone and had agreed that "it would be best for him to stay there and represent our interests in the . . . Conference. . . . This has been a painful decision for all of us." Lucas acknowledged that "diminished fan support" had played a role in the decision, but he refused to place all the blame on Carmody. The university's Center for Business Development and Research had been instructed, he revealed, to study the attendance problem from all angles, including ticket prices, marketing strategies, scheduling, even game times.

The day's events, said Carmody, came as "a surprise to me. I have not made any plans to do anything else. It was a mutual understanding after my talk this morning with Dr. Lucas." He refused to speculate on who might replace him or to offer advice. "Every man has

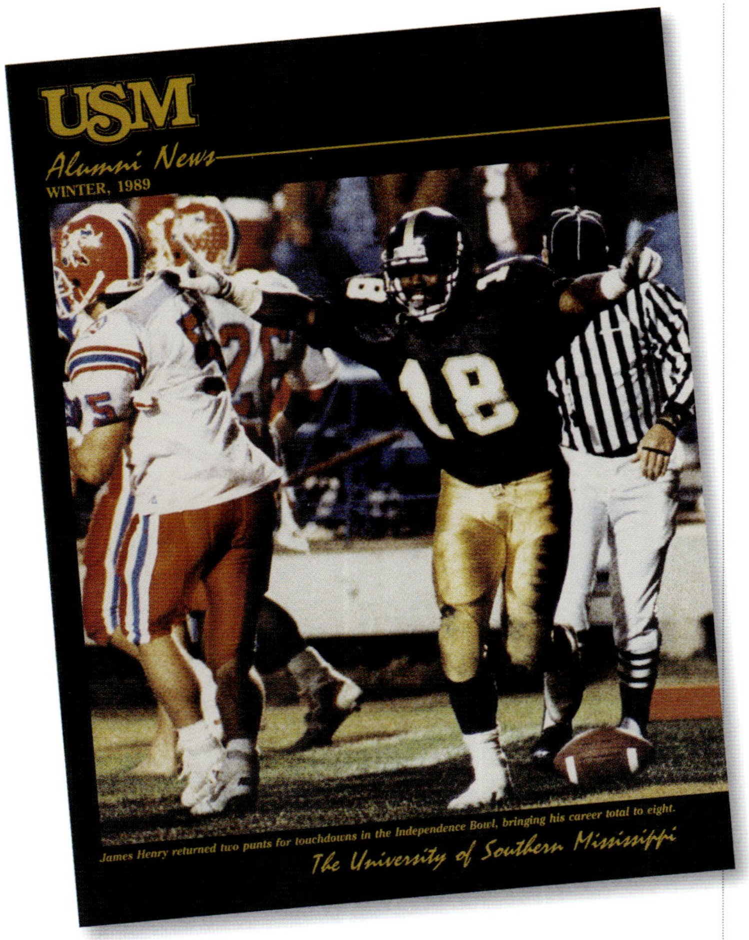

In their first postseason appearance in seven years, the Golden Eagles defeated Texas-El Paso 38-18 in the 1988 Independence Bowl. Defensive back James Henry (#18) scored twice on punt returns to earn most valuable player awards for both offense and defense.

his own ideas." Whoever was chosen, he insisted, would inherit "the best bunch of kids in collegiate football. . . . The situation here is at times extremely difficult. We've been consistent winners. . . . We are very much proud of what we've accomplished at the University of Southern Mississippi." Membership in a football conference, he added, could well be "the salvation" of the program, "if there is one." It turned out to be an insightful and prophetic assessment.

It took only two weeks to find a successor. At a press conference on December 17, Texas A&M assistant Curley Hallman was introduced as USM's new head coach. Growing up next door to Tuscaloosa at Northport, Alabama, Hallman had felt "the influence of Coach Bryant," as he put it, "since my high school days." Yet he never played for the legendary Bear. Instead, he became an All-Southwest Conference defensive back under Bryant disciple Gene Stallings at A&M. A reporter suggested that Hallman appeared to possess the "public relations" savvy necessary "to sweet-talk warm bodies back into M. M. Roberts Stadium." When asked how he would attack the attendance problem, the new coach responded, "By getting out and working hard." Soon after accepting the job, Hallman met with student government leaders, and he had obviously done his homework. "In the last forty-seven years," he told them, "this university has had four losing seasons. That is an unbelievable accomplishment."

In late August, McLellan announced that USM, along with Cincinnati, Virginia Tech, Tulsa, and Memphis State, had entered into an agreement with the Independence Bowl that would send one of those schools to Shreveport as the host team in December. Hallman's debut came shortly thereafter, on his forty-first birthday, September 3, against Stephen F. Austin. The modest 21-7 victory over the Division 1-AA Lumberjacks was punctuated by a halftime show featuring a 310-piece marching band, the largest ever fielded by the Pride. A week later in Tallahassee, on the Eagles' second play from scrimmage, Florida State's Deion Sanders intercepted a Favre pass and returned it 39 yards for a touchdown. The 49-13 drubbing that followed turned out to be one of only two losses that season, the other coming at the hands of Auburn, 38-8 in November. In between were seven victories that secured USM's first bowl bid since 1981.

In a late September shootout at East Carolina, the Eagles found themselves down 42-38 with 1:19 left in the game. Favre then marched his team down the field, completing three of four passes, including a forty-yard, cross-field bullet to Alfred Williams, who said after the game, "I heard it coming. I swear I'm not joking, I heard it." Short yardage quarterback Ailrick Young then came in and lobbed a five-yard touchdown pass to tight end Preston Hansford with twelve seconds left to seal a 45-42 victory. Three weeks later, USM defeated Mississippi State (38-21) for the tenth time in twelve years, and by October 29, only Memphis State stood between Southern and a bowl bid. The clincher came with 39 seconds left and Memphis leading by a point, when Eugene Rowell broke open deep and Favre hit him in stride. The homecoming

Quarterback Brett Favre (1987-90) set school passing records (single-season and career) for attempts, completions, yards gained, and touchdowns.

crowd gasped as Rowell juggled the ball for several steps before tucking it in for a 45-yard, game-winning score.

Two days before Christmas, the Eagles went bowling for the first time in seven years. Their opponent, Texas-El Paso, entered the game a one-point favorite, but USM led 10-7 at halftime. In the third quarter, James Henry broke the game open with two punt returns for touchdowns, giving him a school record eight for his career and earning him the rare distinction of winning player of the game awards for both offense and defense. The 38-18 victory gave USM a 10-2 mark for the year, only the second ten-win season in school history and the first since 1952. Hallman was voted Metro Conference Coach of the Year, but he raised some eyebrows two months later when he interviewed, unsuccessfully, for the vacant head coaching position at the University of South Carolina.

Still, Eagle Fever was back and running high as the 1989 "home" opener against Florida State approached. McLellan had agreed to move the game, originally scheduled for Hattiesburg, to the Gator Bowl when promoters in Jacksonville offered a $525,000 guarantee and national television coverage. The money and exposure seemed worth the sacrifice, especially after Favre hit tight end Anthony Harris with twenty-three seconds left to seal a 30-26 upset of the sixth-rated Seminoles. With Mississippi State coming to Hattiesburg the following Saturday and USM back in the national rankings for the first time since 1981, prospects looked bright. The Bulldogs dimmed them in short order, however, upsetting the eighteenth-ranked Eagles 26-23 in front of a record crowd of 34,189 in Roberts Stadium. Things went downhill thereafter, as consecutive road losses followed at Auburn, TCU, and Texas A&M, and the team limped to a 5-6 finish that produced few highlights after opening day. Perhaps most memorable was a spectacular finish against Louisville on the road. With twenty-three seconds left and the score deadlocked, freshman Vernard Collins blocked a Cardinal field goal attempt, and the game appeared destined to end in a 10-10 tie. Instead, Favre took a final snap with thirteen seconds left, retreated right to evade a defensive lineman, and launched a 79-yard "hail Mary" that Michael Jackson tipped beyond the reach of several Louisville defenders into the waiting arms of Darryl Tillman, who carried it into the end zone as time ran out.

Hopes for a rebound in 1990 suffered a major blow when Favre was injured in an automobile accident shortly before fall practice began. Opening the season at home against Division II Delta State, the Eagles struggled to a 12-0 win behind freshman backup quarterback John Whitcomb. The following Saturday against thirteenth-ranked Alabama in Birmingham, a weak but determined Favre took over the offense midway through USM's first possession. Though he played sparingly, his mere presence seemed to ignite a spark, and after Kerry Valrie returned an interception 75 yards for a touchdown, the half ended 10-10. The game was tied again at 24, when the

In 1991, former Golden Eagle quarterback, team captain, and MVP, Jeff Bower returned to his alma mater to serve as head football coach.

offense began a drive with barely seven minutes left and Favre at the helm. He marched his team from its 20-yard line to the Alabama 35, but the drive stalled there. On came conventional placekicker Jim Taylor, a straight-on relic in a soccer-style age, who nonchalantly nailed a 52-yard field goal with 3:35 to go in the game. The defense held on to preserve the upset and spoil the Alabama head coaching debut of Hallman's old mentor Gene Stallings. Sadly, Taylor's last-minute magic deserted him the next two weeks against Georgia and Mississippi State. His 42-yard effort on the last play of the game in Athens hit the upright and bounded harmlessly to the turf, giving the Bulldogs a hard-fought 18-17 victory. At Starkville, he missed a 47-yarder that allowed State to win (16-13) the final game between the two teams, though USM held a 14-12-1 edge in the series, including 10 wins in the last 14 meetings.

The 2-2 Eagles then reeled off four straight victories, including a 25-13 home win that Louisville coach Howard Schnellenberger labeled "unusual." The Cardinals came into the game undefeated and confident of ending USM's eight-game winning streak in the series, but six minutes into the first quarter, the visitors found themselves down 22-0. Louisville went three-and-out on their first possession, and Tony Smith returned the ensuing punt 45 yards for a touchdown. A fumbled snap led to a two-point conversion, and the Eagles led 8-0. On the next series, linebacker Thad McDowell intercepted a Browning Nagle pass, and two plays later Roland Johnson scampered 47 yards to make the score 15-0. Shortly thereafter, Valrie scooped up a Cardinal fumble and returned it 42 yards to put USM up 22-0 with only 5:51 gone in the game. Despite outgaining the Eagles 347 yards to 142 and sacking Favre six times, Louisville could not overcome the bizarre beginning. "I've never been through a game like this," lamented a bewildered Schnellenberger. "Maybe it was the moon down here in Hattiesburg."

After a disappointing loss at Virginia Tech, USM finished with victories over Southwestern Louisiana and fifteenth-ranked Auburn to earn a berth in the All-American Bowl in Birmingham against North Carolina State. Hallman would not be there, having accepted the head coaching job at LSU two weeks after the Auburn game. On December 2, only six days after Hallman announced he was leaving, McLellan called a press conference to present his replacement, Oklahoma State offensive coordinator Jeff Bower. "Dang, it's great to be here," Bower told the enthusiastic crowd, who understood the full import of the expression only when McLellan explained that the highway patrol, unable to provide an official escort from the capital city, had authorized him to turn on his flashers and head south. They had made it from the Jackson airport to Hattiesburg in an hour and fifteen minutes. The former Golden Eagle quarterback had been team captain and MVP in 1975 and served on Bobby Collins's coaching staff at USM for six years after that. "I've always wanted to be a head coach here," he said. His debut proved bittersweet, however, for it was also Favre's swan song, and the Wolfpack overcame his 341-yard passing performance, a USM bowl record, to win a 31-27 thriller in front of 44,000 at Legion Field.

Golden Eagle basketball also blossomed in the 1980s. The 1980–81 team, led by freshman playmaker Curtis Green and junior forward Joe Dawson, finished 20-7 and gained the school's first berth in the National Invitational Tournament (NIT). Big wins came over Marquette, Oklahoma, Mississippi State, and Memphis State, but a capacity crowd at Reed Green coliseum saw the season end with a disappointing two-point loss to Holy Cross in the opening round of the NIT. After a 15-11 finish the next year, USM encountered a major challenge in 1982–83 with its first season in the Metro Conference, whose premier team, the University of Louisville, had captured the national championship only three years earlier. The Eagles struggled at the beginning, winning only ten conference games in its first three seasons in the league. After a 14-14 mark in 1982–83 and 13-15 the following year, the record sank to a dismal 7-21 in 1984–85. The play of several freshmen, however, and a big home win over Louisville nurtured hopes of a better future. Things turned around dramatically in 1985–86. After heartbreaking near misses at home against top-ranked Memphis State and eventual national champion Louisville, USM won eight of its last ten regular season games. The fourth-place finish in the conference and 17-10 record overall was enough to win Metro Coach of the Year for Turk and a second trip to the NIT for the team. Postseason wins remained elusive, however, as the Eagles dropped a one-point game to Cincinnati in the conference tournament and an 81-71 decision to Florida in the NIT.

With five returning starters and three outstanding transfers, Turk's troops began 1986–87 with high hopes. Despite an impressive win over North Texas State in the school's first appearance on national television, Southern struggled to a 9-2 start and then limped to a disappointing 17-11 regular season finish. A single victory over Virginia Tech in the Metro tournament, the school's first

SOUTHERN TO THE TOP

Derrek Hamilton

The accomplishments of the 1987 NIT champions seemed endless. Randolph Keys garnered the tournament's most valuable player award, and Derrek Hamilton joined him on the all-NIT team. Keys, Casey Fisher, and Kenny Siler entered USM's thousand-point club, and Fisher set a school record for career assists. Even the radio voice of the Eagles, John Cox, a product of USM's department of radio, television, and film, received Mississippi's Sportscaster of the Year award from the National Sportscaster and Sportswriter Association. The 23 wins, the most by a USM team in a quarter of a century, gave Coach M. K. Turk a career record of 163-143. It was a memorable and fitting way to celebrate 75 years of basketball that began on an outdoor dirt court behind Forrest County Hall. In his 1954 tribute to Lee Floyd, Jimmie McDowell had predicted that one day Southern would "become a big-time ball club–a team that may eventually play in Madison Square Garden." Twenty three years later, that prediction came true in spectacular fashion. Team barber and unofficial spokesman Casey Fisher best described what the scrappy underdogs from a former teachers college in south Mississippi had done: "We came, we saw, and we tore the house down."

Casey Fisher

NIT MVP Randolph Keys

In 1989, Clarence Weatherspoon was voted Metro Conference Freshman of the Year.

since joining the league, eased the pain somewhat and earned USM its third NIT bid since 1980. A first-round home matchup with Ole Miss revived the interest of fans, who stood in line for hours as tickets to basketball in Reed Green Coliseum finally became what M. K. Turk had long hoped to make them, a precious commodity. The growing excitement also rejuvenated his players who gave the boisterous capacity crowd everything they could have hoped for, building a commanding 36-point lead before cruising to a 93-75 win. The USM community was stunned when the tournament committee passed over Hattiesburg as a second-round site and sent the Eagles to play St. Louis University in Kiel Auditorium. The team responded with an 83-78 overtime win, but for the second time the committee shunned Green Coliseum, scheduling Southern's third-round battle with Vanderbilt in Nashville. Again, however, the Eagles responded with a win, 95-88, despite squandering an 18-point first-half lead. "The best team won today," said Vandy coach C. M. Newton. "Now they go to New York and we go to class."

All of Mississippi's attention seemed focused on the Big Apple as Turk took his team to Madison Square Garden for a semifinal match with Big Eight power Nebraska. Sophomores Jurado Hinton and Randy Pettus came off the bench to spark a sputtering offense and overcome an early 13-point Cornhusker lead. The 82-75 win put USM in the finals against a powerful LaSalle team. Several hundred fans followed the team to New York, while thousands of alumni and friends throughout the state and the nation watched on cable television as John White made a crucial steal with six seconds to play and then calmly dropped two free throws through the net to seal an 84-80 victory and give USM the first national basketball tournament championship ever won by a men's team from Mississippi.

With four starters returning from the NIT championship, the 1987–88 squad opened with six straight wins on the way to a 15-2 start and the first top-twenty ranking in school history. Then came a four-game losing streak that included a 141-133 double overtime loss at Virginia Tech, the highest scoring game in Metro Conference history. Seven losses in the last ten games dashed any hopes of an NCAA tournament bid, and in the opening round of the Metro tournament, the Eagles sent host Memphis State to the free-throw line a record forty-six times, losing 97-84. Still, USM earned a third straight NIT invitation and beat Clemson at Reed Green before falling to Virginia Commonwealth on the road to finish 19-11. Randolph Keys, Derrek Hamilton, John White, and Casey Fisher all finished their careers in the thousand-point club, but their departure left the cupboard noticeably bare for the following year. With guard Randy Pettus the lone returning starter, the 1988–89 team fell to a forgettable 10-17. The future looked promising, however, as forward Clarence Weatherspoon won conference freshman of the year honors and, with sophomore guard Darrin Chancellor, made the all-Metro second team. They would be joined in 1989–90 by Copiah-Lincoln Junior College transfers Russell Johnson and Daron Jenkins, who bolstered the line-up considerably.

While the men's basketball team was winning the NIT, Kay James's Lady Eagles brought home USM's first Metro Championship trophy in any sport.

Shirley Jones and Joye Lee-McNelis, both of whom had played for Coach Kay James, served together as assistants on their mentor's staff in the 1980s. Lee-McNelis would return as Lady Eagle head coach in 2004.

John Cox and Shirley Jones handled the radio broadcast for the Lady Eagles' first appearance in the Women's NIT in 1982.

USM would close out the decade by hosting the Metro Conference tournament, winning the league MVP trophy, and earning the school's first bid to the NCAA tournament. The 1989–90 campaign began with a preseason NIT contest in Baton Rouge against LSU. Sporting two seven-foot freshmen, one of them named Shaquille O'Neal, and all-American guard Chris Jackson from Gulfport, the Tigers entered the game ranked second in the nation. The six-foot eleven-inch Jenkins held his own against the two big men, scoring 25 points to their combined 26, but Jackson's 37 led LSU to a 91-80 victory. Later against Arkansas State, the team handed Turk his two hundredth career victory. "I remember my first win," he said after the game, "against Southern Benedictine. We won by one point . . . in front of 1,500 fans. . . . I would say things have gotten significantly better." Finishing at 18-10, the Eagles moved on to the conference tournament in Biloxi's Mississippi Gulf Coast Coliseum. Victories over Virginia Tech and Cincinnati set the stage for a championship matchup between USM and perennial conference bully Louisville. Despite a heartbreaking 83-80 loss in front of a third straight capacity crowd, Weatherspoon was named

Metro Player of the Year, and the team finally secured the elusive NCAA bid. Playing in the East Regional at Hartford, Connecticut, the Eagles lost 79-63 to LaSalle, whom they had defeated for the NIT championship three years earlier.

Kay James's Lady Eagles also distinguished themselves in the 1980s, appearing in the AIAW tournament (1981), the Women's NIT (1982), and the NCAA tournament (1985, 1987, 1989, and 1990). The 1984–85 squad hosted the Metro tournament after finishing the regular season at 19-7 to give James her eighth consecutive winning season. Portland McCaskill, who finished the year as career leader in scoring and rebounding, led USM past Louisville and South Carolina to earn a spot in the finals against powerful Memphis State. In one of the most exciting athletic contests ever played on the USM campus, the Tigers edged James's squad 77-75 in overtime. Two years later Southern again made it to the Metro finals, this time against South Carolina. Tournament MVP Lesha Franklin led the Lady Eagles to a 68-66 win that gave USM its first Metro championship in any sport and made 1987 truly a championship year for Golden Eagle basketball.

After a rebuilding season (12-16) in 1987–88, the Lady Eagles closed out the decade with a second conference championship (1989–90) and back-to-back trips to the NCAA. A first round loss at Rutgers ended the 1988–89 campaign at 26-5, but the following year proved to be the most productive in school history. After winning the conference tournament, the 1989–90 team defeated LSU 75-65 to advance to the second round of the NCAA tournament before bowing to perennial women's powerhouse Louisiana Tech. Through thirteen seasons, Kay James's record stood at 238-128, and she was Metro Coach of the Year in 1988–89. During the eighties, six players (Joye Nell Lee, Portland McCaskill, Wilhelmina "Kat" Smith, Sharon Varnado, Renee Magee, and Gina Griffin) joined the thousand-point club. Other memorable Lady Eagles included Diane Backstrom, Bridget Winston, Amy Heiden, Brenda Williams, Lesha Franklin, and Catrina McCants. James had brought USM women's basketball a long way, but the best was yet to come.

Baseball coach Pete Taylor resigned after the 1983 season, and one of his former players, Hill Denson, took over the program. College baseball was coming into its own in the eighties, and USM could hardly hope to compete in a conference with the likes of Florida State without spending much more money on what had long been considered a minor sport. Denson discovered that USM was using only half of the scholarships allowed by the NCAA. His first team won only 13 of 51 games, but it took him only

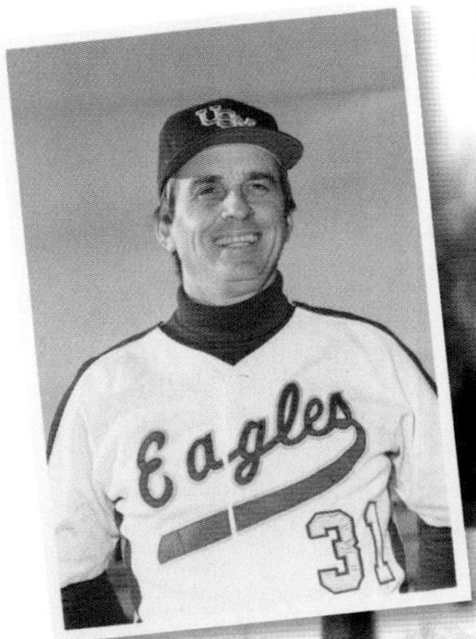

In 1983, former Eagle player Hill Denson succeeded his mentor Pete Taylor as head baseball coach.

Scooter Love (#5) set a school record with 42 stolen bases in 1988.

two more years to produce a winner. Playing in a new facility named for Coach Taylor, the 1985 team finished 28-41; it would be Denson's last losing season. No USM team had ever won 30 baseball games; beginning in 1986, no Denson team ever won fewer. The eighties produced several record holders. Scooter Love stole 42 bases in 1988, and Ive Burnett 85 in his career (1983–86). Fred Cooley ended the 1989 season with 23 home runs and 86 RBIs. Darrell Lindsey's 55 starts, 29 wins, 23 complete games, and 374 strikeouts (1985–88) remain career records. Other notable players included Doug Pearson, Greg Bryant, Greg Conner, Mark Erickson, Sammy Basford, Chris Wagner, Kenny Graves, Kent Willis, Doug Cronk, Kerry Valrie, Tommy Sims, and Chuck Shive. Eight Eagles were drafted, and pitcher Pat Rapp spent eleven years in the major leagues. As the decade drew to a close, USM looked forward to hosting the 1990 Metro Conference tournament in a refurbished Pete Taylor Park.

In 1988, USM was the only university in America to host an exhibit that featured the largest collection of the works of artist Norman Rockwell ever assembled.

By 1990, the NCAA required Division I schools to offer at least seven varsity sports for both men and women. Of necessity, therefore, USM's athletic program expanded steadily during the eighties, but most "minor" sports labored under considerable financial restraints. In 1987, Helen Grant did triple duty, coaching women's volleyball, tennis, and softball. When men's tennis was added the following year, the new coach, Teddy Viator, also took over the women's team. Grant continued with the two other sports, each of which produced but a single winning season during the decade. In 1990, USM participated in eight varsity sports for men (football, basketball, baseball, tennis, golf, indoor and outdoor track, and cross country) and seven for women (basketball, tennis, volleyball, softball, indoor and outdoor track, and cross country). Athletics had become big business, for both the university and the community. A 1989 economic impact study commissioned by the College Football Association estimated that at USM football alone pumped $24.8 million into the Hattiesburg area's annual economy.

After three quarters of a century, student life had become rich and varied. Three new fraternities (Sigma Chi, 1981; Delta Tau Delta, 1984; and Tau Kappa Epsilon, 1986) and two sororities (Zeta Phi Beta, 1982, and Alpha Delta Pi, 1985) had appeared, and there were more than 200 active student organizations on campus. Almost 70 percent of all students shared a total of more than $12 million in various kinds of financial aid; 2,300 students held

October 12, 1989 The Student Printz 3A

Satire on tomfoolery and inflated expectations

FREDDIE 4 HEISMAN

By Fred Horne

As of today, I, Fred Horne, am throwing my cap in the ring (er, figuratively speaking) for the Heisman Trophy. In other words, I'm declaring my candidacy and seeking public support for one of the most coveted prizes in the "civilized" world.

What, a cynic might ask, is the basis for my belated candidacy? Well, since I'm in the middle of Big Gold country where simplistic thinking abounds, I shall explain the obvious.

You see, it's common "knowledge" these day that a university cannot become distinguished or world-class unless it has a bona fide football hero, a.k.a. Heisman Trophy candidate. Earlier this football season, USM quarterback Brett Favre was widely advertised as USM's candidate, but (as we all know by now) he has fallen from "grace" by completing too many passes to the opposition.

Since a Big Gold "crisis" has resulted from Brett's failure to meet world-class expectations, a new football hero is needed forthwith. In other words, somebody has to come to the rescue of our school's "precious image" and reinstate our "distinguished" aspirations. I hereby submit that "Football Freddie" (yours truly) is the man for the job.

From this point on, I will mostly refer to "Football Freddie" in the third person while discussing his background and qualifications.

•

Believe it! USM's "Football Freddie" is for real.

Although "Freddie" may be considered old and spent (as the cartoon below tends to indicate), his gridiron exploits of yesteryear more than make him a viable candidate for the Heisman.

"Freddie's" saga began long ago and far away during his tour of duty in the Far East as a U.S. Marine. The record shows that "Freddie" quickly became a football hero among his fellow Marines because of his uncanny ability to score touchdowns during beach parties (a.k.a. organized brawls) held by the Marine units in which he served.

What was "Freddie's" secret? Well, his fellow Marines never quite figured it out, but "Freddie" was simply the only sober Marine on the beach. While his buddies were preoccupied with distractions like hunting for another keg of brew and beating up on one another, a teetotalist "Freddie" was running for touchdowns and otherwise earning his nickname.

Should "Freddie's" cunning and stealth -- i.e., exploitation of the "enemy's" weaknesses -- be perceived as a knock against his athletic prowess? No way! Just ask the salty Marines that played against "Freddie." They all agree that "Freddie" was tough as leather (as in leatherneck) and lived by the Marine credo of "taking no prisoners" -- especially on the gridiron.

The photo below, which shows "Freddie" scoring a touchdown after cold-cocking a fellow Marine (potential tackler) with his steel helmet, is a good example of USM's Heisman-hopeful at his best.

Besides demonstrating physical toughness, the photo also illustrates "Freddie's" wizardry in camouflage and concealment (i.e., ball-handling ability). Although "Freddie" has possession of the pigskin, it is clearly invisible to the cameraman and, of course, to the drunken Marines who are trying to mug (tackle) "Freddie" before and after he crossed the goal line. (For the record, the pigskin was under "Freddie's" helmet.)

I have one final Heisman plug for "Football Freddie." If versatility is a criterion for selecting the Heisman winner, then "Freddie" should be a shoo-in. You see, there have been numerous so-called "triple threats" (one who runs, passes and kicks with adeptness) who have won the Heisman. But never before has there been a quadruple threat -- that is, until the advent of "Football Freddie."

How could this seemingly impossible phenomenon exist? Well, in keeping with the Marine motto of traveling by air, land and sea (as applied to the gridiron), "Freddie" simply went one better. For example, when faced with a seemingly impenetrable wall of rowdy Marines, "Freddie" would camouflage himself, break out his combat shovel and tunnel underneath the goal line (with the football, of course).

"Freddie's" fellow Marines never figured this one out either; they just shook their heads and dubbed him "Football Freddie."

•

Although Brett Favre hasn't been officially canned as USM's Heisman candidate, we all know the sorry score. That's why I'm calling upon "Chuck" Bennett (USM's official Heisman promoter) to stop crying in his beer about Brett and get on with the task of promoting "FREDDIE 4 HEISMAN." Our university's "world-class" status is at stake.

"Freddie" in his prime

.01

"Freddie" in his -- well...

USM'S "Football Freddie" runs for Heisman

—PAID ADVERTISEMENT—

Throughout the 1980s, graduate student Fred Horne's ubiquitous signs and full-page ads in the student newspaper added a quaint flavor of student protest to an otherwise relatively sedate era in campus life. A letter to the editor of the *Printz* dubbed him the school's "resident attention monger" for his incessant criticism of administration and athletics.

A SECRET GARDEN

Lena de Grummond came to USM in 1965 to teach library science. She had recently retired after a long career as a teacher, librarian, and supervisor of school libraries in Louisiana. To help her students understand the entire process of publication, she began to solicit original materials by authors and illustrators of children's books. Writing as many as a hundred letters a week, all in longhand, she assembled what became the Lena Young de Grummond Children's Literature Research Collection at the McCain Library and Archives. Among the early contributors were H. A. and Margret Rey, creators of the popular "Curious George" series. When Margret Rey died in 1996, she left to the de Grummond Collection a substantial portion of the couple's literary archive, including original manuscripts and illustrations of the mischievous little monkey who delighted children around the world. The early works on Curious George were among the few possessions the Reys had smuggled out of Paris when they escaped to Lisbon by bicycle shortly before the Nazi occupation in 1940. Several hundred items of Rey materials appeared in the 1999-2000 McCain Library exhibit, "Curious George Comes to Hattiesburg: The Life and Work of H. A. and Margret Rey." Under its founder, who retired in 1970, and later longtime curator Dee Jones, the de Grummond Collection became one of the largest repositories of children's literature in North America, containing more than 100,000 published volumes and related material from more than 1,200 authors and illustrators, including Randolph Caldecott, Kate Greenaway, Ezra Jack Keats, and Judy Blume, along with the Reys. It was, in one admirer's words, "Mississippi's own secret garden of children's literature," where one might find anything from a sixteenth-century edition of Aesop's Fables to a hundred different versions of the Cinderella story.

Lena de Grummond (above) founded USM's world-renowned Children's Literature Research Collection now housed at the McCain Library and Archives.

With the support of library director Warren Tracy, de Grummond in 1967 launched an annual book festival that brought together teachers, parents, and librarians to rub shoulders with authors, illustrators, and other noted figures in the world of children's literature. Beginning in 1968, the festival included the awarding of a University of Southern Mississippi Medallion for distinguished contributions in the field. In 2001, the annual Children's Book Festival was named in honor of longtime participant and benefactor Faye B. Kaigler.

The University of Southern Mississippi Medallion for distinguished contributions in the field of children's literature.

By 1985, USM offered club sports, including rugby (below), as well as intramural competition for men and women in more than forty sports.

part-time campus employment, a total annual payroll of almost $3 million. The Commons, which was completely renovated in 1982, hired a registered dietician and added a self-service soup and salad bar and a self-service drink fountain. An active Associated Student Body offered a variety of student government services and events, and the University Activities Council sponsored top-name entertainment. In 1988, the C. W. Woods Art Gallery presented a major exhibition of the works of artist and illustrator Norman Rockwell. USM was the only university in America chosen to host the show, which boasted the largest collection of Rockwell's work ever assembled. Such gallery showings, along with plays, concerts, and recitals provided a wide range of cultural activities for students as well as for the community at large.

By the mid-eighties, USM boasted one of the nation's premier recreational sports programs. For more than a decade, it had steadily progressed thanks to the vision of Chairman Billy Larson of the Department of Physical Education and the steadfast support of Presidents McCain and Lucas. In 1974, Larson had convinced a young "yankee" with four impressive job offers already in hand at least to visit Hattiesburg and interview for the newly created position of director of intramural athletics. Arriving at the old municipal airport in a three-piece suit in the heat of summer, Lou Marciani found Larson waiting for him in a pickup truck with a dog in the back and a box of doughnuts on the front seat. Larson threw the visitor's luggage in back with the dog, thrust the doughnuts into his hands, and took off for campus, pointing out attractions like the site of the soon-to-be-built Cloverleaf Mall on the way. Impressed with Larson's persistence and McCain's commitment to a

In 1988, USM's "Salt and Pepper" bested ninety-four other teams to win the National Invitational Flag Football Tournament in New Orleans.

NBC correspondent and USM alumnus Chuck Scarborough delivers the 1987 commencement address.

first-rate program, Marciani accepted the job and returned to his current position at Buffalo State in New York to tie up loose ends. Physical education professor Jim Townley, whom Larson had dragooned into supervising intramurals in the interim, feared that Marciani would never really show up. When he did arrive and walked into the old sports arena, Townley spied him and came sliding across the gym floor on one knee. "God bless you, son," he said in disbelief, "you're here!" He crossed himself, threw up his hands, and exclaimed, "Hallelujah, he's here, Larson, he's here!" Marciani was hooked. "Ever since then," he later explained, "it's been a love affair with the University for me."

First, he hired a competent assistant, Steve Rey, and with the help of a single graduate student worker, they began to stabilize what had been a volatile intramural program. Then came not only expansion and improvement but diversification. By 1984, when Marciani left to become athletic director at Salisbury (Maryland) State, the multipurpose program included, besides new and improved intramural facilities, an outdoor recreational complex at Lake Sehoy, club sports, campgrounds, and a 144-acre equestrian center. By the end of the decade, Marciani's successor Sid Gonsoulin directed an intramural program that offered competition in forty sports ranging from football and basketball to water polo and Frisbee.

The library, as it had been since Anna Roberts's day, continued to be one of the areas where lack of funds pressed the university hardest. Though the budget for acquisitions almost doubled between 1977 and 1983, it remained largely flat for the rest of the eighties. The overall budget, strained by rising journal costs, failed to meet the threshold for membership in the Association of Southeastern Research Libraries. The 1973 self-study had set a 1985 target of 1.5 million volumes for the library, which would have tripled its holdings. The university did not reach that goal, but it made significant progress, and consultants for the board's undergraduate program reviews found library resources adequate, though problems remained for some graduate programs. The McCain Library and Archives held several valuable special collections including the Sam Woods Collection of rare books and artifacts and the Lena Y. de Grummond collection of children's literature. The library's Teaching-Learning Resource Center established a reputation for excellence and creativity that earned it the 1981 G. Theodore Mittau Award of the American Association of State Colleges and Universities for innovation and change in public education.

"It has been well said," President Lucas noted at the outset of the university's Diamond Jubilee, "that where there is no vision, the people perish. We at The University of Southern Mississippi have a vision, a vision which requires us to stretch our imaginations, to use our resources very wisely, and to work harder, perhaps, than what otherwise might be required. This vision has brought us, over these seventy-five years, from significant but really rather humble beginnings, to a university whose programs and whose people are becoming truly distinguished."

Indeed, the institution's growth and progress had been remarkable. Since the first degree class in 1922, it had awarded almost 65,000 degrees, more than half of them after 1972. It was affiliated with the publication of ten scholarly journals. Its Honors College was one of only fourteen in the United States. It was the first institution in Mississippi with accredited undergraduate, graduate, and continuing education programs in nursing and the first in the nation to offer bachelor's, master's, and doctoral degrees in polymer science. It was one of only fifteen institutions in the nation to offer three fully accredited doctoral programs in psychology, one of only four to hold accreditation in all four fine arts disciplines—art, dance, theatre, and music. Its English department ranked in the top 10 percent in the nation, its dean of home economics was elected president of the American Dietetics Association for 1988–89, and in 1987 a member of its science faculty served as president of the largest professional organization in the world, the American Chemical Society. In 1984, its president was elected to head the 354-member American Association of State Colleges and Universities. In the words of its mission statement, USM now defined itself as "an emerging, comprehensive institution committed to seek and reward distinction among its programs, faculty, students, and services. Its purposes are to provide high-quality teaching, research, and service for the benefit of the people of Mississippi, the Gulf South, and the nation."

Chapter 6

THE UNIVERSITY FOR THE NEW SOUTH

Unveiled in 1988, the new institutional theme "The University for the New South" would be the concrete expression of President Aubrey K. Lucas's inaugural vision of a truly distinguished university.

In announcing the reorganization plan in 1988, President Lucas had used the opportunity to unveil a new institutional theme: USM—The University for the New South. The slogan had originated in a separate ad hoc committee on marketing and public relations, but many of its concrete outlines emerged from the reorganization process: "an inclusive University where qualified students can attend regardless of color, class, religion, or economic background . . . a University which is responsive to the many needs of our state," including "better educational opportunities, improved health care, support for families and children, economic development, and cultural enhancement;" a University with "a proper balance among teaching, research, and service." In short, the University for the New South would be the concrete expression of Lucas's inaugural vision of a truly distinguished university. Out of the fires of crisis and struggle, the institution had once again reached beyond its rich heritage to forge for itself a new identity designed to meet the challenges of a changing world.

A significant expression of the new identity appeared on April 2, 1991, when the university celebrated the opening of a new $19.7 million Polymer Science Research Center. USM's Department of Polymer Science evolved out of the Pan American Tung Research and Development League laboratory, which moved to the campus from Picayune in 1963. South Mississippi and Argentina were the world's major producers of tung oil, and USM worked hard to develop new uses for the product. Ironically, polymer science, under the leadership of Chairman Shelby Thames, became a separate academic department in 1970 shortly after Hurricane Camille destroyed Pearl River County's tung trees. Over the next fifteen years, USM became one of the country's two leading polymer science research institutions and one of only four offering both undergraduate and graduate degrees in the field. During that time the university awarded 150 bachelor's, 50 master's, and 28 Ph.D. degrees (10 in 1985–86 alone) in polymer science. The program perfectly embodied the union of academic distinction and economic development that seemed so essential to the future of both the university and the people it served. Research by members of the department had already led to valuable practical applications, including plastics for artificial hearts.

Beginning in 1986, Mississippi's congressional delegation helped secure sufficient funding to build and equip a new two-story, 86,000-square-foot home for the polymer science program. At groundbreaking ceremonies in

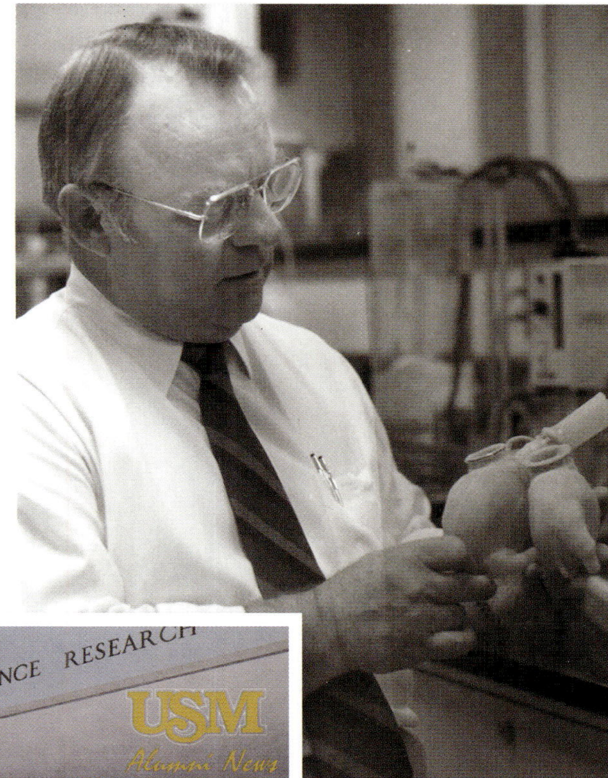

The Center was later named for Professor Shelby Thames (shown above with an artificial heart made from polymers), who pioneered USM's polymer science program.

Ribbon cutting ceremonies for the $19.7 million Polymer Science Research Center featured (from left to right) President Lucas, Senator Thad Cochran, and Representative Gene Taylor. At the April 1991 event, Keynote speaker John Patrick Jordan of the U. S. Department of Agriculture suggested that with the new facility USM's polymer science program could "run with Cal-Tech and MIT any day of the week and twice on Sunday."

In 1991, the university installed a new computerized access system for residence halls.

1988, Lucas noted that the polymer science center would be the "first building on this campus to be constructed principally for the purpose of research." At ribbon-cutting ceremonies three years later, Thames described it as "the most magnificent polymer science facility in America, and probably the world." Lucas praised the congressional delegation, several of whom were on hand, for their support. The day's events, said Representative Gene Taylor, marked "a significant milestone in the history of this University. It signifies that USM is achieving recognition as a major research university."

The capstone came two years later when the Mississippi legislature appropriated half a million dollars for a Mississippi Polymer Science Institute to be headquartered at USM's new center. The institute provided the third component, service, to an extraordinary academic-industrial partnership, which included instruction, by the Department of Polymer Science, and research, enhanced by the sophisticated facilities of the new center. The institute's staff now possessed the resources to do what faculty could not, devote all their energies to assist the rapidly proliferating polymer-related businesses in the state. USM's polymer science program epitomized Lucas's vision of a distinguished university making significant contributions to the development of human capital in the state and region.

Having begun brilliantly, the new decade turned darker, however, and the early nineties would be among the most trying of Lucas's presidency. In the fall of 1991, two rapes spread anxiety throughout the campus and led to costly, and what some considered inconvenient, security measures, including a $70,000 computerized access system for residence halls. The following February, the body of a newborn was found stuffed in a duffel bag in the closet of a Hillcrest dormitory room, whose female resident was ultimately charged with murdering her baby. In December 1992, the eagle mascot, Nugget, was discovered dead in his aviary home. Pellet wounds on his body led to early reports that he had died of lead poisoning caused by a shotgun blast sometime during the previous three to six weeks. The Alumni Association offered a $1,000 reward for information about the shooting. Meanwhile, Nugget's remains were sent to a U.S. Department of Interior laboratory in Oregon for a "forensic necropsy." In July came the shocking, and embarrassing, results: Nugget had died of malnutrition caused by "improper feeding." The mascot's student trainer had left school after the final football game, leaving care of the bird in the hands of an assistant trainer, also a student. The assistant had continued to feed Nugget regularly but did not always remain to see that he actually ate and, without handling him daily, failed to detect a dramatic weight loss. The $5,000 fine USM paid to the U.S. Fish and Wildlife Service and to the National Fish and Wildlife Foundation constituted, the university insisted, an admission of responsibility but not guilt.

More foreboding than all these setbacks, however, was the return of the dreaded budget cuts. The last good year had been 1988–89 (a $5.8 million increase), but that had come in the wake of severe cuts in the mid-eighties. After a 5 percent ($2.2 million) midyear cut in September 1990,

Every university has unsung heroes, those who perform indispensable chores that go largely unnoticed. Polly Stout was officially retired by the 1990s, but her services were still in demand. She had become, as President Lucas put it, "an institution within this institution. . . . She helps us recall when, why, and how things were done, as well as who did them. She has few, if any, peers when it comes to accurate proofreading. She has a never-failing sense of appropriateness in all situations, which has served USM well as she has planned and administered innumerable official functions. Besides all that, Polly is a faithful and generous friend."

Her husband, English professor Wilbur W. Stout, came to Mississippi Southern College in 1944, but she was still teaching at a girls' school in Memphis and visited him once a month the first year by bus. When R. C. Cook became president in 1945, she became Mrs. Cook's unofficial social coordinator and advisor. Over the years, she was assistant director of housing (1956–65), student lounge hostess in the old Southern Hall Annex, and at various times temporary instructor in the Latin American Institute and the departments of English and history. In 1965, she became editorial and research assistant to the president and among other duties prepared every annual university *Bulletin* for two decades. To provide coffee for workers at registration, she once brought two fifty-cup percolators that blew a circuit when she plugged them in, leaving everyone sweltering temporarily in a darkened coliseum.

Polly Stout (left) and Jessie Morrison

Her friend and "partner in crime" was Jessie Morrison, who served as secretary to three presidents. In reference to an expanding personnel office, William D. McCain once wondered aloud why it took an entire staff and a suite to do what Miss Jessie used to handle by herself out of a single desk drawer. She kept a strange ornament on her desk, whose function no one could determine though some said it resembled an instrument of torture.

Though Polly Stout was one of a kind, the nearest thing to an heir was English professor and associate dean of liberal arts Stanley Hauer, who among other things wrote and edited accreditation documents and helped plan inaugurations for a generation.

In 1992, Eagle mascot Nugget was found dead in his cage.

and a 9.2 percent ($3.5 million) cut for 1991–92, state funding per student had fallen 18.4 percent (31.3 percent after adjusting for inflation) since 1988. Forced to eliminate vacant positions to save money, USM by 1991 faced a record fall enrollment with a hundred fewer faculty than had been available three years earlier. Those who remained had received no raises since 1988. The choices were excruciating. In October 1991, the college board approved 5 percent raises for faculty (3 percent for staff) at all state universities for 1992–93 and 1993–94 but left each institution to generate the funds internally without additional appropriations. "This process of budget reallocation," Lucas warned alumni, "will be painful. . . . Every program and function within the University will be reexamined. . . . USM will change, but it will remain committed to providing programs that are nationally competitive and which are needed in Mississippi."

Department chairs were instructed to conduct exhaustive self-studies from which "environmental scanning reports" for each unit would become the basis of recommendations regarding elimination or consolidation of programs. The recommendations would come from an academic affairs program evaluation team (PET) composed of the nine campus deans; the dean at Gulf Coast; the director of university libraries; the presidents of the academic council, the graduate council, and the faculty senate; and eight members of the faculty at large. The scanning reports would also identify superior programs. "It would be pointless," said vice-president for academic affairs David Huffman, "to be all negative. We might as well decide what's important as well as what's not important."

When the scanning reports arrived at Huffman's office, collectively they ran to some 3,600 pages weighing in at twenty- six pounds. In seventeen hours of deliberation over three days, PET members scrutinized "every department, academic major, emphasis area, and degree in the university." Lucas received PET's final report on February 12, 1992, and forwarded it to the college board, noting, "As you can see, the Team has been thorough in its work, and the recommendations would affect USM profoundly." He added that a separate "task force" would soon be recommending specific reductions for "all non-academic budgets." Three days earlier, Governor Kirk Fordice had imposed substantial cuts in the current budget, and USM lost another $2 million.

On February 13, Lucas called a special convocation to announce the PET recommendations. "This is a grim situation," he warned. "I don't want to mislead you by giving any indication that we can handle this financial crisis without the loss of jobs and programs. . . . Personnel will be affected. . . . We must down-size or 'right-size' our operations so that they're in line with these stringent resources." The PET report encompassed "significant consolidation," including elimination of the bachelor of fine arts degree in dance, the master's degree in recreation, the emphasis area in photojournalism, and the entire school of library science. Lucas stressed that the recommendations had not yet been approved, that discussions and opportunities for persuasion would continue. Financial constraints, a *Printz* editorial mused, would bring "fundamental changes" to the university, to its "role in society," as well as "its own mission. . . . The baby boomers have graduated . . . and the college that rode their flash-flood college entry is dealing with enrollment growth that has slowed to a steady but moderate" trickle. "The University for the New South," the author concluded, "is searching for itself." USM was not alone. Mississippi State's counterpart to the PET report called for the elimination of fourteen departments, thirty majors, and seventy faculty positions. *The Chronicle of Higher Education* reported that public universities across the country would receive $80 million less in 1992–93 than they had the previous year.

Every penny seemed precious. In January, the administration had asked IHL for permission to raise student fees for room and board and health services. The following month, night and weekend classes were relocated to restrict the use of seven buildings, saving over $50,000. Another $250,000 was saved by adjusting thermostats three to five degrees and delaying the use of air conditioning until April 15. Student "energy monitors" patrolled buildings each night, turning off lights and closing doors and windows. The administration was seriously considering a proposal to "outsource" physical plant operations to Marriott Facilities Management. In late March, the cabinet approved the final "Plan for Budget Reduction 1992–93," and on April 6, a weary Lucas outlined its contents at yet another special convocation. In academics, the plan called for the elimination, some through consolidation, of two departments, thirteen degree programs, and seventy-two emphasis areas, shaving the budget by more than half a million dollars. Notable casualties included the undergraduate major in sociology and the entire Department of Science Education. Several programs originally targeted for elimination were spared, including the bachelor's degree in dance and the master's in recreation. The school of library science

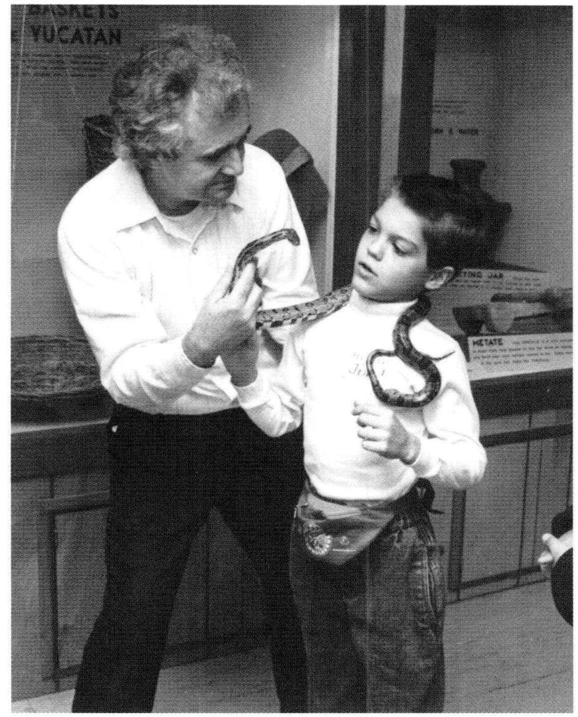

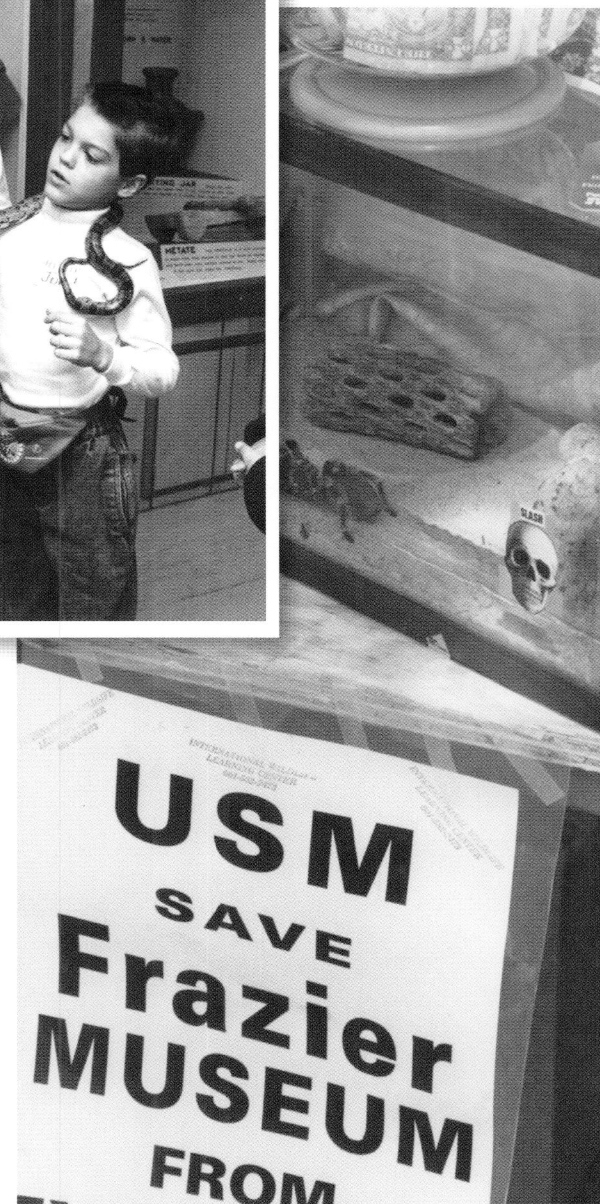

The popular John Martin Frazier Museum of Natural History fell victim to budget cuts in 1992.

also survived but only with the loss of all five of its emphasis areas.

On the nonacademic side, recreational sports, which the 1988 reorganization had shifted to student affairs, now lost its entire budget ($286,000), as did the natatorium ($25,000). Their operations, along with those of the new recreational complex under construction, would come from a $30 per semester increase in student fees. Physical plant would lose $539,000, but director David Anderson's herculean efforts to reduce waste and improve efficiency, including a million dollars already saved in utility costs, staved off Marriott's takeover bid. Other significant savings came from reductions in faculty release time ($413,000) and elimination of a subsidy to athletics ($325,000). The collective nonacademic cuts ($1.6 million) would bring the total reduction in budget to $2,214,823. "This . . . year," the president concluded, "has been the most difficult we have had." Yet not all the news was bad. The otherwise painful five months of self-scrutiny had revealed extraordinary quality in some departments, particularly the master's programs in professional accountancy and nursing and doctoral programs in music, psychology, English, and polymer science. These six would become "centers of excellence," with top priority in funding and faculty. After the IHL board had approved all the proposals, Lucas expressed his gratitude for the grace and harmony with which everyone had endured a difficult process: "We're hoping that the time of cutting has passed."

The most notorious casualty of the budget ax was the John Martin Frazier Museum of Natural Science. From its nook in the basement of Mississippi Hall, the facility hosted thousands of local elementary school students each year with entertaining as well as educational exhibits. Operated under the now doomed Department of Science Education, the museum was scheduled to close at the end of 1992. Outraged, local elementary teachers incited a veritable crusade to save it. Children at Oak Grove Elementary School raised $300 by donating their ice cream money to the cause, but to no avail. The university agreed to continue to provide the space and utilities if an alternate sponsor could be found, and longtime museum director Richard Moore hoped for "a miracle." When none materialized, the director of the USM Foundation, which had established a special account for donations to the museum, sheepishly offered to return the youthful crusaders' money.

Just as the sense of crisis seemed to be receding, another bomb exploded. On June 26, 1992, the United States Supreme Court ruled that vestiges of Mississippi's segregated past remained embedded in its current system of public higher education. The ruling involved a lawsuit filed in 1975 by Jake Ayers Sr. of Glen Allan on behalf of his son and twenty-one other black students. Plaintiffs charged that the state's three historically black public institutions remained largely segregated and suffered from programs, facilities, and funding that had long been grossly inferior to those of their predominantly white counterparts. The Supreme Court sent the case back to the district court in Oxford where it had originated with instructions to presiding judge Neal Biggers that state officials and plaintiffs work together toward remedies that would end the de facto dual university system. Again virtually panic-stricken, the college board in October offered a drastic proposal that would have combined existing universities and eliminated several high-visibility programs. USM would have acquired jurisdiction over Mississippi University for Women but lost programs in engineering technology and social work to an expanded Jackson State University. The plan provoked a statewide uproar that led to the creation of a blue ribbon task force that held public hearings to gauge public sentiment. Support for the board appeared almost nonexistent, and its proposal, said the task force chairman, "has divided our people and caused severe dissension."

Meanwhile, a ghost from USM's own segregated past was coming back to haunt the institution. In September 1991, the Jackson *Clarion Ledger* ran a story on Clyde Kennard, who had tried unsuccessfully to integrate Mississippi Southern College in the 1950s. Based on documents, some published in the article, from the newly opened files of the Mississippi State Sovereignty Commission, the newspaper insisted that Kennard had been wrongfully convicted of possession of alcohol in 1959. USM's African-American Student Organization (AASO), supported by student government leaders, designated October 15 as Clyde Kennard Day and invited James Meredith, who had broken the color barrier at Ole Miss in 1962, to keynote the event. Following Meredith's address, John Webb spoke, recalling that Kennard, his brother-in-law, had once said that while he might never "get to go to that college," he could help open the door for others.

"I believe his trials . . . and disappointments were not in vain. This gathering tells me that the door to USM is open to all students—black and white." Ceremonies concluded with an evening candlelight vigil in front of the student union followed by a panel discussion on "The Legacy of Racism in Academia."

The AASO also called upon the university to honor Kennard in a more tangible and permanent way, and Lucas appointed a committee of faculty, staff, and students to recommend a fitting memorial. "We must remember Clyde Kennard," the president said, "so that we can be reminded that even good intentioned, well meaning people can do wrong when such wrong is accepted, expected and demanded by society." Derek Hopson, the school's first black Associated Student Body (ASB) president, deemed the action "a great step for the university. I think it truly says that we are concerned and we really want to live up to those ideals of being the University for the New South. I just simply urge that we now, on Dr. Lucas' statement, heal our wounds and move on." In February 1992, the committee made several recommendations, including the renaming of the Student Services Building in Kennard's honor. At the second annual Clyde Kennard Day in September 1992, *Student Printz* executive editor Riva Brown received the inaugural Clyde Kennard Award for Outstanding Black Student Leader.

For Black History Month the following February, the university scheduled an elaborate "Celebration of Diversity." Raylawni Branch and Elaine Armstrong Chamberlain, the first black students to enroll successfully at USM, returned to campus to hear Pulitzer Prize-winning columnist Clarence Page deliver the first of an annual lecture series named in their honor. On February 18, 1993, the Student Services Building was rededicated Kennard-Washington Hall in honor of Kennard and Alcorn State University president Walter Washington, who in 1969 had received from USM the first doctoral degree ever awarded to a black student in Mississippi. In what one reporter described as an atmosphere of "quiet reverence and hope

As part of a weeklong "Celebration of Diversity" in February 1993, the Student Services Building was renamed Kennard-Washington Hall. Clyde Kennard, a decorated Korean War veteran, paved the way for later black students with his unsuccessful attempts to integrate Mississippi Southern College. Walter Washington earned from USM the first doctoral degree ever awarded to a black student in Mississippi and went on to serve as president of Alcorn State University.

Donors Larry and Jim Payne (third and fourth from right) participate in groundbreaking ceremonies for the recreational sports and fitness complex named in their honor.

The Payne Center, which opened in 1993, featured a spacious atrium entrance overlooked by workout centers and aerobic rooms; a one-eighth-mile running track; four basketball/volleyball courts; additional courts for badminton, squash, and racquetball; weight rooms; centers for fitness assessment and wellness resources; a first-aid/training room; saunas; and two thousand lockers. In addition to office space, the structure housed meeting and seminar rooms sufficient for one hundred hours of classroom work every week.

for the future," a standing-room-only audience paid homage to Kennard, Washington, and a long list of African American "firsts" at USM. "As each name was called," the *Printz* reported, "more tears were shed until at the end of the list the auditorium exploded into applause for the accomplishments of those on the stage."

Speaking of Kennard, Lucas acknowledged that, "no honor we bestow today can erase or make amends for the tragic events which surrounded his unsuccessful attempts to become a student at USM. By placing his name on this landmark building, we are ensuring that we will remember Clyde Kennard and his role in our institution's history, and we're saying to the world that we apologize for the indignities he suffered." Washington was introduced to a standing ovation. "Whatever I have tried to do since I left this university," he said, "grew out of [the] stimulating experience I had here at Southern." And yet, the changes had been profound. "To come back on this campus," he marveled, "and see a revolution taking place; blacks and whites walking together, living in the same dormitories, here for one purpose: to get a good education . . . and we're going in that direction because of Aubrey

K. Lucas." It had been a "momentous" day, as Elaine Chamberlain put it. "I think it's going to bring about a lot of good and healing, a lot of healing." Lucas declared the celebration "a heartwarming success."

Despite the progress, Mississippi had hardly become a paradise of racial harmony, and the specter of *Ayers v. Allain* still hovered ominously over the universities. Finally on March 7, 1995, after two decades of litigation, Judge Biggers handed down a decision. There would be no closings or mergers, but many programs would be redistributed to increase racial balance, particularly at the three historically black institutions. Miraculously, USM "escaped," as the *Hattiesburg American* put it, "virtually unscathed." The sense of relief within the university community was universal and almost palpable. Faculty senate president Vivien Carter praised the president's leadership. "I don't know how we came out unaffected," she declared, "but I understand that Dr. Lucas' testimony before the courts was very effective where USM is concerned." Indeed, Lucas, testifying very near the end of the two-month long trial, had argued vigorously that shifting sound programs from USM to the historically black universities would neither improve education nor promote desegregation. No one was more pleased at the outcome than Lucas himself. "It's a relief this is finally over," he said. But it was not over. Many details of the settlement remained to be implemented, and the "implications" of *Ayers* would accompany USM into its second century.

By the mid-nineties, thanks in part to a thriving state gaming industry, the budget clouds had also parted somewhat. Between 1984 and 1994, state appropriations for higher education had declined by almost 4 percent. In May 1994, Lucas announced that faculty and staff would receive raises averaging 7 percent for the coming year. In twenty-three years as a college president, he exulted, "I've never seen anything to equal what we received this year," an expected 15.7 percent increase in education and general expenditure funds plus millions more for construction, repair, renovation, and furnishing of facilities.

Despite budget constraints, the university was already enjoying a significant building boom that included, besides the new Polymer Science Research Center, a long-awaited recreational and fitness complex and a major expansion of Cook Library. Planning for the sports facility had begun over a decade earlier, and in a spring 1984 referendum, students overwhelmingly (98 percent) approved a $5 per semester fee to underwrite the cost. By 1989, however, Lucas concluded that "the student funds just won't build the kind of facility we need," and he began to cast about for an alternate source of money. On February 12, 1990, he was able to announce one of the most generous gifts ever made to the university. Jackson businessmen, alumni, and brothers Jim and Larry Payne donated $2 million to complete the recreational sports and fitness complex, along with a pledge of $2 million more for endowments for the college of business administration, athletics, and other programs. "The University of Southern Mississippi is indeed proud to claim Jim and Larry Payne," Lucas said, "two young entrepreneurs whose philanthropy and loyalty to their alma mater are truly exemplary." Their gift would, he added, "be a significant boost in our striving for distinction."

On August 23, 1993, the $7.5 million, 133,000-square-foot Payne Center, named in honor of the donors, opened its doors. Recreational sports soon became the largest employer of students on campus, with more than 400 lifeguards, clerks, and intramural referees. Two years later, the National Intramural-Recreational Sports Association (NIRSA) ranked USM the best of 260 comparable institutions participating in its Natural High Program. By then, the Payne Center had already entertained more than two million visitors, and in 1996, NIRSA named it one of the top 13 fitness facilities in North America.

As construction of the Payne Center was winding down, work was just beginning on a significant addition to Cook Library. Budget cutbacks had hit the library particularly hard. When escalating journal costs forced a moratorium on book purchases in 1990–91, students voted 950-340 in favor of a $5 per semester library fee, and the ASB made a token donation from its own budget, hoping to stimulate private giving to support the library. A $235,000 cut in the following year's budget cost Cook Library four vacant positions, and a 20 percent decrease in funds for student wages led to a comparable reduction in operating hours. Finally in 1992, the legislature earmarked $8.6 million of its bond bill for capital improvements to supplement $4.85 million approved in 1990 for expansion of USM's library. Construction began the following year on a five-story addition immediately north of and connected to the existing facility. When completed in 1995, it gave Cook Library a total of 230,000 square feet of space, making USM's combined library facilities the largest in Mississippi. All operations then moved into the new structure until a thorough renovation of the original building was completed in 1997. In 1995, USM libraries installed an On-line System of Computer Assisted Retrieval (OSCAR) and the following year catalogued the system's one millionth volume. In 1999, OSCAR was replaced by a more sophisticated software system named ANNA in honor of longtime librarian (1926–62) Anna Roberts.

Academics remained the focal point of the university's mission. In 1990, history professor Neil McMillen won a coveted Bancroft Prize for his book, *Dark Journey: Black Mississippians in the Age of Jim Crow*. The following year, the school of nursing celebrated its twenty-fifth birthday with a dinner honoring founding dean Elizabeth Harkins. Since its inception in 1966, the program had produced more than 2,500 graduates, and in 1996 a higher percentage (98.89) of USM graduates passed the registered nurses' licensure examination than did those of any other program in the state.

After a decade of growth, the Center for International Education merged with the Division of Lifelong Learning in 1991 to form the College of International and Continuing Education with Tim Hudson as dean. By the mid-nineties, almost 5 percent of all USM students took advantage of overseas programs, and New York's Institute for International Education, which administered Fulbright Scholarships, rated only three other American universities ahead of Southern in the number of students studying abroad. In 1997, fifty years after it all began with the English Language Institute, USM offered opportunities for study in twenty places around the world and exchange programs with eight foreign institutions.

A $13.5 million addition to Cook Library opened in 1995, making USM's combined libraries the largest in Mississippi. The following year, the library acquired its one-millionth volume, and state senator Steve Seale, university librarian James Martin, and head of cataloging Ann Branton looked on as President Lucas entered it into the university system.

In 1992, *Chemical Engineering News* listed the top fifty American universities receiving federal funds for research in chemistry, and USM ranked twenty-third, ahead of such prestigious institutions as Ohio State, Rutgers, and Texas A&M. No other Mississippi school made the list, and no other from the Southeast made the top thirty. Two years later, external funding for the university as a whole reached a record $29.4 million. "When I came

In 1991, Tim Hudson (left) became dean of the new College of International and Continuing Education. By the mid-1990s, USM ranked fourth in the nation in the number of its students studying abroad, offering opportunities in more than twenty places around the world.

here [1967]," said vice-president for research and extended services Karen Yarbrough, "there was no funded research—none. I think we've changed the research environment of this institution. We've elevated scholarly and creative activities to their proper role."

In 1994, the school of social work celebrated its twentieth anniversary and over the following two years earned accreditation for all its programs from the Council on Social Work Education. The school of home economics changed its name to family and consumer sciences in 1995, and the following year the oral history program became the Center for Oral History and Cultural Heritage. The same year, a leading professional journal ranked USM's school of communication in the top ten nationally in several categories, including doctoral enrollment. Also in 1996, polymer science student Kevin Thigpen of Ellisville won a Goldwater scholarship, the preeminent national award for undergraduates studying mathematics, natural science, or engineering. Between 1994 and 1999, USM would claim seven Goldwater Scholars, and Thigpen would go on to become the first Southern Miss student to reach the finals in the prestigious Rhodes Scholar competition.

Student life also flourished in the nineties. Enrollment for 1991 was 12,348 in Hattiesburg and 13,944 overall, both records. For the decade, graduate enrollment peaked at 2,778 in 1997, as did total enrollment at 14,593. In 1992, the Mississippi Press Association tapped the *Student Printz* for more awards, including the prize for general excellence, than any other campus newspaper in the state. The 1996 student yearbook, edited by Greg Lees, won the school's first All American Award from the Associated Collegiate Press. *The Southerner* also garnered marks of distinction for academic and feature coverage, layouts storytelling, and thoroughness. In 1994 the ASB, which had been the Student Government Association (SGA) until 1974, elected the first woman president since the 1940s. The name SGA was restored the following year, making Cindy Woods the only female ASB president in school history. Students, as they had for decades, complained about inadequate parking. In 1990, with almost 12,000 permits issued for 6,255 spaces, a parking decal constituted little more than a hunting license. The previous year, the university had collected $158,930 in traffic fines on 25,368 tickets. Recommendations by a 1994–95 task force led to some improvements: additional parking spaces, computerized ticketing, and more efficient enforcement. A feasibility study estimated that a four-level campus garage would accommodate 1,387 vehicles but at a cost of approximately $7 million, or $5,000 per parking space. "Pavement, pavement everywhere," a *Printz* columnist lamented, "but not a place to park."

The moral climate had changed considerably since the days of Daddy Joe or even the middle decades of the twentieth century. By the 1990s, the campus clinic offered open access to a container labeled "condoms," though it was soon placed behind the counter after some students abused the "privilege." One anonymous female interviewed by the *Student Printz* confessed that "usually you'd go in and you think nobody is looking and you grab a handful and stick them in your backpack. But I didn't waste them." The cost became prohibitive as clinic workers had to refill the bin as many as five times a day. "Now you have to ask for them," the interviewee complained; "Shoot, I wouldn't do that!" Or as a fellow student, a male this time, put it, "I am embarrassed to ask for them because they know what you're doing with them."

The nineties would prove pivotal for USM's future on the Gulf Coast. In 1992 Joe Holloway, who had served as dean at Gulf Park from the beginning, died unexpectedly. Louis Elias served as interim dean until July 1993, when former Auburn University-Montgomery chancellor James O. Williams was chosen to succeed Holloway. In 1996, USMGC combined its Center of Marine Science at the Stennis Space Center and its Gulf Coast Research Laboratory into a new Institute of Marine Sciences and lured U.S. Department of Energy microbiologist Jay Grimes to direct it. That year, enrollment on the coast topped 1,700 for the first time in thirteen years and only the second time ever. By the end of the decade, USM was poised for major expansion on the Gulf Coast.

As the end of the twentieth century approached, the pace of technological innovation quickened dramatically, but technology was a two-edged sword, creating new demands along with new opportunities. Ten classes on the schedule for spring semester 1994 were available to students at both Hattiesburg and Gulf Park. Compressed video allowed an instructor on either campus to interact with students at the other. Not everyone was pleased, and debate over the issue was heated at the January 1994 meeting of the faculty senate. Longtime history professor William Scarborough scornfully suggested, "If you're going to follow this principle, why don't you just videotape some of the big guns at Harvard and Berkeley and Stanford and send it out all over the country and have standardized tests?" Not all faculty were critical of the new venture. Geology professor Gail Russell declared that, with compressed video, "I can communicate what I need to students on the coast better than I can communicate . . . in Stout Hall to people sitting on the fourth row." Compressed video was only the beginning, however. Electronic mail was available, though little used, on campus as early as 1992, and the Internet came the following year. By 1995, USM had its own website, and soon adapting to rapidly changing technology would be a fact of life for everyone in higher education.

In 1990, President Lucas established a staff council to represent the interests of nonfaculty employees. Three years later, faculty, staff, and their families thronged Roberts Stadium to enjoy food, fun, and fellowship at the first of what became an annual Employee Appreciation Day. Tom Estes resigned in 1990, and James Henderson became vice-president for business and finance. The following year, English professor Maureen Ryan replaced Honors College dean Peggy Prenshaw, who accepted a position at LSU. When Howard Miller retired as director of public safety in 1992, he was succeeded by Keith Oubre, whose father had held the same position in the 1960s and '70s. Dean of student development Joe Paul moved up to

Director of orchestral activities Jay Dean.

vice-president of student affairs when Peter Durkee retired in 1993, and Peter Alexander replaced the retiring Harold Luce as dean of the college of the arts in 1996.

Arts and athletics continued to be the university's most visible faces to the outside world. In 1993, the USM Chorale represented the United States at the International Festival of Choral Song in Nancy, France. Aubrey and Ella Lucas joined the nine-day tour, which included concerts in Paris and Pont-a-Mousson as well as Nancy. "We were thrilled that they were able to be there," beamed choral director William Weinert. "It reflects the wonderful support the School of Music has. Colleagues of mine at other universities were just in awe that the president would be accompanying us to something like this." The following year, professor of classical guitar John DeChiaro was invited to Rome where he played for a large Vatican audience that included Pope John Paul II. In 1996, The Pride celebrated its seventy-fifth anniversary with the marching band's premiere international performance in Dublin, Ireland. Invited by the Lord Mayor, the band marched in the city's St. Patrick's Day Parade and also played at St. Paul's Cathedral.

Also celebrating its seventy-fifth anniversary in 1995–96, the USM Symphony Orchestra enjoyed its first-ever sold-out season, which included a rare university performance by world-renowned violinist Itzhak Perlman and multiple concerts by the St. Petersburg (Russia) State Symphony Orchestra. Director of orchestral activities, and USM alumnus, Jay Dean who, in reporter Sharon Wertz's words, had "swept," into his duties in 1988 "supercharged with energy and big plans," was hardly content to sit on his laurels. For the 1996–97 season, he booked popular clarinetist Pete Fountain and former bandleader for Johnny Carson's *Tonight Show*, Doc Severinsen. Both had appeared at USM before, Fountain to help dedicate Reed Green Coliseum in 1965 and Severinsen two years later. At Severinsen's October 1996 appearance, according to the *Student Printz*, Dean conducted the first half of the concert in traditional fashion, after which "Doc" took over the baton and led the orchestra through a series of "sensitive, sassy, and provocative" Big Band numbers.

Dean of student development Joe Paul (right) replaced longtime vice-president for student affairs Peter Durkee, who retired in 1993.

In April 1995, the Department of Theatre and Dance's production of *Catfish Moon*, written by USM alumnus Laddie Sartin, won a spot in the prestigious American College Theatre Festival. Of the 900 colleges and universities that participated in the state and regional competition, only six survived to perform at the Kennedy Center in Washington, D.C. "It was big stuff," said theatre professor R. B. Hill, who directed the play. "I have never been prouder of this place, even when we beat Ole Miss in football." Of the other nine productions in the Mississippi competition, five were directed by graduates of USM. The National Selection Team, who judged all the regional competitions, heaped special praise on several members of the USM troupe: C. Glen Matthews for individual excellence in acting, Joe Renick for lighting, and the entire cast—Matthews, Canady Vance, Benjamin Craven, and Timothy Xavier Davis—for ensemble acting. Department chair George Crook was especially proud that *Catfish Moon* was the only play of the final six "in which all production and design was done solely by students."

Budget troubles hit the athletic program especially hard. In 1990, USM's football budget of $1.7 million lagged far behind the national I-A average of $10 million and even farther behind the Southeastern Conference average of $12 million. "Sometimes I feel like a son-of-a-bitch at a family reunion," Bill McLellan groused. "Decisions have to be made. . . . Students get mad about tickets and the number of home games. The coaches want money to build a better program. . . . The truth is we pinch a nickel pretty hard around here." In 1995, ticket prices increased (from $14 to $16) for the first time in nine years. When pressed about requiring tickets for small children, McLellan quipped that theaters "wouldn't let them in free." Student attendance had improved, from an average of barely 3,400 a game in 1987 to more than 5,000 in 1990, but the momentum was difficult to sustain. Response to a 1995 promotional gimmick proved disappointing. During selected home games, four full-semester scholarships were to be awarded to students whose names were randomly selected and announced at the end of the third quarter. Only two of the first eight students announced were in attendance and therefore eligible. A *Printz* editorial deemed such apathy disgraceful. "If you went home to Mize or Mendenhall," the editors scorned, "so mama could do your laundry and you could hang out with high school friends, it cost you $1,200. . . . Enjoy your clean underwear."

Jeff Bower's first full season as head coach got off to a promising start that included a second straight win over a ranked Auburn team. A disappointing loss to Louisville in late September, however, foreshadowed trouble, as the 1991 Eagles stumbled to a 4-7 finish with embarrassing losses to Cincinnati, Tulsa, East Carolina, and Louisiana Tech. The 1992 team improved to 7-4, coming within a whisker of upsetting eventual national champion Alabama (17-10) in Birmingham and highly rated Florida (24-20) in the Swamp at Gainesville. Sandwiched around the Alabama loss were victories over Memphis State (23-21) and Louisiana Tech (16-13), secured by Johnny Lomoro field goals, each on the last play of the game.

The Department of Theatre and Dance was invited to present its production of *Catfish Moon* at the Kennedy Center for the Performing Arts in Washington, D.C., in 1995. The play, one of only six chosen for the honor out of nine hundred in the American College Theatre Festival competition, was written by Southern Miss alumnus Laddie Sartin.

The true freshman's 52-yarder in the season opener at Memphis was his first collegiate kick, and Bower threw him into the fray with the advice, "Do it just like practice." Things ended on a high note when the Eagles stole a squeaker (13-12) at Virginia Tech, but a midseason loss at Northern Illinois probably cost them a shot at postseason play.

Hopes ran high for 1993, but a daunting schedule began with Pittsburgh in what Bower deemed "the biggest home opener" he could remember at USM. To encourage student attendance, the game, originally scheduled for the Saturday before Labor Day, had been moved to Thursday night. Despite national television coverage by ESPN, attendance was the largest at home since the Mississippi State game four years earlier. Radio voice of the Eagles John Cox relinquished his broadcast booth to ESPN and did the play-by-play from the photographers' deck in front of the press box. Unfortunately, Johnny Majors's Panthers spoiled the party, upsetting the favored Eagles 14-10. "Even though we didn't win," McLellan said after the game, "it brought us together." The newfound unity would be sorely tested over the course of a season that soon turned nightmarish. Following a 44-37 win over Northeast Louisiana at home, the Eagles dropped seven of their next eight games before the misery finally ended with a 30-30 tie against Tulsa on the road. The 3-7-1 record (Alabama was later forced to forfeit its 40-0 win) of 1993 proved to be Bower's worst. The turning point perhaps came a year later, as the Eagles, 5-5, closed out the 1994 season in Baton Rouge. To avoid another losing

The Atlanta Falcons chose running back Tony Smith in the first round of the 1992 NFL draft with a pick that they had ironically acquired from Green Bay in exchange for Falcon quarterback Brett Favre.

Brett Favre became USM's most celebrated professional football player, leading the Green Bay Packers to two Super Bowls, including a championship in 1997. Among his many NFL records were three Most Valuable Player Awards. In 1993, his Golden Eagle jersey was officially retired during ceremonies at M. M. Roberts Stadium.

season, they faced one of the most difficult tasks in college football, beating LSU in Death Valley. Down 18-17 with the game winding down, tight end Scott Harper made a circus catch at the LSU 12-yard line, but three plays and two sacks later, the ball was back at the 32. Chris Pierce then quieted the raucous home crowd by calmly drilling a 52-yard field goal to give USM a 2-point lead. The Tigers got one more chance but missed a 50-yard effort of their own as time expired. The victory clinched the first of what turned out to be 14 straight winning seasons for Bower. Ironically, it also sealed the doom at LSU of the man he had replaced four years earlier, head coach Curley Hallman.

On April 24 of the next year, USM took what McLellan called "the most important step . . . in its athletic history." At Harry Caray's restaurant in Chicago, commissioner Mike Slive announced the formation of a new conference (eventually named Conference USA)that included, along with Southern Miss, DePaul, UNC-Charlotte, South Florida, Marquette, Alabama-Birmingham, St. Louis, Tulane, Memphis, Louisville, Cincinnati, and Houston (the league later added East Carolina, Army, and TCU). More significantly, in the fall of 1996 the latter five would join USM in its first competition for a conference football title since 1951 with the winner receiving an automatic bid to the Liberty Bowl in Memphis. Slive also announced the signing of a five-year contract under which Fox Sports Net would televise a conference game of the week. Though the new league's immediate strength would be in basketball, where Louisville, Cincinnati, and Marquette had all won national championships, the prospects for Golden Eagle football were unparalleled. "Players all want to compete for a championship," said Bower, "wear championship rings, play in bowl games and play on television." Except for football, conference play would begin in the fall of 1995.

USM's final season as a football independent was erratic. It began with a refurbishing of Roberts Stadium that eventually included the transformation of the driveway beneath East Stadium into Eagle Walk, a gold-painted replica of a gridiron festooned with banners commemorating memorable players, seasons, and bowl appearances. The team's pregame parade, led by band, cheerleaders, and mascot, through the Eagle Walk into the stadium became a popular ritual for all home games. The home opener against Northern Illinois was moved to Thursday night, August 31, and dubbed "Sellout '95." Under the direction of a marketing consultant, a "Dream Team" committee sold almost three hundred blocks of tickets to area businesses and organizations. The result was the third largest crowd in school history, 33,092, who reveled in a 45-13 victory in which Fred Brock blocked a punt, caught a touchdown pass, returned a kickoff 95 yards for a touchdown, and finished the night with 204 all-purpose yards. The following week's 24-20 loss to thirteenth-ranked Alabama in Birmingham was almost unbearable. The Eagles led 20-10 at halftime and 20-17 with less than two minutes to play, when Tide quarterback Brian Burgdorf completed a fourth-down pass to Toderick Malone deep in Alabama territory. Facing another fourth down

The Eagle Walk debuted in 1995 and became the scene of a popular pregame tradition.

at the USM 35 with 17 seconds on the clock, Burgdorf again found Malone, this time in the end zone. Young defensive back Patrick Surtain, who got turned around on the play and lost coverage, would later redeem himself many times over, but the taste at Legion Field that afternoon was exceedingly bitter. After a 24-21 win at Utah State, USM traveled to Bloomington for its first game against a Big Ten opponent, Indiana. Two missed extra points and a blocked field goal handed the Hoosiers a 27-26 victory, and the Eagles dropped three of their next five contests, two of them on last-second field goals. Facing road games at Memphis and Southwestern Louisiana to close the season, Bower had reached the turning point in his career as a head coach. Two years earlier under similar circumstances, his team had collapsed down the stretch, but the 1995 squad ended the year with two gritty victories that gave him his first back-to-back winning seasons.

Reminiscent of the victory over Gene Stallings and Alabama six years earlier, the Golden Eagles began 1996 by spoiling the debut of new Georgia head coach Jim Donnan. Without crossing the goal line, they eked out an 11-7 decision thanks to three Johnny Lomoro field goals, a safety, and a game-ending goal line stand. After a 20-10 loss to Alabama and wins over Utah State and Southwestern Louisiana, Southern Miss played its first conference football game in forty-five years, a 24-7 win at Louisville. On the eve of a Thursday night ESPN contest at East Carolina two weeks later, Bower made what one sportswriter called possibly "the most controversial coaching decision of his career." To shake up a hitherto sputtering offense, he surprised everyone, including the ECU defense, by starting former third-string quarterback Lee Roberts. The daring switch to a redshirt sophomore who had played in only one series all season, marked a defining moment of the Jeff Bower era. After missing on his first throw, Roberts reeled off a school-record 13 straight completions, finishing 14 of 16 (87.5 percent, also a school record) for 229 yards and a touchdown in a convincing 28-7 victory. Roberts's performance catapulted him from obscurity to stardom. Over the next two and a half seasons, he would break almost every school passing record, including many held by Brett Favre, and help restore Golden Eagle football to a prominence it had not enjoyed since the early 1980s. By November, Southern Miss, now ranked twentieth in the AP poll, was only a win at Houston away from the C-USA championship. Defense took the night off, as the two teams combined for 1,049 yards of total offense in a game that went to overtime tied at 49. After Houston scored a touchdown on its possession, Brandon Francis caught a fourth-down swing pass

but fell inches short of the goal line giving Houston a 56-49 victory. Roberts threw for 398 yards, another school record, and Kendrick Lee caught 10 passes for 260 yards, also records, but the defense could not stop Cougar running back Antowain Smith, who rushed for 231 yards and six touchdowns, including the game-winner in overtime. The two teams would share the league title with 4-1 records, but the loss cost USM a bowl bid as well as its national ranking. The 8-3 record, however, the best since 1988, was a sign of better things to come.

The offensive line opens a big hole for running back Eric Booth in USM's season-opening 11-7 victory "between the hedges" in Georgia's Sanford Stadium.

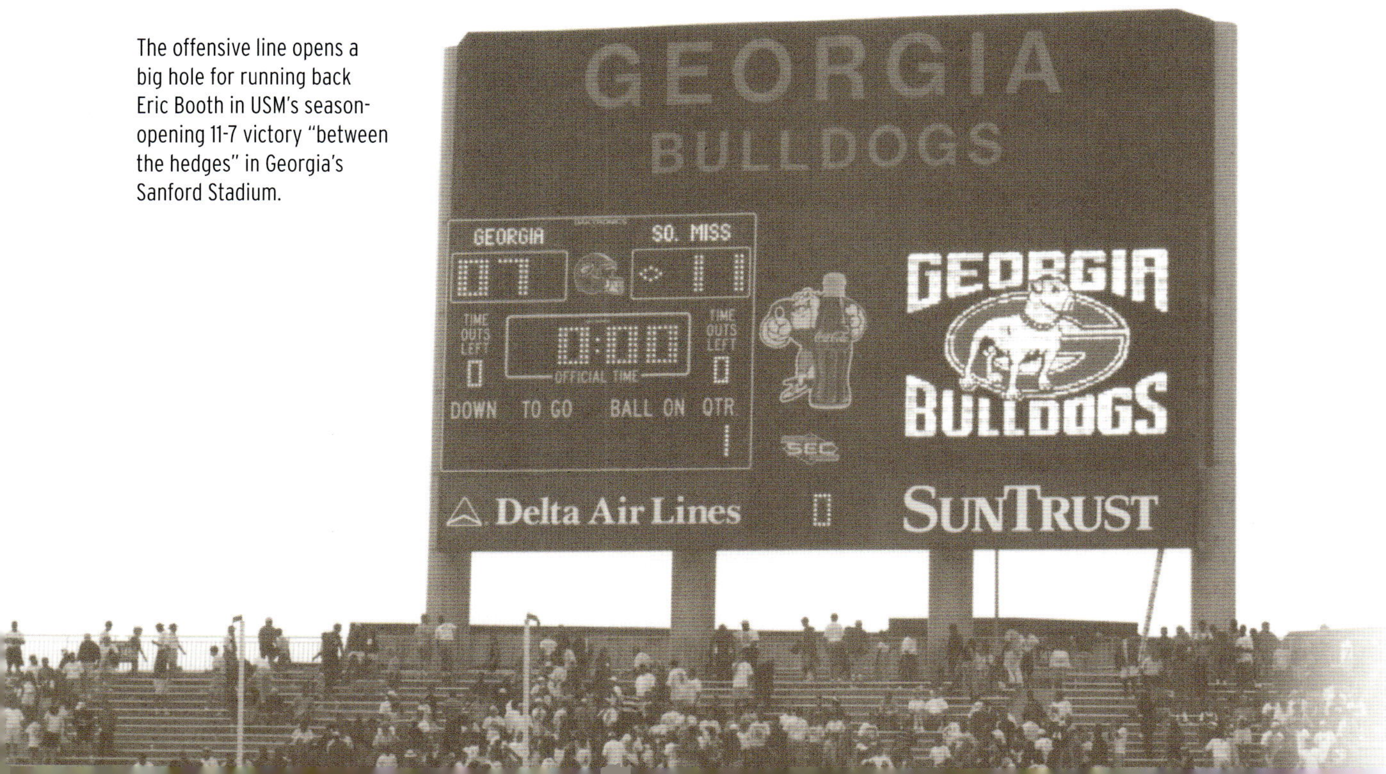

Quarterback Lee Roberts (1995–98) broke numerous school passing records, including many held by Brett Favre, and led the Eagles to two Conference USA championships and two bowl appearances.

In women's basketball, Kay James's thirteenth season produced a mediocre 17-12 record in 1990–91, but it also marked the debut of perhaps the most dominating athlete in any sport in USM history. Janice Felder led the team in scoring and rebounding and won freshman of the year honors in the Metro Conference. Over the next three years, she led the Lady Eagles to three twenty-win seasons, two regular season conference titles, three appearances in the Metro tournament finals, and two trips to the NCAA. She became only the second basketball player to win three Metro MVP awards, the other being USM's Clarence Weatherspoon. The 1991–92 team finished 21-10, won the conference tournament, but lost a first-round NCAA visit to Rutgers. Despite winning the regular season conference championship, the following year's squad failed to secure a return trip to the NCAA after losing to host Louisville in the Metro tournament.

James began 1993–94 with 381 career victories, 296 of them at USM. A win streak to open the season added eight more, and on February 19 the Lady Eagles defeated Tulane 89-66 to give James her four-hundredth victory, during which Felder also became the school leader in career rebounds. Three days later against Northwestern State of Louisiana, James pulled her star with 7:43 left in the game, thinking she had broken the women's scoring record. Realizing that she had only tied the mark, James sent her back in and forbade anyone else to shoot the ball. When Felder fed Sules Walker for an easy layup, James glared and threatened to "kill her" if she gave the ball up again. By season's end, she had amassed 2,275 career points, 139 more than men's leader Nick Revon. Despite a Metro tournament loss to Virginia Tech, the Lady Eagles earned host privileges in the NCAA, first against Tennessee State, winning 86-72, and then Western Kentucky. A thrilling three-point victory over the Hilltoppers vaulted USM into the "sweet sixteen," but the most successful basketball season in Golden Eagle history came to an end in Piscataway, New Jersey, with a 78-64 loss to Connecticut. The team finished 26-5 and sixteenth in the AP poll, and James was voted into the Mississippi Sports Hall of Fame.

After winning two straight regular season conference titles, USM slipped to third in 1994–95 but rallied to win the league tournament. On March 8, 1995, in the last Metro Conference women's basketball game ever played, the Lady Eagles beat host Louisville 95-83. The 21-9 season ended with a heartbreaking 96-95 overtime loss to SMU in the first round of the NCAA tournament. The following year, Brandy Reed was player of the year in Conference USA's inaugural season, but the team finished second in the league and lost to Memphis in the conference tournament. The 22-8 record was enough, however, to earn the eighth NCAA bid in twelve years, and after an opening round win over Utah, the Lady Eagles were eliminated by perennial women's powerhouse Louisiana Tech. It had been a remarkable era, producing,

Coach Kay James holds Janice Felder's jersey, which was retired after the 1993-94 season. Felder led the Lady Eagles to three twenty-win seasons, including an appearance in the "sweet sixteen" of the NCAA tournament in 1994, and remains the only woman to claim three Metro Conference MVP awards.

Fan favorite and three-time Metro Conference MVP Clarence Weatherspoon finished his career (1989–92) as the all-time leader in rebounds but fell seven points short of Nick Revon's scoring record.

in addition to Felder, four of the school's top twelve career point leaders: Patricia Nash, Nedra Hosey, Tanya Bullock, and Alexis Hall.

With four starters returning from the only NCAA tournament team in school history, M. K. Turk's men entered the 1990–91 season ranked nineteenth in the country and favored to win the Metro Conference. A season opening upset of number six Alabama sent expectations soaring, but a disappointing loss at Tennessee Tech two games later brought them back to earth. Then came a ten- game win streak, the longest since 1967–68, which included a first-ever triumph over Louisville at Freedom Hall. In early February, USM was 17-2 and ranked ninth in the AP poll. Then, inexplicably, things fell apart, as the Eagles lost five of their last seven games, though the 21-6 record clinched the first men's basketball conference title since 1952. Despite a first round loss in the Metro tournament, the team earned a bid to the NCAA east regional at College Park, Maryland. For the second year in a row, however, USM played poorly in the tournament, falling to North Carolina State 114-85. Clarence Weatherspoon was again Metro MVP, and he and Darrin Chancellor made first team all-conference, while Bernard Haslett made the all-freshman team.

Beginning in 1991–92, Golden Eagle fortunes took a hard turn. After a remarkable run of five postseason appearances in the previous six years, Turk would see only one winning season in the next five. The Metro Conference took its lumps, too, as Florida State, South Carolina, Cincinnati, and Memphis all withdrew, and the league risked losing its automatic bid to the NCAA for five years. The addition of the University of North Carolina-Charlotte (UNCC), South Florida, and Virginia Commonwealth in April 1991, reduced the penalty to a single year. Despite his team's 13-16 record, Weatherspoon closed out a remarkable career, winning his third consecutive Metro MVP trophy. Early in the season, he eclipsed Wendell Ladner's career record for total rebounds, and he finished the year with 2,130 career points, only seven shy of Nick Revon's twenty-eight-year-old mark.

The most prolific scorers in USM men's basketball history, Clarence Weatherspoon (left) and Nick Revon.

Despite a 10-17 finish the following year, Turk broke the school record for career victories. An 86-59 triumph over Alcorn State on December 15, 1992, gave him 247 wins, surpassing Lee Floyd's mark, which had stood since 1971. In 1993–94, USM ended the regular season 13-13 against the twenty-eighth most difficult schedule in the nation. The Metro tournament returned to Biloxi that year, and Turk's squad earned a spot in the finals with victories over Tulane and UNCC, both of whom had swept the Eagles during the regular season. Though Louisville won the championship 69-61, Southern squeaked into the NIT field only to be eliminated by Clemson in the first round. In 1994–95, the Eagles for the first time defeated Ole Miss and Mississippi State in the same season. They also swept Louisville but finished 6-6 in the final season of Metro Conference play. After wins over Virginia Tech and top-seeded UNCC in the tournament at Freedom Hall, USM squared off against Louisville in the last Metro basketball game ever played. It was a bittersweet moment. "The new conference is going to be fantastic," Turk said, "but . . . the Metro has been so good to all of us." The final matchup was also fitting. "Denny Crum and I were around for the first Metro Tournament," Turk pointed out, "in 1976—he was head coach at Louisville and I was an assistant at Memphis State—and we were around for the last one. It was awfully special." The Cardinals won 78-64, but USM earned its seventh bid to postseason play in ten years, against St. Bonaventure in the NIT. A 75-70 loss gave the Eagles a 17-13 record for the year. Damien Smith joined Glenn Whisby as a second team all-Metro pick, and Kelly McCarty made the conference all-freshman team.

USM's first season in Conference USA would turn out to be M. K. Turk's last. December brought frustrating losses to Mississippi State, in overtime, and Ole Miss, in double overtime. Two months later, the team handed their coach his three-hundredth victory, a 62-46 win over St. Louis at Green Coliseum. In the first round of the conference tournament, the Billikens turned the tables, eliminating the Eagles 61-44 and ending their season at a disappointing 12-15. An injury-plagued Damien Smith again made second team all-conference, and Anthony Richards was voted C-USA freshman of the year. On March 12, Turk announced that he was retiring. "I sat down with Bill McLellan," he said, "and a coaching change came up. I said it might be a good idea." McLellan conceded that it had been an agonizing decision. "Times change," he said, "and it ain't what you've done, but what are you going to do . . . we have to have more attendance." Lucas, too, acknowledged his ambivalence about the move. "I wanted M. K. Turk as our coach for as long as he wanted to be here," the president confessed, "because I just admire him that much and have a lot of affection for him. We need more M. K. Turks here at Southern Miss. But life doesn't always work out that way."

Following several disappointing seasons, Coach M. K. Turk (far right) resigned in 1996. During twenty seasons, his teams won 301 games, more than one-third of all the victories in Southern Miss men's basketball history.

Turk betrayed no bitterness, bowing out with the same dignity and affability that had characterized his remarkable career. "I've been around since dirt," he said, "and it's time for me to start on something else. It's not a sad day." He was in some ways the victim of his own success. "When I first came here," he noted, "we were hopeful to be in consideration for an NIT bid. Last year, I apologized for going to the NIT and not the NCAA. The standards are high, and they should be." Turk claimed more than one-third of all the school's victories in men's basketball, but one achievement stood out. "Winning the Metro was big," he said. "Beating top ranked opponents was big. Joining the Metro was big. Joining Conference USA was big. Winning the NIT was bigger. . . . It gave our university more national exposure than any other event in the history of the school . . . academic or athletic, because that team received headlines coast-to-coast." Lucas agreed, emphasizing that "winning the NIT title gave us national visibility that the school had never had."

It took less than three weeks to find Turk's successor, Iowa State assistant coach James Green. The selection of an Ole Miss graduate raised some eyebrows, but Green came with a strong recommendation from his boss, whose USM credentials were impeccable. Tim Floyd's father, Lee, had coached, and won, more basketball games at Southern Miss than anyone except M. K. Turk. As an assistant at Idaho (also under Floyd), Alabama, and Texas A&M, the new Eagle coach had earned a reputation as an outstanding recruiter. Introducing him at the March 31 press conference, McLellan deadpanned, "If he can recruit Mississippi boys to Moscow, Idaho, he can surely get players to come across the Leaf River to Hattiesburg." Green, who welcomed both "the opportunity" and "the challenge," promised to recruit good students as well as good athletes. "We want the kind of person that will sit in the front of the class, not the back," he said. "We will look to recruit competitive people that love USM. We want players that will reflect well on this university and this community."

In 1996, Iowa State assistant James Green was introduced as the new head coach for men's basketball.

Under Hill Denson baseball blossomed in the 1990s. The turning point came in 1990, when USM hosted the Metro Conference tournament in an expanded and refurbished Pete Taylor Park. An 8-0 start, the best in school history, earned the first ever national ranking. After a midseason slump, the team rebounded to win 12 of its last 14 games and 2 more in the Metro tournament, enough to secure its first ever NCAA bid. The trip to the regional in Baton Rouge proved eminently forgettable with a single victory over Louisiana-Lafayette sandwiched between lopsided losses to Southern Cal (23-5) and Houston (15-3). Still, it had been an amazing season. The record 42 victories (against 25 losses) included wins over Mississippi State, Ole Miss, Florida, Florida State, and LSU. Kevin Young led the team in *every* offensive category except walks, batting .379, with 96 hits, 13 home runs, 75 RBIs, and 17 stolen bases. Damon Pollard was equally dominating on the mound. His 21 starts, 13 wins, 152 strikeouts, and 148.1 innings pitched remain single season school records, while the 11 complete games and 3 shutouts claim at least a share. Remarkably, John Gilligan's 11 victories tied the record for second most wins in a season.

The following year was almost as good, lacking only some of the marquee victories. Another midseason swoon, which included three losses each at Tennessee and Florida State, left USM 16-16 in early April, but a

Playing in an expanded and refurbished Pete Taylor Park, Hill Denson's baseball Eagles hosted the 1990 Metro Conference tournament. Behind the hitting of infielder Kevin Young (second photo from left) and the pitching of Damon Pollard (third photo from left), the team posted a record forty-two wins and earned the school's first trip to the NCAA tournament.

23-5 finish got them back at least to the NCAA bubble. Three Metro tournament wins, before bowing to South Carolina, produced a 42-22 record that garnered a second postseason bid, this time to Austin, Texas. Unable to bounce back from a disheartening 6-5, 11-inning loss to Long Beach State in the opening game, the Eagles sleepwalked through a humiliating thrashing from the host Longhorns, 18-2. The stars of 1991 included pitchers Marc Kubucki, Mark Carson, and Tony Phillips. Kubicki still holds the record for appearances in a season, 41, while Phillips's 13 saves ranks second, as does Carson's 11 wins, which matched Gilligan's total from the previous year. On the offensive side, Scotty Jurich set a single season record with 279 at-bats, and Todd Nace's .392 average and 105 hits rank eighth and fifth respectively.

After 1991, Hill Denson, like M. K. Turk, struggled to overcome the expectations engendered by his own extraordinary accomplishments. The years that followed produced great players but no 40-win seasons, no championships, and no NCAA appearances. In 1992, Bill Selby's 23 home runs tied Fred Cooley's 1989 mark, and two years later Tommy Davis hit .403, second only to Wilson Plunkett's record .453 set twenty years earlier. A two-time all-American, Davis also finished with top ten single season totals in hits, home runs, and RBIs. In 1994, the Boston Red Sox chose him in the second round of the major league draft, the highest ever for a Southern Miss player. He, Young, Selby, John Bale, and Chad Bradford eventually made it to the big leagues, and twelve other Eagles were drafted between 1990 and 1996. Between 1992 and 1993, attendance at "the Pete," as it came to be called, more than doubled to an average of 1,792 per game, ranking 12th out of 292 Division I baseball programs. Thereafter,

In 1994, the Boston Red Sox drafted two-time all-American Tommy Davis in the second round of baseball's major league draft, the highest ever for a Southern Miss player. He was one of seventeen Eagles drafted between 1990 and 1996.

Southern Miss became a fixture in the attendance rankings in NCAA baseball, prompting Conference USA to award its inaugural baseball tournament to "the Pete" in 1996.

Perhaps no one personified the USM legacy of pluck and perseverance as did Marshall Bell, the school's first black head coach. In 1979, athletic director Roland Dale needed two additional sports to maintain the university's Division I status in the NCAA, and he persuaded Bell, a 1971 graduate, to return and start a track program. He arrived in August barely a month before the first meet. Building from the ground up, he began with a $26,000 budget and two scholarships spread among seven athletes. Ole Miss launched its program the same year with a budget six times larger. "I established a foundation," Bell said, "by signing distance runners because they could run cross country, as well as indoor and outdoor track." For almost twenty years he labored without a facility, his team practicing at Hattiesburg High School and competing on the road. Somehow, he made it work. Within a decade, he had an all-American in Kenny Glenn, and astonishingly, in 1992, still without a home track, his teams captured both the men's and women's Metro Conference championships. Dale compared it to "having a Rhodes Scholar without having a library." Bell won Metro coach of the year honors, and the men's team won the title again in 1993. Two years later, construction began on a state-of-the-art track complex, and by 1996 work was far enough along that members of national teams from Kenya and Malawi were able to use the facilities to train for the summer Olympics in Atlanta. Finally on March 29, 1997, after eighteen "homeless" years, the Southern Miss track team hosted its own meet, the inaugural USM Invitational. "I'm like a kid in a candy factory," Bell beamed. Six weeks later, Conference USA held its 1997 Track and Field Championships at USM's new facility. Having seen a dream come true, Bell retired in June, and the new track was named in his honor.

Other minor sports continued to struggle, though tennis standout Katie Kocsis was Conference USA MVP in 1996, and Phil Meadows made the all-conference team in golf. Helen Grant was able to give up coaching responsibilities in volleyball after a 24-16 season in 1990, but not until seven years and four coaches later did the team produce another winning record. Grant was finally able to concentrate on softball, but it fell victim to budget cuts in 1992, and she became senior women's administrator and compliance coordinator for athletics.

In April 1995, USM earned high marks from a SACS committee that visited campus as part of the university's reaccreditation process. Southern Miss earned not only reaccreditation but commendation for "the high quality of its faculty," who were, according to the reaffirmation committee's report, "well qualified . . . and highly motivated." The visitors praised "USM's commitment to its own future," and its "general attitude of mutual trust and respect," noting that "almost everyone gave a great deal of credit for this spirit to the University's President, Dr. Lucas. His openness, sense of humor, optimism, confidence and commitment have helped build an environment that bodes well for USM's future." Within months, that encouraging assessment would taste bittersweet.

Summers on college campuses are usually somewhat uneventful, especially during the dog days that follow mid-July. At USM in 1995, the dog days were anything but uneventful, and the events that unfolded were historic. They began with the modest bequest of an unassuming eighty-seven-year-old black woman. Oseola McCarty had spent most of her life washing and ironing other people's clothes. A native of Wayne County, she moved to live with her grandmother and an aunt in Hattiesburg at the age of five. When the aunt became ill, Ola, as everyone called her, dropped out of school in the sixth grade to help with the family's laundry business. "I didn't go back," she later recalled, "I just washed and ironed." She never married, never owned a car, and after 1947 lived in a small wooden frame house that she inherited from an uncle. There she continued to

For eighteen years, track coach Marshall Bell (inset) labored without a home facility. Remarkably, both his men's and women's teams still won conference championships in 1992, and he was named Metro Coach of the Year. USM's new state-of-the-art track complex (above) was completed in time to be used by national teams from Kenya and Malawi training for the 1996 summer Olympics in Atlanta. Linje Nankhuni, leader of the Malawi team, remained in the fall to do graduate work in sports administration and to continue training. "It was love at first sight," he said of the university and its facilities.

Oseola McCarty's generosity made her famous. In 1995, after almost seven decades of earning a quiet living by washing and ironing other people's clothes, she donated the bulk of her life savings to USM. As her banker Paul Laughlin put it, "She reached out to help, and by helping she became a star." That year, she won the nation's second highest civilian award, the Presidential Citizens Medal, reserved for Americans who "have performed exemplary deeds of service for their country or their fellow citizens." The ensuing months were a whirlwind of celebrity appearances (*The Today Show, Good Morning America, The Oprah Winfrey Show*) and interviews with scores of news organizations (*Time, Newsweek,* the *New York Times*). The following year, she helped carry the Olympic torch on its way to Atlanta, released the famous ball at Times Square on New Years Eve, and received an honorary doctorate from Harvard. As her pastor Woodrow Armstrong said, she had "become the sweetheart of the nation." In 1998, she received the first honorary doctorate ever awarded by The University of Southern Mississippi.

Fittingly, fame itself profited others more than herself, as her "generosity," in Aubrey Lucas's words, "inspired many other people to add to her gift so that additional

Stephanie Bullock of Hattiesburg (left) was awarded the first Oseola McCarty Scholarship in 1995.

needy and deserving students may benefit from collegiate study." By the time of her death at the age of ninety-one, her Foundation endowment had grown to almost $600,000. On September 25, 1999, her body lay in state in the rotunda of the Lucas Administration Building, after which mourners gathered for a celebration of her life in Bennett Auditorium. One of the maxims from her book, *Simple Wisdom for Rich Living*, provided a fitting epitaph. "There's a lot of talk about self-esteem these days," she had written. "It seems pretty basic to me. If you want to feel proud of yourself, you've got to do things you can be proud of. Feelings follow actions." By her own measure, Oseola McCarty had departed with ample grounds to feel good about herself.

Oseola McCarty carrying the Olympic Torch in 1996.

take in laundry for a living. From her grandmother, she had learned the value of hard work and thrift. "I'd put money away and save it," she said; "when I got enough, I went to [the bank] and put it in."

As the years passed, she "began to think about what to do with" her little nest egg. And then it came to her: "I want to help somebody's child go to college." After her doctor insisted that she retire in December 1994, Paul Laughlin, the trust officer at her bank, advised McCarty that she probably had more in her account than she could reasonably spend in the years likely left to her. He suggested that she consider making provision for the distribution of whatever might be left at her death. He lined up dimes on his desk to represent her potential estate divided into tenths. After designating the portions she wanted to leave to a cousin and to her church, six dimes remained unallocated. That, she told Laughlin, was to go for college scholarships. "She said she wanted to leave the bulk of her money to USM," he recalled, "and she didn't want [anybody] to come in and change her mind." Laughlin made arrangements for 60 percent of her estate to be placed in an irrevocable trust administered by the USM Foundation. The six dimes turned out to represent $150,000. "I don't know that I have ever been as touched by a gift to the university as I am this one," Aubrey Lucas declared.

He invited McCarty to the annual fall convocation on August 29 to introduce her to the faculty and staff. Though she had lived in Hattiesburg for more than three-quarters of a century, she had never before been on campus. By that time, the news media, smitten by her story, had turned her into a national celebrity, and from all over the country donations were pouring in to the Foundation seeking to match her gift and enable the first McCarty Scholarships to be awarded in their namesake's lifetime. The president began his remarks by reading several tributes written about her. His actual presentation of her to the assembly touched off a thunderous and sustained standing ovation, after which he presented to her a framed letter from another president that read in part, "Hillary and I were moved by your gift to the University of Southern Mississippi. Your unselfish deed is a remarkable example of the spirit and ingenuity that made America great."

The mundane catalogue of convocation commonplaces that followed seemed anticlimactic until a single casually spoken sentence caught the ears of those dutiful enough to be still attentive: "Let me now discuss with you my professional plans," said Lucas. What followed was a bombshell. "I have informed Commissioner [Thomas] Layzell and members of the Board of Trustees that I will leave the presidency of this University on December 31, 1996." Audible gasps were followed by stunned silence. He continued. "Please notice that I did not say anything about retirement, for I wish to continue to do meaningful work for our University after leaving the presidency. Notice also that I did not say 'step *down*' from the presidency," for that implies that the presidency is above or superior to other positions in our University, and over these twenty years you have taught me better than that."

To dispel misconceptions, Lucas emphasized that his decision was not a response to any disappointment or illness. "I am in very good health," he reported, "and my mind is no worse or better than it has ever been." He still enjoyed his work, he said, and believed that USM's future had never looked brighter, but "very few long-term presidencies . . . end happily. . . . The time to step aside is when things are going well and when there are two or three colleagues who truly regret to see you do it." He was making the announcement so early, he confessed, because "if I don't go public with these plans, I may change my mind. . . and that will not be in the best interests of our University." Moreover, he wanted to be sure, he said, that the faculty and staff first heard the news from him and not from some other source. "Whatever success I have enjoyed as your president," he said, "is attributable largely to you. You are part of my larger family; therefore, you should be in on this decision." Also there was still much he wanted to do, he said. "*There will be no lame duck presidency.* You and I cannot even think about slowing the enviable momentum which our University now enjoys. . . . Let us go now to make the 1995–96 academic year the best one yet in the history of our University."

Early in 1996, the college board designated five of its members to serve as a search committee for Lucas's successor. Board member Carl Nicholson of Hattiesburg articulated the anxieties of everyone associated with USM when he said, "This is probably the most important search I've been a part of in my twelve years on the Board." By June, the committee had narrowed a field of eighty-three applicants

In August 1995, Aubrey Lucas announced that he would relinquish the presidency at the end of the following year.

to four, each of whom visited the campus for a rigorous round of interviews with the various constituency groups. Outspoken as always, history professor William Scarborough undoubtedly overstated the case when he asserted that "the general consensus with no exceptions is disappointment in the candidates." Nonetheless, his displeasure signaled what the presidential aspirants were up against. A *Printz* editorial suggested that "one of the major reasons for the controversy over the presidential candidates is that Dr. Lucas' shoes will be hard, bordering on impossible to fill. To put it simply, everyone loves Dr. Lucas. . . . We just hope his successor will ensure the university continues to grow and be distinguished." Lucas had made USM "a very democratic institution," said Scarborough, "by listening to students, being sensitive to minorities and establishing rational tenure procedures for faculty." He would be a hard act to follow.

A BOWTIE AFFAIR

Despite faulty memories to the contrary, Aubrey Lucas did not always wear bowties. "Years ago," he recalled, "I guess I did those things I thought looked professorial. I even tried to smoke a pipe one time, but Ella put a stop to that." He got the idea of wearing bowties during a trip to California, he said, and bought his first one at a San Francisco men's store in 1982. Bud Ginn insisted that "Ella had to tie it [for him] for years." Once, he said, the entire cabinet plotted to attend a meeting wearing bowties, but they couldn't tie them either. "The experts in dressing for success," Lucas once noted, "say that only clowns and professors should wear bowties–and I guess I qualify on both counts." In any case, the familiar sartorial insignia became part of his persona, and Homecoming 1996 was christened "A Bowtie Affair" in his honor.

Aubrey Lucas and his first lady Ella

By the time the board met in Hattiesburg in July to make its choice, a consensus had emerged in favor of Mercer University provost Horace Fleming. The vote was six to two, with Nicholson and fellow board member Jake Mills from Tupelo voting against the majority. "I don't think we ever had us all agree on any new president," said board president James Luvene of Oxford, and the two dissenters insisted that their opposition had not been personal and pledged their full support for the new president. Fleming had been the only candidate with "no negatives," said board member Nan Baker. "His strength of character was a key." In the judgment of search committee chair and USM alumnus Marlin Ivey, he "had all the qualities . . . we were looking for."

At its April 1996 meeting, the college board announced that the Administration Building would be named for Aubrey Lucas. Transparently unsuspecting, he responded modestly, "I am deeply honored." It was only the beginning. Over the ensuing months, accolades for the outgoing president tumbled one upon the other in profusion. An entire expanded special edition of the *Student Printz* paid tribute to the man and his legacy, page after page of patently heartfelt expressions of affection, respect, and gratitude. Bud Ginn, who served many years in the Dome, reminisced about his longtime boss:

> I've seen him so tired he couldn't function, but he'd go home and greet people at a reception and just get rejuvenated. He loves people and has more stamina than any person on this earth. . . . He listens with both his brain and his heart. . . . What sets him apart from most every president I know is that he knows everyone's name. He also knows their salaries. He really cares about what happens to people, from the person who picks up the garbage to the person giving a lecture. . . . He doesn't believe gossip. If you can't verify it, don't bother to tell him. He'll ask, "Do you really know that's true? If not, then it's not worth talking about." He can really chew you out in his own way, but you always come out feeling OK. You don't feel disregarded. He holds you responsible but doesn't micromanage.

Police chief Keith Oubre recounted just such an incident. He had changed the name of his department from public safety to police without informing the president. Soon afterward, Lucas saw a police car on campus and casually inquired whose it was. When told it was USM's, he exclaimed, "Oh, no, we don't have a police department." Oubre said that he and Joe Paul were summarily "summoned" to the Dome. "I saw a side of him I hadn't seen before, but it all worked out well." Ginn noted that Lucas was a stickler for "the social graces," illustrated by a summer day he remembered the two of them spent with Tom Estes roaming the streets of New Orleans in search of a conference table for the Honor House. "It must have been 108 degrees," Ginn recalled, "but he wouldn't let us take off our ties. He said it wouldn't look right." Lucas applied his standards of propriety as rigidly to himself as to anybody. "There are days I can see the stress in his eyes or the set of his jaw," Ginn said, "but you can't tell it in his manner." A tribute from the Division of Student Affairs best captured the poignancy of the moment: "Your vision illuminated our path; your encouragement allayed our fears; your selflessness helped us to distinguish ourselves. You leave us with the conviction to carry on. For all these gifts we thank you."

In an interview with Sharon Wertz of the *Alumni News*, Lucas offered some reflections of his own. He "could not have served with as much energy or as long," he said, without the support of his wife Ella. "She has a steady personality, thinks clearly, makes sure I eat as I should and think as I should." Her selfless support liberated him to concentrate on building the "distinguished university" that he had envisioned in his inaugural address in 1975. "In his own indefatigable fashion," Wertz observed, he had "led USM to a new level of academic credibility. The University has . . . become a major league player in a broad spectrum of research, service, economic development, cultural, and athletic areas. . . . At sixty-two, he still has the energy, drive, and boyish grin that has won friends, loosened purse-strings, and opened doors during his long tenure. He is a study in contrasts—elegant but down-home, relaxed but no-nonsense, charming but shrewd."

In 1996, the college board announced that the USM Administration Building would be named in honor of retiring president Aubrey Lucas.

Like his predecessor "Daddy Joe," Lucas put the students first. "The emphasis must be on what happens to" them, he insisted. Young Lani Pike understood. A 1990 graduate from USM-Gulf Coast, she decided to attend commencement only at the last minute and kept a diary of the experience. She had never before seen the main campus, and she was dismayed when graduation marshals hurried her along, "not even looking at me. Then I encountered the warmth and sincerity of Dr. Lucas. He shook my hand, looked directly into my eyes and smiled broadly, as if I were his own child. He said, with affection, 'And graduating with honors! That's wonderful.' I felt deeply touched by his sincerity." The report of the SACS reaffirmation committee acutely summarized USM's experience in the 1990s: "We believe it bears repeating that USM has done an excellent job in maintaining and developing quality under difficult circumstances and with inadequate resources. Its ability to maintain high faculty morale, broad-based commitment to the University, and a practical idealism in pursuit of its goals is impressive. We share the broadly held view that much of this can be credited to the leadership and personality of President Lucas."

Chapter 7

CHARTING THE FUTURE

OSEOLA McCARTY HALL

Hardy Hall on USM's Gulf Park campus.

Joe Cook's unceremonious ouster in 1928 had stirred deep anxiety within the State Teachers College family. The students called him "Daddy Joe," and respect as well as affection for him ran deep and wide throughout the college community. For seventeen years, he had provided stability and continuity; he was the only president anyone associated with the institution had known. In his departing address, Cook sought to allay everyone's fears. "As the years go by," he assured them, "presidents will come and go, but this college will remain on the job." In retrospect, those words seem as appropriate for 1997 as they had been sixty-nine years earlier. Aubrey Lucas, like Cook, had been universally revered and respected, and after twenty-one years as chief executive, more than anyone in the school's history, he was the only president many among the faculty and staff had known. Indeed, for more than four decades, only two men, Lucas and William D. McCain, had presided over the institution. Except for a handful of old-timers, the former's succession of the latter in 1975 was the only presidential transition anyone could recall. Barely a decade later, those who remained would have witnessed four more.

The first came at eight o'clock on the morning of January 3, 1997, when new president Horace Fleming arrived at the newly refurbished Lucas Administration Building for his first official day at work. Meeting with reporters later that day, he set the tone for his administration, noting that USM "is a student-centered . . . University." He hinted that upgrading technology would be a top priority and revealed that he had already commissioned "a study . . . to determine the feasibility of mounting a major . . . fund-raising campaign." Promising to elaborate on these and other plans at a convocation later in the month, he said that meanwhile he intended to conduct "management by walking around," eliciting from faculty, staff, and students their ideas and aspirations regarding USM's future.

When Horace Fleming arrived for his first official day at work on January 3, 1997, he was only the third president to do so in forty-two years.

At the promised convocation on January 23, Fleming paid tribute to his predecessor. "The selection of a successor to Dr. Aubrey Lucas," he said, "was—and is—a defining moment in the history of USM." Under his leadership, the university had risen "to a place of prominence nationally in higher education," and while "following" him would be a "challenge," Fleming acknowledged, his "record of accomplishment" had been "one of the attractions of USM." The new president stressed that his primary commitment would be to "compensate our faculty and staff adequately. . . . For me, there will be no higher priority." He reiterated his commitment to be student-oriented and pledged to nurture a "learning environment" distinguished by "the holistic education of our students and the advancement of knowledge generally." Civic responsibility would also be a priority, he said. "We must be actively involved in the expanding range of community and economic development activities of our state and community." In summary, he emphasized quality. "We cannot be all things to all people. What we do, we must do well."

Having outlined the general principles that would guide his presidency, Fleming turned to specific operational priorities. "The single most important thing that we can now do," he suggested, "is to reflect upon where USM has been, where we are now, where we want to go, and how we will get there. We need a strategic plan. But, more importantly, we need a strategic vision for the next 10 years." To that end, he shared his intention to appoint a blue ribbon "Commission on the Future of the University." He also announced that in light of the impending consultant's report on the feasibility of a capital campaign, he would soon name a committee to search for a new vice-president for university advancement.

Restating an earlier theme, he pledged to "work hard to see that we have the technology we need—not an easy task in view of other things competing for available dollars." That insight would return to haunt him later as the pool of available dollars diminished and the competition intensified accordingly. He concluded by affirming his commitment to shared governance. "We are a team. . . . I need your support. I also need your constructive criticism. My door will always be open to you. We also need to 'prop each other up' from time to time and always support each other professionally and personally. That is what the USM family is all about."

The new president would get to earn his spurs early. The university had appealed an October 1996 decision by the National Council for Accreditation of Teacher Education to place USM's teacher education programs on probation. During Fleming's first month in office, NCATE denied the appeal. David Huffman, vice-president for academic affairs, emphasized that except for the issue of field experiences, all the problems cited were "non-programmatic and . . . don't directly impinge on student learning." Though the programs remained accredited pending a reevaluation in 1998, probation was an embarrassment. The president pledged that "we will do what is necessary to make sure we continue to have a premier program." Indeed, the following year NCATE lifted the probation, thanks in large measure, according to the dean of education, to Fleming's "commitment to quality teacher preparation," which "set the tone" for the university's response.

Fleming had described his "style of leadership" as strategic rather than operational. "I will delegate authority broadly," he said, "while I focus more upon the acquisition of resources and the charting of a . . . course for the further evolution of the University." The NCATE affair, however, offered the first indication that internal operations would absorb more of his time and energy than he had hoped. Personnel turnover would plague Fleming throughout his administration. By April, he found himself facing the unexpected chore of replacing four deans: Tyrone Black in business, James Schnur in education, and Robert van Aller in the graduate school, all of whom announced their desire to return to the classroom, and Allison Yates in health and human sciences, who would become director of the new Center for Food and Nutrition Research.

In July, Huffman resigned to return to teaching, and his duties were temporarily assigned to vice-president for research and planning Karen Yarbrough. When Yarbrough announced in December that she, too, would retire the following June, Fleming decided to create the office of provost to assume responsibility for academic affairs as well as to act as second in command in the president's absence. The new post would allow Fleming, as he put it, "to get out and do some things that need to be done and yet be assured there is someone on campus coordinating daily operations." Searches for those positions had not even begun when vice-president for business and finance James Henderson announced his resignation. By the time Alumni director Ron Phillips added his name to the retirement list in April, the university was already searching for three senior-level administrators.

Meanwhile, Fleming had hired a part-time technology consultant, John McGowan, who found that academic computing, administrative computing, and telecommunications all reported to separate vice-presidents. In May 1997, he became acting chief technology officer and began "re-engineering" technology campus-wide. Shortly thereafter, all technology services were merged into an office of technology resources (OTR) under McGowan, who reported directly to the president. Preparing for the requirements of year 2000 (Y2K) compliance, McGowan warned, along with the need to "expand, improve, and streamline" operations generally, would cost "millions," but "through it all, Southern Miss has set its sights on striving towards, reaching, and maintaining status as a true cutting-edge university that will offer its students, employees, and alumni the best that the world has to offer."

Such an ambitious, and expensive, vision was destined for controversy, and presidential support would prove essential. Addressing the Y2K problem alone would cost an estimated $2.4 million, but "we have no choice," Fleming insisted, "but to move the dollars to this critical need." Murmurs began when OTR purchased PeopleSoft, a computer package that would facilitate not only Y2K compliance but also "a full redesigning of many areas of campus." Implementation began in 1998 with construction of a "core network" designed eventually to connect "every branch of the University system," including USM

In 1997, Ron Phillips retired after serving a decade as director of the USM Alumni Association.

Gulf Coast. At fall convocation that year, Fleming predicted that technology would become the institution's "greatest single program expenditure," perhaps as much as $20 million over the next five years. By April 1999, when McGowan could boast that USM was ready for Y2K, the original cost estimate had more than doubled to $5 million.

In the fall of 1998, Southern Miss offered its first Internet course, and a year later, more than fifty such classes were available. While some old-timers grumbled, many instructors and most students welcomed the innovation, and soon several buildings offered computer labs, including one available around the clock in Cook Library. In 2000, OTR began implementation of a new EagleAir network, which would eventually allow wireless internet access from virtually any building on campus, including dormitories. The project earned a feature article in *The Chronicle of Higher Education*, which in turn attracted inquiries from other universities contemplating "going wireless" themselves. By that time, the Fleming administration had spent or committed more than $10 million toward enhanced technology.

At the annual fall convocation in September 1997, Fleming unveiled his Commission on the Future of the University. Cochaired by history professor Marjorie Spruill Wheeler and alumnus Keith Cobb, former CEO of Alamo Rent A Car, Inc., the panel included thirty-six members representing faculty, staff, students, alumni, and friends of the university. Its mission, the president said, was to "weave USM's core values, capabilities, traditions, resources (current and projected) and, most important of all, our ambitions for tomorrow into a living document." Its report, due in the spring, would become the centerpiece of Fleming's formal inauguration and his administration.

At the end of his first year in office, the new president received generally high marks for his performance. He had particularly endeared himself to the campus community in July when the college board had granted all the presidents a 10 percent raise. Fleming diverted $10,000, almost all of his increase, to an annual donation to the USM Foundation for the benefit of faculty and students. At that point, a local reporter observed, he enjoyed "a near-unanimous show of support." External funding was up 13 percent, construction was under way on new buildings for liberal arts and theatre and dance, and he had approved a student proposal for a pedestrian brick plaza at the center of campus. Fall 1997's enrollment topped the previous year's record by 3.3 percent, and in September the IHL board approved the school of nursing's return to separate college status. Fleming declared in a December interview, "We've had a great year." Karen Yarbrough described the president as "an excellent listener." Everyone, she added, had "underestimated how much information you have to transmit to a new leader in order for him to have an opportunity to make decisions with a full background about a subject. . . . He's been a sponge in trying to absorb as much knowledge as he can from every constituency." In a different context, soaking up information could appear less virtuous, as SGA president Brooks

John McGowan became director of the new office of technology resources in 1997.

Moore hinted when he observed that Fleming was "decisive enough, but sometimes he puts things off because he wants to include the entire university in a decision."

A week of activities, including the report of the Commission on the Future, was planned around Fleming's inauguration on April 16, 1998. Inaugural committee cochair Stanley Hauer stressed that "the centerpiece of an inauguration is not the president, it's the institution. It's not a celebration of one man, it's a celebration of all of what we are." Fleming agreed. "I regard the inaugural," he said, "as symbolic of the continuity of the university and consider this the ideal moment to talk about the future." In an interview with the *Student Printz*, Hauer urged students to attend "what is potentially a history-making speech by the president. This won't be the typical inaugural or commencement fluff. This will be a substantial speech with the president reacting to the important issues concerning the university. It stands to be one of those tiny handful of moments that will change the history of the institution." In anticipation of the commission's report, Fleming said, "Questions about our future are too important for me to try to answer alone. . . . I am looking for committed, innovative, dedicated people who want to do something big in their lives and who are much smarter than I am."

On April 14, the commission presented a twenty-page document emphasizing three basic themes: a student-centered environment, teamwork and collaboration, and service to the community by meeting societal needs. Many of the recommendations were fairly standard

Aubrey Lucas and his successor, new president Horace Fleming, at the latter's inauguration April 16, 1998.

(increase compensation for faculty and staff, expand library holdings, recruit and retain more minority faculty) or reflective of the university's existing strengths (promote a global perspective through exchange and study abroad programs, promote the arts, recruit and retain quality faculty). Several, however, were bold or innovative and would bear particularly rich fruit and help reshape the institution's mission: strengthen the focus on economic development and entrepreneurial studies, increase opportunities for academic-industrial partnerships, develop a space utilization plan, improve the health and well-being of people in the university's service area, enhance the freshman year experience and develop service learning opportunities for students, expand the presidential scholars program, and pursue Carnegie Research II status. Perhaps the report's most significant recommendations concerned the Gulf Coast, where, the commission declared, "USM stands prepared to offer four-year, degree-granting programs at such time as legislative and Institutions of Higher Learning authorization and funding are provided."

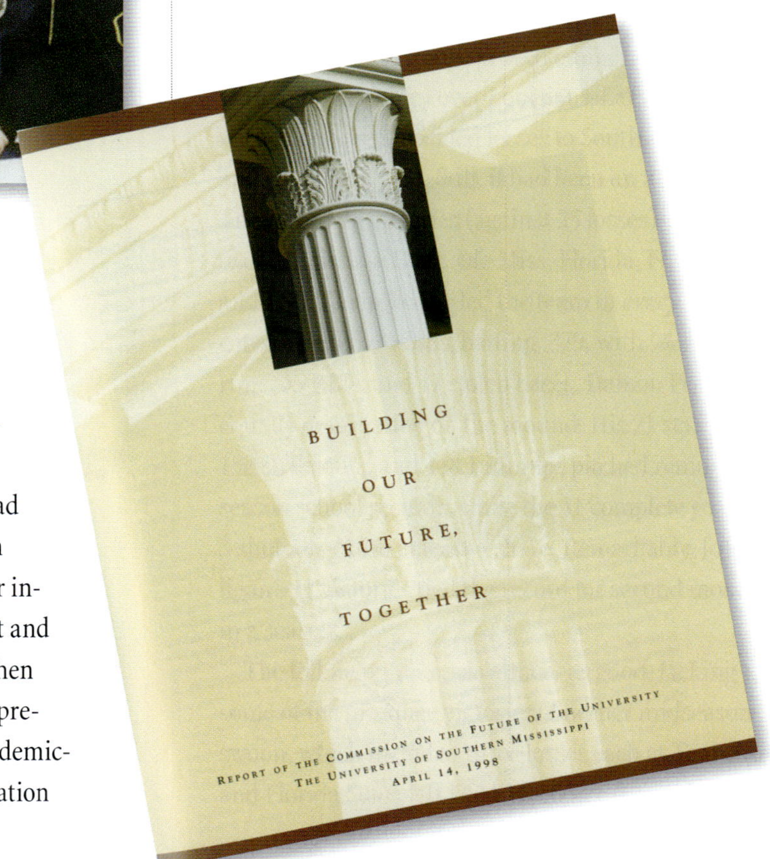

Fleming responded with praise and gratitude to the commission and to others who had contributed to its labors. "There are fundamental and significant areas of need in Mississippi," he said, "particularly in public education, public health and well-being, and economic development. . . . We will call upon each college and school within the University to embrace dual missions—one . . . dedicated to traditional concepts of scholarship and teaching and the other dedicated to visible, direct contributions to the social, economic, and cultural well-being of our state and our society, with emphasis on these three critical areas of need." The next task, he suggested, would be to convert the commission's vision into a concrete strategic plan that would provide a blueprint for "The Southern Miss Model." Though gratified by a 13 percent surge in enrollment over the previous five years, he said, "We do not seek to be the largest university in Mississippi. But we do intend to be the best that we can be. . . . We cannot be all things to all people. . . . Quality, quality, quality; we will not sacrifice quality. What we choose to do, we will do well."

President Fleming and his administrative team: (seated, left to right) Joe Paul, vice-president for student affairs; Lynda Gilbert, vice-president for business and finance; Myron Henry, provost; Don Cotten, vice-president for research; (standing) Bud Ginn, vice-president for administrative affairs; Fleming; Curt Redden, vice-president for advancement; and James Williams, vice-president for USM Gulf Coast.

By summer, Fleming was able to introduce his new administrative team. In March, new vice-president for advancement Curt Redden joined Lucas holdovers Bud Ginn, vice-president for administrative affairs; Joe Paul, vice-president for student affairs; and James Williams, USM Gulf Coast dean since 1993, who had been given the title vice-president in February. In June, Myron Henry was named provost; he had most recently held the same post at Kent State University in Ohio. Two months later Donald Cotten took over as vice-president for research, and Lynda Gilbert became vice-president for business and finance. Gilbert had held a similar position at the Arkansas Agricultural Experiment Station, and Cotten had been a longtime professor and administrator at USM. At a press conference in August, Fleming introduced the old and new vice-presidents as the "team that will lead us to the next level."

Not all the personnel changes were at the cabinet level. Earlier in the summer, new deans had been named for business administration, William Gunther, and education and psychology, Carl Martray. Jayne Perkins replaced longtime registrar Danny Montgomery, who retired in the fall, and Bob Pierce became only the third executive director of the Alumni Association in school history. An alumnus himself, Pierce had earlier been

Under new Alumni Association director Bob Pierce, the *USM Alumni News* gave way to an enhanced and expanded publication, *The Talon*.

assistant director of development for athletic fundraising. Upon his departure to join a private marketing firm in 1995, he told *Student Printz* reporter Scott Walker, "I can't rule out the fact that I may one day be back at Southern Miss." Walker presciently responded, "The university could only hope to be so lucky." As Alumni director, Pierce promised to "attempt to control sudden outbursts of passion for USM," but that devotion to his alma mater and his determination to "push Southern Miss to the limits of its potential" would become renowned. To him goes much of the credit for two early innovations, one official, the other less so. In 2000, the *USM Alumni News* gave way to an expanded and more colorful publication, *The Talon*, whose enhanced graphics and new name were pitched to a broader readership. The informal modification issued from Pierce's agreement with others that to the outside world, the institution's unique identity was inseparable from the name Southern Miss, which, in preference to all others, including USM, he sought to make the standard term of reference for the university.

One of the new provost's first tasks was to lead the effort to transform the report of the Commission on the Future into a strategic plan. In December 1998, Fleming appointed a twenty- member strategic planning committee, chaired by Henry and charged with developing a rough draft that was to include a recommendation on a capital campaign. Four months later, the committee presented a document that proposed eighteen major initiatives divided into two categories. The first included commitments to attain Research II status in the Carnegie Foundation's ranking system, to continue to improve technology, to pursue dual campus status for USM Gulf Coast, to consolidate the Center for International Education's (CIE) reputation for national leadership in its field, to secure resources for construction of new facilities, and to undertake a major fund-raising drive. The second set of objectives included more vigorous promotion of diversity among faculty and staff, maintenance of statewide leadership in teacher training, increased community partnerships and public service efforts, and modification or even elimination of programs where appropriate. The plan would set Southern Miss on a course to become "a national university for the Gulf South." It would also, said Fleming, provide the basis for launching an ambitious capital campaign. "Our task now," he concluded, "is to bring the strategic plan to life through annual planning and resource allocations tied to it."

At the midpoint of his four-year contract, Fleming noted two issues that would receive particular priority in the immediate future: expansion of USM Gulf Coast and consolidation of the university's efforts in community and economic development. Regarding the latter, three existing programs, all with roots in the early 1980s, converged in 1998 to create a new Department of Economic Development. In the spring of 1980, the Department of Geography and Area Development first offered a master of science degree in economic development, the only such graduate program in the country. Nine years later, professors Ron Swager and Richard Larkin secured a federal grant to create a Center for Community and Economic Development with the dual mission of supporting the economic development activities of communities and agencies, especially in south Mississippi, and providing practical experience to USM students studying economic development.

Meanwhile, in 1982 the College of Business Administration (CBA) created an International Business Center under director Eddie Lewis. Six years later, in conjunction with CIE, Lewis developed a Japanese studies program, under which USM students earned credit while studying abroad and also got to meet and interact with Japanese executives and other business professionals. The same year, CBA and CIE launched a Latin American executive development program that brought businessmen from Central America to USM to take business courses and to explore potential trade relations between their home countries and Mississippi. In the early nineties, CBA and CIE established a similar program for Japanese executives. Midwife for that venture was Michyna Sawada, a former official with the Japanese Ministry of Education whom Lewis had met during one of her visits to Japan. Sawada persuaded Yasuto Kaetsu, founder of Kaetsu Women's College in Tokyo, to host a reception for friends and associates of USM in Japan. An exchange program between Kaetsu and USM soon emerged; Kaetsu himself toured the Hattiesburg campus in 1994, and President Lucas reciprocated the following year. By 1997, fifteen Kaetsu students, including two volleyball players, were enrolled at Southern Miss. The following year, Eddie Lewis became USM's first Kaetsu Distinguished Professor in International Business, thanks to a $250,000 endowment provided by the Kaetsu Educational Foundation. She was also awarded an honorary professorship by Kaetsu College. The Kaetsu-Southern Miss partnership, said Lewis, reflects USM's "commitment to be the best international business program in the region and one of the top programs nationwide."

Eddie Lewis (pictured here with Yasuto Kaetsu, founder of Kaetsu Women's University in Japan) pioneered USM's Japanese studies program. Founding director of USM's Center for International Business, in 1998 she became the first to hold the Kaetsu Distinguished Professorship in International Business, endowed at Southern Miss by the Kaetsu Educational Foundation.

The American Economic Development Council transferred its Economic Development Research Institute from Ohio to USM in 1998 and its professional journal, *Economic Development Review*, a year later. "We are bringing all of our economic development efforts into one focused unit," said President Fleming. "Then we will work hard to strengthen that unit through our mission priorities: teaching, research, and service." In September 1998, the Department of Geography and Area Development moved from liberal arts to become part of a new Department of Economic Development in the College of International and Continuing Education. Dean Tim Hudson added associate vice-president for administrative affairs to his title, and former Alumni Association president Robert Ingram was named executive director of economic development. The department would "offer a learning environment that is," said Hudson, "interdisciplinary, global in scope, analytical in content, and practical in implementation." A year later, David Kolzow became chair of the new academic unit, which now offered a Ph.D. in international development.

Even before taking over as president, Horace Fleming had linked USM's role in economic development to the expansion of USMGC. His predecessors, he said, especially Aubrey Lucas, had built "a solid foundation" at USMGC, and "now, colleagues express to me their desire to 'move up to the next level.' This is going to be one of my top priorities." During Fleming's first year as president, USMGC celebrated its twenty-fifth anniversary, and in May he delivered the commencement address at the first such ceeremony held at the Gulf Park campus since 1973. "These are exciting times for USM Gulf Coast," said Dean James Williams. "We are at an all-time high in enrollment, our academic offerings are the most extensive ever . . . and there is a surge of interest for higher education on the coast."

That surge of interest prompted a special legislative appropriation that allowed the IHL board to hire a New York consulting firm to conduct a formal study of higher education needs on the coast. In his inaugural address in April 1998, Fleming heartily embraced the Commission on the Future's recommendation that USMGC add freshman and sophomore courses to its existing offerings. Inauguration events included a special recognition ceremony on the coast during which he revealed that Harrison County and several of its municipalities had committed $2 million toward construction of a new multi-million-dollar classroom facility at Gulf Park. Several months later at its annual summer retreat, the college board received and discussed the consultant's report, which recommended "an enhanced University of Southern Mississippi presence on the Gulf Coast with substantial independence and flexibility in adapting continuously to local conditions."

Acknowledging that "community colleges should continue to be the primary provider of lower division courses," the report affirmed that "continuing demand for a four-year university," as well as some of the report's own recommendations, "make it likely" that USMGC would begin to offer freshman and sophomore courses. A survey of "key Coast constituencies" revealed that of all proposed "arrangements for the delivery of higher education," most respondents "tended to support a comprehensive USM . . . and an expanded Upper-Division/Graduate USM on the Gulf Coast." Such a course involved certain "political . . . constraints," however, as reflected in the report's suggestion that "all steps should be taken to capture the capabilities and willingness of other Mississippi institutions to collaborate." To that end, the recommendations included establishment of "a multi-institutional center with USM Gulf Coast the lead institution." Finally, the consultants stressed the urgency of the situation: "It is critical that implementation of the recommendations contained in this report begin as soon as possible."

In 1997, USM Gulf Coast celebrated its twenty-fifth anniversary. Two years later, the IHL board voted to allow admission of freshman and sophomore students at USMGC, making Southern Miss the state's only dual-campus university.

After two years in office, Fleming considered impending expansion on the coast to be his "biggest accomplishment." At its January 1999 meeting, the IHL board bestowed dual campus status on USM, with Hattiesburg as the main residential, comprehensive site, supplemented by a nonresidential, metropolitan branch at Gulf Park. USMGC was authorized to admit 150 freshmen in the fall and to increase the freshman class by 150 each fall for five years to a maximum of 750. "The long-term gain," Fleming stressed, "is more access and more opportunity for people on the Gulf Coast and not at anyone else's expense." Foreshadowing the theme of a soon-to-be launched capital campaign, Fleming echoed the consultants' warning against delay. "We cannot afford to lose a minute," he said; "now is our time." While expanding its own operations, the university would also administer on the coast a multi-institutional center, under which any university in the IHL system could offer programs not available through USM.

Delays would come, however, as the community colleges and other institutions remained unconvinced that USM's expansion would not come at their expense. The first hurdle appeared in March when federal district judge Neal Biggers enjoined USMGC from admitting freshmen, suggesting that proposed freshman admission standards for USMGC might conflict with guidelines he had established for the *Ayers* settlement over which he was presiding. The attorney for plaintiffs in that case also charged that USM's expansion would divert funds needed for the settlement. Ironically, four white board members agreed. The Jackson *Clarion Ledger* reported that a "deeply split board voted 6-4 to defend the expansion plan," and three of the dissenting trustees took the "extraordinary action," as they put it, of refusing to allow the board's counsel "to represent us individually in regard to this particular motion." One board member suggested that the support for expansion, which had originally passed by a 7-5 vote, was rooted in "election-year politics." Indeed, attorney general, and potential gubernatorial candidate, Mike Moore had paved the way for expansion in November 1998 by ruling "that the IHL Board has the authority, in its discretion, to designate the Gulf Park Campus facility and/or other sites on the Mississippi Gulf Coast as campus or part of the campus" of USM. A week after issuing that ruling, Moore spoke on the Hattiesburg campus and declared, "I am in full support of a four-year facility. The coast needs to have more higher education options, and USM is a perfect school for that."

Within a month after Biggers had approved revised admission standards and lifted his injunction in November 1999, the state community and junior college board filed suit to halt expansion. Undeterred, USMGC erected a billboard on Highway 49 that proclaimed, "Now Admitting Freshmen," and by May fifty-four had enrolled. They would have to wait more than two years to take classes, however, as the case dragged on until February 2002, when the Mississippi Supreme Court finally ruled in USM's favor. The billboard went back up, and freshmen attended classes at Gulf Park for the first time in the summer of 2002. By fall, the freshman class numbered ninety-three, but USM received barely a tenth of the $2 million Fleming had requested for the expanded operations on the coast. Gulf Park did, however, enjoy two new state-of-the-art facilities, a $5.65 million Advanced Education Center, which had opened in January, and a $7.65 million Library. It was the most ambitious building project ever undertaken at USMGC and the first to benefit from state funds. Academic dean Joe B. Hill predicted that the improvements would "transform the presence of USM on the Gulf Coast, making us look like a modern, metropolitan university and not an afterthought." Volunteers, including Vice-president James Williams, formed a human "chain of knowledge" to help transport books from old Cox Library to the new facility, which was seven times larger and dwarfed the existing collection of 73,000 volumes. A "Bricks to Books" project was launched to fund additional book purchases through the sale of commemorative bricks that would pave the entranceway to the new Library with the names of donors.

Meanwhile, significant developments occurred in existing programs. In 1998, the Institute of Marine Science established new academic departments, in marine science at the Stennis Space Center and in coastal sciences at Gulf Coast Research Lab (GCRL) in Ocean Springs. Twelve researchers at GCRL were granted professorial rank and tenure, marking, in Fleming's words, "a major step in merging the traditional research laboratory into the academic structure of Southern Miss." The same year, construction began at Cedar Point, a 224-acre site near GCRL that Jackson County had donated to Southern Miss in 1995. Part of the site was to house a marine animal and ecosystem health research center that would be, according to Institute director Jay Grimes, "the preeminent

A turn-of-the-century construction boom featured a new $11.5 million Liberal Arts Building (upper right), a $12.7 million theatre and dance facility (lower right), a $3 million home for the DuBard School for Children with Language Disorders (above), and a $125,000 computerized sign at the southeastern corner of campus adjacent to Hardy Street and Highway 49.

marine sciences institution on the Gulf of Mexico." The remaining 109 acres of wetlands was to remain undisturbed. In 1999, the department of marine science at Stennis began offering the nation's only master's degree in hydrographic science, which involves mapping the ocean floors for navigation and other purposes. "It's going to . . . train the next generation of hydrographers for the Navy," said department chairman Denis Wiesenburg. Three years later, grants of $2.4 million from the U.S. Department of the Navy and $600,000 from the Naval Oceanographic Office enabled Southern Miss to create and administer a national Hydrographic Science Research Center at Stennis, which became the locus of the greatest assemblage of working hydrographers and oceanographers in the world. That same year, the Institute of Marine Science became the College of Marine Sciences, making USM one of only ten institutions in the country with similar emphasis on marine-related sciences.

On the Hattiesburg campus, Fleming inherited from Lucas two major construction projects, an $11.5 million Liberal Arts Building and a $12.7 million facility for theatre and dance. Their completion in 1999 began a construction boom that rivaled McCain's "dusty or muddy" era of the 1950s and '60s. The following year, a bricked pedestrian plaza opened, connecting Owings-McQuagge Hall with The Hub. Student government leaders, who had proposed the project in 1996, envisioned "an identifiable place on campus," said vice-president for student affairs Joe Paul, "that students could enjoy, remember, come back to and tell their children about." Vice-president for business and finance James Henderson liked the prospects for improved safety from both reduced vehicular traffic and enhanced lighting. Financed from the reserve accounts of auxiliary services, the $767,000 cost was eventually repaid through the sale of commemorative bricks for the plaza engraved with donors' names.

Fleming's first fall marked the third consecutive year of an ongoing housing shortage, and planning began for the first residence hall built on campus since 1968. Completed in 2001, the $13.6 million dormitory, which housed almost four hundred students, was named for Oseola McCarty. Fleming would depart in 2001 with additional construction projects totaling almost $125 million either in progress or on the drawing board. In 2000, the university

TRAGEDY AND REMEMBRANCE

In September 1997, popular dean of students Tom Shoemaker died tragically as a result of an automobile mishap while visiting family in North Carolina. "All of us . . . are shocked and saddened by this tragic news," said vice-president for student affairs Joe Paul. "Our student leaders have lots of love and respect for Tom, and they are feeling lots of grief right now." Student Government Association president Brooks Moore observed that "from training student leaders to counseling students in distress, Dr. Shoemaker's door was always open. He valued our opinions and encouraged us to go for our dreams. Our concerns were his number one priority. [USM's reputation as a] friendly and dedicated university with a personal family setting started in his office and filtered throughout the campus culture."

"Dr. Tom," as the students knew him, first came to Southern Miss as assistant dean of students and director of Greek life in 1992. A scholarship endowment for Greek students was established in his name, and Panhellenic Council president Courtney Zito reflected that "it was like we used all that Dr. Tom taught us to raise money for the scholarship fund that would allow us to give back some of what he had given us." In 2001, a portion of the brick plaza in front of The Hub was designated Shoemaker Square in his honor.

Tom Shoemaker

The portion of the brick plaza immediately in front of The Hub was designated Shoemaker Square in 2001.

Oseola McCarty Hall, the first dormitory built on campus in more than three decades, opened in 2001. The $13.6 million facility, which could accommodate almost four hundred students, was named in honor of the institution's most celebrated benefactor.

engaged a consultant to direct a campus committee appointed to develop a master plan for future physical expansion. "We're hemmed in," the president had told a reporter the previous year. "We're an urban campus. We've got to effectively utilize the available land without being wasteful. At the same time, we've got to respect the environment." Referring to the perennial parking problem, he suggested that a multilevel campus garage seemed inevitable: "some day, we're going to have to stack cars."

Under Fleming, Southern Miss continued its ongoing pursuit of national distinction in academics. Doctoral programs were added in nursing (cooperatively with the University Medical Center in Jackson), coastal sciences, international development, nutrition and food systems, administration of justice, and audiology. In 1998, the undergraduate degree in sociology was restored after a six-year absence, and the board approved a new bachelor's degree in museum studies for art, one of only four in the Southeast. The same year, two prominent consultants termed the nutrition and dietetics program, which had trained more than half of all dieticians practicing in the state, "the best-kept secret in the United States." In 1999, Mississippi's first interdisciplinary program in African studies emerged, thanks to a $360,000 grant from the U.S. Department of Education. Its study abroad component gave Southern Miss seventeen such programs, enrolling more than six hundred students each year. Also in 1999, the university began offering an interdisciplinary graduate minor in women's studies. Three years later, the departments of journalism and radio, television, and film became part of a new school of mass communication and journalism while the remaining unit from the old School of Communication, speech communication, became an independent department within liberal arts.

Polymer science continued its reign as USM's most visible academic entity nationally. In 1999, the program sought to change its name to the School of Polymer Science and Engineering, but Mississippi State protested vigorously. "MSU feels very strongly," said commissioner Tom Layzell, "about the use of the word engineering in the school and the degree." In a controversial 7-4 vote, the college board allowed Southern Miss to add "engineering" to its graduate degrees but not to its program's name. Instead, it became the School of Polymers and High Performance Materials. Shelby Thames stressed that "all of our other competing programs have engineering in their title. Now we're somewhat on the same playing field with those guys . . . as long as we have 'engineering' in our degree titles."

In 1996, Lucas had requested that the board name the Polymer Science Research Center in Thames's honor. "Under his leadership," Lucas asserted, polymer science had "become the most notable academic department in the state of Mississippi. . . . He has put us on the map." At the April 1998 ceremony, Thames praised keynote speaker Senator Thad Cochran: "He's the man that carried the water; if there's ever anybody who deserves credit for this building, it's him." He also credited Lucas and his predecessor William D. McCain, as well as former dean of the university Charles Moorman for their unflinching support in the face of strenuous opposition

The pedestrian brick plaza opened in 2000, offering an attractive and spacious environment that would, in the words of vice-president for student affairs Joe Paul, "enhance the tradition of The Hub being the focal center of the campus." To improve safety, vice-president for business and finance James Henderson instructed designers to make it "bright enough that you can go out there and do surgery in the middle of the night."

from most of his colleagues in the chemistry department. "He's a visionary," said current polymer science chair Robert Lochhead. "When he founded this program, the chemists and the physicists and the engineers never thought of polymer science as a sub-discipline. He set the pattern for the department." Though it had been his "dream," Thames said, "I had a lot of help. I was fortunate enough to have the idea and have nerve enough to stick my neck out." He recalled that when he initially met with the president, "it took us about thirty minutes to decide to put the department in motion," but McCain added a stern warning, "Thames, don't embarrass me."

Lucas disclaimed any knowledge of polymer science, "but I know a good deal about polymer scientists," he said. "They work very hard, they demand a lot of themselves and their students, and they expect a lot from their president in terms of support." In a revealing quip, Thames had once told an interviewer, "I'm not interested in studying the sex life of the tsetse fly. I want to do something." Both his comments and Lucas's would turn out to be fraught with irony. In the complex milieu of a major university existed disciplines whose subject matter appeared more remote from utility than even the romantic proclivities of tsetse flies, but they, too, might expect presidential support for their labors, however seemingly esoteric. Thames would find it difficult to consider such labors valuable or strenuous, though he would also later find himself in a position that required him to deal with the expectations of an entire university community. The results would be unpleasant for everyone.

By the late nineties, Southern Miss students also were beginning to earn national distinction. In 1998, biochemistry major Paul Sykes became the school's second Rhodes Scholar finalist, and two years later Lance Brown fulfilled one of Aubrey Lucas's fondest dreams by claiming USM's first Truman Scholarship, one of only seventy-five awarded nationally to support graduate study for students seeking careers in government or public service. USMGC senior Scott Neilson's perfect score on the CPA examination in 2001 earned a Gold Medal and placed him in the top 1 percent of accounting students in the country. That year, Fleming's last, the percentage of Southern Miss students passing professional licensing examinations was extraordinary: nursing, 92; speech-language pathology, 94; medical technology, psychology, and school leaders licensing assessment, 100. After several years of steady

In 1998, the Polymer Science Research Center was named for Shelby F. Thames, and Senator Thad Cochran delivered the keynote address

DR. GIFTED EDUCATION

Frances Karnes came to USM in 1973 as an assistant professor in the Department of Research and Human Development. Distressed over inadequate opportunities for gifted children in local schools, she began to lobby lawmakers to correct the deficiency. The following year, an amendment to existing legislation expanded the definition of programs for exceptional children to include gifted programs. In 1979, she became the founding director of USM's Center for Gifted Studies. In addition to its academic offerings, the center established semiannual workshops for public and private school teachers, Saturday and summer programs for gifted students, a yearly Parenting Gifted Children Conference, and a leadership studies program with annual competitions in speaking, writing, and the arts. Karnes also helped found and for years led the Mississippi Association for the Talented and Gifted. Suzanne Bean, (pictured right with her mentor) professor of education at Mississippi University for Women and a former Karnes student, described her as "a positive and tenacious role model" for advocates of gifted education.

Frances Karnes

Michael Herrington attended his first Southern Miss program for gifted children at the age of eleven, and for several years he was a regular at both the Saturday and summer sessions. He later returned to Hattiesburg to practice hematology and oncology. "I think the center's programs pull a competitive spirit from the students," he said. "The gifted program allowed me this type of competitive experience before entering medical school." In 2001, Dr. and Mrs. Herrington made a substantial donation toward the establishment of an endowed chair in gifted studies in Karnes's name at Southern Miss. The Frances A. Karnes Center for Gifted Studies, as it was renamed in 1999, celebrated its thirtieth anniversary in 2009.

growth, enrollment dipped slightly in 1998 and, partly as a result of more rigorous academic requirements for returning students, again the following year. The slide ended in 2000, however, and the following year overall enrollment topped fifteen thousand for the first time.

Turnover among administrators remained a problem. In 1999, Bud Ginn, who had served in the Dome for almost two decades, retired as vice-president for administrative affairs. Barely midway through his third year as provost, Myron Henry suddenly resigned in January 2001 to become full-time professor of mathematics. Fleming declined to comment on what he regarded as "a personnel issue," but criminal justice professor and faculty senate member Don Cabana acknowledged that as the school's first provost, Henry had taken on "a difficult job." His decisions had on "some occasions" encountered "very strong disagreements" from more than a few members of the faculty. To replace him, Fleming chose Anselm Griffin, whose former duties as dean of the graduate school fell to Donald Cotten, who also retained his position as vice-president for research.

In 1999, the Kaplan *Newsweek* College Catalogue rated USM as a "top school" in several categories, including "best value for your money." Based on a national survey of high school guidance counselors, the catalogue also ranked Southern Miss among the best in extracurricular activities, individual academic attention, basic liberal arts education, and study abroad opportunities. An even more significant rating came the following year, when the Carnegie Foundation for the Advancement of Teaching listed USM among the 150 schools in its highest classification, "Doctoral/Research Extensive Institution." Cotten explained that the new Carnegie status "opens the door" to research dollars for which "we have not been historically competitive." Indeed, between 1997 and 2002, funds generated from external sources tripled, from $20.6 million to $62.7 million. In 1998, the USM Research Foundation was established to facilitate the transfer of such gifts as Solutia, Inc.'s donation that year of $1.4 million worth of technology, patents, and other intellectual property to the polymer science department. Nor did the growing emphasis on research come at the expense of teaching. "At our institution," Provost Griffin insisted, "research and teaching are so locked together, they are inseparable. . . . It's all part of the same activity."

In 1998, a decade after being separated from the Alumni Association, the USM Foundation provided more than $830,000 in scholarships to almost 450 students, including 30 Honors College Presidential Scholars. Six endowed professorships generated more than $2.5 million annually, and the Foundation claimed more than $40 million in total assets. Perhaps the most unusual came from 1964 graduate Gene Carlisle, who in 2000 donated one of his forty-six Wendy's franchises to the university. Southern Miss leased the property back to the Carlisle Corporation, which continued to operate the restaurant with a portion of the sales going to the university. By 1999, more than two hundred donors had committed $30 million through a Founders' Society which allowed them to give to the Foundation through estate planning.

Like administration, athletics underwent a significant changing of the guard in the late 1990s. M. K. Turk had retired in 1996, and a year later Hill Denson and Marshall Bell followed suit. Denson had put Southern Miss baseball on the map with 468 victories, 12 winning seasons, 2 trips (the school's first) to the NCAA tournament, and attendance annually among the nation's best. At a June 4, 1997, press conference, Denson joked, "I have always enjoyed beating [Mississippi State coach] Ron Polk. He is expected to announce his retirement later today, and, just so I can beat him one last time, I'm announcing mine first." Athletic director Bill McLellan immediately named Denson's assistant and former Eagle catcher Corky Palmer as the new coach. Alabama assistant Wayne Williams replaced Bell, who had coached USM's track teams since their inception in 1979. Following three disappointing seasons, including an 11-17 record in 1998–99, her worst in 22 years at the helm, Kay James's career at Southern Miss ended in March 1999. "The team's had some great seasons," said associate athletic director Helen Grant, "but the last couple of years have been .500-seasons. . . . We felt it was time to make a change." In the school's athletic history, only baseball's Pete Taylor spent more years as a head coach than James, and she had directed arguably the most successful program in any sport since Pie Vann's retirement in 1968. She had once said modestly, "I want to be remembered as a Christian coach who loved her players and did her best to represent this university well." Her successor was Liberty University head coach Rick Reeves.

Employees watch as President Fleming and alumnus Gene Carlisle take a turn at flipping burgers in USM's own commercial restaurant. Carlisle, a 1964 graduate and successful entrepreneur, donated one of his many Wendy's franchises to his alma mater in 2000. The Carlisle Corporation continued to operate the establishment under lease with a portion of the revenues going to the university.

Also in 1999, McLellan retired after thirteen years as athletic director. Blunt and businesslike, he had not always been "Mr. Congeniality," but the athletic program had made significant strides under his leadership. The budget had grown from $2.7 million in 1986 to more than $9 million, and in 1998 Eagle Club membership topped three thousand, raising a record $1.1 million for athletic scholarships. Plans were under way for a multi-million-dollar athletic center to replace the Fairchild Field House, which had seen no major expansion since the M-Club sponsored additions in the late eighties. McLellan had played a critical role in the emergence of Conference USA. "Bill is the dean of our athletic directors," said commissioner Mike Slive, "and his contributions . . . were invaluable, especially in football where his national reputation lent great credibility to our young league." During McLellan's tenure, the graduation rate for athletes was higher than the university average in all but one year. While many schools had sacrificed quality for quantity to achieve gender equity, McLellan insisted, "If we can't be competitive, then I don't want to put a team out there." The Office of Civil Rights' principle of "proportionality" required the percentage of female student-athletes to reflect that of the student body, and in 1996 only 9 of 107 Division I-A schools met the requirement. With a population almost 60 percent female, Southern Miss found it especially difficult and expensive to maintain competitive programs. Nonetheless, women's soccer was added in 1997, and softball was in the midst of its first season since being discontinued in 1992 when McLellan announced his retirement.

In 1997, former Golden Eagle catcher and coaching assistant Corky Palmer was named head coach for the Southern Miss baseball team. In 2001, the playing field at Pete Taylor Park was named for retired coach Hill Denson, whose legacies included the popular "Right Field Roost," where rabid Eagle fans cooked, cheered, and made life miserable for opposing outfielders and relief pitchers.

McLellan's replacement was Northeast Louisiana athletic director Richard Giannini, who came to Southern Miss with thirty-two years of experience in athletic administration and sports marketing. His career included stints at Duke and his alma mater Florida, as well as the NCAA. He said that his top priority at Southern Miss would be development. "I will be a tireless worker," he pledged, "to take this university to a higher level. I'll be the first guy to meet people for fundraising. . . . Vision is expensive, but I'm going to get the fundraising done." His second goal, he said, would be marketing; "If we don't have people in the seats then we can't succeed." During the summer of 1999, he spoke to fifty groups and five thousand people, and by the end of his first year he had raised $8 million

for facilities. In 2000, a separate foundation was established for athletics, and a year later Eagle Club funding approached $1.5 million. Also in 2001, a new baseball clubhouse and office complex (later named for donors Charles "Bubba" and Sharon Rogers, Scott Thames, Clay and Cindy Thames, and Nick and Gigi Welch) opened at Pete Taylor Park. The $800,000 facility was totally funded by private contributions. The same year, a new softball complex was completed and ready for use in 2002. In the fall of 2002, the football team, administrative personnel, and coaches for most sports moved into a new $9.3 million Athletic Center.

Nineteen ninety-seven would be a bittersweet season for Jeff Bower. In an ironic April interview for the school newspaper, his wife Debbie described him as "an incredible family man. . . . Those two little girls are the most important things to him. Every coach needs to have daughters." Five months later on the eve of the first home game, the elder, seventeen-year-old Kristen was killed in an automobile accident. Bower's handling of painful personal tragedy earned him a measure of admiration that no professional accomplishment could ever match. "This is a death in our family," said running back Harold Shaw. "He is like a father to all of us. When he hurts, we hurt too." And the hurt was long and deep. "I don't know if the pain will ever stop," Bower later said. "I don't know that you ever get over it. You just learn to deal with it a little better." He dealt with it by pouring himself with renewed dedication into what he had left, his family and his team. A prominent national columnist noted that by "the manner in which he handled the ultimate adversity, Bower became much more than a coach; he became a sterling example of everything that is right in the profession."

Under athletic director Bill McLellan, Southern Miss made significant progress toward gender equity without sacrificing quality.

During the summer of 1997, the athletic department decided to capitalize on tradition by reviving the old stadium nickname, and "The Rock at Southern Miss" was painted prominently beneath the press box. The season began with a hard-fought road loss at defending national champion Florida (20-6) followed by a dominating performance (24-7) at Illinois, the first win ever over a Big Ten team. By the time Houston came to Hattiesburg for Homecoming in mid-November, USM was 6-3 and unbeaten in the conference. The theme for the year, "unfinished business," had pointed to this matchup which had been so costly the year before. The Eagles did indeed take care of business, with a 33-point shutout that clinched a Liberty Bowl bid and at least a share of the C-USA crown. The regular season finale at Memphis was one for the record books. Harold Shaw's 188 yards made him the first 1,000-yard rusher in a decade, and Sherrod Gideon's 6 catches gave him 54 for the year, one more than Cliff Coggin's forty-eight-year-old single season record. Lee Roberts's 16 touchdown passes also tied Brett Favre's single season mark.

In early December, Bower, who had interviewed for the head coaching job at Wyoming, turned down an interview at Arkansas. "I am flattered that they had expressed an interest in me," he said, "because it is a compliment to this program. . . . Southern Miss is where I want to be. . . . I want to be a part of all the great things that are about to happen at USM." By that time, Eagle Fever was approaching epidemic proportions in anticipation of the trip to Memphis to face Pittsburgh in the first bowl appearance since 1990. By early December, Alumni director Ron Phillips reported that "the demand for rooms and tickets is far beyond anything

Fundraising and facility improvement became a major priority for Richard Giannini (lower right), who replaced the retiring Bill McLellan (upper right) as athletic director in 1999. Within three years, the Rogers, Thames, and Welch Baseball Center (above), a new softball complex, and a $9.3 million Athletic Center (below) had been constructed.

we have ever imagined or experienced." Upwards of 20,000 Southern Miss fans turned Liberty Bowl Stadium into what John Cox's predecessor Bill Goodrich had loved to describe as a sea of gold. "I looked up behind me early in the game," Bower said, "and I got chills." His players did not disappoint, cruising to the largest margin of victory in Liberty Bowl history, 41-7. The defense's three touchdowns and Gideon's three touchdown receptions also set bowl records. At 9-3 the team finished the year ranked nineteenth in the country, and 13 Eagles made all-conference, 8 of them on the first team. Patrick Surtain won defensive MVP honors, and Bower was C-USA coach of the year.

The Golden Eagles began 1998 ranked in the top twenty-five, but they did not stay long, losing at thirtheenth-ranked Penn State and to number seventeen Texas A&M at The Rock for the first 0-2 start since 1976. After a 55-0 win over Southwestern Louisiana, came a disappointing 21-7

The old stadium dormitory had been known by its residents as "The Rock." Seizing on that tradition, Roberts Stadium was officially dubbed "The Rock at Southern Miss" in 1997.

conference loss at Tulane, marred by costly turnovers. The team rebounded to win six of the remaining seven games and finish 7-4, but the season ended on a sour note with a 42-35 defeat at the hands of Idaho in the Humanitarian Bowl in Boise. Adalius Thomas was C-USA defensive MVP, and running back Derrick Nix was conference freshman of the year. Gideon broke several school records for receiving, as did Roberts for passing, including his coach's old mark for career completion percentage.

In 1997, the Eagles won a second Conference USA championship and humbled Pittsburgh 41-7 in the Liberty Bowl.

After convincing wins over Tulane and Northwestern State to open 1999, the Eagles traveled to Lincoln to play fourth-ranked Nebraska. The defense held the Cornhuskers to 185 yards of offense and their fewest first downs, eight, in any game since the 1960s. Despite four Southern Miss turnovers, two of them for touchdowns, it took a last-minute interception of a Jeff Kelly pass inside the Nebraska 10-yard line to preserve a 20-13 Husker victory. A standing home crowd ovation for the valiant Eagle effort turned many of the USM faithful into fans and friends of the respectful Husker nation. The following week, turnovers again spelled doom for the Eagles in a 23-6 loss at number five Texas A&M.

Five victories in the next six outings vaulted Southern Miss into the top twenty and set the stage for a showdown for the Conference USA title at Louisville. Late in the game with the score tied at 27, an Eagle drive stalled at the Cardinal 37-yard line, and Jamie Purser came on to punt. Bower seemed to be severely reprimanding wide receiver Shawn Mills, who stood barely inbounds with his back to the line of scrimmage. When the ball was snapped, Bower yelled, "Go," and Mills raced down the sidelines as Purser faked the punt and lofted the ball to him 26 yards down field for a first down. Several plays later with 1:07 left on the clock, Brant Hanna kicked a 27-yard field goal that left Louisville fans stunned, coach John L. Smith crying, "foul," and Southern Miss Conference USA champions for the third time in four years. Soon dubbed "Mills Kills," the play had been designed, and cleared with the officials, by defensive coordinator Dave Wommack. The Eagles and their fans would get to ring in Y2K in Memphis with a Liberty Bowl matchup against Colorado State.

In 1999, alumnus Lamar Reynolds was honored for attending two hundred consecutive Southern Miss football games. The streak, which began with a 52-9 Homecoming victory over Texas-Arlington on October 3, 1981, finally ended at 230 in 2001.

In an ugly contest in front of the third largest crowd in the bowl's history, the two teams combined for 19 penalties and converted only 8 out of 36 third downs. CSU led in total yardage, but the Eagles hung on to win 23-17. Several notable careers ended that night. Sherrod Gideon and Todd Pinkston finished as the most productive pass catching combination in school history, ranking first and second in career receptions, receiving yardage, and touchdown catches. Adalius Thomas won his second C-USA defensive MVP award, and Bower was again coach of the year. The team finished with the highest final ranking in school history, thirteenth in the ESPN-*USA Today* poll and fourteenth in the AP.

USM started the 2000 season ranked twenty-second in the country but opened with Tennessee, Alabama, and Oklahoma State, all on the road. The Vols won the first game, but it was not decided until the Eagles failed to recover an onsides kick with 55 seconds left and bowed 19-16. After an open date, Southern Miss shut out the Crimson Tide 21-0 at Legion Field and then drubbed the Cowboys in Stillwater 28-6. By November, the Eagles were 6-1 and ranked thirteenth with Louisville coming to The Rock for Homecoming. The two teams fought to a third quarter tie at 21 when the Cardinals erupted for four touchdowns and rolled to a 49-28 win. USM's, and

Bower's, football fortunes seemed to turn on that loss. Since 1995, Southern Miss was 39-15 with an amazing 24-2 conference record, second only to Florida State's dominance of the Atlantic Coast Conference. From that point through the following seven seasons, the record was 53-38 and 39-20 in C-USA. After winning three of the first four league titles, the Eagles won only one in the next eight years. A week after the Louisville loss, they struggled to a double-overtime win against a mediocre UAB team and then squandered a 24-7 lead to lose at Cincinnati. The regular season ended at 7-4 with a 14-9 loss to East Carolina in a rain-soaked quagmire at The Rock. Southern Miss had dropped more conference games in three weeks than it had lost in the previous four and a half seasons. A thrilling 28-24 upset of LaDainian Tomlinson and thirteenth-ranked TCU in the GMAC Mobile Bowl eased the pain somewhat, but the season had been disappointing, and it was a portent of things to come. Defensive end Cedric Scott shared C-USA's defensive player of the year award, the fourth in a row by an Eagle. The following year's squad, playing without an injured Derrick Nix, struggled to a 6-5 record, the worst in six years, and sat out the postseason for the first time since 1996. Quarterback Jeff Kelly finished his career with the best completion percentage in school history and second only to Brett Favre in passing yards and total offense. He also won the Orrin Swayze Award as the top banking and finance student in the state of Mississippi and a C-USA scholar athlete of the year award.

Southern Miss rang in the new millennium in Memphis against Colorado State in the 1999 Liberty Bowl. Michael Villalonga (#49) and T. J. Slaughter await the coin toss with visibly grim determination that led to a hard-fought 23-17 victory. At number thirteen in the national polls, the 1999 Eagles finished with their highest ranking since joining football's major college division in 1963. Adalius Thomas (#97) won his second straight conference defensive MVP award, and Bower was again coach of the year. Sherrod Gideon (#11) and Todd Pinkston (#80) became the most productive pass catching-duo in school history.

In the late 1990s, the Nasty Bunch got nastier than ever under defensive coordinator John Thompson (center), and assistants Tyrone Nix (between Thompson and head coach Jeff Bower), and Joe Robinson (far right).

On December 18, 1997, Southern Miss named a coach for its recently revived softball program. Lu Harris had twice taken Nicholls State to the NCAA tournament before moving on to coach a professional team. Several players she had recruited to Nicholls transferred to be with her at USM, and two of them, pitcher Courtney Blades and shortstop Amy Berman, would play their way into the Southern Miss Legends Club for athletes. The 1999 team started 3-3 but won 47 of its next 50 games, 8 of them against ranked teams, and 4 tournament championships. In March they became the only first-year team to earn a top 25 ranking. After playing their first 40 games on the road, they returned to Hattiesburg to host the Lady Eagle Invitational tournament, winning all five games, the only ones played at home all season. More than 1,100 fans turned out for game two in which Blades recorded her one thousandth career strikeout. "It was some of the biggest crowds I've ever played in front of," Berman said. "I had chills when I took the field."

A 48-6 regular season finish earned a berth in the NCAA regional at Baton Rouge, which the Lady Eagles won propelling them into the College World Series in Oklahoma City. Two heartbreaking 1-0 losses, the first to second-ranked and defending national champion Fresno State, ended the Cinderella season at 52-9. The team finished eighth in the nation, and Berman and Blades were first-team all-Americans. Blades's 497 strikeouts set an NCAA record, and Berman led the team in hitting (.456) and home runs (15). Chrystal Stevens and Jennifer Ford also hit above .400, and Ford led the team with 60 RBIs. Harris was named South region coach of the year.

Rated fifth in the preseason poll, the 2000 Lady Eagles got off to a rocky 0-4 start, though every loss was to a top 5 team. A 24-game win streak down the stretch clinched Conference USA's inaugural regular season softball championship with the league's first tournament slated for USM's temporary home field at Oak Grove's Optimist Park. The pitching staff tossed shutouts in all three games, and Southern Miss headed back to Baton Rouge for another NCAA regional. Blades won her second regional MVP award, and catcher Kenya Peters joined her on the all-tournament team. In the championship game, the Lady Eagles defeated host LSU to earn a second straight trip to Oklahoma City. In the opening game against second-seeded Arizona, Blades pitched only the fourth perfect game in Women's College World Series history. Losses to eventual champion Oklahoma and UCLA, sandwiched around a win over Alabama, ended the season at 63-13. Erin Johnson joined Blades on the all tournament team, and Blades won the Honda Award for the nation's most outstanding college softball player. She also broke her own season record for strikeouts with 663 and set new NCAA career marks for strikeouts and victories. Of her 95 wins, 50 had been shutouts, 14 no-hitters, and 3 perfect games. After the season, Harris accepted the head coaching job at the University of Georgia, and Giannini chose Gay McNutt, who had taken Northwestern (Louisiana) State to two NCAA tournaments, to replace her.

McNutt inherited a fairly bare cupboard, with only two starters and eleven other players returning. Nonetheless, her scrappy 2001 squad fought their way to a 43-18

Coach Lu Harris (right), pitcher Courtney Blades (left), and shortstop Amy Berman (above) led the softball Eagles to the Women's College World Series in 1999 and 2000.

regular season record and won the school's second straight C-USA tournament title. Felicia Gonzales was tournament MVP and conference pitcher of the year, and she, Tammy Edwards, and Channika Gant were first-team all-C-USA selections, while Melissa Cundiff and Heather Bell made the all-freshman team. Returning to the Baton Rouge regional for the third straight time, the Lady Eagles lost their first two games to end the season at 46-21.

James Green ran a tight basketball ship. "I just believe that without discipline," he said, "you cannot have a good program." Anthony Richards noted that "practices are more intense. . . . Everything is hard, fast, and just all out." Green had little patience with free spirits. "We got rid of the sweat bands, T-shirts and girdles under the shorts," he explained. "We don't need individual attention; we need team attention." He believed in defense. In the fourth game of 1996–97, his team held South Alabama to 36 points, the fewest scored against a Southern Miss team in 34 years. That first squad struggled, however, finishing 12-15. Despite being picked tenth out of twelve teams in Conference USA, the 1997–98 Eagles raced out to a 13-2 start, the best since 1990–91. A five game losing streak followed, however, in the midst of which Green flew into a rage after a 79-67 loss at Memphis. Richards took the outburst personally and quit the team, as did football player Adalius Thomas, who was the first USM athlete to play both sports since 1963. Neither player accompanied the team on the flight to Tampa for the next game against South Florida. Thomas discounted Green's tirade, saying he just wanted to concentrate on football and classwork. Richards would rejoin the team

Seniors Rod Agee, Kelly McCarty, and Jimmy Floyd led the 1997–98 basketball Eagles to twenty-two wins, the most since the NIT championship team in 1987.

the following year. Led by seniors Kelly McCarty, Rod Agee, and Jimmie Floyd, the Eagles bounced back to win nine of the next twelve games, including two in the conference tournament. A loss to Auburn in the NIT hardly dimmed the accomplishments of what Green described as "the most rewarding team that I have ever been involved with." The 22 wins (against 11 losses) were the most since the NIT champions of 1986–87.

Despite the return of Richards and the addition of Indiana transfer Neil Reed, the Eagles slipped to 14-16 in 1998–99. An early home loss to Jackson State and an eight-game losing streak, the longest in fourteen years, were especially embarrassing, though Reed, who averaged 18 points a game, made the all-conference second team. The following year's squad improved to 17-12, and Giannini extended Green's contract through 2004, noting that "his players represent Southern Miss well on the court and in the class room, and that's a reflection of his leadership abilities." Transfer David Wall led the team in scoring and earned second team all-conference honors. After the season, the NCAA granted Vandarel Jones, who had not qualified academically and sat out his freshman year, a fourth year of eligibility. A recent rule change restored non-qualifiers' lost year of eligibility if they graduated within four years of entering school. Jones not only graduated on time but won a C-USA scholar athlete of the year award in 2001. Making the most of the opportunity, he led the 2000–1 squad to a share of USM's only C-USA title ever in men's basketball. Though early elimination from the conference tournament cost the Eagles a trip to the NCAA, Jones was voted the league's most valuable defensive player, and Green was coach of the year. A first round NIT loss at Mississippi State (75-68) ended the season at 22-9, but Jones set the school record for career field goal percentage, and Mel Cauthen finished third in career assists.

Kay James's Lady Eagles slipped to 13-14 in 1996–97, the first losing season in almost a decade, though Nedra Hosey closed out a remarkable career leading the team

In 2001, Vandarel Jones led the Eagles to a share of the only men's C-USA basketball championship in school history.

in scoring, assists, and steals. The following year's team struggled to a 14-13 finish despite an outstanding performance by Melody Reed, who led in scoring and rebounding. Also, junior LaShonda Jackson Smith, the school's all-time leading three-point shooter, scored her one thousandth point as a Lady Eagle. An 11-17 season in 1998–99, James's worst and last, overshadowed a brilliant year by Angela Atterberry, who led the team in scoring, rebounding, assists, and steals. Rick Reeves took over the program in 1999 and led Southern Miss to its first postseason appearance in four years. A televised game against Houston in February drew the largest crowd ever for a women's game in Reed Green Coliseum. The team finished 17-13, losing at Georgia Tech in the first round of the Women's NIT. Atterberry ended her career as the tenth leading scorer in school history. The following year, Angela Johnson joined her in the thousand-point club, but the team sank back to 12-16.

Corky Palmer wasted little time getting the baseball team back into postseason play. His first squad in 1998, led by the hitting of Jeremy Schied and Cliff Wren, posted a respectable but unspectacular 30-28 mark. The 1999 team got off to a 17-5 start and won a record 27 games at home, including USM's one thousandth victory. Michael Artman's .408 batting average, 106 hits, and 33-game hitting streak all rank in the top three in the record book. Dusty Haley led the team in home runs and RBIs, Josh Walker won 9 games while losing only 1, and reliever Tyler Kee registered 10 saves in 39 appearances, the second most in school history. The 38-21 record at the end of the conference tournament was good enough for a spot in the NCAA sub-regional in Tuscaloosa, where the Eagles won two over South Alabama but lost twice to the host Crimson Tide to finish 40-23. Despite notable performances by Haley, Darren Welch, Chris Finnegan, and Jeff Cook at the plate and Chad Rogers and Shea Douglas on the mound, the team slipped to 32-26 in 2000 and 27-32 the following year, the first losing season since 1985.

The 1999 baseball team won forty games and appeared in the NCAA tournament for the third time in school history.

In other sports, a major soccer publication ranked USM's 1997 squad, led by Stacey Hall and future head coach Gail Macklin, the fifth best first-year team in the country. Founding coach John Vincent left in 2000 and was replaced by Matt Clark. In 1997 and 1998, Tosha Barnicoat and Shalini Job led the volleyball team to its first ever back-to-back winning seasons, and Barnicoat was a first team all-C-USA selection in 1998. Santiago Restrepo replaced coach Steve Sykes, who left in 2000

Tosha Barnicoat won all-conference honors in 1998, leading the volleyball team to its first-ever back-to-back winning seasons, and a major publication ranked USM's 1997 soccer squad the fifth-best first-year team in the country.

after compiling a 66-65 record in three seasons. The men's tennis team finished second in the C-USA tournament in 1997, and Stefan Feyen (1997), Toby Simpson (1998), Dirk Rinehart (1999), and Miikka Kangas (2000, 2001) made first team all-conference. David Jansson was C-USA freshman of the year in 1999. Two golfers made all-conference, Greg Howell in 1998 and Tim Yelverton in 2001 and 2002. The track team produced two all-Americans in 2000, Wenston Riley in the 110 meter hurdles and Jason Wilson in the decathlon. Riley repeated in 2001.

Symphony director Jay Dean continued to be a tireless, and relentless, promoter of both the arts and the university. When he had first proposed bringing Itzhak Perlman to USM, he recalled, "Everyone laughed at me, both here and in New York." His persistence paid off, however, and Perlman's visit opened other doors. Ray Charles, who had performed on campus in the sixties, returned in 1998, and the world's premier cellist, Yo-Yo Ma, appeared the following year. Perlman returned in 2001, as did Doc Severinsen, who launched the symphony's 2001–2 season with a televised event called "Night of a Thousand Trumpets" featuring almost a thousand trumpeters recruited by Dean and his staff from high school, college, and professional orchestras in thirty-two states and three foreign countries. Dean quipped that when he first suggested the idea of "a night of 1,000 trumpets," Severinsen responded, "A thousand trumpets, huh? I can still probably play louder than all of them." The theatre department's production of *The Rimers of Eldritch* in 2000 won regional competition in the American College Theater Festival and earned the right to perform at the Kennedy Center in Washington, D.C. It was an encore for theatre professor R. B. Hill, who had also directed the Southern Miss production of *Catfish Moon*, which won the competition in 1995.

On April 20, 2001, the university announced the most ambitious fund-raising effort in school history: The Campaign for Southern Miss—Our Time Is Now. Susan Hollandsworth of the Foundation would direct the campaign, and President Emeritus Lucas would chair a charter leadership committee that would recruit other volunteers. "Our goal is 100 percent participation," said vice-president for university advancement Curt Redden. Priorities, which had been derived from the 1999 strategic plan, would include merit scholarships, faculty and staff development, expansion of USMGC, libraries and technology, athletics, and increasing Founders' Society membership to five hundred. Redden revealed that almost half of the targeted $100 million had already been given or pledged during the "quiet phase" of the seven-year campaign, which had begun within months of Fleming's arrival in 1997. The public effort would conclude on June 30, 2004.

It was not the most propitious moment to launch a capital campaign. In Fleming's first budget cycle, 1998–99, the university enjoyed a $12.1 million (11.1 percent) increase, but by the spring of 2000 the state's economy was in the midst of a deepening slump. Staring at a possible $11 million cut for IHL in the coming year, the university began bracing for its share of the shortfall. Almost forty vacant faculty and staff positions were eliminated; a 1.5 percent internal tax was placed on auxiliary services; and $1.1

million was set aside to cushion any additional cutbacks. "We persevered in the face of adversity before," said provost Myron Henry, "and we will again, but there's no doubt we'll have challenges and some of this will be painful." USM's budget for 2000–1 was $1.5 million less than the previous year. By January 2001, substantial mid-year cuts seemed imminent, and the college board was seriously considering a declaration of financial emergency. The latter would give presidents almost unlimited discretion over their budgets, including the authority to eliminate both programs and personnel. Fleming criticized the idea openly. "I'm not going to whistle past the graveyard," he said, but "it's a dire situation when you must declare a financial emergency. It takes decades to recover." In February, Fleming was instructed to reduce expenditures for the current year by almost $4 million (6.58 percent).

The board was scheduled to review Horace Fleming's contract in June 2001. Instead, the issue was delayed for a month as the trustees wrestled with details of the resignation of Mississippi University for Women president Clyda Rent, who had been under fire from her faculty for more than two years. Meanwhile, rumors surfaced that some Southern Miss alumni, particular supporters of the athletic program, were bombarding the board with faxes and telephone calls requesting Fleming's removal. Others quickly rallied to the president's defense. Political science professor Joe Parker warned that "it would be a disaster if he's fired over the failure to give athletic supporters everything they want. It will mark USM as a football factory. . . . It will be like a hanging on the square for future

Itzhak Perlman, shown above rehearsing with director Jay Dean and the USM Symphony Orchestra, returned to campus in 1998, and the world's premier cellist, Yo-Yo Ma (right), appeared the following year.

In 2001, President Horace Fleming and Curt Redden, vice-president for advancement (standing), announced a $100 million capital campaign, the most ambitious fundraising effort in school history, to be directed by USM Foundation officer Susan Hollandsworth and campaign chairman Aubrey Lucas (seated).

presidents. . . . I'm convinced now he's in trouble." Fleming insisted that he was not half-hearted in his support of athletics. As part of the strategic planning process, he had appointed an athletic enhancement task force and commissioned it "to chart a course . . . that will take us to [the] next level," that level being in "the top 20 overall in the nation with respect to competitiveness." His choice of Richard Giannini to replace Bill McLellan as athletic director won widespread approval, and he had supported Giannini's recommendation to create a separate foundation for athletic fundraising. In a 1997 interview with the *Hattiesburg American*, he had deemed athletics "an important part of the educational process," but he had also insisted that the program would have to carry its weight financially. "We have a budget to balance," he said, and though anticipating no such dilemma, he warned that he would not "move any money from any other program area to athletics, because that is not appropriate."

Funding had always been an uphill battle for Southern Miss, and the recent IHL cuts had particularly ravaged an athletic budget already reeling from two years of substantial deficits. The addition of women's soccer (1997) and softball (1998) to meet gender equity requirements had increased expenses by $700,000 and contributed to the decision to eliminate men's cross country and indoor track in 2000. "It will take every available resource," Giannini stressed, "to balance the budget and to maintain the current competitive level of our athletic teams." In 2001, Fleming chose not to exercise a board-approved option to increase student fees designated for athletics.

USM

Some boosters feared that the administration's general development policy drained potential donations for athletics into other areas of the university. "A lot of folks wonder what they're doing," former Eagle Club director Ben Willoughby said regarding the university's fundraising strategists. "It seems like the only thing that some of them are good at is going to meetings and drinking designer water and eating boiled shrimp that somebody else has peeled."

Most of the campus community stood behind Fleming. The student government leadership, the staff council, the faculty senate, and the executive committee of the Foundation board all spoke out or passed resolutions of support. Individual expressions of support were often less than ringing, however. "There are members of the faculty who have had individual policy differences with the president," said Don Cabana, president-elect of the faculty senate. "That's normal. This is much bigger . . . . It's crucial to this institution. You don't change horses in the middle of a budget stream like this." Another faculty member noted that "there was some argument about the budget cuts . . . but I think the situation is improving. What we need is some continued leadership and if Dr. Fleming is willing to be more communicative and allow us in the decision-making, then I think it's salvageable." What the local newspaper called a "divided" Alumni Association board issued a statement rather than an endorsement. Acknowledging the IHL board's "legal authority" over the president, it requested that Fleming be accorded "the respect and dignity to which he is entitled as President of the University" and that the trustees "base any decisions on what is best for The University of Southern Mississippi."

Longtime university benefactor, and former college board president, Bobby Chain discounted the suggestion that opposition to Fleming was limited to a handful of athletic boosters. "I like Horace Fleming," he said, "but this is deeper than athletics. It originated on the campus." Indeed, only a few months earlier, controversy over the handling of budget cuts had brought the dreaded phrase "no confidence" to the lips of some members of the faculty senate. Cabana insisted, however, that the senate leadership "never took it up in any serious vein. We killed it. It was one or two folks." Staff council president Mary Sumrall perhaps best articulated the prevailing campus sentiment. "I grew up with two sisters and a brother," she said. "We fussed and we squabbled, but if somebody outside the family jumped on one of us, they had to deal with all four of us. That's the way this university is."

Most members of the college board withheld comment. President Bill Crawford bemoaned the public nature of the controversy. "When it gets in the paper," he said, "it doesn't help the institution, the president or the board." Reflecting on the recent troubles at MUW, he added, "There seems to be an industry that criticizes presidents." Roy Klumb, who had vigorously opposed USM's expansion on the coast, stated that his decision on Fleming would not be based on that issue alone. The press speculated on other areas of criticism that the board might explore in its evaluation of Fleming's performance: athletics, the expensive upgrade of technology, the rapid turnover among administrative personnel, and what the *Hattiesburg American* described as "whiny and unpresidential" criticism of the board regarding budget cuts.

The board's formal review of the president's performance was scheduled for Thursday, July 19. Fleming later recalled that commissioner Tom Layzell informed him on Wednesday night that he could expect to be grilled about athletics and technology expenditures. The next day, the trustees interviewed him for two hours behind closed doors. Emerging to greet well-wishers waiting anxiously outside, he quipped, "It's kind of like a wake, isn't it?" For three more hours in executive session, the board deliberated his fate, before recalling him to offer a one-year extension rather than the conventional four-year contract. He declined. Explaining his decision to the crowd outside, he termed the proposed one-year contract "an invitation to fail. . . . The board has not given me what I think is necessary to be effective." Supporters responded with a standing ovation, commending his decorum, which one student said "proved our point about how classy Dr. Fleming is. His decision proved his love for the university."

Within a month, Don Cabana's report on the annual board retreat heightened anxieties. Representing the Southern Miss faculty senate, he heard, he said, "a great deal of discussion fostered by the presidents of Ole Miss and Mississippi State about whether the state can afford four comprehensive universities." Board president Bill

Crawford insisted that such discussions "shouldn't be viewed as threatening. . . . There wasn't anything that was anti-USM." Board member Bryce Griffis of Sturgis lamented the "us against them" mentality, accusing Cabana of "trying to stir up another mess when we're trying to cool everything down." Cabana remained skeptical. "To have a discussion at all that revolves around whether the second largest university in the state should be comprehensive would make one fretful. I think it is something the faculty ought to be concerned about. . . . It was fairly clear what the tone of the meeting was."

The board did win applause for choosing Aubrey Lucas to serve as interim president while a national search was conducted for Fleming's successor. On August 30, two days before Lucas was to take over, Fleming, who had refused to elaborate on his differences with the trustees, broke his long silence. He was highly critical of "an IHL system" that he said was "on the verge of being dysfunctional. It's a contentious system." He pointed particularly to a television interview in which Roy Klumb had revealed that he and fellow board members had been discussing Fleming's problems months before his formal review. "Nobody came to me," Fleming said. "Is it the object of this board to stand by and watch the presidents fail? If it is, that's a dereliction of duty." The crucial point of contention, he argued, was leadership, which he carefully distinguished from management. "The board doesn't know my management style," he insisted. "It's the faculty, staff, students and volunteer leadership who know my management style. The board looked them in the eye and said, 'Forget it.'" In terms of leadership, his style had been aggressive, he suggested, which had made some board members uncomfortable. "When I came here," he said, "I was told two things—we need a strong advocate and we need to move to the next level. I think I probably got nailed for being outspoken, but I don't regret it. . . . If you're a strong leader and people disagree with you, you have a management problem." A *Hattiesburg American* editorial conceded that "it would be easy to interpret some of Fleming's statements as a case of sour grapes." However, "there's just one problem with that approach," the editor countered. "In too many cases, Fleming's criticisms are right on target."

It was time to look ahead, Fleming said: "Nothing will be gained by continuing to debate the IHL Board's decision. . . . We need to make sure there are people on the board who understand our university. I would say, get to the board, get very close to the board." It was later revealed that he had been retained for a year as consultant to the board and the university on technology issues and USM's capital campaign. His $134,000 fee "sounds like severance pay," one faculty member scorned. "The behavior of the Board is an embarrassment; they've acted like a bush-league operation. He wasn't good enough to be president, but a 'consultant.' Sounds more like alimony in a divorce case." In a farewell letter in the *Student Printz*, Fleming thanked the faculty, staff, and students "for the opportunity . . . to be part of the Southern Miss family . . . and for affording me the honor of serving as president of one of the finest universities in the world!" He and his

In 2006, the first class of Southern Miss Luckyday Scholars graduated.

With limited monetary resources, USM could hardly afford to be just another university. "We keep working harder and smarter than the competition," said recruiting officer Mathew Cox, "to attract academic scholars and sell them on Southern Miss, not the money. Second, we find our niche . . . our unique attraction–one that separates this University from the others–and hammer that point home." By the early 1990s, that niche revolved around leadership and service. Each year, hundreds of high school seniors competed for membership in "a unique program that does more than give students a slap on the back and a scholarship check." Leadership scholars at Southern Miss not only received substantial financial aid, but participated in a required academic leadership seminar and a variety of other campus activities. By 2002, the program boasted a 94 percent freshman retention rate and had produced four successive Student Government Association presidents.

Frank R. Day

Meanwhile in 1997, the university established an office of community service learning with a full-time coordinator, the only one of its kind in the Southeast. The Southern Miss program became a model for other universities, and in October 2000 USM received a grant from the Corporation for National Service to create a Mississippi Center for Community and Civic Engagement. The Center was to promote community engagement activities across the state through conferences, seminars, and twenty Lighthouse Partnership programs to foster integration of service learning into local school curricula.

About the same time, the legacy of a visionary Jackson businessman enabled the university to expand its niche on a grand scale. Beginning in 1994, Frank R. Day's Luckyday Foundation anonymously provided college scholarships for students from Jackson's Bailey Magnet School, and several attended Southern Miss. Day (above) died in 1999, and two years later his Luckyday Foundation awarded USM the largest gift in the university's history. Beginning in the fall of 2002, the Foundation would annually fund $2,000 scholarships for 100 incoming USM freshmen, 10 of whom would receive an additional $4,000 for study abroad. Since the scholarships were renewable for four years, the grant would eventually support 400 Southern Miss Luckyday Citizenship Scholars each year, the equivalent of a $16 million donation. Based on demonstrated leadership skills as well as financial need, the scholarship requirements included a strong community service component. "The Luckyday program," said vice-president for student affairs Joe Paul, "is exciting and unique in all of higher education because it is far more than just a financial award to outstanding students. It is a citizenship program that will help these students maximize their academic experience through community service learning and foster among these scholars a lifelong commitment to civic engagement."

In 2006, the first class of Southern Miss Luckyday Scholars (opposite page) graduated, and the program won a Silver Award for Excellence from the National Association of Student Personnel Administrators.

In the 1990s, community service and service learning became integral parts of student life at Southern Miss.

family would be, he said, "Golden Eagles for life! Our time is now!" He challenged the entire Southern Miss community "to come together as never before—and with a strength and determination unparalleled in our history—to achieve the vision set forth by our Commission on the Future."

That vision had been, as he had repeatedly stated, the "centerpiece" of his presidency. He saw it as his legacy. He had arrived in Hattiesburg more than four years earlier facing, as he himself acknowledged, two major challenges. The first, "following Aubrey [Lucas]," would have been formidable for anyone. It was, as Bobby Chain put it, "like trying to follow Bear Bryant at . . . Alabama." The report of the Commission on the Future had been his blueprint for meeting the second challenge, "finding out how to get to 'the next level.'" Some of the report's recommendations had already been achieved: the attainment of Carnegie Doctoral/Research Extensive status; implementation of a comprehensive strategic planning process; development of a master plan for physical growth; and establishment of Mississippi's first Office of the Freshman Year Experience. Significant progress had been made toward other goals laid out by the Commission: record enrollment for 2001, including a 13 percent increase in freshmen with ACT scores of 25 or higher; the addition of 23 new degree programs; growth in external research funding from $20 million in 1997 to $51 million in 2001; procurement of the largest donation in school history to underwrite the Luckyday Citizenship Scholars program; gifts or pledges constituting half of the capital campaign's goal of $100 million; and improvements in technology that, though controversial, kept the institution from falling, in the words of former dean of administration Eugene Saucier, "light years behind."

Fleming's most daring and potentially most significant achievement, one which contributed profoundly to his troubles with the board, was his relentless pursuit of expansion on the Gulf Coast. Despite a razor-thin margin of support from the trustees, determined opposition, including legal action, from other institutions in the state, and even resistance from some of USM's own, he persevered. Though he would not enjoy the satisfaction of presiding over it, a true multi-campus Southern Miss would perhaps become Horace Fleming's most tangible and enduring legacy. Even those who sought his dismissal paid tribute to his decent and humane character. A staff member remembered sitting at the hospital bedside of her seriously ill infant and hearing the telephone ring. It was Fleming. Following a compassionate and encouraging conversation, he offered his assistance if needed and left his home telephone number. "I don't know many presidents who would do that," the young mother asserted. On the eve of Fleming's departure, Lucas described him as "beloved" and lauded his forbearance: "I'm finding the faculty and staff are healing quite well; I think Dr. Fleming has a lot to do with that."

His most appreciative admirers were the students, for he had always stressed that making Southern Miss a "student-oriented university" was his top priority. *Student Printz* editor Jared Head's description of his final interview with Fleming well captures their sentiment. Arriving early, Head anticipated a brief and stiff formality. Instead, the president came out of his office asking, "Where's my friend Jared?" Spying his guest, he crossed the room and extended his hand. "A firm handshake was my first impression of him," Head noted. A lengthy and unhurried "get to know you session" followed. Before the young journalist could pose a question, "He asked where I was from," Head recalled, "what my future aspirations were, if my wife was a student and why I chose to come to Southern Miss. . . . He gave me his undivided attention for almost an hour. It was one of the most profound interviews that I have been involved in." And after it was over—"the last impression I got of Fleming: a firm handshake."

Perhaps, as one critic charged, Horace Fleming was "in over his head" as president of USM, or as another put it, the "job is just too big for him to handle." Others were more charitable. "He came in at a bad time," said Eugene Saucier, "and he had an awful lot of problems that took an awful lot of money to solve." The turn of the millennium had brought with it excruciatingly difficult circumstances, especially in funding. "Never in my thirty years in higher education," Fleming said, "have I seen such stress as we have endured in the last two years. No one can devise a satisfactory plan to reduce spending by $13.5 million in eighteen months and expect to maintain—much less advance—programs and retain people. We have all done the best we could. . . . I think The University of Southern Mississippi has come through this remarkably well, under very difficult circumstances. We have suffered, and we will continue to suffer—along with everyone else—while the economy is in a downturn. But we must not be deterred. We have great potential, so long as we do not allow fear to dictate our course—or shortsightedness to dim our view of the future we envision."

President Fleming was devoted to sustaining USM's reputation as a "student-oriented" university.

The board had decided that Horace Fleming was not the man to lead Southern Miss into that future, but he had done much to help chart the course.

Chapter 8

STEADFAST THROUGH THE STORM

COCHRAN
CENTER
SERVICE ZONE
TOW ZONE

WALKER
BUILDING

Southern Miss entered the new millennium as a dual-campus university, and the fortunes of Hattiesburg and the Gulf Coast became increasingly intertwined. No one could foresee that not far over the horizon lurked a calamity that would forever bind them together in mutual suffering and succor. In 2004, the Office of Naval Research granted the department of marine science $1.6 million to establish a Central Gulf Ocean Observing System (CenGOOS). Operations began with the launching of a single buoy equipped to monitor, among other things, atmospheric pressure, wind speed, and waves. Barely a year later, those natural forces would coalesce into a shrew with the deceptively demure-sounding name Katrina. On the way to inflicting unprecedented devastation on much of the Gulf South, especially Mississippi and New Orleans, she unleashed her most violent fury on Station USM-3M01. In the richest tradition of the institution whose name it bore, the little buoy soldiered on, dutifully recording invaluable data while being tossed about by category five winds and waves. Such perseverance in the face of seemingly insurmountable odds symbolized the proud heritage of Southern Miss.

Meanwhile, in September 2001, Aubrey Lucas returned to the helm of an institutional ship already buffeted by the treacherous winds of all too familiar financial uncertainty. "Everybody I talk to talks about the need for additional funds," he said, "whether it's in the arts or athletics or academic programs or student affairs. All over campus, we really are strapped for money." Optimistic as always, however, Lucas sought to rally the apprehensive troops. "USM is doing exceedingly well despite the funding challenges," he insisted. "We know what we have and we've got to live with it." Shortly before leaving office, President Fleming had revealed plans for a $10 million national economic development center and had announced a $1 million grant from the French government to help transform an ancient abbey in Pontlevoy into USM's new European studies center. During Fleming's final year, faculty generated a record $50.1 million in external funding, and in 2001 fall enrollment for the first time topped 15,000.

Southern Miss students joined millions around the country in a candlelight vigil in memory of the victims of the tragedy of September 11, 2001.

On April 13, 2002, the board named Shelby Thames USM's eighth president. Trustee Bill Crawford praised "his wealth of experience and strong leadership style," and commissioner Tom Layzell noted that he possessed "the type of local, national and international perspectives on challenges and current trends in higher education that are necessary for effective leadership today." That style and those perspectives would eventually become highly controversial. At least one member of the board had reservations and expressed them candidly. "We're looking for a consensus builder," said Virginia Shanteau Newton, who had chaired the search committee. "This is a very fractured university family." The only trustee with a Southern Miss degree, she had her doubts about Thames. "I really do question the ability of Dr. Thames to rally the troops because of fear of retaliation," she said, casting the only vote against him, a lonely symbol of portent and pathos. "I literally put my heart and soul into this search," she said. "My commitment to Southern Miss is steadfast." Pledging her full support to Thames, she added, "I hope it all works out well."

The faculty's reaction seemed to vindicate her fears. In the midst of the search process, a dormant local chapter of the American Association of University Professors (AAUP) was revived, partly at least out of fears of a

Thames presidency. Chapter president and history professor William Scarborough articulated the members' anxiety. "Understand," he said, "we all have a great deal of respect for many of the things he's done. The one concern that we have, and it seems to be virtually universal, is that his managerial style seems to be autocratic rather than democratic." Of approximately six hundred faculty members, one-third participated in an AAUP survey regarding the presidential finalists. Only fourteen found Thames an "acceptable" candidate, while 85 percent deemed him "unacceptable." At the dedication of the Polymer Science Research Center in 1998, Thames had reflected on his long association with USM. "I came here when I was an eighteen-year-old kid," he mused, "in 1954. . . . All three of my children . . . received degrees here. My little granddaughter will start here in the fall. This is a place that's dear to my heart. This is my university."

Literary historian Robert Heilman suggests that tragedy and melodrama offer different approaches to experience. In one, "we put the erring man in his place"; in the other, "we put ourselves in the erring man's place." Tragedy pits "one potentiality" within man "against another"; melodrama pits "man . . . against another man." The story of Shelby Thames's presidency would betray elements of both. There were some who wanted to put what they considered an erring man in his place, who saw potentiality only through the lens of the past, a past from which they bore wounds that made the thought of a successful Thames administration unbearable. They wanted him to fail, and he knew it.

In November 2001, Chi Omega Sorority staged its fiftieth annual holiday Songfest, the oldest continuous Greek philanthropic tradition at Southern Miss.

What issued from the confluence of those desires and that knowledge was classic tragedy. Shelby Thames's devotion to USM was genuine, and he had achieved much for the institution and for himself. Yet the attributes that drove those achievements—boldness, determination, relentless assault against all obstacles—unless sufficiently tempered by more irenic sensibilities could prove problematic in the hands of a president. Thames groped for the distinction between resistance from concrete circumstances and the resistance of complex personalities, and he did so in the face of opposition that was often implacable. He and his detractors brought out the worst in each other, and each interpreted the other's words and actions in the worst possible light. In between were many who suffered collateral damage.

At the outset, Thames did have support, some of it enthusiastic, among the students, staff, and especially alumni. The *Hattiesburg American* predicted that his "presidency may turn out to be a major factor in solidifying South Mississippi's political power." During the summer of 2002, "power-brokers" from throughout the state descended on alumnus Ray Sims's Hattiesburg ranch for a benefit "cook-out" for the USM Foundation. Their "presence," said state senator Ron Farris, "was directly attributable to their long-standing relationship and respect for Shelby Thames. I absolutely believe that the respect Shelby has brought to the table will benefit the whole area."

The day after Thames took office, a *Student Printz* editorial urged him and his critics to find common ground.

"He will have to work with faculty, staff and students," said the editors, "just as they will have to work with him. It is now up to the university community to make things work." Most pressing was a budget squeezed between $4 million in midyear cuts and $2.4 million in increased fixed costs. Faculty and staff faced a third consecutive year without raises as IHL allocated Southern Miss $3 million less for 2002–3 than the previous year. At the outset of his presidency, Thames faced the unenviable, but necessary, chore of eliminating thirty-two vacant faculty positions and issuing thirteen university employees their pink slips. The college board approved an 8 percent rise in tuition for all state universities, but Thames boldly requested, and received, a separate additional increase for USM. "Everybody, including the board," said faculty senate president Don Cabana, "is tired of having to deal with tuition hikes. But he tackled this issue when no one else has. That money is critical to the university. I have to really give him some kudos for having accomplished that." Thames insisted that despite the budget woes, "the University of Southern Mississippi is healthy. It is a vibrant university that looks forward to the future."

In 2002, Shelby F. Thames became USM's eighth president.

In July, Thames made wholesale administrative changes. He named Jay Grimes provost to replace Anselm Griffin, who departed for Georgia Tech, and he appointed Tim Hudson to the newly created position of provost for the Gulf Coast campus. Donald Cotten resigned, and his responsibilities were divided between James Hollandsworth, who now became dean of the graduate school, and Angeline Dvorak as vice-president for research. Alumna Lisa Mader replaced Bud Kirkpatrick as director of marketing and public relations, and Susan Hollandsworth became interim director of development pending a national search for a vice-president for university advancement to replace Curt Redden, who resigned to enter private business.

Thames stressed that Hudson's appointment reflected USM's status as a dual-campus university. Dvorak had been president of Mississippi Technology Alliance and the Institute for Technology Development in Jackson, where she had worked with Thames developing a company to market paint derived from polymer research. He praised her "educational and business background," which he said, "provides a combination of skills that will be invaluable to her as our vice-president of research." That background, which included a stint as president of Ashland Community College in Kentucky, would later become a lightning rod for controversy and the catalyst for campus-wide upheaval. At the time, however, senate president Cabana speculated that "generally everyone is pleased with" the new appointments, though "my guess would be that if the faculty had their druthers, some of these positions maybe would have involved some searches." Thames described them as "all very, very, good people."

In his first few months as president, Thames had defused some of the antipathy that had greeted him as a candidate. A September meeting with the faculty senate, his first, offered an opportunity to solidify the progress he had made. Instead, in the words of a *Printz* editorial, it "was an opportunity missed, as Thames confirmed rumors of a confrontational leadership style and poor people skills, setting an abrasive tone for his tenure at USM." He had already indicated that his approach to the budget problem would involve priority and efficiency. He sought to identify those programs with the potential to be, he said in what would become one of his favorite phrases, "world class" and "focus on those pockets of high quality . . . while bringing up supporting programs at the same time." The measuring stick would be productivity, and of course his model was polymer science. "The key is," he said, "whatever I've been able to accomplish, I've kept at it. . . . People in general have a tendency . . . to start off for three or four days and work real hard and all of a sudden, they lose their focus. . . . We can't afford to lose our focus."

Apparently, he feared that USM harbored more than its quota of "people in general." The anxious but hopeful senators heard him outline plans to institute a new document to measure faculty efficiency. "Convince me

In January 2003, President Thames announced a sweeping and controversial reorganization of USM's academic structure, consolidating nine colleges into five.

what you are doing in your field is recognizable and valuable," he said. "It doesn't have to be tied to dollars but that would be helpful." The student newspaper charged that apart from its mercenary overtones, Thames's scheme of requiring "professionally distinguished faculty members to fill out report cards for themselves on how efficient they are is simply insulting." Senator William Scarborough from history questioned the universal applicability of a standard instrument to measure productivity. "You cannot quantitatively compare individuals in different areas of study," he warned. The emphasis on "economic development and grants," he suggested, "has nothing to do with people who are writing about philosophy and poetry. Some people in the administration, because of their background in science, do not understand what people in liberal arts do for research." Scarborough's comments reflected widespread suspicions among liberal arts professors that Thames doubted the diligence of their labors, and the fact that many of them found ample time and energy to criticize his policies relentlessly could only have reinforced whatever doubts he did entertain. Over the course of his presidency, his doubts and their suspicions would perversely reinforce each other, as his most vocal and unyielding opposition emanated from the liberal arts faculty.

The issuance of the new "faculty activity report" the following spring only heightened professors' fears, especially those in liberal arts. In addition to the conventional categories of teaching, research, and service, faculty productivity would now be assessed in a fourth area, economic development. Thames sought to allay fears in an email memo to the faculty. "I am sensitive to your concerns," he wrote, "and want to address them in order to eliminate any miscommunication or misunderstanding regarding the intended use of the report and the goals of this administration." He insisted that "departmental and faculty review" would remain "the primary means of evaluating faculty performance," that the activity report would merely be an additional factor in the existing process. Reaffirming his oft-repeated commitment to making "the Southern Miss faculty . . . the best paid in Mississippi," he explained that collectively "the reports" would constitute a valuable "tool for quantifying overall faculty accomplishments to the legislature when requesting funds for faculty raises. We need this type of information to be an effective advocate for you." Conceding that complaints about a "'one size fits all' form" were "well-taken," he promised that "faculty input will be extremely beneficial" in the process of revision, and he encouraged faculty to make their "thoughts and suggestions known." He also acknowledged that "the availability of external funds varies with disciplines and not all faculty members will achieve the same financial result." That acknowledgment was buried, however, at the end of a long paragraph emphasizing the urgency of outside funding to the university's future, especially in terms of salary increases.

Thames's assurances of sensitivity and flexibility concerning the activity report seemed sincere, but they came on the far side of a bigger controversy that had seriously eroded his credibility with most faculty. During a state of the university address on January 17, 2003, he announced a sweeping reorganization of USM's entire academic structure. In what a reporter described as "a tense nineteen-minute power point presentation," Thames revealed that effective July 1, the nine existing degree-granting colleges would be compressed into five. The old colleges "and their leaders have served our students well," he said, but the streamlined arrangement would leave "five robust colleges, which hold the promise of improving academic, administrative and budgetary effectiveness at Southern Miss, allowing us to better serve our students." He maintained that the changes involved no reduction of programs or tenured faculty positions and would allow one to two million dollars to be shifted from administration to instruction. National searches would begin immediately for deans of the new colleges, and the current deans, who learned that their posts were being eliminated only minutes before the convocation, were invited to apply.

The reorganization was a turning point in Thames's relationship to the faculty. Theatre professor Stephen Judd later noted that from the very beginning "most faculty, myself included, had deep doubts" about his presidency, "but we wanted to make the university work. The real open questioning of Dr. Thames' administration happened when the deans got fired." Illustrative of Judd's point was the fate of Terry Harper, a popular history professor for almost forty years, who had since 1983 served as an equally popular and effective dean of liberal arts. Harper now found himself deposed, not with the trappings of an honorable and discreet resignation, but summarily, his dismissal couched not in the language of gratitude befitting years of faithful service, but in terms of the exigencies of efficiency, delivered verbally only minutes before it was announced to the world. As the initial shock of the announcement wore off, campus response was swift and intense. Appearing before the faculty senate that same afternoon, Thames "became visibly angry," according to the *Student Printz*, "at criticism he had failed to consult with, nor even make mention to, faculty or students his restructuring plan." The newspaper also reported that he had earlier informed supporters in the community about his plan while deans whose positions were about to be eliminated were kept in the dark until the last minute. Some student comments were favorable. "Dr. Thames has stuck his neck out for us," said one. "I like how he's putting students first."

The relationship between Thames and the faculty continued to deteriorate. In late April, Cabana resigned as president of the faculty senate because he was troubled, he said, by the "increasingly hostile tone and substance of Senate debates" and by "demeaning comments that question the integrity of presidents and provosts without factual information." The senate, he warned, was "on a path that will only lead to escalating conflict with administration officials." He was particularly distressed by talk of a "no confidence" vote. "This topic needs to die the death it deserves," he advised. By that time, the public image of the Thames administration had become largely defined by his conflict with the faculty. In an article subtitled "Driven or Dictatorial?" *Clarion Ledger* reporter Andy Kanengiser suggested that "even some faculty members think a vocal portion of the faculty is gunning for Thames, who has shaken up things on this campus." Polymer science professor Robert Lochhead explained that his longtime colleague "likes to get things done—and quickly. The challenge is that academia likes a lot of discussions." Lochhead, as dean of science and technology, had been one of the casualties of the reorganization. It had been, he said, a "disturbing" experience. Kanengiser speculated that the controversy swirling around Thames had not diminished his standing with "his bosses," the IHL board. Trustee Scott Ross stated, "I think Dr. Thames has done exactly what we expected him to do. I'm not surprised by the quick pace he's followed with the reorganization and emphasis on economic development. He has the odd notion of expecting a day's work for a day's pay. His style probably rubs some academics the wrong way. A lot needs to be done. He has the best interests of that university in mind."

Early in May, the senate requested that Thames meet with a "facilitator" to improve communications with the faculty. "We don't need a facilitator," he insisted. "We just simply need to sit down and have open, viable discussion. We're mature professionals." In the fall, the president did accept an SGA proposal that he meet monthly with students on their turf. "I want students to get to know Dr. Thames like I do," said SGA president Jared Loftus. At the first of these "Tuesdays at 2 with Thames" in Seymour's Grill, the president began by asking how many of those present believed that the university's enrollment would grow to twenty thousand. When all the students raised their hands, he beamed, "You think like I do. That's the USM spirit."

In June 2003, Thames suddenly announced that he was transposing the provosts. He realized, he said, that their initial appointments had raised eyebrows, since Grimes "knew so much about the Gulf Coast," and Hudson was "more comfortable" with the Hattiesburg campus. The method to his madness had been conscious and "strategic," he explained, for "each now has an appreciation for a part of Southern Miss which each knew little about prior to these assignments. . . . It is now time to take advantage of this learning process," or as one campus wag called it, "administrative cross-training." As of July 1, Grimes would return to the coast, and Hudson would move into the Dome. Later in the summer, deans were named for the new colleges: Elliott Pood in arts and letters, Rex Gandy in science and technology, Harold Doty in business and economic development, Joan Exline in health, and Willie Pierce in education and psychology. Exline and Pierce were internal interim appointments, pending ongoing national searches.

As 2003 wound down, conditions on campus, while still tense, seemed somewhat calmer. The fiscal year began, for the first time since 2000, with a budget increase, though slight. In October, the faculty generated a monthly record $13.3 million in external funds, and the capital campaign was closing in on its $100 million goal. Construction was complete or under way on a $5 million renovation of Walker Science Building; a new $3 million facility for the DuBard School for Language Disorders; a $7.5 million athletic field house and training facility; a new women's softball field; a $423,000 outdoor fitness trail; the final phase of a $1.2 million 3-D Art Building; a $6 million addition to the Polymer Science Research Center; a $7.9 million International Center; and the $30 million first phase of a new student life center. At Gulf Coast Research Lab, NASA was supporting and helping to fund a $6 million Geospatial Center and research program that opened near the end of 2002, and planning had begun for a major expansion of the J. L. Scott Marine Education Center and Aquarium at Point Cadet. In May 2003, commencement at Gulf Park for the first time included doctoral graduates. At fall convocation, Thames announced that preliminary figures indicated a record enrollment of more than sixteen thousand, making Southern Miss the largest university in the state.

The apparent calm only preceded a more violent storm foreshadowed by an embarrassing repudiation of the landmark enrollment. Officials at Mississippi State, which had been the largest university in the IHL system for almost two decades, challenged the accuracy of USM's enrollment figures, as did the Southern Miss chapter of the AAUP. In the face of mounting public criticism, the university conducted an internal audit of its process for reporting enrollment and in December acknowledged that its initial figures for the fall semester had indeed been inaccurate. What proudly began the semester as the largest university in Mississippi with 16,662 students contritely shrank by December to 15,579, well below MSU's 16,173. Provost Hudson also stressed that no student had suffered "academic or financial" loss because of the "unfortunate" incident, but the damage to the institution's image was incalculable. A local newspaper reported that "some sources close to the College Board questioned whether USM had deliberately falsified its enrollment record." AAUP criticism of the "scandal" was relentless. "This doesn't pass the smell test," scorned local president Frank Glamser.

Sometime during the fall, the *Hattiesburg American* received what reporter Janet Braswell described as "a plain brown envelope with no return address." Inside was a photograph of Thames "with a slash mark across it" on a compact disc labeled "Stop Shelby." The "technically sophisticated" CD contained several satirical episodes, including an "elaborate" parody entitled "Czar Wars" about "evil Shelboo and his court of like-minded followers assembled to crush the rebellious faculty." Behind the scenes, however, something much more serious than satire was brewing, and the fury of the tempest that was about to engulf Thames and his faculty antagonists would dwarf the squalls that had preceded it. Ironically, the focal point involved the person in charge of perhaps the most successful aspect of his administration, economic development.

Thames sought to make USM "an economic development machine for South Mississippi," and by the end of 2003, he had made a good start. Plans were well under way for the $10 million national economic development center, now named in honor of Senator Trent Lott, who in 2002 helped secure a $2 million congressional appropriation to start the process. Despite escalating costs and contentions between Thames and national coordinating chair Bobby Chain over construction delays that hampered fund-raising efforts, groundbreaking ceremonies took place in February 2005. Sadly, the site chosen for the facility required demolition of the old sports arena, whose walls had once echoed with the excitement of Fred Lewis's Golden Giants, countless memorable intramural contests, and gleeful local youngsters participating in summer activities of the National Youth Sports Program.

Twenty thousand gallons of American Pride, an environment-friendly paint developed by polymer science research at Southern Miss, helped refurbish the Pentagon after the terrorist attack of September 11, 2001.

Polymer science continued to illustrate the scope of the university's research potential for economic development. To repair the Pentagon following the tragedy of September 11, 2001, the Department of Defense purchased 20,000 gallons of American Pride, a paint developed by polymer science research at Southern Miss. In 2003, television's Discovery Channel featured Southern Miss in an episode of its *Champions of Industry* series devoted to education. USM had been chosen, said one of the producers, because "the energy and drive it devotes to its research and economic development effort . . . have brought significant benefit to the university's and the state's economic growth. Additionally, we were delighted to find their marine sciences program has a national and international reputation far beyond that which our own research uncovered." About the same time, Angeline Dvorak, vice-president for research, added "economic development" to her title.

On December 11, 2003, Frank Glamser lunched at McDonald's. The professor of sociology and president of the local AAUP chapter returned to campus to find what he described as the equivalent of "a bomb" sitting on his office floor just inside the door. It was a manila envelope

In 2004, the old sports arena was demolished to make way for the Trent Lott National Center for Excellence in Economic Development and Entrepreneurship.

with his name and AAUP handwritten on the front. Inside was a sheaf of documents that demonstrated, according to the anonymous letter attached, that Dvorak had misrepresented her affiliation with the University of Kentucky English department. The next morning, on the advice of a friend well versed in workplace ethics, Glamser delivered the package and its contents to the office of the president. He also left a letter to Thames explaining how he had come to possess the papers and foreswearing any desire on the part of the AAUP to get involved in the issue raised. "I assume," he added, "you will handle it appropriately." Thames, who was ill during much of December, later said that he took the matter "very seriously" and asked Dvorak to reassess the accuracy of her resumé. She, and associates she said, examined it scrupulously and could find nothing out of order. She and Thames moved on to other business and never responded to Glamser, she said, because "I didn't know there was anything to clarify." When the president failed even to acknowledge receiving the information, Glamser said he reluctantly decided that the AAUP must act and appointed a committee to investigate the charge. As chair, he chose English professor Gary Stringer because of his reputation for being, as a *Chronicle of Higher Education* article put it, "careful and deliberate." Stringer's wife, Mary Ann, as acting dean of the College of the Arts had been one of the casualties of Thames's reorganization in 2003.

On January 16, 2004, a local television station reported that questions had emerged concerning Dvorak's credentials. At a tense press conference four days later, an irate Dvorak defended her resumé and threatened legal action against anyone who questioned its veracity. She explained that as president of Ashland Community and Technical College (1997–2000), she had been granted tenure in her field, English, through the University of Kentucky, whose board of trustees at the time of her appointment also governed the state's community colleges. "Never in my wildest dreams," she later declared, "would I have thought someone would interpret that I was trying to pass myself off as a person in the department of English at the University of Kentucky. I don't even know where the department is. I've never even been there." The complexity of the relationship between her faculty status and her precise duties at Ashland increased when the Kentucky legislature later separated the community colleges from the university. She noted that state law nonetheless allowed her to retain her tenure through the university rather than the new Kentucky Community and Technical College System. The confusion was further compounded by variations in the specific description of her complicated faculty status in her biography on the Southern Miss web site, in university news releases, and in separate versions of her curriculum vitae. Since leaving Ashland, Dvorak insisted, "I have consistently identified any and all relationship with The University of Kentucky as being solely affiliated with my duties and responsibilities as a community college president." Moreover, she charged, the real target of the investigation was not her but the Thames administration: "At the end of the day for the AAUP, Angie Dvorak is just the flavor of the month. I'm just . . . collateral damage." She had not granted access to her "personnel information" to anyone from AAUP, she warned; "after today, if you have any questions about these issues, you can talk to my lawyers."

The import of her actually earning tenure at a four-year institution hinged on the role she now played in tenure decisions at USM. "It seems clear to the faculty," said senate president-elect David Beckett, "that people who are judging whether people should be tenured or not should be themselves tenured." On January 22, Stringer presented his findings to a meeting of the local AAUP chapter. Dvorak's and the university's claims about her tenure record, he concluded, were "misleading." Stringer's report along with relevant documents was forwarded to Thames, the college board, and the faculty senate and made available to the media. Thereafter, press interest in the story gradually diminished, and "we thought it was a dead matter," said Glamser. Meanwhile, Thames instructed Jack Hanbury, the university's director of resources and risk management, to investigate further. Several weeks later, Hanbury met separately with Glamser and Stringer concerning their investigation of Dvorak. When he began to probe about their methods of soliciting information, each refused to answer without the advice of legal counsel. Afterward, both were summoned to separate meetings in the president's office. Early the next morning, Friday, March 5, Thames informed them that he had initiated termination proceedings against them and that their computers had been confiscated and the locks on their offices changed. They could arrange with the chief of campus police to retrieve personal belongings. Stringer's office contained material related to his editorial work on the *Variorum Edition of the Poetry of John Donne*, a quarter of a century's labors that had brought prestige as well as almost a million dollars in support grants to the university.

At a tense press conference in January 2004, vice-president for research and economic development Angeline Dvorak denied charges that portions of her resumé were misleading.

THE STUDENT PRINTZ

Thursday, January 22, 2004 | http://www.usm.edu/printz | Vol. 88, Issue 30

Dvorak defends credentials

BY RACHEL QUINLIVAN
Executive Editor

USM Vice President Angie Dvorak defended her academic credentials Tuesday and said she will sue "whoever is at fault" for making false accusations about the validity of her resume.

The vice president of research and economic development responded after Frank Glamser, president of USM's chapter of the American Association of University Professors, said the group had formed a committee to

"At the end of the day for the AAUP, Angie Dvorak is just the flavor of the month," she said. "I'm just the collateral damage."

DVORAK

Dvorak said neither Glamser nor any known member of the AAUP asked for information regarding her tenure status while serving as

about these issues, you can talk to my lawyers," she said.

She would not specify who her lawyers are but said a lawsuit was being prepared. As of Wednesday, no lawsuit had been filed in the Forrest County Circuit Court or U.S. Federal Courts by Dvorak, and Lisa Slay Mader, director of marketing and public relations, said the university had not filed suit.

Dvorak's biography on USM's Web site said, "Dvorak served as president and CEO of Ashland Community College in Ashland,

University of Kentucky."

USM President Shelby F. Thames said in a statement Tuesday at the time Dvorak was hired as president, all community colleges were operated exclusively by the University of Kentucky, and tenured faculty appointments for community college were made through the university's board of trustees.

Dvorak was awarded tenure on July 1, 1998. Although in 1997, the Kentucky legislature passed a bill, which brought all of the state's community colleges under one

the University of Kentucky.

But Glamser said he, nor the AAUP, ever made any claims.

"We're in the process of investigating this," he said. "At no time have we charged them with anything."

Glamser also said he did not release any information to the media.

"In fact, the vita shown on WDAM has a different format than the one we have," he said.

Glamser received an anonymous packet of information, including university press releases and Dvorak's resume, on Dec. 11,

never heard back from them. After consulting with the AAUP's executive committee, Glamser said they decided to begin an investigation.

Mader said Thames had reviewed the packet and that was the reason for his statements at the news conference. She also said the resume included in the packet and being used by the media was not prepared by Dvorak, but said, under the advisement of her lawyers, Dvorak would not be releasing her resume until after the AAUP meet-

THE STUDENT PRINTZ

Tuesday, March 9, 2004 — http://www.usm.edu/printz — Vol. 88, Issue 39

No Confidence

Faculty Senate votes after two suspensions

GLAMSER

STRINGER

Chad Applebaum/Photo Editor

Above: Shandi Shiver, left, a junior nursing major, and Cameron Beach, a junior history major, hold protest signs outside of the conference room in the administration building Monday before USM President Shelby F. Thames spoke during a press conference. Right: Thames talks during a press conference Monday.

Coming this week

Today

12:15 p.m. Student Forum with President Shelby F. Thames in Commons rooms A, B and C

4 p.m. Student-organized protest in front of the Administration Building

Wednesday

5 p.m. All-faculty convocation in Mannoni Performing Arts Center. Faculty will need to bring their IDs in order to vote.

Friday

2 p.m. The Faculty Senate has called a special session and will be held in the Hall of Honors.

In This Issue...

How classes were affected - page 2
Faculty Senate Resolution - page 3
Shelby F. Thames fires back - page 4
The Printz Editorial
Board speaks out - page 4
Students and Faculty respond - page 5

Students speak out against terminations

By Vicki McDonald, News Editor

In Other News

James Green resigns

Green's eight years as head basketball coach came to an end Friday, when he resigned his coaching position effective immediately. See page 10

Hub City Happenings

Hattiesburg offers a wide range of activities, from nightlife to downtown restaurants. With a lively art scene and great food, there has never been a better time to visit downtown. See page 6

In a terse official statement, the university confirmed that Stringer and Glamser had been suspended with pay pending the outcome of the termination process. In a later lengthier communication, Thames stated that IHL policy granted the two professors ten days to request a hearing and that he had "strongly encouraged them to do so." Because legal restraints prohibited USM from commenting on the grounds for such a personnel action, he also urged them "to agree that the hearing be open . . . so that everyone can hear the facts and see the documented evidence." His decision to act had been personally "difficult," he said, but it was based on "solid evidence" discovered during "an extensive six-week investigation . . . that included . . . review by outside attorneys, who advised us that the facts constituted grounds for termination." As a tenured professor himself, Thames stressed, he understood "the gravity of this situation." While tenure protected valuable rights, it "does not absolve people of responsibility for inappropriate actions and violations of law." He appealed to the university community to "reserve judgment and allow the system to work" and in the meantime not to allow "distractions to derail our efforts in the classroom, lab or field. We are here to educate. Let us not forget that."

In March 2004, faculty and students protested the firing of tenured professors Frank Glamser and Gary Stringer.

As news of the suspensions spread, the campus erupted in indignation. Later in the day, an emergency meeting of the AAUP's executive board attracted some two hundred faculty and students, whom Stringer cautioned "to be very measured and cunning in the response you make. There is no point in being rash." A legal defense fund was organized, and Glamser promised that "if . . . my guardian angel takes out the administration tonight, you'll get your money back." A group styling itself "Concerned Students of Southern Miss" began circulating a petition requesting that the two professors be reinstated. Within a week they had almost two thousand signatures. A hastily-called session of the faculty senate on Sunday took on the air of a religious camp meeting as one speaker after another condemned Thames to thunderous applause. History professor and alumnus Andrew Wiest, whom Thames had recently cited as an administration supporter, spoke emotionally of his deep devotion to Southern Miss. The firing of Glamser and Stringer, he said, hit him "like a sledgehammer. . . . I'm worried when I stick my key in my office door in the morning. That's how palpable the fear has become." He urged his colleagues to vote "no confidence," and all forty senators did so.

Criticism was coming from beyond the campus, too. "This looks very serious to me," said Bobby Chain. "I think the university will get unusually bad publicity—possibly nationally—on this. I wish there could have been a way to handle it in a more dignified way." On Monday morning, Thames held a press conference to explain his actions. Students and faculty, some carrying signs of protest, jostled with reporters and cameramen for space in the crowded Lucas Administration Building. Chants of "impeach Thames" and other interruptions at times echoed through the cavernous rotunda forcing the president to stand helplessly mute until the noise died away. He accused the AAUP of using the Dvorak controversy to "form a collective bargaining unit" and to expand its membership. His comments, especially the assertion that opposition came from a vocal minority, evoked derisive laughter. "The man is a clown," scorned Noel Polk. "If he weren't so powerful, he would be doing comedy. It was one ridiculous line after another." Thames criticized faculty for inciting the students, singling out a junior history professor whom he accused of canceling class to allow his students to protest. "That's a damn lie!" shouted Doug Chambers, who had indeed canceled a class but, as he later explained, because he had been summoned for jury duty. The entire episode was, in the words of a reporter, an "embarrassing spectacle."

The following day, hundreds gathered for a "Tuesday against Thames" protest organized by Concerned Students of Southern Miss. Others reserved judgment. One student carried a sign saying, "No facts, No opinion . . . Go Thames." Until all the details became public, he declared, "I'm supporting the president." On Wednesday, Thames loyalists organized a counterdemonstration at the Ogletree Alumni House. The crowd, which reporters estimated at anywhere from fifty to three times that many, included Jeff Bower. "I'm not here to pass judgment on anyone," the popular football coach said. "This administration has been very supportive of our athletic program and our student athletes, and I'm very appreciative of that." A student in attendance complained that all the protest had brought "education" to a halt "to pursue the political messages of a few professors. It saddens me to know students have been used as political posters." The same day, Thames met with students in the University Commons and opened himself to questions. A local editor described the audience as polite but largely skeptical and their inquiries as "relentless" and "pointed." At one point, he reported, the beleaguered president told them, "Most of y'all don't believe this, but I do have friends."

Sensitive to complaints about the impact of the suspensions on students, Thames flirted with the idea of allowing the professors to complete the semester. On Wednesday, however, USM public relations officer Lisa Mader quoted Thames as saying, "I cannot with good conscience return these two individuals to the classroom." She also disclosed that "the charges" against the professors "referenced acts . . . that may be violations of criminal law" and that Thames had again "implored" Glamser and Stringer "to open the hearing and put the evidence on the table." Their attorney, Michael Adelman, accused the president of "trying to . . . taunt or dare our clients to release the charges." They had refused to do so, Glamser said, "because that would permit the Thames administration to unleash all the resources of their PR machine against us in the court of public opinion. I can assure you that neither Dr. Stringer nor I have intentionally or knowingly done anything unethical or illegal."

That afternoon, the executive committee of the Alumni Association board condemned "unfruitful diversions" and implored "both sides to get beyond their emotional energies." The official statement, later endorsed by both the full board of directors and the Association's past presidents council, declared, "It is obvious that all who are involved in the controversy . . . have caused some detriment to the University." The statement urged "the IHL Board to thoroughly investigate the facts and to resolve this matter in a most expedient manner, and to make the facts available to the public! Delay and a lack of public advisement will only exacerbate the situation." On Wednesday evening, almost 70 percent of the full faculty turned out for senate-organized convocations in Hattiesburg and at Gulf

Park. "Barring a miracle," Glamser told the Hattiesburg gathering, "our academic careers are over. Even if we go to the courts, relief will be many years away." Stringer insisted that he was "not a saint" and did not "wish to be a martyr, but this is not the great white throne of judgment and Shelby is not God." Ninety-three percent of those voting at the two convocations approved a resolution of no confidence, which also urged the board to halt the termination process, reinstate the two professors, and restore "freedom of speech, academic freedom and freedom from retaliation."

On Thursday, provost Tim Hudson revealed that the president had not consulted him before the decision to suspend Glamser and Stringer. Thames claimed that he had bypassed the provosts, as well as the deans and chairs, because he "did not want to expose them to the unfair unwarranted criticism to which I have been subjected." He pointed out that the new, and controversial, faculty handbook authorized the president to "initiate personnel actions involving members of the instructional staff," though he had originally proposed shifting "much of that authority to the department chairs and the deans." Myron Henry, he said, who represented the senate on the committee that revised the handbook, "insisted that only the President should have the authority to initiate termination proceedings against tenured faculty." Thames insisted that the administration "has followed, and will continue to follow all University and IHL rules and regulations." Hudson expressed dismay at the manner in which Glamser and Stringer had been dismissed, and he supported efforts to allow them to complete the semester. On Friday, the two professors formally requested a hearing. "What a week!" exclaimed a *Hattiesburg American* editorial on Sunday, describing the saga that had unfolded since March 5 as "raucous, contentious and extremely unsettling."

As the newspaper had predicted, the turmoil was far from over. In an interview with the *American* the following day, Dvorak predicted that the controversy had destroyed her academic career. She would continue her duties at USM as long as allowed, she said, but "in academia . . . no one ever recovers" from accusations of misrepresenting credentials. "I feel like I worked pretty damn hard [to have] to start all over." In this and other interviews since the accusations had first surfaced, reporters described Dvorak in such terms as "visibly angry, her fists clenched and her lips pressed tightly together," "her eyes red, her fingers clenched tightly," "fight[ing] back tears." One faculty member expressed sorrow that she felt mistreated, "but if she and Dr. Thames had been willing to talk with us about this earlier on, we might have had a conclusion more amenable to everybody." Another suggested that "when this had all come out, if she had said, 'oops, sorry, I don't mind changing that,' this would have all died." Dvorak later declared that she was paying "a mighty high price" over differences of "interpretation, particularly when . . . they could have just asked me a question, and I'd have been glad to have told them." A former president of the AAUP chapter observed that "she didn't have to apologize, just say it was possibly misleading. But instead of doing that, she flew off the handle and threatened to sue people." Indeed, she stubbornly refused to recant the threat of legal action, warning ominously, "I always finish what I start." The exchanges between Dvorak and her critics illustrate how far past each other the two sides were talking. Neither could see themselves as sinning as well as sinned against, for vindication required undiluted malevolence on the other side. To acknowledge any responsibility for the impasse would have humanized the opposition in a conflict in which for many the tragic world of flawed human beings was dissolving into a melodramatic world of angels and demons. Such a struggle could end only in the enemy's abject surrender.

Letters to the editor of the local newspaper reflected a public opinion deeply divided, and technology had vastly expanded the scope of public debate. "Thanks to the Internet," the student newspaper noted, "everyone has a voice." Within days after the story broke, several web sites offered both supporters, but especially critics of the administration, clearinghouses for both information and opinion. Some observers saw fault on "both sides," who had, according to one member of the *Hattiesburg American*'s online editorial board, "stepped into the fray with name calling, accusations and self righteousness. The complete lack of civility and professionalism is very disheartening." Another lamented the "apparent breakdown of open and honest dialogue on both sides. . . . If either side feels they must emerge the victor, then our community is sure to be the loser." One letter writer wondered emphatically, "Where is the college board?" Indeed, no official response came from the trustees until March 15, when IHL issued the following statement: "Whenever a matter generates such an outpouring of interest, the board takes it seriously. Consequently, the board will discuss this issue this week in a careful and appropriate manner." Individual members, with the exception of Roy Klumb, had said little publicly about the controversy. Outspoken and clearly sympathetic with the president, Klumb even wrote a guest newspaper column condemning the "lynch mob" out to get Thames. He reminded readers, "This is the same set of folks who threatened a vote of no confidence on Dr. Fleming and. . . raised holy h___ when Dr. Fleming was released a year later."

Former Mississippi Supreme Court Justice Reuben Anderson presided over a hearing regarding the dismissal of professors Glamser (left) and Stringer.

The board finally met to discuss the matter on March 18 and solicited the counsel of Attorney General Jim Hood. On April 1, the faculty senate issued an open letter to Thames "as a way of restating our concerns to him and sharing those concerns with the public." While his treatment of Glamser and Stringer was "without parallel at America's best universities," they insisted that the vote of no confidence involved far more than that single grievance. "Rather," the letter stated, "the collapse of faculty confidence in your presidency reflects alarm about two years of ill-conceived decisions and management practices, several of which we highlight here." In addition to those already discussed publicly, the items that followed included "implementing an invasive technology policy that allows seizure and impoundment (for any reason!) of computers used in faculty offices," employing a "risk manager" when the university already had a "full-time legal counsel," imposing "an ill-conceived drug and alcohol policy" that subsequently had to be withdrawn, granting "stealth raises . . . to selected administrators and faculty," and "creating an environment so negative that significant numbers of respected and experienced colleagues are choosing to leave the university." The same day the senate published its letter, the college board scheduled the two professors' hearing for April 28 and accepted Hood's recommendation that Reuben Anderson, Jackson lawyer and former justice of the state supreme court, preside. At a second student-faculty protest on April 6, one speaker vowed, "We're not backing down, we're not going home, we're here to stay and Thames is leaving . . . He isn't the president of this university anymore, he just doesn't know it yet."

The hearing, scheduled for two days, opened amidst a near-carnival atmosphere. In Meeting Room B on the second floor of the R. C. Cook Student Union, eager spectators quickly claimed the fifty seats available to the public, as the crew from USM broadcasting services set up its audio and video recording equipment. Another 150 squeezed into the ground floor game room to watch a live transmission of the proceedings from the hearing room upstairs. Others listened to the campus radio station, which also broadcast the event live. In the Union lobby, supporters of the suspended professors sold T-shirts to raise money for the legal defense fund, which had already collected almost $30,000. Some wore "Impeach Thames" buttons, and others simply milled about with idle curiosity. At 9:44 A.M., Anderson called the session to order with an apology for the late start, which he insisted would not happen again. James Keith of the Jackson law firm of Adams and Reese served as counsel for the administration, and Adelman and American Civil Liberties Union attorney Robert McDuff represented the professors.

The administration accused Stringer and Glamser of "making statements that were untrue, dishonest, or misleading . . . engaging in malicious conduct . . . misusing state property, including the University's computer system . . . disclosing the social security number and other confidential information about . . . Dvorak, a student, and another member of the faculty . . . engaging in insubordinate conduct; and engaging in unprofessional conduct . . . including attempting to disrupt working relationships among the faculty and administration and undermine confidence in the administration and the University." Following opening statements by Keith and McDuff, Thames took the stand shortly after ten o'clock.

His testimony quickly confirmed what many of his critics had suspected; he had authorized investigators to scrutinize the electronic mail of Stringer, Glamser, and others. For almost two hours, Keith questioned him about emails and other evidence that substantiated the administration's charges, he insisted, and justified his actions. The two professors' "witch hunt," as he labeled it, to discredit Dvorak began not in December but as early as July when Stringer began to make inquiries about her tenure status at both Michigan State and Kentucky. Stringer was "irked," Thames said, reading from one of the emails, because of Dvorak's role in denying promotion to a Southern Miss colleague in English. Stringer, he added, had repeatedly misrepresented himself, to secure information, and Glamser had attempted unethically to manipulate the editor of the student newspaper with promises of favorable letters of recommendation as a reward for stories critical of Dvorak and the administration.

An employee of the Kentucky community college system testified by affidavit that she had responded to Stringer's request for information regarding Dvorak's tenure status because she believed, based on his use of her social security number, that he was acting in an official capacity for USM. She stated that she would not have done so otherwise. Thames also read an email in which *Printz* editor Rachel Quinlivan told Glamser, "That most certainly was a bag of goodies you gave to us today. All of you did fabulous work checking it all out. I can't imagine how they are going to talk their way out of this." At the close of Thames's testimony, Anderson declared an hour's recess for lunch and summoned the parties and their lawyers to meet with him in an adjacent room. They remained closeted for more than three hours as everyone else waited anxiously for the hearing to resume. At approximately three o'clock, the principals reemerged, and Anderson read a breathtaking statement. The two sides had agreed on a settlement, he announced, and all involved "believe it is in the best interest of the faculty, staff, alumni and students of the University of Southern Mississippi to put this matter behind us. We welcome the opportunity to heal the wounds of the university and to engage in constructive and positive efforts to move this university forward. We consider this matter concluded and we will not make any public comments." Anderson refused to reveal details of the agreement until the college board had approved it, but he allowed the two professors thirty minutes each to respond to the charges and to Thames's testimony.

Glamser denied that he made any inquiries regarding Dvorak before receiving the anonymous packet on December 11. The "bag of goodies" referred to in Quinlivan's email, he said, was the press kit on the investigation of Dvorak that the AAUP made available to all media. Moreover, she was an exceptional student, and his offer of favorable references was based on the quality of her stories not their slant. In a subsequent column, Quinlivan deemed Thames's comments "personally insulting." She had "very strong opinions about this administration," she continued,

> opinions I have held since several upper level administrators insulted the work of both me and my staff, used intimidation tactics in their conversations with the *Printz* staff and told me on several occasions stories I was working on were "non-stories" or something "students wouldn't care about." Some of those insults were emailed to the *Printz* account; perhaps those administrators would like their emails published or broadcast as mine were. But my opinions have been kept private, shared only with those I trusted, including Dr. Glamser. I have never written an editorial about this administration, instead choosing to work as a reporter, not as a columnist. Just because I am a journalist doesn't mean I don't have an opinion, and just because I have an opinion doesn't mean I can't report the news objectively.

Objectivity had by that time become a difficult virtue for almost everyone at Southern Miss.

Glamser declared emphatically his conviction that had he not spoken out about the enrollment "scandal" as well as the Dvorak controversy, he would not be facing dismissal. Stringer, too, contended that he was being punished for exercising academic freedom. He had never misrepresented himself, he insisted, and he had already obtained the information about Dvorak by telephone before he listed her social security number in any email. He testified that the number had been written on a yellow "sticky note" attached to a copy of Dvorak's resumé that mysteriously appeared in his mailbox in early January. With that copy of the resume in front of him as he drafted the email to the community college official in Kentucky, he unconsciously listed the social security number, he explained. "It's probably the bibliographer in me, the scholar. . . . I footnote. . . . I do it without thinking. I would have had exactly the same information if I hadn't."

Supporters of the professors remained confident that they would be reinstated. "I can't imagine," said English professor Anne Wallace, "they would have agreed to any settlement that would not bring about some kind of restitution to what happened to them." Such hopes were dashed two days later when the college board approved the settlement and released details of the agreement. The university would end "termination proceedings" and pay Stringer and Glamser their current nine-month salaries for two more years, after which the institution would bear no obligation to employ them. During the two years, Southern Miss would "not provide any office facilities, office supplies, or otherwise facilitate their physical presence on campus or their research projects," except for Stringer's work on Donne. Matching support for that project would continue under terms required by an existing external grant, though Stringer would be free to secure sponsorship from another institution, in which case USM's support would cease. Both professors relinquished the right to sue the university or the board, and the university agreed to attempt to dissuade Dvorak from filing suit against either of them. The professors also promised "to refrain from offering public criticism or commentary about the University's internal administrative operations during the term of this agreement."

In the words of one reporter, Thames had "silenced" perhaps the most "vocal critic of his administration . . . Glamser, but will have to pay him and. . . Stringer for two years." Board member and lawyer Amy Whitten observed that "trials result in winners and losers. Settlements result in winners." Stunned and disappointed, many among the USM faculty hardly felt like winners. Some were even angry and tossed about such terms as "sellout" and "betrayed." The *Hattiesburg American* reported that before the hearing, Stringer, his wife, and Glamser had all prepared retirement papers just in case. Most of the campus community remained distressed but sympathetic. "They took on the challenge," said Myron Henry, "and paid the price emotionally, physically and financially." Another speculated that "there was enormous pressure brought to bear here . . . you can't ask two individuals to save the world. . . . Obviously there's a power differential."

Anger was largely reserved for Thames, especially his monitoring of private emails, which one faculty member termed "outrageous" and another "scary." Alumni and donors were also angry. Bobby Chain suggested that perhaps his own emails to people on campus had been intercepted. "I hope some of them were," he said. "I'd be mad as hell. . . . There's no winners in this situation but there is a loser and that is the university as a whole," which he feared had received "a national black eye. . . . I think we're really damaged." Donor Marcia Hartwig rejoiced that Stringer and Glamser were "out of the fire" but deplored a situation that left "the rest of us . . . to deal with an exceedingly flawed administration and two years of bitterness and very little hope." She and her physician husband Geoffrey had recently canceled a substantial annual scholarship donation and pledged a comparable amount to the professors' defense fund. "I feel let down by this settlement," she said, "and someone needs to pick up the torch again."

Speculation began immediately regarding the administration's capacity to recover from the latest fiasco. The *Hattiesburg American* concluded that "this incident underscores the fact that Thames faces very real questions about his ability to lead the state's second largest university." Acknowledging that his policies seem "to have saved money, streamlined operations and made accountability a part of academic life," the editors noted that during his tenure the school had also "lurched from one controversy to another." To survive, they advised, he would have to make significant changes. In May, he accepted the deans' proposal for a President's University Council to improve communication between the administration and the campus community. Consisting of eighteen members divided equally among faculty, staff, and students, the council, he said, would supplement, not supplant, existing representative bodies, with whom he also pledged to work and communicate more effectively. He insisted that no emails were currently being monitored and accepted the council's proposal that he seek the attorney general's counsel before implementing any future scrutiny. He also created a "President's Page" on the university web site, which eventually included a periodic newsletter, the "President's Update," as well as summaries of cabinet meetings. Distressed that his actions had "generated controversy," he insisted, "It has never been my intention to cause our university harm or unrest. . . . I have committed my life to advancing our university, and as your president, I will continue to devote my full attention to working with you while Southern Miss becomes firmly established as a world-class institution."

Study abroad opportunities included the popular Vietnam studies program led by history professor Andrew Wiest (left).

On May 7, the faculty senate adopted a resolution petitioning the board to replace Thames. Reporter Janet Braswell noted that the "enthusiastic outrage" of the earlier no confidence vote had mellowed into profound "sorrow." Stephen Judd remarked that "certainly among the old hands, people do love the university. Even me, I came here six years ago when it was really a special place. It's certainly become a sadder place. We're watching wonderful people who've been here years leave early. A lot of the culture that older, established faculty members created has gone away." Former legislator and longtime Southern Miss administrator Eugene Saucier added his voice to those calling for the president's removal. In a guest column in the *American* on May 16, he asserted that Thames lacked both "the temperament" and "the people skills" requisite for the job. "He is incapable of seeing any way but his as the right way," Saucier said, "and, like an elephant, never forgets what he perceives as an injury done to him. I have known him for nearly forty years and was instrumental in helping him rise in the university, though I deeply regret that fact. The bottom-liners and power-brokers who put Shelby in as president will, if they do not demand his resignation, live to regret it."

On May 20, the board met with Thames for two hours in executive session. "They didn't . . . invite a single faculty member in there," Myron Henry complained. "It's amazing. One has to wonder if the board is even interested in communicating with faculty." The trustees were "encouraged," according to a terse official statement, "by the accomplishments that USM has achieved under Dr. Thames' watch, and by the efforts being made to rebuild the university community and to address the problems of unrest. The board continues to support the president as he implements his plan." Any plan, declared a skeptical Henry, must articulate "trust in capital letters. It's one thing to talk about trust and another to have it." In June, Glamser announced his retirement, exercising a provision of the settlement that allowed him to receive his two years' compensation as a consultant to the university rather than an employee. "I don't want to discuss it or give reasons for it," he said. "I am officially retired. My status is consulting." Stringer accepted a position at Texas A&M, taking his Donne project and grant with him. The same month, Dvorak resigned as vice-president to focus exclusively on her duties as president of the university's research foundation, especially development of a proposed new innovation and commercialization park. Thames denied that the reassignment had anything to do with the recent controversy and to replace her as vice-president promoted associate vice-president for research and technology transfer Cecil Burge.

And so ended the most contentious episode at USM, certainly since the 1960s if not ever. Wounds were deep and widespread, and bitterness and mistrust lingered. Many questions remained unanswered, for the settlement had foreclosed cross-examination of the principals, and its terms had silenced them, at least for the foreseeable future. Most mysterious, lurking half-forgotten in the shadows of obscurity, was the anonymous principal who perhaps held the key to all the other mysteries, the incident's sinister "Deep Throat." His identity, like that of the infamous "Blackbird" of the 1920s, remains concealed, but unlike his predecessor, he was no youthful prankster. The "bomb" he planted on the floor of Frank Glamser's office was wantonly destructive. Ironically, the institution in whose interest everyone purportedly, and perhaps sincerely, acted suffered the most damage. Out of the mouths of, if not babes, at least idealistic and confused students came the most poignant postmortems. Rachel Quinlivan, who had helplessly watched her name dragged into a public controversy, reflected on the outcome. "This university," she wrote in a May column, "is going through a difficult time period. A string of events has destroyed values and good opinions, but most importantly it has damaged the reputation of a university that indeed is, in some respects, world-class." SGA president Jared Loftus, who had seen Thames from a closer vantage point than most students, articulated the dilemma of the noncombatants. "I gained a lot of respect for him," Loftus said, but "when [faculty] are telling you totally different sides and say they're 100 percent sure, it's hard to know. It blurs things up, that's for sure."

Apart from the lingering internal tensions, the university faced continuing budget constraints. In June, the board authorized the "outsourcing" of food services and bookstore operations to private companies and approved a 6 percent tuition increase, though Thames warned that the revenue generated would be absorbed by rising operational costs. Salary increases would have to come from elsewhere. Though faculty and staff had received but a single 2 percent raise, and that midyear, since 1999, Thames reaffirmed his commitment to enhanced compensation as his top priority. "We must pay productive people well for their hard work," he declared, but he also repeatedly stressed that doing so depended upon improvements in enrollment, retention, operational efficiency, and external grants. Therefore, he insisted, "it is everyone's responsibility to increase enrollment, improve retention, and make absolutely certain that our class offerings are second to none. We all play a part in that responsibility chain. Similarly, it is everyone's responsibility to increase external funding," as supportive colleagues if not as actual grant writers.

Unfortunately, the months of administrative controversy had overshadowed exciting things happening elsewhere in the university. In 2003, history professor Andrew Wiest's Vietnam studies program won the Institute of International Education's Andrew Heiskell Award for Innovation, and the following year history colleague William Scarborough's *Masters of the Big House* won the Richard Wright Literary Award. Also in 2004, Frederick Barthelme, director of USM's acclaimed Center for Writers, joined John Updike and three others as a finalist for the prestigious PEN/Faulkner award for fiction. In 2005, Southern Miss awarded its first Ph.D. in nursing, and medical technology major Elizabeth Herrington recorded the nation's highest score on the American Society for Clinical Pathology Board of Registration examination. By that time, USM's Center for Sustainable Health Outreach had helped train almost a thousand volunteer health advisors working among poor and minority communities in Mississippi and Alabama.

Under director Bob Pierce, the Alumni Association was pursuing an ambitious agenda. More than half of all Southern Miss alumni had graduated since the old student handbook, *The Drawl*, had ceased publication in the late seventies, and in 2002 a Tradition Enhancement Committee recommended its revival. The previous year, the Student Alumni Association had sought to expand and diversify its membership by changing its name to The Legacy. The revamped student organization, the new committee, and the reissued handbook played instrumental roles in an effort to educate students and alumni alike in the institution's history and traditions. The Legacy initiated new traditions to perpetuate the memory of older ones: having freshmen repaint the Eagle Walk before the first football game each fall; supporting other athletic events with a weekly theme painted on the "Little Rock" between the District and McLemore Hall; ritually burning, at the first fall Friday Night at the

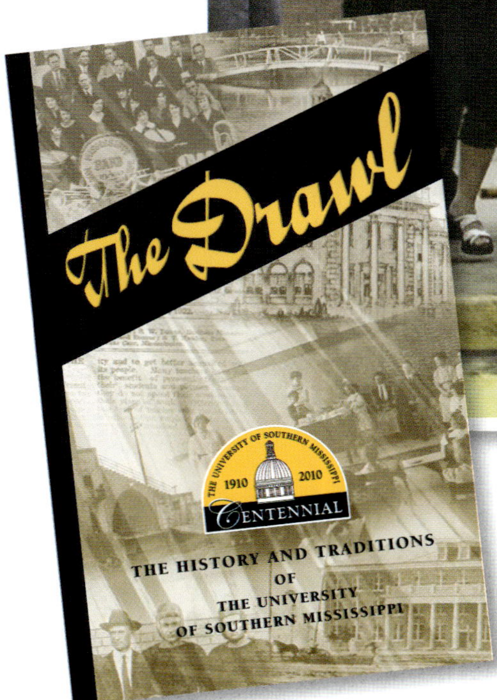

A Tradition Enhancement Committee and a revamped Student Alumni Association, which became The Legacy in 2001, helped the Southern Miss Alumni Association restore old traditions, including revival of the old student handbook, as well as foster new ones, such as Friday Night at the Fountain, painting the "Little Rock," and repainting the Eagle Walk.

Fountain, T-shirts and hats from other schools swapped by students for Southern Miss replacements; and hosting an annual Legacy Lecture Series. In 2004, Association president Rex Kelly and presidents-elect Danny Mitchell and Rosemary Aultman spearheaded the development of a revolving strategic overview process that facilitated long-range planning and led to several initiatives: administrative reorganization that included the addition of an associate director for external affairs; establishment of interest-based constituent societies and regional alumni ambassadors to supplement the work of local chapters; publication of an annual report to increase alumni awareness of Association activities; and a proposal to renovate and expand the Ogletree House. That same year, the first Legacy Scholarships, funded in part by proceeds from an annual Homecoming golf tournament, were awarded to children or grandchildren of active members of the Alumni Association.

In 2005, at the Mississippi Coast Coliseum in Biloxi, opera tenor Placido Domingo appeared in concert with the Southern Miss Symphony Orchestra in what director Jay Dean described as "the most significant musical event ever to have occurred in Mississippi."

Upon returning to the presidency in 2001, Aubrey Lucas had noted that "two areas in the university . . . relate it better to the outside constituency than any other . . . arts and athletics." In promoting the former, symphony director Jay Dean outdid himself in 2004–5. The symphony orchestra's season opened in October with renowned flutist Sir James Galway and in April 2005 brought to the Mississippi Coast Coliseum what Dean described as "the most significant musical event ever to have occurred in Mississippi." An opera tenor who appealed to popular audiences, Plácido Domingo was, the director said, "the number one classical music performer in the world, period." He would appear in only six American cities in 2005, and one would be Biloxi, where he would perform with The University of Southern Mississippi Symphony Orchestra in what was cosponsored by Beau Rivage Resort and Casino and billed as "The Concert Event of a Lifetime." Luring the most famous tenor in the world to Mississippi once again proved, as Dean put it, that at Southern Miss "the unattainable is possible." The icing on the cake came after the first rehearsal when Domingo said of the Southern Miss orchestra, "No amount of advanced expectation could have prepared me for what I discovered . . . a veritable treasure trove of truly outstanding young musicians from so many parts of the world."

In athletics, the new millennium belonged to baseball, but not immediately. The 2002 Eagles finished 36-22 behind Jeff Cook, who led the team with 16 home runs and 108 RBIs, and Shea Douglas, who won 10 games and struck out 108. They and Allen Winningham, who hit .366, made first team all-conference. The following year's squad won more games than any in school history and began an unparalleled string of postseason appearances. Clint King led in hitting with a .394 average and 77 RBIs, and he and Cook each hit 23 home runs. Starting pitcher Bob McCrory won ten games and struck out 90, while Austin Tubb recorded 10 saves with a 1.45 ERA. Southern Miss won the C-USA regular season and tournament titles and hosted the school's first NCAA regional tournament. After a first round loss to Southern University of Baton Rouge, Eagle bats exploded the next day, eliminating Murray State 18-0 and Southern 18-1. Baylor

Jarrett Hoffpauir set school records in 2004 with 109 hits and 92 RBIs.

The 2003 baseball Eagles won more games (forty-seven) than any team in school history, winning the Conference USA regular season and tournament titles and hosting USM's first NCAA regional tournament.

squeezed out a 3-2 victory in the championship game, but USM finished 47-16 and ranked as high as fifteenth in postseason polls. Cook was a C-USA scholar athlete, and Corky Palmer was conference coach of the year.

Jarrett Hoffpauir had a remarkable year in 2004, batting .405 and setting school records with 109 hits and 92 RBIs. He was also the nation's most difficult strikeout, fanning only 8 times all season. The team swept three games from an Ole Miss squad ranked in the top ten, and Cliff Russum tossed a no-hitter against Eastern Illinois, striking out 15 batters. Anthony DeWitt posted a 10-3 record, and Austin Tubb had 10 saves and an ERA of .93 out of the bullpen. Fighting their way out of the losers' bracket after a first round loss in the conference tournament, the Eagles ran out of gas in the championship game, bowing to TCU 3-1. Seeded second, USM won its first game in the Baton Rouge regional but lost the next two to finish 45-19. Hoffpauir and Tubb were voted to several all-America teams, and they along with Ryan Frith and Matt Shepherd made first team all-C-USA. With those four players gone and injuries to pitchers Cliff Russum in the preseason and Mike Cashion early in the year, prospects for 2005 dimmed considerably, but the hitting of Marc Maddox, Brad Willcutt, and Jason Lowery and the pitching of Patrick Ezell and reliever Daniel Best took up the slack. After going 39-17 in the regular season, the Golden Eagles hosted the C-USA tournament for the first time since 1996, falling again to TCU in the championship game. A third straight trip to an NCAA regional, this time in Oxford, proved short and disappointing as the team dropped back-to-back games to Oklahoma and Maine to finish 41-21. Daniel Best's .46 ERA set a school record, and he joined Willcutt and Maddox on the all-C-USA first team. Maddox was also a Conference USA scholar of the year.

Armed with a new slogan, "Anyone, Anywhere, Anytime," and an apparently healthy Derrick Nix, the football team began the 2002 season with three straight home wins. The opening game against Jackson State drew a record crowd of 35,169, and Nix keyed victories in the other two with 201 rushing yards against Illinois and 196 against Memphis. The Eagles lost five of the next eight, however, including conference losses to TCU, Louisville, and Tulane. The Louisville loss, the third in a row to the Cardinals, was especially bitter. Playing at home with a national television audience watching on ESPN, Southern Miss squandered a 17-3 halftime lead and missed on three late field goal attempts, including a 32-yarder that would have forced a third overtime. A closing win over East Carolina at The Rock secured the team's fifth bowl bid in six years, and Derrick Nix's 139 yards put him within 11 of Ben Garry's career record of 3,595. No one knew that Nix had willed his way to the most productive season of his career (1,194 yards) playing with kidneys that were barely functioning. Diagnosed with a degenerative disease that would eventually require a kidney

In 2003, the university unveiled a new athletic mark and a new official shade of gold. Alumnus Rodney Richardson, whose RARE Design firm developed the logo, said that it was intended "to create a classic athletic identity inspired by a strong tradition modernized to reflect the Southern Miss spirit of perseverance and achievement."

Despite playing with a degenerative disease that would eventually require a kidney transplant, running back Derrick Nix had his most productive season in 2002, rushing for 1,194 yards. Unable to compete in the Houston Bowl because of the illness, which was diagnosed following the regular season, he fell eleven yards short of Ben Garry's career rushing record of 3,595 yards.

transplant, he would never get the chance to break Garry's record or to showcase his talents in the NFL. Playing without him, the team fell to Oklahoma State 33-23 in the Houston Bowl, but linebacker Rod Davis won USM's first Conerly Trophy given to the best college player in Mississippi. Exemplifying everything good about Southern Miss football, Nix won the team's Heart of the Eagles Award. "The heart of the Eagles," Bower said, "that's what he's all about."

The 2003 season began and ended poorly, but in between, Southern Miss captured its fourth Conference USA championship. After an embarrassing 34-2 loss to the University of California at Berkeley and wins over UAB and Memphis, USM hosted Nebraska in the most anticipated and celebrated game ever played in Roberts Stadium. The outcome was disappointing, as the Cornhuskers humbled Southern Miss 38-14 in front of a record crowd of 36,152 and a national television audience on ESPN. The Eagles rebounded to win five of the next six setting up a C-USA showdown against TCU at The Rock in late November. Neither team had lost a conference game, and the ninth-ranked Horned Frogs were playing for a bid to the Bowl Championship Series (BCS). USM jumped out to a 31-6 lead, but the visitors recovered two onsides kicks and stormed back to within three points. Following an Eagle field goal, cornerback Greg Brooks forced a crucial fumble on TCU's next possession, and Southern Miss went on to win 40-28. A victory over East Carolina the following week secured the conference title and a third bid to the Liberty Bowl in seven years. Utah spoiled the trip to Memphis with a 17-point shutout in which the two teams converted only 4 of 31 third downs between them. Eight Eagles made first team all-conference, and Bower won his third coach of the year award. Rod Davis passed Clump Taylor to become the most prolific tackler in school history with 526.

In the opening game of 2004 in Lincoln, Nebraska, Southern Miss took advantage of five turnovers to stun the Cornhuskers 21-17. The turning point came midway through the third quarter when linebacker Naton Stewart returned an interception 49 yards for a touchdown. After Dustin Almond's 46-yard scoring pass to Marvin Young

put the Eagles ahead, the defense delivered a last-minute goal line stand to seal the victory. Four more wins, including a 39-35 overtime thriller over Houston at home, and a lone loss at Alabama put the midseason record at 5-1. Things went downhill thereafter, however, beginning with a 52-34 drubbing by Cincinnati at The Rock that broke USM's 13-game conference win streak. The regular season ended at home against highly-ranked California in a game that had been rescheduled because of Hurricane Ivan in September. A fourth quarter touchdown pulled the scrappy underdogs within a point, but the Golden Bears blocked Darren McCaleb's extra point attempt and returned it 80 yards to go up by three. Cal running back J. J. Arrington, whose 261 rushing yards was the most by an opponent in school history, set up an insurance touchdown with a 56-yard carry late in the game. The loss dropped the Eagles to 6-5, which was good enough to qualify for the New Orleans Bowl where they downed North Texas State 31-10. Despite the disappointing record, linebacker Michael Boley won the Conerly Trophy and was named C-USA player of the year on defense as was kick-returner John Eubanks for special teams.

During the summer of 2005, Conference USA lost nine members, including Louisville, Cincinnati, and TCU, but

Football 2003 provided a rollercoaster season of highs and lows. A record crowd turned out for Nebraska's historic visit to The Rock in September only to witness a disappointing 38-14 loss. After a 3-3 start, the Eagles finished the season with six straight wins, including a 40-28 upset of ninth-ranked TCU, after which fans tore down the goalposts, and coach Jeff Bower received the traditional victory shower.

The 2004 season began with a 21-17 upset of Nebraska in Lincoln (left) and ended with a 31-10 victory over North Texas State in the New Orleans Bowl. Linebacker Michael Boley (right) won USM's second Conerly Trophy and sixth C-USA defensive MVP award.

gained six new ones. With all members now football institutions, the realigned league went to two divisions whose winners would meet in a championship game. Hurricane Katrina played havoc with the 2005 season, forcing USM to postpone its opening game against Tulane and sending the Eagles to Memphis to prepare for the following week's game at Alabama. The University of Memphis generously provided housing and use of its facilities for the week, but the stress took its toll, and the Crimson Tide triumphed 30-21. It took a miraculous overtime win at Marshall late in November to preserve a winning season, as the team stumbled to a second consecutive 6-5 record and a return to the New Orleans Bowl. Playing in Lafayette because of Katrina, Southern Miss defeated Arkansas State 31-19. Linebacker Kevis Coley became the seventh Golden Eagle in ten years to win C-USA defensive player of the year honors, and twin brother Trevis, along with George Batiste, Eubanks, and punter Luke Johnson joined him on the all-conference first team. Southern Miss placed eight players on the Conference USA team of the decade: Boley, Davis, Patrick Surtain, and Adalius Thomas on defense; Nix and Sherrod Gideon

Students waving "dot posters" to distract opposing free throw shooters became a familiar sight in Reed Green Coliseum.

on offense; and Eubanks and Eric Booth on special teams. Bower was selected coach of the decade.

In basketball, several incidents in 2001–2 illustrated the virtues and the frustrations that marked James Green's last three seasons at Southern Miss. On the eve of the conference opener at Memphis, he benched leading scorer Elvin Mims for violating a team rule. "We teach the game and we teach life," he explained. "If that means we play without our best player, then we'll play without our best player." His team lost by 22 points. A week later, USM held UAB to the fewest points in Blazer history, and Mims came off the bench to score 25 points and spark a 50-36 victory. Later at Tulane, the Green Wave hit a desperation three-pointer at the buzzer to force overtime and went on to win 66-61. At Cincinnati, Green's team suffered the worst loss in school history 89-37. With no chance to make the conference tournament and only pride to play for, the seniors rallied their teammates for a win over South Florida to finish 10-17.

Another losing season (13-16) followed in 2002–3, though USM evened the score with Cincinnati, upsetting the Bearcats in the C-USA tournament. Despite a stellar year by Charles Gaines, who led the team with double-digit averages in scoring and rebounding, the Eagles suffered through a third straight losing season in 2003–4. On March 5, 2004, as the locks were being changed on the offices of Frank Glamser and Gary Stringer, Green announced his resignation. It came the day before the season ended and followed conversations involving the coach, the athletic director, and the president. "James

Southern Miss basketball entered a new era in 2004 with head coaches Larry Eustachy for men and former Lady Eagle player and assistant Joye Lee-McNelis for women.

Green is a quality person," Giannini told a press conference. "In a very competitive Conference USA, he led the team to a conference championship and two NIT appearances. He has been a leader off the court, as well, achieving high graduation rates among his student athletes. I appreciate James' dedication to Southern Miss." The next day, Green watched from the stands as longtime

Sonja Brown (2001-3) broke every school record for blocked shots, including most in a single game (eleven) against Hampton in December 2002.

assistant Jeff Norwood coached the final game, a 63-50 loss to East Carolina.

Three weeks later, Giannini held another press conference to introduce new head coach Larry Eustachy. The new Eagle boss brought a 260-145 record over 13 seasons as a head coach, most recently at Iowa State where he took his team to the Elite Eight in 2000 and won national coach of the year honors. He also brought some baggage, having departed Iowa State in 2003 amidst charges of inappropriate behavior off the court. His first Southern Miss team got off to a 9-2 start that included the first 100-point game in a decade and an 88-84 upset of LSU at the Mississippi Coast Coliseum in Biloxi. What followed bordered on collapse, as the Eagles won only twice more and finished 11-17. Things got worse in 2005–6 with the first 20-loss record in 21 years (10-21). "This is as frustrated as I've ever been at any time in coaching," Eustachy said at one time during the season. One bright spot was the play of freshman Courtney Beasley, who led the team in scoring.

Rick Reeves's Lady Eagles also continued to struggle with losing seasons in 2001–2 (11-17) and 2002–3 (14-15). Leading scorers were LaTasha Sumerall and Dana Jones. Sumerall led the team in steals both years as did Sonja Brown in rebounds. Brown also broke all school records for blocked shots, including 11 in a game against Hampton in December 2002. In 2003–4, Deondra Carter made the C-USA all-freshman team and led the team to its first winning record in four years, 14-13. It was not enough for Reeves, who resigned at the end of the year with a 68-74 record in five seasons. His successor was former Eagle player and assistant coach Joye Lee-McNelis, who in 13 seasons at Memphis had won four straight C-USA championships and made 8 postseason appearances. "I'm excited about coming home," she said. "My number one

Coach Joye Lee-McNelis's first recruiting class included Kendra Reed (top photo) and Amber Eugene, who would be instrumental in restoring the fortunes of Southern Miss women's basketball. As four-year starters, both would score more than a thousand points in their careers.

priority is to take the program back to the lofty heights that it enjoyed during Coach Kay James' tenure." It would take time, however. Led by Shannon Stueber and Emer Foley, her first squad struggled to a 9-19 record. The 2005–6 team, with no seniors and all but five freshmen, improved to 14-15. Two of those freshmen, Kendra Reed and Amber Eugene, would be instrumental in the rebuilding process. Reed led the team in scoring and Eugene in rebounding, while the only junior on the squad, Kristin Chaney, led in assists and steals.

After two losing seasons, the softball team seemed on its way to a third with a 5-11 start in 2004. Seven of those first 16 games were against ranked teams, however, and a midseason win over Mississippi State seemed to ignite a spark. A three-game sweep at Houston followed, "and that's when the players started really to believe," said coach Gay McNutt. After three wins at East Carolina, Southern Miss returned home for the final regular season series against league-leading Louisville needing another sweep to clinch a C-USA championship. A last-inning

In 2004, the grass surface of Roberts Stadium was replaced by a new artificial Momentum turf, which in October was renamed Carlisle-Faulkner Field in honor of alumnus and benefactor Gene Carlisle.

two-run homer by Sarah Boyd won the first game 4-2, and pitcher Danielle Wymer handcuffed Cardinal hitters 6-1 in the second. A solo home run by Auriel Jenkins decided the final game 3-2 and gave USM a 19-4 conference record and a third C-USA championship. Winless in the conference tournament, the Eagles still received a bid to the NCAA regional at Stanford, where they dropped 2 of 3 games to finish 33-26. Jessica Holaway, who had won 15 games in each of the previous two seasons, won 18 in 2004 and ended her career ranked third in wins, shutouts, and strikeouts behind Courtney Blades and Felicia Gonzales. Jenkins was MVP in the conference and McNutt coach of the year. The record slid to 29-32 the next year and 29-38 in 2006, but in the latter season Ashley Brenan, Charity Butler, Ashley Davis, and Jessica Huerta all closed out memorable careers. Davis finished with 193 hits, the most in school history.

In other sports, men's indoor track was restored in 2002 after a two-year absence, and Cedric Norman made all-American as an indoor and outdoor high jumper in

A DREAM COME TRUE

"I always dreamt," Sue Pace recalled, "of a member-driven, community-based organization that allowed retired adults to satisfy their thirst for knowledge." In 1991, Aubrey Lucas gave her a chance to make the dream come true. As director of continuing education at USM, she convinced President Lucas that with $3,000 she could inaugurate a project in which "seasoned adults . . . could learn from each other through peer-taught programs." Lucas provided the seed money, Pace and ninety-four charter members provided the vision and energy, and the Institute for Lifelong Learning (ILR) was born. Membership quickly outgrew the Institute's facilities at its Peck House headquarters, and a 1999 building fund campaign raised $750,000 for renovation and expansion. The new Asbury Annex featured a large meeting room for ILR's luncheon lecture program and other social activities and three additional classrooms for its seminars and five-week, member-led personal enrichment courses on topics ranging from horticulture to music therapy. In 2005, the Bernard Osher Foundation granted the Institute $100,000 and the possibility of additional support if membership reached five hundred in three years. ILR gratefully changed its name to the Osher Lifelong Learning Institute (OLLI), and by 2008 membership approached 550. The Osher Foundation responded with a $1 million grant. "Because of this endowment," said Pace, "there will be earnings available so that our grandchildren will have a place to learn and enjoy friendships when they become 'seasoned adults.'" The following year, Susan Bone replaced Pace, who declared, "I am excited to retire and enjoy OLLI as a member. All these years and I have never been able to take a class."

2004. Bridget Files, Andrea Bush, Amy Truong, and Nikki Tribble led the 2003 volleyball team to the best season in school history with a 27-6 record, 11-2 in Conference USA. The team finished third in the league, and Santiago Restrepo was coach of the year.

In 2003, athletic director Richard Giannini announced an ambitious plan for sweeping improvements in athletic facilities, including major renovation and expansion of Reed Green Coliseum, luxury suites for both baseball and football, new facilities for tennis and Olympic sports, and additions to the softball and track-soccer complexes. "It's something we have to do," he said. "Maintaining the status quo is not an option." The following year, Roberts Stadium received a new artificial Momentum turf, which was rededicated that October as Carlisle-Faulkner Field in honor of alumnus and benefactor Gene Carlisle. The following month, expansion plans suffered a setback when Hattiesburg voters rejected a "tourism tax" that would have provided $12 million in funding for the athletic improvements and renovation of Bennett Auditorium. Construction continued, however, as Giannini pledged to secure funds elsewhere.

On June 30, 2004, the capital campaign that had begun under Horace Fleming in 1997 ended successfully with more than $107 million received in gifts or pledges. The total included $38 million for athletics, $28 million for scholarships, $16 million for faculty and staff development, and $14 million for USMGC. An additional $44 million worth of intellectual properties was donated to the Southern Miss Research Foundation. In August, new vice-president for research Cecil Burge reported that external funding had increased for the sixth year in a row to almost $70 million. Despite higher tuition, fall enrollment rose slightly in 2004, including significant increases in first-time freshmen (7.5 percent), transfers (12 percent), and USMGC (17 percent). The Honors College welcomed 31 freshmen (including 6 National Merit finalists) with ACT scores of 31 or higher, up from 17 the previous year. From 57 percent in 2002, the college's retention rate for first-time students had jumped to 98 percent.

Not all the news during fall 2004 was good. In *U. S. News and World Report*'s annual ranking, USM fell from a third- to a fourth-tier university. Thames blamed the drop on the provost office's failure to provide the magazine with "complete and accurate information," including a report on the graduate program. "This is a most unfortunate situation," he said, "that cannot be allowed to happen again. . . . We will be in discussions with all components of our university to ensure accuracy and accountability of data retrieval and reporting." In November, Hattiesburg voters rejected the tourism tax that would have supported improvements to university facilities. Most alarming was notification in December that the Southern Association of Colleges and Schools had placed USM on probation for deficiencies in its assessment of distance learning programs. "We take our SACS accreditation very seriously," said Thames, "and we will remedy this situation," but for at least a year, until SACS met again the following December, the

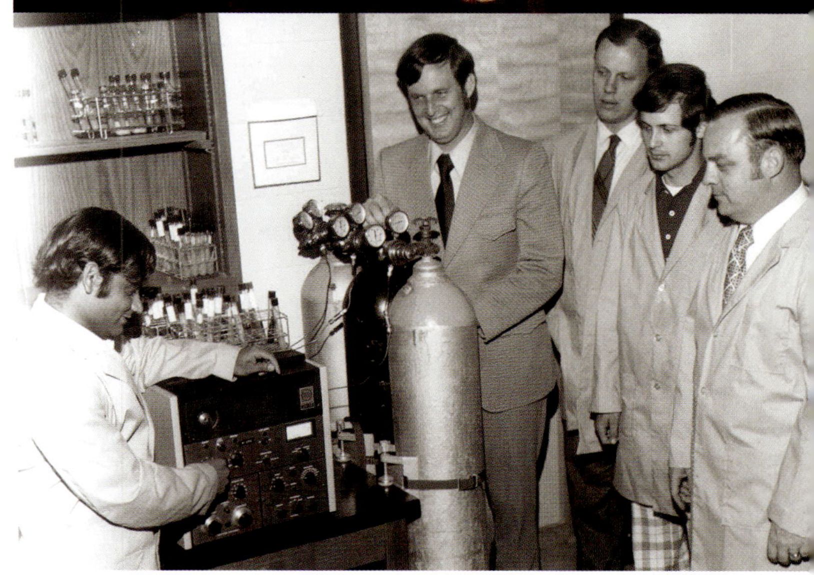

In May 2005, President Shelby Thames announced that the college board had approved his request to remain at his post for two more years, after which, he said, "I will return to my first love—the lab."

university would labor under the acute embarrassment of academic probation.

By early 2005, rumors were again circulating that Thames's job was in jeopardy. On January 28, the faculty senate for three hours heatedly debated another proposed no confidence vote and five days later voted 39-2 in favor of a resolution asking the board to initiate a national search "to find a successor to Dr. Shelby F. Thames" in time for "a smooth transition of leadership" when his contract expired in May 2006. The resolution also pledged that in the interim "USM faculty members will do all they can . . . to help remove USM from SACS probation." According to senate president David Beckett, the sponsors of the resolution "purposefully left out the words 'no confidence.'" When asked if he intended to step down in 2006, Thames responded, "Why would I retire? I'm having more fun than I've ever had in my life."

Suddenly on May 19, however, Thames announced that the board had granted his request to remain at his post until May 2007. In a prepared statement, he explained that the one-year extension of his contract would allow him to finish "many important projects" while affording the board ample time "to conduct a national search for a successor . . . to whom I hope that I can pass the baton for a long, successful term." He had sought the presidency, he stressed, "for one purpose only: to facilitate change—fiscally and organizationally. . . . Just as the world we live in has changed dramatically, universities must also change to remain relevant. . . . The commissioner and board of trustees know that I love this university." When a new president was chosen, he said, "I will return to my first love—the lab. I will also continue to be found in the stands at Southern Miss athletic fields for years to come. . . . I'm not on the road to retirement."

Several of the "important projects" Thames wanted to complete involved construction. Indeed, as his old nemesis the faculty senate later conceded, "physical improvements at the Hattiesburg Campus are quite noticeable."

The new $7.9 million International Center opened in 2005.

The five-story, 42,000 square foot International Center had recently opened with a dining facility on the first floor. The addition to the Polymer Science Research Center was finished along with a $750,000 annex to the Peck House. Construction was under way on the student life and economic development centers, and a fundraising campaign for renovation and expansion of the Ogletree House was poised to begin. Three quarters of a century earlier, surveying the fruits of a similar construction boom, Joe Cook had deemed "the building of correct ideals in the souls of young men and women far more important than the building of houses with bricks and mortar." On August 29, 2005, Hurricane Katrina unleashed a brutal vindication of Cook's dictum, spawning countless reminders of both physical frailty and spiritual resilience. For people in the Gulf South, storms are a fact of life, and old-timers who could remember Camille believed they had seen the worst. Katrina chastened them. Her category 3 winds and unprecedented tidal surge left a swath of devastation whose magnitude was almost inexpressible. Once a category 5 monster, she had mercifully diminished before coming ashore near Buras, Louisiana, her lethal northeast quadrant raking the Mississippi coast. Creeping inland, she spewed hurricane force fury over Hattiesburg and beyond.

Three days without power and water, USM's main campus sustained damage estimated at $20 million. The roofs of forty buildings required repair; six, including the emblematic dome of the Administration Building, had to

Hurricane Katrina left her mark on the Hattiesburg campus. The roofs of six buildings, including the Lucas Administration Building, had to be replaced.

be replaced. With 27,000 cubic yards of debris scattered about, clearing alone cost $500,000. Selflessness abounded, as the office of student affairs, under vice-president Joe Paul, became the nerve-center of efforts to meet the needs of students most directly affected by the tragedy. Almost a thousand had to withdraw, while more than a hundred temporarily transferred in from institutions paralyzed by the storm. Disaster accomplished what had seemed impossible only days before, as three years of rancor and discord dissolved into unity of purpose under Thames's leadership. He was determined to keep the school open and to protect jobs, and his persuasive insistence that "we will be better than before," heartened a shaken and anxious university community. Remarkably, classes resumed in Hattiesburg on September 12, only two weeks after the storm.

Prospects seemed bleaker for USM-Gulf Coast, where the extent of devastation was astounding. At Gulf Park, the storm surge had swept past the former provost's home and swallowed the first floor of the older buildings fronting the beach. The provost's home, which had recently

Katrina damage at Southern Miss facilities on the Gulf Coast was astounding. Of the stately old provost's home at Gulf Park, which had recently been converted into a coffee house, only the front steps remained. The unprecedented storm surge completely gutted the J. L. Scott Marine Education Center and Aquarium at Point Cadet in Biloxi.

ALUMNI HEROES

In 2006, several Southern Miss graduates received accolades for their roles in the aftermath of the Katrina disaster. Both the coast *Sun Herald* and the New Orleans *Times-Picayune* won Pulitzer Prizes for public service. The staff of the former included fifteen USM alumni led by publisher Ricky Mathews, who on the eve of the storm sent a team to Columbus, Georgia, to print the newspaper there. The *Sun Herald* never missed an issue and distributed 20,000 free copies every day for a month. "At the end of the day," said Mathews, "we serve the community. In the days after the storm we were the only way people could get the news." Three other alumni, Chuck Cook, Ted Jackson, and Leslie Williams worked for the New Orleans paper. *Picayune* editor Jim

CNN reporter Kathleen Koch.

Sun Herald publisher Ricky Mathews.

Amoss praised his entire staff but singled out photographer Jackson, who, he said, "braved extraordinary circumstances to capture some of the most memorable images." Jackson had already won a Pulitzer for his photography in 1997.

Honors College alumna Kathleen Koch's CNN documentary on recovery efforts in her hometown of Bay St. Louis prompted more viewer responses than any such broadcast in the network's history. She said that covering Katrina was the most important assignment in her career. In April 2006, she returned to campus to join longtime journalism professor Gene Wiggins as the first two inductees into the Southern Miss School of Mass Communication and Journalism's new Hall of Fame.

been converted into a coffee house, was gone, and even the new Library and the Advanced Education Center on the north side of campus had to be gutted. At Point Cadet in Biloxi, destruction was total. What was left of the J. L. Scott Marine Education Center and Aquarium had to be demolished and its operations moved to the Gulf Coast Research Laboratory in Ocean Springs. Even there, conditions were "mind boggling," in the words of biologist Jim Franks, who had ridden out Camille as a

Pat Joachim, associate provost for USMGC, led a heroic recovery effort, refusing to surrender even a semester to Katrina's malice. Miraculously, on October 10, 2005, barely six weeks after the storm struck, classes resumed in makeshift facilities at the former Garden Park Hospital in Gulfport, which became the Southern Miss Gulf Coast Student Services Center.

graduate student at GCRL thirty-six years earlier. "This," he concluded, "was much worse." Farther east, Cedar Point held up better but still sustained almost $100,000 worth of damage. Miraculously, no Southern Miss employees were killed, but 128 lost their homes.

In the aftermath, leadership fell to Pat Joachim, who only days earlier had been coaxed out of retirement to become associate provost in charge of USM-Gulf Coast. Administration there had been largely unsettled since the university reorganization in 2003 when the college of marine sciences had been disbanded. Vice-president James Williams retired that summer, and Jay Grimes returned to the coast as provost. The following February, Ken Malone had been appointed to the newly created post of chief of operations. When Tim Hudson left the university in August 2004, Grimes became provost for both campuses, headquartered in Hattiesburg. It was after Malone resigned in the summer of 2005 that Joachim took over, temporarily she thought, as associate provost. She faced the Katrina crisis with a gritty optimism befitting the institution's heritage. Refusing to surrender the semester, she supervised the transfer of Gulf Park operations to the former Garden Park Hospital in Gulfport, which the university's research foundation had recently acquired. A portion of the facility, supplemented by several portable structures, was converted into a Gulf Coast Student Services Center with 50,000 square feet of classroom and office space. Amazingly, on October 10, classes resumed amid the clatter of continuing construction, operating on a compressed, summer-like schedule. Squeezed into an area one-sixth the

With extensive damage at the Ocean Springs Gulf Coast Research Laboratory visible in the background, Southern Miss biologists resumed operations only days after Katrina. For more than thirty years, GCRL had maintained an uninterrupted data base of monthly fish samples collected from a series of stations in the Gulf. September 2005's samples were collected on time and at all stations.

size of Gulf Park, students studied or lounged between classes at computer stations on tables lining the halls. "We've not had to compromise our instruction delivery or content," said a proud Joachim, who paid tribute to a faculty and staff whose loyalty and determination remained unflinching in the midst of personal suffering and loss.

For more than thirty years, biologists at GCRL had maintained an uninterrupted data base of monthly fish samples from a string of stations along the Gulf. Within days of the storm, they were back on the water collecting September's samples on time and at all stations. Lab faculty and staff processed the samples in outdoor makeshift facilities in between classes, which began there in modular units on September 19, and periods of voluntary cleanup work. Southern Miss facilities at Jackson County and the Stennis Space Center in Hancock County sustained minimal damage, and classes resumed at those sites on October 10. At Keesler, with half the base flooded and most available buildings converted into shelters, classes were canceled for fall semester.

In the months that followed the catastrophe, USM became the recipient of a worldwide outpouring of sympathy and aid: $5,000 from Kaetsu University in Japan; phone cards for Gulf Coast faculty and staff from the University of North Dakota staff senate; $35,000 from Rotary International for Gunter Library at GCRL; $15,000 for student assistance collected from individual donors at Emporia State University in Kansas. The university also served as a conduit for relief to others: books from schools in south Florida for libraries on the coast; book bags full of school supplies for students in Gulfport; band instruments from the University of Illinois for coast schools. Other items included clothes, blankets, computers, even Christmas toys and prom dresses, as well as money. Teams of students from universities as far away as Canada joined Southern Miss students in volunteer relief work in Hattiesburg or on the coast.

Most poignant were efforts by members of the USM family to relieve their stricken fellows. The faculty senate organized weekend trips to help coast employees in cleanup work. "It was like the cavalry arriving, just in time," said one coast professor. "When there's so much to do, and you're standing there throwing away your possessions, it tends to paralyze you and . . . slows your progress. . . . Because of the volunteers from the Hattiesburg campus and others, my house was probably saved." Gulf Park history professor Pat Smith, who helped coordinate the work, suggested that the emotional comfort meant as much as the physical labor. "Total strangers have reached out to help with unimaginably nasty . . . and difficult tasks," he noted, "cleaning out a house that has been ruined by foul flood waters, cutting up giant trees, dragging a whole house full of furniture to the street, helping a person who has lost it all to sort through the rubbish to salvage a few photos or personal remembrances of life pre-Katrina—it's amazing that human beings will rise to such gifts."

Immediately after the storm, the Alumni Association set up an electronic bulletin board as a means of communication for those searching for missing family members. Later, the Association temporarily waived dues for victims of the disaster and worked with the registrar's office to replace hundreds of diplomas lost in the storm. In the months that followed, other branches of the university provided valuable services to the recovery effort. Researchers from the department of geography and geology hurried to collect "perishable" data on the physical dimensions of storm's impact. On the Hattiesburg campus, the counseling center's caseload swelled 400 percent above normal, and director Jacqueline Wiebe praised her staff's "exceptional dedication to students' needs . . . often at the expense of their own needs." The college of business and economic development established a Gulf Coast Business Assistance Center that linked local businesses struggling to recover with the volunteer services of economic development professionals from around the world. Eventually, the university designated and honored a formal hurricane hall of fame for those who had made exceptional contributions to relief and recovery. In some sense, however, the "Heroes of Katrina" were merely representative of an institution whose history had always been marked by ordinary people rising to extraordinary challenges. Thanks to their efforts and those of countless unnamed others, Southern Miss, like the tireless little data buoy that bore its name, remained steadfast through the storm.

Amidst the greatest natural disaster in U.S. history, The University of Southern Mississippi remained, like the little data buoy that bore its name, steadfast through the storm.

Chapter 9

CREATIVE, BOLD, DETERMINED

2003
10
BOWL
1990
BOWL
1988
31
70
68
NEW ORLEANS
BOWL
2005
SOUTHERN MISS
1

In 2006, The University of Southern Mississippi anticipated a new president as well as a new century, and the Alumni Association appointed a transition team to "assist" in the presidential search process. Ironically, that future-oriented task began with a backward glance that revealed how far the institution had come in its rapidly closing first century. A school that for its first ten years offered only certificates and diplomas now awarded more Ph.D. degrees than any university in Mississippi and claimed the state's only Southern Regional Education Board Level 1 designation for comprehensive academic quality. The "sober-faced homesick group" of 227 that Willard F. Bond described from 1912 had grown to a student body of more than 15,000, and a faculty that began with 17 now numbered more than 600. The institution boasted almost 120,000 alumni, more than half of whom had graduated since 1990. One of the five original buildings, which had collectively cost $178,591, was about to be renovated and expanded for more than $3 million, and the largest construction project in school history, a $34 million student life center, was almost complete. Veterans of "the stump age" would hardly have recognized the place.

The university also bore scars from its recent past, especially from Katrina, which had provided a defining experience for the current generation. Total damage estimates approached $300 million. The state's congressional delegation helped secure passage of legislation under which USM received $27.5 million for student financial aid, and during spring semester of 2006, almost 4,000

Former presidents Bill Clinton and George H. W. Bush organized a relief fund that raised more than $100 million for victims of Hurricane Katrina. At a ceremony in New Orleans, Clinton announced a distribution that included $1.5 million for Southern Miss. Sitting with Bush and USM president Shelby Thames (far right) is University of New Orleans chancellor Timothy Ryan.

students qualified for assistance. The USM Foundation established a Katrina Relief Fund, which within a year had collected over $230,000 from individual and corporate donors. The athletic department raised another $117,000 for student athletes. The road to recovery was slow and arduous. Fall 2005 enrollment fell to 15,030, well below the previous year's record 16,035, but it included 143 Honors College freshmen, a 68 percent increase since 2003. On the coast, only 65 percent of those originally enrolled remained in school after Katrina. University Libraries established a Katrina Research Center designed to be the premier repository for information related to the disaster. It was to include a comprehensive oral history project conducted by the Southern Miss Center for Oral History and Cultural Heritage.

By the summer of 2006, semblances of normality were beginning to return, even on the coast. In June, the annual Discovery Sea Camp returned to the J. L. Scott Marine Education Center, now operating out of modular classrooms at Gulf Coast Research Laboratory, and more than 700 youngsters attended the various sessions over the course of the summer. The center had also resumed many of its community outreach activities, including visits to local schools, teacher workshops, and field-trip mini-camps. Fall 2006 enrollment at USMGC was almost back to the pre-Katrina level. On the first anniversary of the storm, Thames promised the people of the coast that USM had not forgotten them. "Today," he pledged, "we reaffirm our commitment to continue playing a vital role in . . . recovery by providing quality academic programs across the Gulf Coast, the state and the region." The college board announced its commitment to rebuild Gulf Park but also revealed plans for an additional campus centrally located somewhere along the Interstate 10 corridor. By the fall of 2007, the Advanced

First Lady Laura Bush speaking at ceremonies designating USMGC's J. L. Scott Marine Education Center as a national Coastal Ecosystem Learning Center in 2007.

A new $30 million student life center, named for Senator Thad Cochran, opened in September 2006. The four-story, 237,000-square-foot facility included the second largest Barnes and Noble college bookstore in the Southeast and a technology atrium adorned by Southern Miss professor of art and design Bill Baggett's mural, *University's Bounty*.

Education Center had reopened for limited day classes at Gulf Park, and plans were under way for a new technology learning center there that would house the popular toy library, which had served handicapped children on the coast free of charge since 1990. "What has been accomplished, when you consider what we have been through," beamed a proud Pat Joachim, "is simply amazing. The future belongs to Southern Miss."

Early in 2006, a relieved Thames announced that SACS had lifted its probation, and a year later the university received its standard ten-year reaffirmation of accreditation. In the spring of 2006, it was announced that the new student life center would be named in honor of Senator Thad Cochran. "Senator Cochran has been a great friend to Southern Miss," Thames said, "and we feel this is a fitting tribute to someone who has worked tirelessly for this university as well as for higher education in Mississippi." In September, after fourteen years of planning and construction, the facility opened with a weeklong celebration. The four-story, 237,000 square-foot center featured an elaborate student dining area, a grand ballroom, a presidential suite, meeting rooms, a technology atrium, and the second largest Barnes and Noble college bookstore in the Southeast.

Sadly, the opening of the Cochran Center also marked the demise of the J. B. George University Commons, and veteran catering director Kim Busche penned a poignant eulogy. "There are years of memories from this square in the center of campus," she wrote. It had probably been the most used facility on campus, hosting everything from formal fund-raising dinners to food fights. "This evening when we lock the doors," Busche said, "this tired but strong building will have finished its tour of duty. . . . There is no fanfare . . . No bells and whistles. Just hungry students eating dinner. . . . Mission accomplished." Another restaurant had also recently opened in the

With the opening of the Fresh Food Company in the Cochran Center and conversion of the old power house into a restaurant, the campus boasted no fewer than seven dining facilities. The old J. B. George University Commons, which had served students for almost half a century, was ultimately demolished to provide additional green space for the central campus.

In January 2008, ground was broken for renovation and expansion of the Ogletree Alumni House.

renovated old power house, and students could now find food and refreshment in no fewer than seven locations around campus.

Shortly before Katrina, the Alumni Association had announced a fund-raising campaign to expand and renovate the Ogletree House. Campaign cochairs, Aubrey Lucas and Lou Ann Poynter noted that "the building is a symbol of all that is good about Southern Miss: her history, her legacy, her alumni and her bright future. The building needs to be restored, but, more importantly, all that it stands for deserves to be elevated to a new level of greatness." Ogletree's death in June 2005 heightened the significance of the project. The campaign, which was suspended after Katrina, resumed in January 2006 and reached its $3 million goal two years later. Groundbreaking took place on January 18, 2008, with the work scheduled for completion in the summer of the following year.

In early 2006, Alumni Association president Danny Mitchell appointed past president Rex Kelly and state auditor Phil Bryant to lead the fifteen-member presidential transition team. Acknowledging the college board's authority to make the final choice, Kelly observed that "the alumni of Southern Miss have a large stake in the outcome of the presidential search and, therefore, have chosen to provide a forum for dialogue, discussion, research and resolution." Mitchell declared, "Controlling our own destiny is an absolute must." The IHL board had recently come under fire for conducting such searches amidst what some considered a shroud of secrecy, refusing to release the names of applicants, including the

In 2006, Scott Ross (left) and other members of the college board's USM presidential search committee visited campus for a day of "listening sessions" with various university constituency groups.

finalists. The board of directors of the Alumni Association, however, formally "endorsed the IHL process," with the understanding that confidentiality applied only to the names of applicants, that all other aspects of the search would be open and transparent.

The process began when the commissioner and the board visited Hattiesburg for a day of "listening sessions" with various campus constituency groups. Over the summer, the transition team met separately with fourteen such groups while compiling the results of a survey mailed to all alumni. After analyzing all the information at its disposal, the team developed a presidential profile that emphasized commitment to academic integrity and experience in higher education, particularly regarding resource development, strategic planning, and collaborative administration. In summary, the report concluded that "the University needs a dynamic person who will unite students, faculty, staff, alumni and the community around a common vision." In the early weeks of 2007, a local advisory committee sifted through scores of applications and forwarded its recommendations to a board search committee. After several rounds of interviews, the board on March 27 announced its preferred candidate, who turned out to be, surprisingly, a woman, an alumna, and an experienced university president.

Martha Dunagin Saunders had been since 2005 a popular and respected chancellor at the University of Wisconsin-Whitewater. Published scholar, award-winning teacher, and experienced administrator, she had worked her way through the ranks of higher education from adjunct instructor to chief executive. With an undergraduate degree in French from USM, a master's degree in journalism from the University of Georgia, and a Ph.D. in communication theory and research from Florida State, she had also served as dean of arts and sciences at the University of West Florida and vice-president for academic affairs at Columbus State in Georgia. She would be the first woman to lead one of Mississippi's comprehensive universities, if she could survive the grueling round of campus interviews scheduled for April 5.

On May 21, 2007, alumna Martha Dunagin Saunders succeeded Shelby Thames as president of Southern Miss.

She need not have worried. On the eve of her appearance, a faculty senate officer told a reporter, "I've talked to a lot of faculty and staff today, and there is great excitement on campus—I mean tremendous. . . . We can't wait to meet her in person." Saunders negotiated the ten-hour gauntlet of constituency group meetings with an impressive combination of charm and candor, promising to "build trust, build a team, and build a campus." The process resembled "an Oprah love-a-thon," in one reporter's words. At the end of the day, it took the board little time or deliberation to name her, unanimously, as the institution's ninth president. It was in many ways an inspired choice. It shattered the glass ceiling of higher education in Mississippi, and not only did Saunders fit the transition team's profile, she brought to the task the

SECRET ADMIRERS

Sometime in the fall of 2005, vice-president for student affairs Joe Paul received a mysterious letter requesting that he look underneath a water fountain on the seventh floor of a building honoring someone with seven letters in his last name. He compliantly went to the proper location in the Johnson Science Tower, where he found a check designated for a "deserving student affected by Hurricane Katrina."

Equally mysterious was the appearance in November of a large decorative stone on the lawn of Danforth Chapel. The rock bore an emblem with a leaf surrounded by seven stars and the date 1877. Believing it to be a fraternity prank, union and programs director Barbara Ross conducted a little detective work and discovered the existence of an organization calling itself The Gold Leaf. "A group of individuals," according to one of the society's letters, "has taken an oath to commit itself to the betterment of The University of Southern Mississippi." Other individuals and groups on campus also began to receive correspondence from The Gold Leaf, often accompanied by a check, usually for $777.77. Apparently, the significance of the number seven derived from the 227 students and 17 faculty members present at the school's opening on September 18, 1912. The date 1877 possibly reflected the origin of the Mississippi Teachers Association, which played such a crucial role in the institution's founding. Another of the society's letters stated, "Our mission is being accomplished through the making of financial and other gifts to individuals associated with the university whom we believe bring honor to the university through their work and lives. Membership in the Gold Leaf is and will always remain anonymous so that the focus of the gift will be on the recipient." A separate but apparently companion organization, The Society of 1910, also emerged. "As students past and present," said one of its statements, "we are driven by our overriding founding principle; to work in all things for the betterment of The University of Southern Mississippi." Ross suggested that it would be fitting for the first named meeting room in the Cochran Center to be The Gold Leaf Room, and on July 7, 2007 (07-07-07), she received a check (the first of seven totaling the $25,000 required for the naming opportunity), designated, of course, for room 227.

SOCIETY OF 1910

Esse Quam Videri

heartfelt affection of a daughter. The following day's *Hattiesburg American* headline read "Saunders to the Top," and a *Student Printz* editorial shortly thereafter gushed, "We have a major crush on Saunders."

The enthusiasm was overwhelming but not universal. A member of the Foundation board, while promising his full support, cautioned that "what goes on in a Division III university and what goes on in a Division I university are worlds apart. . . . I just think there are going to be challenges, and she better be ready to put on her Nikes and start running." As on campus, however, most in the community were elated. "She's one of us," said Bobby Chain. "I think the board made a wise decision." Dean of the College of Health Peter Fos, who had chaired the local advisory committee, said that he and his colleagues had "sort of an intangible feeling she could bring the campus together and push it at the same time." Saunders lent credence to that judgment when she stated, "I spend a lot of time making sure I get the right people around the table, but when the need arises I can be pretty authoritarian . . . . One of the things I never take for granted is the intellectual resources on a university campus. None of us is smarter than all of us. If we can sort of get the herd moving in the same direction we can do anything."

Meanwhile, the clock was ticking down on the Thames presidency. During his last weeks in office, Thames joined in an effort to diminish a dark stain on the university's past by clearing the name of Clyde Kennard. The *Clarion Ledger* had recently published a series of articles on the case, one of which included a sworn affidavit by the man whose lone testimony had been the basis of Kennard's conviction for accessory to burglary in 1960. Johnny Lee Roberts told investigative reporter Jerry Mitchell that Kennard was innocent and that he had earlier been intimidated into testifying otherwise. Students affiliated with the Southern Miss Center for Human Rights and Civil Liberties launched a petition drive to secure a posthumous pardon, but Governor Haley Barbour, the state parole board, and the Mississippi Supreme Court declined to act. The Court suggested that despite the absence of a statutory basis for pardon, "there may be alternate remedies available."

In May 2006, Thames and Aubrey Lucas joined fourteen other prominent Mississippians in petitioning the Forrest County Circuit Court to reverse the forty-six year old verdict. Governor Barbour, who had earlier proclaimed March 30 (ironically the ninety-sixth anniversary of the founding of Mississippi Normal College) "Clyde Kennard Day" in Mississippi, offered a separate supporting petition. "This," he said, "is the appropriate, constitutional way for this innocent man to be exonerated." By that time, the student petition had secured more than 1,500 signatures from faculty, staff, and students. On May 17, in the same courtroom where Kennard had been convicted, Judge Robert Helfrich ruled in favor of the petitioners. "Because this matter did begin here, it should end here," he said. "To me, this is not a black or white issue; this is a right or wrong issue. To correct that wrong I am compelled to do the right thing and declare Mr. Kennard innocent, and his conviction is hereby null and void." Thames called it "a wonderful day for race relations in Mississippi."

Barely a week before his contract as president expired, Thames participated in groundbreaking ceremonies for a new $30 million innovation and commercialization park. "I've dreamed a long, long time about this day," he said. Formally announced in 2003, the park was really an extension of Thames's vision of university-industry collaboration that began over three decades earlier with the creation of the polymer science program. Senator Cochran had helped secure an initial federal grant of $2 million that helped persuade Hybrid Plastics, Inc., a leader in "nanotechnology," to move its operations from Fountain Valley, California, to Hattiesburg. A *Los Angeles Times* editorial lamented the loss, warning that "if California hopes to keep small high-tech companies from moving to Hattiesburg . . . it must do a better job at matching the city's other drawing cards—increasingly important basic research being conducted at the University of Southern Mississippi's polymer/chemistry department."

The Hattiesburg Area Development Partnership, which had helped lure Hybrid Plastics, funded the development of a master plan, which called for closing the university golf course to make way for the park. The same year, the Southern Miss Research Foundation created Noetic Technologies, Inc., to promote the university's portfolio of intellectual properties among companies with the potential to turn research into marketable products and services. The 2007 groundbreaking was for the park's first facility, a $22 million National Formulation Science

4:35
ROCK104 THE OFFICIAL FLAGSHIP STATION OF SOUTHERN MISS FOOTBALL
MISS
SOUTHERN MISS

The foregoing line from Robert Frost's "The Oven Bird" aptly captures the pathos surrounding the demise of the B. O. van Hook Golf Course. The land on which it was built had originally been the college farm, part of the large tract of Lamar County land that J. J. Newman Lumber Company donated to Mississippi Normal College in 1910. For years it lay largely undeveloped until English professor Wilbur W. Stout discovered among its tall pines the ideal setting for a natural amphitheatre. As a graduate student at the University of North Carolina, Stout had become acquainted with Frederick Koch's Carolina Playmakers, especially their productions of outdoor folk theater. After coming to Southern he hoped to develop a similar outdoor drama patterned after Paul Green's "The Lost Colony" or Kermit Hunter's popular Cherokee epic "Unto These Hills." Beginning in 1956, the

college slowly transformed the site into an attractive recreation area that included a forty-acre lake. The outdoor theater never materialized, though retired army colonel and MSC graduate student E. A. Wink wrote a script, "Red Eagle," an Indian saga based on the early settlement of the Mississippi Territory. In the late fifties, when construction of Pinehaven Apartments destroyed the old golf course, a new one was built just south of Lake Sehoy, as the new lake was called in honor of the Creek Indian princess who was a leading character in Wink's play.

Many Hattiesburg residents played their first round of golf on the hilly pine-studded layout that was later named for math professor and longtime USM golf coach B. O. van Hook. The "back nine" included infamous "heart attack hill" on the par four fifteenth hole, survival of which often prompted the celebratory swilling of, in the early days, contraband beer. During the 1960s and '70s, aspiring young professional golfers sometimes knocked around the course tuning up for the Magnolia Classic played at the nearby Hattiesburg Country Club. In 2004, the course was closed to make way for a high-tech innovation and commercialization park. On March 31, the last day of operation, 120 of the old faithful gathered at "the Goat Ranch," as they called it affectionately, for a farewell tournament and elaborate funeral ceremony complete with hearse and kilted bagpiper playing "Amazing Grace." The honor of a final drive off number one tee fell to seventy-seven-year-old James Ray Carpenter, former president of the Professional Golfers Association of America and for twenty-six years van Hook's resident pro.

Perhaps, as chief financial officer Greg Lassen put it, "it makes sense to use this land in a way that better serves the university and the Hattiesburg community." For devotees of "the Goat Ranch," however, the price of progress was the diminution of a venerable thing.

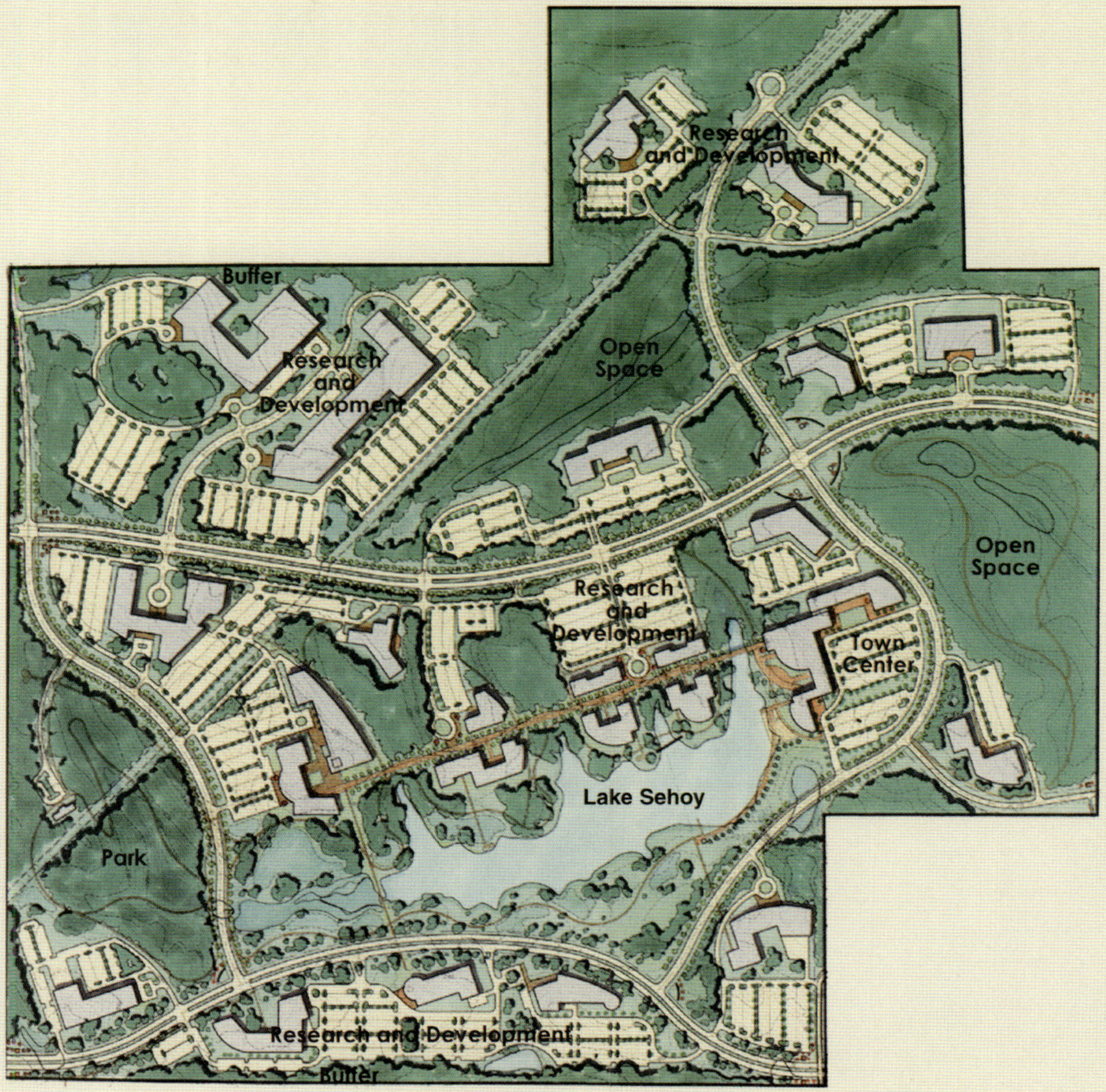

Laboratory funded by a grant from the U.S. Department of Commerce. In October 2008, the park was rechristened The Garden, and Viridis Development Company announced its commitment to construct a $25 million office and research facility, whose first tenant was scheduled to be the Southern Miss Research Foundation. The Garden, Thames boasted, would enable "a company, an individual entrepreneur, University researcher, staff member, or even student, to go full circle from the formulation of an idea in the lab to the creation of a viable and marketable commercial product. It is a virtual one-stop-shop for entrepreneurs." With the potential to become Mississippi's version of California's Silicon Valley or North Carolina's Research Triangle, the innovation and commercialization park, more than anything else, symbolized Shelby Thames's contribution to Southern Miss.

Controversy and opposition dogged Thames to the end. In late 2006, he received a "letter of reprimand" from IHL commissioner Tom Meredith for "failure to obtain the permission of the Mississippi Department of Archives and History prior to demolishing Weathersby Hall and the ROTC Building on the Hattiesburg campus." Some lauded him for saving money by replacing old and structurally unsound edifices with attractive and rare green space, while others criticized the loss of the seventh oldest building on campus (the ROTC facility) which had been the original home of Wimpy's. On the eve of his departure, his relentless antagonists, "concerned that the written history may feature only events and successes as they are portrayed by the . . . Administration," felt "compelled" to issue "A Faculty Senate View" of the Thames legacy. The document catalogued a thirteen-point "set of negative impacts" that the faculty body considered "representative of the real Thames legacy." After recounting the all too familiar train of painful and contentious issues of the recent past, the report concluded that "this list of significant events will be vividly remembered by the hundreds of faculty members whose personal and professional lives were adversely affected during the five-year Thames reign."

Two weeks later, an official university press release summarized Thames's presidency, noting that "the hallmarks of his personal philosophy—hard work and innovation—mark the legacy of his administration." Often what the senate considered "negative actions," such as academic reorganization, Thames deemed signal achievements. External funding, which had doubled during his tenure, from $51.1 million in 2000–1 to $102 million in 2006–7, "defines the culture of academic excellence at Southern Miss," he declared. The rising Trent Lott Center and the promise of the innovation and commercialization park, the statement said, bore witness to the university's enhanced role in economic development. A master campus and facility plan that he had commissioned a year earlier was, said associate vice-president for student affairs Sid Gonsoulin, "a remarkable collaborative effort, led by Dr. Thames. With his leadership and drive, he has left a monumental planning document that will guide our success for years to come." Thames's proudest accomplishment, however, was his leadership during the Katrina crisis. "We shall always remember with gratitude," said Aubrey Lucas, "Dr. Thames' timely actions after Hurricane Katrina, which gave assurance to our colleagues on the Gulf Coast that they would have jobs." Whatever else Southern Miss employees lost in the storm, Thames insisted, "I was determined that they could count on their jobs . . . being secure." Pat Joachim, too, praised "his leadership," without which, she said, "we could not have overcome the obstacles in our way to recovery."

Thames's had been a stormy presidency, and the words of a freshman *Printz* columnist well capture its ambiguity. "Some would have us try to completely erase the memory of him from campus," she wrote, "but honestly, it doesn't seem fair to the positive legacy he has left us." Thames acknowledged that he had made mistakes. "Nobody's perfect," he said, but "I have no regrets at all. None whatsoever." When asked how he would advise his successor, he warned, "You can't bleed in a sea of sharks. That person is going to have to not be afraid to make a decision." As was his wont, he spent his last days working as if he had just begun. "He continues to give us assignments," said provost Jay Grimes, "and ask whether this or that's been done. He's just been typical, lovable Dr. Thames."

The new president took over May 21 and a few weeks later, at the first Freshman Preview session, personally welcomed the first wave of students who would enter under her leadership in the fall. Aware that the orientation activities would engulf them in advice, Saunders promised to refrain from adding to the deluge, except for two exhortations. "Finish what you start," she urged, "because it doesn't count until you've got a degree. But while you're here, ride all the rides—do everything that's available to you as a student." Not averse to her own advice, she wore herself thin the first year attending almost every university event imaginable while allowing the community to size her up by speaking to civic gatherings at every opportunity. "Saunders clearly believes in the power of showing up," the *Hattiesburg American* observed, "and at every appearance, she has emphasized a message of optimism." Her diligence paid off, as Alumni Association director Bob Pierce reported to his constituents in 2008: "I can assure you that in my more than 10 years of serving in this position, and I believe most faculty, staff, and students would agree with me, I have not felt more engaged and more optimistic about the future of the University."

While building trust was important, Saunders found building a team urgent. Three of the five colleges were already without deans, as were the University Libraries and the Honors College, and provost Jay Grimes and vice-president Joan Exline resigned in June 2007. Saunders quickly named associate dean of arts and letters David R. Davies as dean of the Honors College and biology professor and veteran administrator Bobby Middlebrooks as interim provost. Following national searches, three new deans were named early in 2008: Denise von Herrmann in arts and letters, Lance Nail in business, and Carole Kiehl in University Libraries. At the same time, David Wolf filled the restored position of vice-president for university advancement. By the summer, a streamlined executive cabinet was in place. It included holdovers Joe Paul in student affairs, Cecil Burge in research and economic development, chief financial officer Joe Morgan, and Pat Joachim from USMGC. Newcomers included Wolf and provost Robert Lyman. While not part of the cabinet, executive assistants Chad Driskell (external affairs) and longtime faculty member Mary Dayne Gregg (articulation and planning) provided valuable counsel.

As for building a campus, Saunders got even more than she bargained for. Two weeks after naming her president, the college board chose a site for the new Gulf Coast campus, 200 acres donated by the owners of Cross Creek, a major development project on Interstate 10 just north of Long Beach. "It's not too often as a president," she said, "you have the opportunity to start a campus from scratch. . . . The opportunities are staggering. When you consider the population on the Gulf Coast, the shipyard, Stennis—we're going to be a driving force for those opportunities." Cross Creek, which met the board's criteria of being accessible, visible, and centrally located, would become USMGC's main campus. Gulf Park would remain a vital component of Southern Miss on the coast, accommodating "stand-alone" operations such as a proposed

A series of community-campus core dialogues in 2007 solicited university stakeholders' perceptions of Southern Miss and their aspirations for its future.

new entertainment industry center. The school of mass communication and journalism's film program moved from Hattiesburg to the coast in August 2007, and the undergraduate major in entertainment industries was set to follow when an adequate building was available. Dean of arts and letters von Herrmann announced, "The plan is to build a state-of-the-art facility on the Gulf Park campus. That will require some significant resources, and we'll be pursuing industry partnerships to help with that."

In the summer of 2007, Saunders approved a master plan for the Hattiesburg campus. She was "impressed," she said, with the labors of a diverse committee led by Sid Gonsoulin, which had been at work for more than a year, soliciting ideas and opinions from interested parties on and off campus. Faculty senate president Stephen Judd commended the committee for its "close attention to how students, faculty, staff, and visitors move through the space," which had contributed, he suggested, to a proposed environment "that is humane, harmonious and functional." The plan designated five campus "districts" (north, central, west, historic, and recreation/athletic) and envisioned new facilities for the colleges of health, education and psychology, and business; expansion of the music and theatre buildings; 8,000 additional parking spaces, including two multi-level garages; a campus hotel; new tennis courts; an Olympic sports building; and additional classroom and office space. "It is definitely doable," Saunders concluded. "We can make progress incrementally and make minor adjustments as we go." Gonsoulin declared, "This transformative plan will

In March 2008, Martha Saunders was formally inaugurated as USM's ninth president.

reshape the University for the next 10–15 years, and continue the Southern Miss tradition of a dynamic, student-centered campus." It offered, he added, "a framework for orderly growth and development of capital improvements that are responsive to the University's current and projected needs."

Among Saunders's top priorities were strategic planning and environmental responsibility. As a prelude to the planning process, she commissioned a community-campus core dialogue project to explore stakeholders' perceptions of Southern Miss and their aspirations for its future. In the fall of 2007, a university dialogue team, guided by a consultant, gathered information through eleven discussion sessions involving more than 350 faculty, staff, students, alumni, and community leaders in Hattiesburg and on the coast. The dialogues crystallized around four areas of strategic focus—"image development, connection to the community, top flight education experiences, and a culture of healthy minds and bodies"—and five forces that defined people's perception of the institution's identity—"a spirit of humanity, self-efficacy, collective individualism, connection to heritage and tradition, and commitment to diversity." Out of those concepts emerged a new institutional theme: "Southern Miss, Where Inspiration Meets Innovation: Creative—Bold—Determined."

That theme and the ideas behind it would shape Saunders's administration, and she articulated them in her inaugural speech the following March. Turning controversy to advantage, she drew her title from a national sports commentator's catty observation regarding the university's recent change in football coaches: "just who does Southern Miss think it IS?" It was "a provocative question, to be sure," she suggested, but an appropriate one for an institution approaching its hundredth anniversary. She had already hinted at the answer in her introductory remarks when she declared, "I am honored today to serve my alma mater . . . one of the finest institutions of higher learning in the world." To elaborate, she employed terminology drawn from the recent dialogues:

> So Just Who Does Southern Miss Think It IS?
>
> I can sum it up in three words: Creative. Bold. Determined. . . . I believe that the forces of innovation that make Southern Miss, Southern Miss, are much the same forces that make Mississippi, Mississippi, and the Gulf South, the Gulf South. There is a spirit of humanity here, as evidenced in our resourceful response to Hurricane Katrina. There is a belief that we can do anything we set our minds to . . . with or without permission. We understand better than most that if we are going to make things happen for ourselves, we are going to have to link arms as a team and pull together. . . . Our differences open our options for innovative solutions, while our traditions keep us grounded in common purpose. We can bring out the best in our students, our communities and ourselves. . . . May God bless Southern Miss for all it has been and for all we will make it—together.

Like her predecessors, she stressed that Southern Miss should be a student-centered university. "Getting admitted, getting registered, getting financial aid and getting parking should be easy," she said. "The biggest challenge our students should ever feel should be in the classroom."

In 2008, President Saunders signed the American College and University Presidents Climate Commitment and created an office of sustainability under Larry Lee (pictured far left) to monitor the university's efforts, as she put it, "to minimize our environmental footprint."

Shortly before the inauguration, Saunders had appointed a strategic planning committee, which she chose to lead herself along with associate provost William Powell as cochair. To assist the committee, she also created an enrollment planning council and a budget model task force. By early 2009, an overview document, "Designing Our Future . . . Together," outlined the planning process for each area of strategic focus. It also contained statements on mission—"to cultivate intellectual development

The Village, an $18 million residence complex for sororities and senior female scholarship holders, opened in 2007.

and creativity through the generation, dissemination, application and preservation of knowledge"—and vision—"Southern Miss will emerge as the premier research university of the Gulf South, engaging and empowering individuals to transform lives and communities."

The goal of nurturing "a culture of healthy minds and bodies" received early attention when Saunders signed the American College and University Presidents Climate Commitment in April 2008. "We will think ecologically," she declared, "with a commitment to actions that reduce, reuse, and recycle. Our buildings will be designed with the environment in mind. Our physical plant will re-think operations to minimize our environmental footprint." A climate commitment council would coordinate those efforts and monitor university compliance with the requirements of its pledge. Shortly afterward, the president established an office of sustainability, which she said would be "the key to meeting the university's climate commitment. I am really happy with the enthusiastic way the campus has embraced this project. We aim for Southern Miss to become the model of sustainable thought and practice within our state and region."

In the fall of 2007, sororities moved from antiquated Wilbur Panhellenic dormitory into a new $18 million residence complex, The Village, which also housed senior female scholarship holders. About the same time, planning began for a construction project even larger than the Cochran Center, a proposed $37.7 million gated dormitory complex on the north side of Fourth Street opposite Bond Hall. Two years later, ground was broken for the four four-story structures that would accommodate almost 900 students in attractive double-occupancy rooms. Deemed Century Park, the complex was scheduled to open in 2010, the university's one-hundredth birthday. Consistent with the master plan, it would be the first Silver LEED (Leadership in Energy and Environmental Design) certified residence facility on any campus in the state and "the first of several construction phases," according to director of residence life Chris Crenshaw, "dedicated to providing state-of-the-art living communities for the students of Southern Miss." The dormitory complex eliminated almost 500 parking spots, and in the summer, construction was scheduled to begin on a 1,200-space garage. Due to open in 2010, the $14–16 million project would employ a privatized funding model using parking fees to repay the cost over thirty years.

In 2006, Lou Marciani, director of the school of human performance and recreation, and Walter Cooper, former dean of health, physical education, and recreation, spearheaded the creation of a Center for Spectator Sports Security Management (CSSSM) at Southern Miss. A year later, the U.S. Department of Homeland Security awarded the center $3.5 million to train personnel at more than one thousand institutions around the country. In 2009, CSSSM was designated a national center and began conducting training certification workshops for NCAA institutions using the sophisticated facilities of NFL stadiums as host sites. In 2008, The Hague University in the Netherlands became the thirteenth international exchange opportunity for Southern Miss students, and polymer science major Justin Poelma became USM's seventeenth Goldwater Scholar as well as a finalist for the prestigious Marshall Scholarship. That fall, the university welcomed a record 57 presidential scholars, including nine national merit finalists. Also in 2008, Aubrey Lucas was yet again lured out of retirement as interim replacement for commissioner of higher education Tom Meredith, who had resigned under fire. Lucas's reputation for integrity helped restore credibility to an Institutions of Higher Learning system that had recently seen more than its share of controversy. A year later, he was able to return to retirement when the board chose Southern Miss alumnus Hank Bounds as the new commissioner. The IHL also honored USM dean of students Eddie Holloway as Mississippi's Black Educator of the Year in 2009.

Groundbreaking for Century Park, a $37.7 million dormitory complex, took place in 2009.

USM's outstanding art facilities include the sculpture program's iron-pouring cupola, the largest of any university in the country.

Southern Miss boasts a fully accredited and nationally competitive program in dance.

Convention South magazine billed the Southern Miss Arts Gala "Atlantis" as its top event for 2007.

In 2009, the Southern Miss Symphony Orchestra received a Mississippi Arts Commission Governor's Award for Excellence for Leadership in the Arts.

Composer-in-residence Luigi Zaninelli.

The arts also continued to flourish at Southern Miss. In 2006, longtime band director Thomas V. Fraschillo became the first Mississippian ever elected president of the American Bandmaster's Association, and composer-in-residence Luigi Zaninelli's opera *Snow White* made its world premiere on campus and its European debut at the renowned Teatro del Maggio Musicale Fiorentino in Florence, Italy. The following year, "Partners for the Arts" celebrated ten years of town-gown cooperation in support of the university's arts programs and enhanced cultural opportunities for the people of south Mississippi. In 2008, senior Bernadette Birzer received the International Sculpture Center's Outstanding Student Achievement in Contemporary Sculpture Award. In the face of declining state revenues, the Southern Miss Symphony Orchestra in April 2006 launched a Five in Five program to raise $5 million in time for the university's centennial celebration

In 2006, the Pride and Dixie Darlings entertained Packer fans at Green Bay's Lambeau Field.

in 2010. The funds were to help support a scholarship endowment that enabled the orchestra to attract students from around the world. "Our orchestra recruits internationally," said director Jay Dean, and indeed, more than half the group's musicians came from abroad and over the years included students from Spain, Russia, Bulgaria, China, Japan, and especially Latin America. For a dozen years, Dean held recruiting auditions in Mexico City. In addition to donations from individuals and organizations, the Five in Five program shared proceeds from special events, including a second USM performance by Sir James Galway, this time accompanied by his equally accomplished flutist wife Lady Jeanne; a "United in Song" concert featuring Dionne Warwick, Patti LaBelle, Patti Austin, and others in a tribute to songwriter and alumna Tena Clark; and an "Atlantis Gala" that *Convention South* magazine deemed its Top Event for 2007. In 2009, the symphony orchestra won a Mississippi Arts Commission Governor's Award for Excellence for Leadership in the Arts.

Biloxi's Damion Fletcher had not been one of the big recruiting prizes in Mississippi high school football's "year of the running back" sweepstakes in 2005. Weighing only 170 pounds, he signed with Southern Miss and became the big surprise of the 2006 football season. In an opening day loss at Florida, he rushed for 89 yards to earn a starting spot the next week. This time he gained 116 yards against Southeastern Louisiana, and he never looked back, topping the 100-yard mark six more times on his way to breaking every freshman rushing record at USM and most in Conference USA. The following week, he had 177 yards and three touchdowns in a 37-17 home win over North Carolina State. Despite losing playing time to a midseason knee injury, he totaled 1,388 yards, eleventh in the nation and second best all-time at Southern Miss. Running behind all-conference linemen George Batiste and Travis Cooley, he and fellow freshman Tory Harrison keyed USM's first 2,000-yard rushing season since 1987. Quarterback Jeremy Young added 1,769 yards passing to help break the school record for team total offense with 4,635 yards. The Eagles won the C-USA eastern division but bowed to Houston, whom they had beaten 31-27 earlier at The Rock, in the championship game. A third consecutive bowl win, 28-7 over Ohio in the GMAC Mobile Bowl, left the record at 9-5 for the year. Fletcher and tight end Shawn Nelson, along with Batiste and Cooley, made the all-C-USA first team, and kicker Darren McCaleb set school career records for both number and accuracy in field goals and extra points.

Freshman sensation Damion Fletcher (#25) rushed for 1,388 yards in 2006. He would eventually become the most productive running back in Southern Miss history.

Linebackers Gerald McRath and Tumbo Abanikanda corral a Tennessee running back in 2007. Despite a disappointing 7-6 record on the year, McRath captured USM's eighth C-USA defensive MVP award in eleven years.

With 17 starters returning, including 9 on defense, the Eagles entered the next season a consensus pick to win Conference USA. *The Sporting News* ranked them twenty-fourth preseason and rated Southern Miss with the best pregame atmosphere, the best home-field advantage, and the best fans in C-USA. The high expectations would make the disappointments of 2007, several of them in front of national television audiences, all the more frustrating. After an opening win over Tennessee-Martin at home, USM traveled to Knoxville to play the big Tennessee in front of 106,000 at Neyland Stadium. Leading by six near the end of the half, the Eagles allowed Tennessee to convert a critical fourth down play and take the lead 17-16. The Vols went on to win 39-19, but Bower regrouped his troops for a 28-21 victory over East Carolina on the road the next Saturday. Two weeks later, Boise State rolled up 506 yards of offense and embarrassed the Eagles 38-16 in a Thursday night ESPN game at Bronco Stadium. Southern Miss then returned home for a Wednesday night ESPN 2 matchup against winless Rice.

What should have been a breather turned into an exercise in futility. Redshirt freshman Martevious Young, who got the starting nod at quarterback because of injuries to Jeremy Young and backup Stephen Reaves, broke his leg on the third play of the game. Playing in severe pain from badly bruised ribs, Reaves threw four interceptions, which along with two lost fumbles spotted Rice a 31-7 fourth quarter lead, but the Eagles refused to quit. Reaves, who completed 24 of 44 passes on the night, engineered touchdown drives of 80 and 95 yards, each

Flanked by daughter Stephanie (left) and wife Debbie, football coach Jeff Bower announced his resignation in November 2007. His 17 seasons and 119 victories rank second only to Pie Vann in school history.

followed by a two-point conversion, to pull USM to within eight points. Following an onsides kick, Reaves marched his team 57 yards for another score, but this time the two-point attempt failed. After forcing the Owls to punt, Southern Miss got one last opportunity, but Reaves fumbled with 1:07 left, and Rice ran out the clock to hand Bower and his players a crushing 31-29 defeat.

Again the Eagles bounced back to win three of the next four, but the loss was another nationally televised home game, this one on Sunday night against Central Florida. Following a 37-7 victory over UAB, Southern Miss dropped its third game of the year at The Rock, squandering a fourth quarter lead to lose to Memphis for the third time in four years. To heighten the insult, the Tigers' winning score came on a 52-yard touchdown pass by former Hattiesburg High star Martin Hankins with 1:04 left in the game. For a third time in 2007, Bower rallied his players from a bitter defeat to win their last two games, but only 17,705 fans showed up for the home finale, a 16-10 nail-biter over Arkansas State on a dreary Saturday two days after Thanksgiving. On Monday came a surprising, and to some shocking, announcement: Jeff Bower had resigned.

"A contingent of fans," as a local sportswriter described them, had been increasingly critical of the coach for several years, and Internet message boards gave them a new medium by which to vent their displeasure. After the Rice game, discontent spilled over to the rank-and-file fans, and the Memphis loss opened the floodgates. People mailed their season tickets back to the athletic office in protest. "Rumors began to swirl," according to the local newspaper, "that the big-money donors were about to pull the plug on the cash machine if Bower was not replaced at season's end." At a hastily called press conference on November 26, Bower, flanked by his wife and daughter, read a prepared statement. "Southern Miss has been a significant part of my life and my family for a very long time," he said. "To have played here, to have received my education here, to coach here and now to have my daughter in school here, we are very blessed. After meeting with Richard Giannini this morning, we came to a mutual decision that I have resigned as the head football coach at Southern Miss." He thanked supporters, especially his players and assistant coaches, and in an emotional conclusion declared, "I am proud that we have run a clean program. We have run it with integrity, we've won games, and most importantly, we graduated our student-athletes. There comes a time in any situation that you must move on. I want you to know that there is a lot of fight left in Jeff Bower. I'm not done yet."

Bower would coach the team in the Papajohn's.com Bowl in Birmingham, Giannini revealed, against old foe Cincinnati. Acknowledging that the fan base was deeply fractured, he pleaded for unity. "Whoever the coach is," he said, "[fans] . . . need to rally behind this program. I've been disappointed our fans have been the way they've

To succeed Bower, athletic director Richard Giannini chose Oklahoma State offensive coordinator Larry Fedora.

been. I hope they rally behind Jeff [and the team] when they go to Birmingham. They deserve it. . . . Jeff Bower has made this a lot better program for the next person. . . . It will be a benchmark." President Saunders stated, "Coach Bower has made important contributions to the growth of the football program and we owe him our thanks. He has earned a prominent place in Southern Miss athletic history. Now, we are looking forward to even greater levels of excellence in the years to come." Fan reaction ran the gamut, from outrage to exuberance. Most were divided, frustrated with recent disappointments on the field but deeply appreciative of Bower's contributions and especially his loyalty. A *Printz* columnist captured the ambiguity. "Jeff," he wrote, "I didn't realize how much I liked you until you were gone. Good luck." Prospects for healing the wounds and unifying the fan base hinged on the choice of a new coach.

Giannini, who conducted a whirlwind search personally, seemed to have hit the jackpot, as more than a thousand fans packed the Cochran Center ballroom on December 12 to greet new coach Larry Fedora. The enthusiasm was almost palpable; handsome, articulate, and brimming with energy, Fedora said all the right things, and the crowd roared with approval. He began with a quote from General George Patton: "Instead of waiting to see what might develop, attack constantly, vigorously, and viciously. Never let up, never stop, always attack." The "attack" slogan would become the new theme of Golden Eagle football. Fedora challenged fans to pack The Rock and be loud and obnoxious. He had obviously done his homework, as his concluding remark brought the house down: "I believe the flagship university in the state of Mississippi resides in Hattiesburg. I believe we can make the nation recognize there's a force to be reckoned with at Southern Miss."

Meanwhile, the news of Bower's departure left his players stunned and confused. "He's a great man," said senior lineman Chris Clark, "I'll tell my kids about him. . . . He was a father for me for five years." Accolades for Bower, and criticism of the decision, poured in: from former players, from colleagues, and from the media, whose general condescending tone was reflected in the soon infamous query, "Just who does Southern Miss think it IS?" The team, determined to send him out on a winning note, fell short, bowing to the twentieth-ranked Bearcats 31-21. Gerald McRath won USM's eighth C-USA defensive player of the year award, and he, Matthew Chatelain, Martavius

Prince, and Brandon Sumrall made first team all-conference. Fletcher won the Conerly Trophy, and his 1,586 yards broke the school single-season rushing record.

The Jeff Bower era had abounded in irony. It began and ended with a bowl loss at Legion Field in Birmingham. When he was hired, he had been offensive coordinator at Oklahoma State, and he was replaced by an offensive coordinator from the same school. A strict disciplinarian, he had dismissed his share of players and assistants, yet those who stayed were fiercely loyal to him, and he gave more than one troubled player a second chance and watched him redeem himself. He considered the press, as one reporter put it, "a necessary evil," but journalists respected him and rallied to his defense in the end. There was nothing ambiguous about his accomplishments, however. He had served his alma mater loyally for 29 years, coaching 11 of the 18 bowl games in school history. Among active head coaches, only Penn State's Joe Paterno, Florida State's Bobby Bowden, and Virginia Tech's Frank Beamer surpassed him in longevity at one institution. USM's 14 consecutive winning seasons trailed only Florida State, Michigan, Florida, and Virginia Tech. He had dominated Conference USA, winning four championships, three coach of the year awards, and coach of the decade. Perhaps most significantly, as he himself said, "I'm most proud of what we've done in the classroom—our graduation rate. I think we've done a pretty darn

The home opener in 2008 featured $30 million worth of renovations and additions to Roberts Stadium, including 34 luxury suites in the south end zone.

Damion Fletcher (#25) finished the 2008 season with 4,287 career rushing yards, the most in Mississippi collegiate history. With a year of eligibility remaining, he already owned almost every Southern Miss record for rushing. Fletcher, quarterback Austin Davis (#12), and wide receiver DeAndre Brown led the Golden Eagle offense to more than thirty school records in 2008.

good job." Like M. K. Turk and Kay James before him, he was in many ways a casualty of expectations generated by his own success. Sportswriter and Southern Miss alumnus Rick Cleveland summarized his legacy succinctly, "Bower . . . has won with class and dignity."

Fedora wasted little time making his mark, assembling a staff that even with a late start signed what some considered the best recruiting class in school history. It included wide receiver DeAndre Brown of Ocean Springs, the top recruit in Mississippi and one of the most prized in the country. Fedora's bold prediction of a full house for the spring game failed to materialize, but the record crowd of 11,136 was still impressive and reflected a renewed excitement among fans. The 2008 home opener showcased more than $30 million worth of additions and renovations to Roberts Stadium, particularly an expansion of the south end zone that featured 34 luxury suites and a Touchdown Terrace with club seating. Also, a new club-level Eagles' Nest was added on the east side along with a rooftop plaza connecting the east and west upper concourses. Since 1999, Giannini had overseen construction and renovation projects worth more than $100 million generated through gifts, endowments, pledges, and suite leases.

Beginning with season ticket sales, records fell like rain in 2008, but it was a rollercoaster season that included the longest losing streak in 32 years. Fedora's attacking spread offense showed up in spades on opening night against Louisiana-Lafayette, breaking the school record for a single game with 633 total yards. Fletcher had 222

The 2008 New Orleans Bowl marked USM's eleventh postseason appearance in twelve years. In the first quarter, Conference USA freshman of the year DeAndre Brown broke the single-season school record for pass receptions but then suffered a grisly injury (above). The Eagles went on win 30-27 as Michael Magee blocked a Troy field goal attempt in overtime to give Southern Miss its fifteenth-straight winning season.

yards rushing, and freshman sensation DeAndre Brown caught a 30-yard touchdown pass to spark a 51-21 victory. Auburn brought the Eagles back to earth the next week 27-13, holding Fletcher to 29 yards. After a 27-24 win at Arkansas State, the team went into a five-game tailspin, beginning with back to back conference losses to Marshall and Texas-El Paso at The Rock. Against the Miners, Fletcher ran for a career high 260 yards that moved him ahead of Ben Garry as the school's all-time rushing leader, but the game slipped away 40-37 in double overtime. Number 15 Boise State then handed Southern Miss its third straight defeat at home 24-7, and a 45-40 loss at Rice made it four in a row. Against the Owls, redshirt freshman quarterback Austin Davis completed 32 of 61 passes for 461 yards, all school records, and Brown had 12 receptions for 221 yards and four touchdowns, also a record. Another loss at Memphis left the Eagles 2-6, staring at the first losing season in 15 years.

The skid finally ended with a 70-14 thrashing of UAB, in which Davis ran for a school record five touchdowns and threw 60 yards to Brown for another. Fletcher had 86 yards on his first three carries, putting him over 1,000 for the season and 4,000 for his career. After he left with an injury, Tory Harrison carried for 137 yards, and V. J. Floyd added 118. The Eagles then defeated Central Florida 17-6 in Orlando and eventual conference champion East Carolina 21-3 at The Rock. Against the Pirates, Davis and Brown teamed up for yet another record, a 97-yard touchdown pass, the longest in school history. A closing win at SMU eased Southern Miss into the New Orleans Bowl, its

The baseball Eagles had not missed the NCAA tournament since 2002, and after 2005 the string continued behind such stars as Marc Maddox (left) and Brian Dozier (#12).

seventh straight postseason appearance and eleventh in twelve years. Brown entered the game against Troy tied with Sherrod Gideon for most receptions in a season, and in the first quarter, he broke the record and his leg. The grisly injury looked career-threatening, and though it turned out to be a clean simple fracture, Brown faced a long road to rehabilitation.

Meanwhile, Troy returned a fumble for a touchdown on the game's second play from scrimmage, and the Eagles responded with a 64-yard scoring pass from Davis to Gerald Baptiste on a flea flicker play. With barely a minute and a half gone in the game, the score was 7-7. The half ended tied at 17, but the Trojans scored the only points of the third quarter and led by 10 with nine and a half minutes to play. Southern Miss rallied to send the game to overtime but had to settle for a field goal on their first possession. Troy's ensuing drive also stalled, and Michael Magee came flying almost literally off the corner to block the field goal attempt and preserve the win 30-27 and extend the winning season streak to 15. Fletcher ended the year with 4,287 yards and 21 100-yard games for his career, both school records. Davis alone broke more than 15 offensive records, including most passing yards in a season 3,128. The team's 5,636 yards of total offense was also the most ever in a season. Brown was C-USA freshman of the year, and he, Fletcher, and Gerald McRath made the all-conference first team. Four other Eagles joined Brown on the all-freshman team.

In 2006, the baseball team slipped below 40 wins (39-23) for the first time in four years but still made the NCAA tournament. The regular season included a split with Ole Miss and a sweep of Mississippi State, the first in over a decade. The Eagles lasted only three games in the conference tournament but still made it to the regional in Tuscaloosa, where again they exited in three games, losing twice to a Troy team they had swept earlier at The Pete. Senior Marc Maddox led the team with 18 home runs and 70 RBIs, ranking him first and second for a career in those categories. He and Toddric Johnson made first team all-C-USA. Ryan Belanger and Cliff Russum won eight games each, and Daniel Best became the career leader in saves with 13 on the year. Sophomore Trey Sutton, whom Palmer described as "the best pure hitter I've ever coached," led the team with a

.375 average. The 2007 squad won its first 8 and its last 10 regular season games and earned a fifth straight postseason bid. The Eagles beat UAB to open the C-USA tournament but lost Sutton to a knee injury and dropped the next two. They defeated Troy in the Oxford regional but then lost to host Ole Miss and Sam Houston State to finish 38-21. The pitching staff, led by starters Belanger, Barry Bowden, and David Clark and relievers Patrick Ezell and Tyler Conn, combined for a sparkling 3.79 ERA. Sutton and Belanger were first team all-conference selections.

During the offseason, Palmer speculated that "in a given year, with the right circumstances," the Eagles might yet make it to the College World Series. "Of course, you have to earn it," he added, "but that is the goal." Despite a third straight split with Ole Miss, a win over Alabama, a sweep of Mississippi State, and the first series win ever by a C-USA team at Rice, 2008 was not to be the year. Plagued with injuries, Southern Miss literally limped through much of the midseason. After an opening round win over Central Florida in the conference tournament, the Eagles lost two of the next three, all against Marshall. Palmer took his team to its sixth consecutive NCAA regional, this time in Baton Rouge, where they downed the University of New Orleans in game one to earn a winners' bracket matchup with host LSU. The Tigers, whose visit to The Pete earlier in the year had drawn a record Southern Miss crowd of 5,658, had won 23 games in a row and were too hot to handle. Back to back losses to the second-ranked team in the nation ended the Eagles' season at 42-22. Conn's 18 saves on the season led the nation

In April 2009, baseball coach Corky Palmer announced that he would retire at the end of the season. Assistant Scott Berry was named to replace him.

and earned him first team all-American honors, and he, Bowden, and James Ewing made all-C-USA.

After a 7-0 start in 2009, the season turned somewhat sour with only six wins in the next 15 games. Just as things seemed to be turning around, Brian Dozier broke his collarbone in a win over Jackson State. Leading the team with a .394 average and only 20 hits shy of Sutton's career record, he was also, in Palmer's words, "the best defensive player I have coached in 32 years." Two weeks later, Palmer announced that he would retire at the end of the season, insisting that his decision had nothing to do with the disappointing record. "I love baseball," he said, "but I just don't have the energy anymore to attack this job like it needs." Longtime assistant Scott Berry was named as Palmer's replacement. The team stumbled to a 32-22 regular season finish, winning only 9 of the final 19 games. Hosting the C-USA tournament, the team rallied for three wins before bowing to Rice in the championship game. With 35 victories, the Eagles squeaked into the NCAA field as possibly the last team chosen, giving them a motto for the postseason, "You should have never let us in." A win over Elon and two out of three over host Georgia Tech gave them the regional title and a first ever super regional against Florida in Gainesville. With a sweep of the Gators, the dream came true; Southern Miss was on the way to Omaha and the College World Series. A heartbreaking 7-6 loss to Texas put them in the losers' bracket, and North Carolina ended the Cinderella story, taking the second game 11-4. It had been a remarkable run, and it earned the highest final national ranking ever at number

Behind Conference USA freshman of the year Jeremy Wise, the 2006-7 men's basketball team won twenty games for the first time since 2001.

eight. Todd McInnis was C-USA pitcher of the year, and he and Bo Davis, who led the team with a .359 average and 14 home runs, made the all-conference team. Joey Archer and Corey Stevens combined for 122 RBIs, and the team's 83 double-plays set a school record and led the nation.

In 2006–7, Joye Lee-McNelis's third season, the Lady Eagles broke even at 15-15. Amber Eugene led the team in scoring and rebounding and Kristin Chaney in assists and steals. Forward Lauren Pittman broke into the starting lineup as a freshman. Prospects for the following year looked bright, with four returning starters and three promising transfers, Andrea Barber from Barton County (Kansas) Community College, Pauline Love from Jones County Community College, and Stephanie Helgeson from Purdue. Liz Biland was the lone senior. After a 17-12 regular season, the team won two games in the conference tournament before bowing to top-seeded Texas-El Paso. For the first time in eight years, the Lady Eagles made it to the postseason, hosting Arkansas-Little Rock in the first round of the NIT. A 67-57 win secured the first 20-win season since 1995–96 and another home game, this one against in-state rival Mississippi State, who had defeated USM 77-56 at Reed Green earlier in the year. After trailing by 15 with ten minutes to go, Southern Miss fought their way back, and won 62-61 on Love's three-point basket with two seconds left. A third round loss at Michigan ended the season at 21-14. Love led the team in scoring and rebounding and made first team all-C-USA. Barber led in assists and steals, and Amber Eugene and

In 2008, the women's basketball team reached postseason play for the first time in eight years. Pauline Love led the team in scoring and rebounding that year and the next as the Lady Eagles produced back-to-back 20-win seasons for the first time since 1996.

Kendra Reed both broke into the thousand-point club. The next year's squad started 9-1 in the conference but stumbled at the end, losing four of the last six. A 65-54 overtime loss to Central Florida in the conference tournament championship left them sitting at home for the postseason, but it was another 20-win year (20-12). Love

Carlton Devan Palmer won 963 games as a head baseball coach, but the most memorable came late and unexpected. When he announced his retirement on April 29, 2009, USM's string of postseason appearances appeared to be in jeopardy. "Corky will go down in the record books," said Richard Giannini, "as one of the most successful coaches in any sport at Southern Miss." Little did he or anyone else know how that success would be crowned in the weeks ahead. The 445 wins and seven NCAA tournaments already under Palmer's belt at Southern Miss seemed satisfying enough. "It's been a privilege to coach here," he said, "and it's the only job I've ever wanted." His players had something else in mind.

Barely making the NCAA field, they survived a slugfest against Elon in the opening round of the Atlanta regional. It was "one of the wildest games I've ever been a part of," Palmer said, as the two teams combined for eleven home runs. An 8-0 Eagle lead

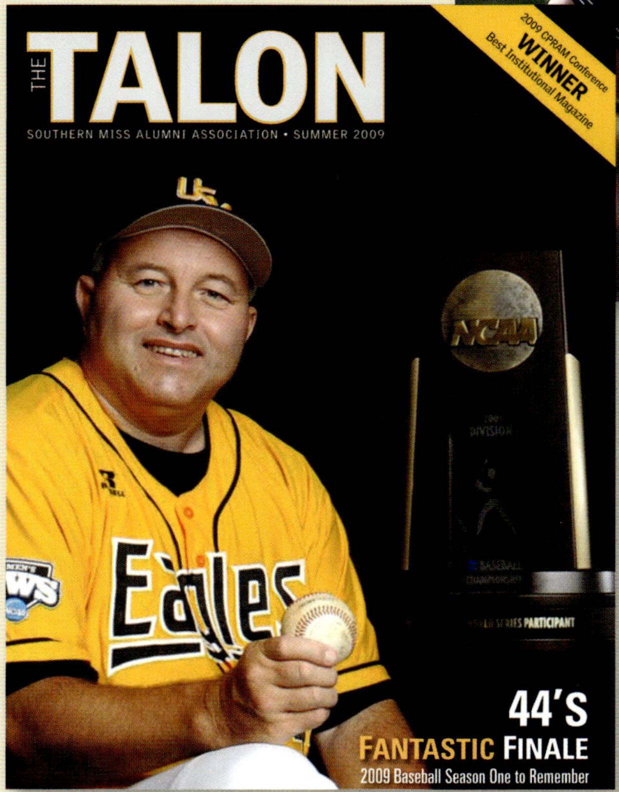

evaporated quickly, and the Phoenix led 13-12 after eight. USM scored five in the ninth, however, and hung on to win 17-15. In the second game, J. R. Ballinger pitched the most innings of his career, eight and one-third, to defeat host Georgia Tech 10-7, but the Yellow Jackets took the next one 10-3. The Eagles put the rubber game away early, scoring nine runs in the second inning on their way to a 12-8 victory and a trip to Gainesville for a super regional against Florida. Freshman shortstop B. A. Vollmuth's four home runs earned him regional MVP honors.

The opener in Gainesville was a see-saw affair, but Jonathan Johnston pitched three and two-thirds scoreless innings out of the bullpen to nail down the victory 9-7. The Eagles fell behind 6-1 in game two but battled back to take the lead in the eighth. After Adam Doleac's clutch pinch-hit loaded the bases with one out, Joey Archer singled home the tying runs. Tyler Koelling then hit a double-play ball, but Florida's first baseman mishandled the relay, and Doleac scored the go-ahead run. The Gators put a runner on in the ninth, but the game ended on a double-play, and Collin Cargill, who had just earned his team-leading thirteenth save, disappeared in a pile of ecstatic gold-clad teammates. With a thousand Southern Miss faithful chanting, "Corky, Corky, Corky," players responded by dousing him with the conventional Gatorade bath.

The trip to Omaha was disappointing. Leading top-seeded Texas 5-4 in the eighth inning, Eagle relievers lost their bearings. Seven of the last eleven Longhorn batters reached base without a hit, scoring three runs, including the game winner, on bases-loaded walks. An 11-4 loss to North Carolina in game two ended the season, and Palmer's career, but it had been quite a ride. "We had a magical season," Palmer beamed. "I'm real glad these guys let me work a little longer; it wasn't me, it was them."

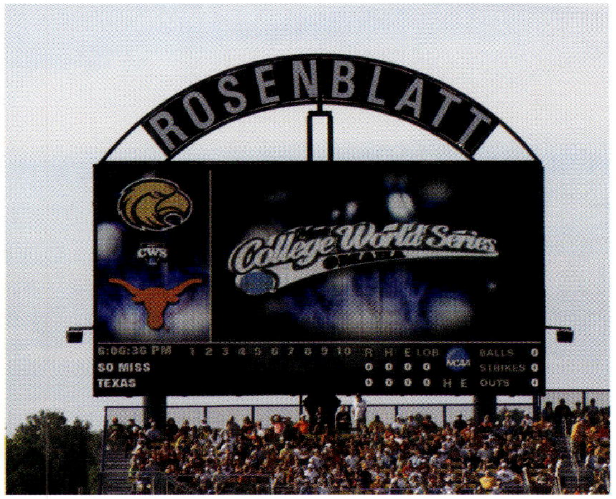

The oak trees planted by President Joe Cook were already almost half a century old when these Golden Grads had roamed the campus as students in the 1950s.

again led in scoring and rebounding and made first team all-conference.

Larry Eustachy's men began 2006–7 with 11 wins in their first 14 games, including a 56-54 thriller over Auburn at home. Freshman Jeremy Wise's 17.5 points a game led the Eagles to a 20-11 record, but an early exit from the conference tournament cost them a postseason bid. Wise was C-USA freshman of the year. The following year, freshman R. L. Horton, the *Clarion Ledger*'s "Mr. Basketball," joined four returning starters, and the Eagles began the season 11-3. Despite winning seven of their last ten games and two in the conference tournament, Southern Miss again missed out on the postseason with a 19-14 record. Wise again led the way, recording his one-thousandth point and averaging 18.7. The 2008–9 team beat Ole Miss by 19 and started 4-2 in C-USA but then lost 10 of the next 11 and struggled to a disappointing 15-17 finish. Wise again led in scoring, and Courtney Beasley and Craig Craft closed out their careers averaging in double figures.

In other sports, Howard Dobson replaced softball coach Gay McNutt after an 18-38 season in 2007. The following year, Jennifer Fox broke the school record for career RBIs, and the team improved to 25-30 that year and 26-28-2 in 2009. Other new coaches included Ricci Luyties in volleyball, Jerry Weeks in men's golf, Kevin Stephen in track, and Scott Ebke in soccer. Track produced three more all-Americans, Raquel Washington in 2006 and Cornelius Duncan and Tanika Liburd in 2007. The men's golf team recorded its highest finish ever, second, in the 2008 C-USA tournament. Individually, Paul Apyan finished third and made the all-tournament team. The student academic enhancement program under Tracy Robinson helped keep Southern Miss ranked among the nation's best athletic programs in academic performance.

In 2007, alumna Jennifer Duke Payne returned to Southern Miss to coordinate the celebration of the school's centennial scheduled for 2010. "As the excitement grows and plans develop," said President Saunders, "we lay the foundation for not only the celebration, but also the creation of Southern Miss history." She appointed a fifty-member centennial committee, led by Alvin Williams, Rex Kelly, and honorary chair Aubrey Lucas, that would, in Payne's words, "help shape a celebration that will both honor our institution's proud past and highlight its promising future." The centennial theme, "A Treasured Past—A Golden Future," reflected that purpose. The foregoing pages catalogue manifold reasons for Southern Miss friends and family to treasure their past. As Joe Cook had long ago noted, "When this institution was created, there was . . . grave doubt in the minds of the people whether such an institution was needed." From those "really rather humble beginnings," as Aubrey Lucas later described them, the little normal college grew into a modern, multipurpose university.

The century-long path had been littered with challenges that engraved perseverance on the institution's character and burned resilience into its soul. It had overcome much: doubts, depressions, wars, natural disasters, human follies, and politics. In the midst of an advertising campaign for athletics, a junior marketing professor had expressed it well. "We're going to tell people what our traditions are," he declared, "and they've been the same since we turned the first shovel of dirt to build the place. We know what it means to care about people, and we know about hard work. Our teams are perfect examples of those traditions." Founded to make life richer for the people of Mississippi, the university had resisted the lure of the ivory tower and made public service integral to its identity. A client of its Children's Center for Communication and Development once exclaimed, "I drive 142 miles every day to bring my son. I'd drive 500 miles a day if I had to. These people are that good." Alumni Association associate director Jerry DeFatta noted that "while the centennial is just cause for Southern Miss alumni to celebrate, it should also serve as a reminder that our greatest achievements have come only when we have picked ourselves up by our bootstraps and worked hard." He might have been thinking of Pat Joachim, leading USM Gulf Coast back from the heartache and ruin of Hurricane Katrina affirming confidently, "The future belongs to Southern Miss."

President Martha Saunders and vice-president for advancement David Wolf display the largest cash gift in Southern Miss history, a $6 million anonymous donation received in 2009.

Regarding that future, Providence seemed to have smiled with a special benevolence in turning Martha Saunders's heart toward home. In the face of a difficult economy, she insisted that "we need a hopeful outlook. . . . We have much to celebrate and few problems we can't solve if we put our minds together. . . . To be sure, our ambitions exceed our resources. That's a good thing, I think." Events appeared to vindicate her optimism. Early in 2009, the university received its largest single cash gift ever, $6 million from an anonymous donor. Saunders stressed that "we cannot answer any questions about the motivations or interests of the giver, but I would like to think he or she has observed our progress as a university and believes in what Southern Miss is all about." Such progress was well reflected that fall in the Honors College's highest enrollment ever, 550, which included 52 presidential scholars, among a record incoming freshman class of 160. For all the marvelous growth and development, the institution had in some ways come full circle. From "Daddy Joe" to "Aunt Martha," it was still a family place.

In 1921, resident dramatist Alma Hickman had written *Memory (A Masque)* for the dedication of the old memorial streetcar station. In it, the title character warns that "only those who live in the Past, the Present and the Future live completely," a truism brought home to the institution in the words of another prominent character, Spirit of the Normal College: "Only a few years ago was I born of the love, the dreams, and the toils of noble men and women. I rejoice in the splendid present and look forward to a glorious future when I shall fulfill more perfectly the great mission for which I was created." Thankful for a treasured past, a generation poised at the dawn of the institution's second century would do well to embrace Miss Alma's hope that "the Mississippi Normal College and her children shall ever cherish the dream of a golden future" and dedicate to it "all we have and are."

NOTE ON SOURCES

The information in this volume, including quotations, was derived largely from public sources. Most useful were university publications, particularly campus newspapers (the *Normal College News, State Teachers College News,* and, since 1927, the *Student Printz*), yearbooks (*Neka Camon* and *The Southerner*), and the *USM Alumni News* (after 1999 *The Talon*). Local newspapers, especially the *Hattiesburg American*, the coast *Sun Herald*, the Jackson *Clarion Ledger*, and the *Jackson Daily News*, were also consulted extensively. Selected gleanings from collections in the university archives, including oral histories, added color, detail, and verification. For athletics, annual media guides for various sports were helpful, as were John P. Bacon's 1967 USM master's thesis, "A History of Intercollegiate Athletics at the University of Southern Mississippi, 1912–1949" and Sigfried Fagerberg's 1970 Ph.D. dissertation, "A History of the Intercollegiate Athletic Program at the University of Southern Mississippi." *Rock Solid: Southern Miss Football* (University Press of Mississippi, 2004) by John Cox and Greg Bennett was indispensable.

ACKNOWLEDGMENTS

Many people contributed to the making of this book, and in listing some of them, I trust that those who remain unnamed will not feel slighted. The staff of USM's McCain Library and Archives was always patient and gracious, even when my requests reached nuisance proportions. Diane Ross and Cindy Lawler helped facilitate use of the university archives in ways too numerous to count; Laura Capell and Amanda McRaney digitized hundreds of photographs; Jennifer Brannock, Danielle Bishop, Kalani Hoffman, Peggy Price, and several student assistants endured months of my presence and what must have seemed incomprehensible methods of research; Ellen Ruffin helped me do justice to the de Grummond Children's Literature Collection; and no one exploring the history of The University of Southern Mississippi could fail to profit from the labors of Yvonne Arnold. For information and photographs on athletics, I am deeply indebted to John Cox, Jack Duggan, Shirley Jones Hill, John Thomas Shields, and Lenore Shields Griffin. Others who helped with information and photographs include Danny Rawls, Kelly Dunn, Albert & Associates, Joe Bailey, Steve Rouse, Steve Coleman, George Clark, Van Arnold, Topher Bostick, Stan Hauer, Jay Dean, Lou Marciani, Mary Sumrall, Cecil Burge, Barbara Ross, Shelia White, and Maureen K. Martin. I owe a special debt to David Tisdale whose proofreading saved me from several blunders. Polly Odom and Jewel Tucker of the USM President's Office helped in immeasurable ways and never let on that I was often in the way. The staff of the Southern Miss Alumni Association was always cheerfully accommodating despite my status as an interloper. I am grateful to President John Hilpert of Delta State University for allowing a leave of absence to undertake this project. I am also thankful for the professional labors of Craig Gill, John Langston, Anne Stascavage, and others at the University Press of Mississippi, as well as designer Dean Cavalier and copyeditor Tammy Rastoder.

The contributions of several people deserve special comment. The support of Alumni Association Director Bob Pierce, notwithstanding my quaintly loose conception of deadlines, was unflinching. Assistant to the President Mary Dayne Gregg, especially her advice and counsel, was as indispensable to me as she is to the university at large. It would be impossible to overstate what Centennial Coordinator Jennifer Payne has contributed to this volume; quite simply, without her there would be no centennial history. I will always treasure President Martha Saunders's confidence that I could do justice to the story of this great institution; she made the book possible. Finally, no one sacrificed more for this project than did Mary Jane Morgan, who had to hold things together alone for far too long.

INDEX

Page numbers in **bold** indicate illustrations.